NEW PROCLAMATION

NEW PROCLAMATION

YEAR A, 2007–2008

ADVENT THROUGH HOLY WEEK

MARY HINKLE SHORE
HERMAN C. WAETJEN
RICHARD L. ESLINGER
MELINDA A. QUIVIK

DAVID B. LOTT, EDITOR

FORTRESS PRESS
MINNEAPOLIS

NEW PROCLAMATION
Year A, 2007–2008
Advent through Holy Week

Library of Congress Cataloging-in-Publication Data

Library of Congress Cataloging-in-Publication Data is available.

ISBN-13: 978–0–8006–4257–0

The paper used in this publication meets the minimum requirements of American National Standard for Information Sciences—Permanence of Paper for Printed Library Materials, ANSI Z329.48-1984.

Manufactured in the U.S.A.
11   10   09   08   07   1   2   3   4   5   6   7   8   9   10

Contents

CONTENTS

The Season of Epiphany
Herman C. Waetjen

The Season of Lent
Richard L. Eslinger

Holy Week
Melinda A. Quivik

Calendar

PREFACE

For over three decades Fortress Press has offered an ecumenical preaching resource built around the three-year lectionary cycle that provides first-rate biblical exegetical insights and sermon helps, a tradition that this new edition of *New Proclamation* continues. Focused on the biblical texts assigned by the three primary lectionary traditions—the Revised Common Lectionary (RCL), the lectionary from the Episcopal Book of Common Prayer (BCP), and the Roman Catholic Lectionary for the Mass (LFM)—*New Proclamation* is grounded in the belief that a deeper understanding of the biblical pericopes in both their historical and liturgical contexts is the best means to inform and inspire preachers to deliver engaging and effective sermons. For this reason, the most capable North American biblical scholars and homileticians are invited to contribute to *New Proclamation*.

New Proclamation has always distinguished itself from most other lectionary resources by offering brand-new editions each year, dated according to the church year in which it will first be used, and featuring a fresh set of authors. Yet each edition is planned as a timeless resource that preachers will want to keep on their bookshelves for future reference for years to come. Both long-time users and those new to the series will also want to visit this volume's new companion Web site, www.NewProclamation.com, which offers access not only to this book's contents, but also commentary from earlier editions, up-to-the-minute thoughts on the connection between texts and current events, user forums, and other resources to help you develop your sermons and enhance your preaching.

This present volume of *New Proclamation* covers the lections for the first half of the church year for cycle A, from Advent through Easter Vigil. In addition, this latest edition of *New Proclamation* continues the time-honored series format while introducing some new, user-friendly elements. These established and new features include the following:

- *New Proclamation* is published in two volumes per year, with a large, workbook-style page, a lay-flat binding, and space for making notes.

- Each season of the church year is prefaced by an introduction that provides insights into the background and spiritual significance of that season, as well as ideas for planning one's preaching during that time.
- The application of biblical texts to contemporary situations is an important concern of each contributor. Exegetical work is concise, and thoughts on how the texts address today's world, congregational issues, and personal situations have a prominent role.
- Although each lectionary tradition assigns a psalm or other biblical text as a response to the first reading, rather than as a preaching text, brief comments on each responsive reading are included to help the preacher incorporate reflections on these in the sermon.
- A bulleted list at the beginning of each chapter provides a brief look at the key themes of that day's assigned texts.
- Boxed quotations in the margins offer thoughts from other writers to illuminate the texts further and to stimulate the preaching imagination.

As has become the custom of *New Proclamation,* the writers for this latest edition represent both a variety of Christian faith traditions and multiple academic disciplines. Mary Hinkle Shore, a Lutheran professor of New Testament who has her own preaching Weblog, brings her creative voice to the seasons of Advent and Christmas. Herman Waetjen, an esteemed Presbyterian New Testament scholar, thoughtfully addresses the texts for 2008's relatively brief season of Epiphany. Richard Eslinger, a Methodist professor of homiletics, not only provides expert exegesis on the Lenten texts, but also provides provocative guides to building sermons around those lessons. And Melinda Quivik, a Lutheran professor of worship and preaching who was intimately involved in the creation of the brand-new *Evangelical Lutheran Worship* for the ELCA, guides preachers through the intricacies of Holy Week preaching. We are grateful to each of these contributors for their insights and their commitment to effective Christian preaching, and are confident that you will find in this volume ideas, stimulation, and encouragement for your ministry of proclamation.

David B. Lott

THE SEASON OF ADVENT

MARY HINKLE SHORE

THREE ADVENTS

Students of the church year often speak of the "two advents" we observe during this season. The first one has to do with baby Jesus. With biblical texts, hymns, and liturgical elements of worship, we prepare for the celebration of our Lord's birth. In Advent, we imaginatively anticipate the incarnation, even though we testify that the miracle of the Word becoming flesh has already happened in the birth of Jesus of Nazareth. In Advent, we also anticipate the return of Christ in judgment. Waiting and watching of this sort has nothing of the make-believe quality of the first kind of waiting. (Imagine if we had little thrones on which to place little Christ the King figurines, as we have little mangers in which to place little baby Jesus figurines on Christmas Eve.)

Meditating on Christ's return inspires less sentimentality than imagining his birth, but properly understood, neither event is "cute" or sentimental. Both of them signal God moving toward humanity for the purpose of setting things right. Whether we are imagining the incarnation or the last judgment, our Advent texts proclaim a God who does not stay distant from creation or impassive in the face of creation's need for redemption, prosperity, and peace. Instead, God answers the cries of his people and God will, in Christ, lead them home.

In addition to these two advents, the church has sometimes spoken of a third. Our everyday lives unfold between the incarnation and the return of Christ to judgment. The third advent names the daily coming of Christ into our individual and communal lives with judgment and mercy—and with a vision for how we might live in such a way that our lives bear witness to the hope we have for the future and to the justice God will establish for all humanity. In Advent, we read Scripture to proclaim salvation as nearer to us than when we first believed, to speak of time as fulfilled, and to pray for God to deliver God's people *now*. The season inspires us to reflect not only on (1) the past coming of Christ as a baby, and (2) the future return of Christ to judgment, but also on (3) the present arrival of Christ in the midst of "the hopes and fears of all the years."[1]

The texts for Advent work on all of these levels. Notice how they call us to watch for God's intervention, not just in a distant future but now, even as the stories they tell are read and preached in the assembly. As Beverly Gaventa observes, "When we say, 'the time is right for a revolt,' we do not mean that revolts happen before lunch or in June, but that an intolerable situation has developed over a period of time. *Now* it must be changed."[2] What is God doing *now* in your context, and how do the Advent texts give voice to that?

Notice also the unbelievably grand dream for the future that these texts articulate. Preachers get so used to familiar texts that we stop hearing them. "Oh right," we say to each other, "Second Sunday of Advent, it must be the peaceable kingdom," but we do not actually stop to imagine what it would be like for us not to be afraid of snakes, or what it would be like to watch a cat and a bird play together without either of them baring a claw or thinking of lunch. We sing the Magnificat and rarely ponder what it might mean if the mighty really were cast down from their thrones and the lowly lifted up. Jack Roeda encourages us to think differently of the end for which we wait when he writes, "While it is true that it is the end of a violin when some hooligan takes it and smashes it to the ground, it is also the 'end' of the violin when a violinist takes it in hand and plays the Bach 'Chaconne.'"[3] Notice in Advent that every Sunday we read a text that imagines the "end" in terms of economic justice, prosperity, and peace.

Advent urges upon us a vision of a new world, a vision which stirs in us a holy restlessness for the complete transformation of ourselves and all things, and which assures us that we live toward, not the sputtering end of things, but toward the day when "all shall be well."
—Guy Sayles[4]

Finally, notice the reversal: God's power is made perfect in weakness. Years ago, when a choir I sang in was sounding a little too loud and heavy on the lyric, "Unto us a child is born," the choir director stopped us and said, "People, we're singing about a *baby* here." We go back to the birth of Jesus each Advent, not to pretend for four weeks that Jesus has not been born yet, but to remind ourselves of the astonishing news that God would choose such vulnerability for our sakes. Notice the baby. God will do amazing things through him.

Notes

1. Phillips Brooks, "O Little Town of Bethlehem," *Evangelical Lutheran Worship* (Minneapolis: Augsburg Fortress, 2006), 279.

2. Beverly Roberts Gaventa, "Homiletical Resources: Advent as Apocalypse," *Quarterly Review* 6 (1986): 59.

3. Jack Roeda, "I Can't See the Caboose," *The Reformed Journal* 36 (1986): 4.

4. Guy Sayles, "Preaching Advent Hope While Millions are Reading the *Left Behind* Series," *Journal for Preachers* 28 (2004): 16.

FIRST SUNDAY OF ADVENT

DECEMBER 2, 2007

REVISED COMMON	EPISCOPAL (BCP)	ROMAN CATHOLIC
Isa. 2:1-5	Isa. 2:1-5	Isa. 2:1-5
Psalm 122	Psalm 122	Ps. 122:1-2, 3-4a, 4b-5, 6-7, 8-9
Rom. 13:11-14	Rom. 13:8-14	Rom. 13:11-14
Matt. 24:36-44	Matt. 24:37-44	Matt. 24:37-44

KEY THEMES

• Visions of God's future inspire God's people to live godly lives in the present.
• God intervenes in the everyday lives of human beings.
• God's future includes praise from all peoples and peace among nations.

FIRST READING

ISAIAH 2:1-5 (RCL, BCP, LFM)

As a whole, the book of Isaiah alternates announcements of judgment on the people of Israel and hope for their renewed life. In large measure, Isaiah 1–39 announces the judgment of God on a people whose life together fails to bear witness to their relationship to the holy and merciful Yahweh, while Isaiah 40–66 proclaims the restoration of those on whom the judgment of God has come. Just as the book weaves together these two themes—judgment and restoration—so does Isaiah 1:1—2:5. Here in miniature, at the beginning of the book, we read the message of the whole.

Isaiah begins with an oracle of judgment that imagines the country desolate and the cities burned out (1:7). When people seek God, God will not respond: "When you stretch out your hands, I will hide my eyes from you; even though you make many prayers, I will not listen" (1:15). Then, after this dreadful threat to turn away from God's people, God turns back. Today's first lesson is a word of hope placed at the end of that first statement of judgment from Isaiah. The contrasts are marked: the text moves from Jerusalem as a burned-out city to Jerusalem as a

4

destination for the nations and a place where all may learn the ways of the Lord. Instead of a picture of God who refuses to heed supplication, Isaiah 2:1–5 proclaims God as One who attends to needs, One who listens and renders decisions as a judge between the nations.

Because God is rendering just decisions, the nations dismantle their war machines. Elsewhere in Isaiah, we read that "the fruit of righteousness will be peace; the effect of righteousness will be quietness and confidence forever" (Isa. 32:17, NIV). This is exactly the order of things in Isaiah 2. People will be treated fairly and will not, therefore, be inclined to take up arms. "The nations will not need to defend against each other, because Yahweh will establish a *pax Jerusalem* through which all will be safe and prosperous."[1] Some might argue that Isaiah's anthropology is optimistic here. Would not humanity be bent on war and destruction even if justice and fairness were the order of the day? Perhaps, but even skeptics have to admit that justice, safety, and widespread prosperity have a better chance of resulting in peace than injustice, danger, and disparity of wealth.

The text's two imperatives make it clear that the oracle of renewal is for both Israel and the nations. Gentiles will say to one another, "Come, let us go up to the mountain of the LORD" (2:3). The prophet says to his own people, "O house of Jacob, come, let us walk in the way of the LORD" (v. 5). Both groups are exhorted to live by the word of the Lord. Even so, there is at least one significant difference between the sentences: the prophet's words to his people are in the present tense, while the words from members of the nations to one another will happen in the future. Israel, listening as it is to the prophet's words before the devastation and renewal of Jerusalem and knowing the way of the Lord, has a chance to live godly lives ahead of the Gentiles. By walking in the way of the Lord, they will live as if that future, when Gentiles seek the word of the Lord and nations beat their swords into plowshares, has already arrived.

Isaiah summons us in these days to a new and vibrant hope, a hope on the move, a hope that grabs hold of our lives, gives us momentum and power, and moves us ahead on the journey to God's future. The prophet reminds us that Advent is as much about *what* we watch for as *how* we wait.
—Christine Roy Yoder[2]

RESPONSIVE READING

PSALM 122 (RCL, BCP)
PSALM 122:1–2, 3–4A, 4B–5, 6–7, 8–9 (LFM)

Psalm 122 offers the picture of an individual swept along with a crowd of pilgrims on the way up to Jerusalem. Probably a festival has brought everyone to the Temple. Energy and joy pulse through the words, as the tribes converge on the holy city "to give thanks to the name of the LORD" (v. 4). Yet, as in so many psalms, to pray this one is to begin with one thing in mind and end with another. At the start, the psalmist is glad about his pilgrimage and his own kinsfolk. At the end, the same voice is praying for the peace of Jerusalem and interceding for all who love the holy city, including, as Isaiah and the newspapers both remind us, both the tribes of Israel and many from all the nations of the world.

SECOND READING
ROMANS 13:11-14 (RCL, LFM)
ROMANS 13:8-14 (BCP)

Isaiah calls on hearers to walk in the way of the Lord in the present time. Likewise, Paul informs his readers that "the night is far gone," and he exhorts readers to "live honorably as in the day" (Rom. 13:12-13). As Isaiah had issued his call when miles of desert still lay between the Israelites' current reality of exile and their homecoming, so Paul urges the Romans to live their lives as if the new age had not just begun to dawn but was present as the full light of day.

Whether the reading for the day begins with verse 8 or verse 11, Paul offers a window here on how eschatology and ethics inform each other in his thought. The text works both back and forward from Paul's announcement that "you know what time it is, how it is now the moment for you to wake from sleep. For salvation is nearer to us now than when we became believers; the night is far gone, the day is near" (13:11-12a). The dawn of salvation is the warrant for Paul's hearers to love others, whether that command is put in Old Testament terms ("You shall love your neighbor as yourself") or christological terms ("Put on the Lord Jesus Christ, and make no provision for the flesh, to gratify its desires").

For Paul, the resurrection of Jesus signaled the beginning of a whole new age. Paul imagined himself and his readers situated at the dawn of that age, while the risen Christ lived and reigned "ahead of them," as it were. Yet it was as if Christ was doubling back on the road, coming soon from the future back to meet his own. He was drawing near, just as at daybreak the sun seems to grow closer and closer to popping over the horizon to shine on those who, moments before, had been living between the first light of dawn.

> [Paul] expects [his readers] to be up before day breaks fully; this theme, with its echoes of the Easter morning stories, resonates through the early Christian sense of new creation, new life bursting through the wintry crust of the old world. It is, he insists, time to wake up.
> —N. T. Wright[3]

The apocalyptic thought that is key to this passage of Scripture is often seen as frightening, irritating, or irrelevant to preachers and their audience. Was Paul wrong about the times in which he lived? If so, how can we expect him to be able to speak (on the topic of Christ's return, anyway) to ours? How is this material to be appropriated today, when still we wait for the full light of day, and when, more than ever, that wait seems likely to stretch on indefinitely?

Romans 13:11 offers at least a partial response to these questions. The point of saying, "Salvation is nearer to us now than when we first became believers," is not to proclaim anything about the day and hour of the Messiah's return. Rather, the word *nearer* testifies that something redemptive is and has been happening all along, even though the exact nature and timetable of that redemption are often hidden from us. Concerning the day of salvation, Paul does not know or claim to know the "when." He knows only the "what" of it: that day will be characterized not by excess, exploitation, or wrangling, but instead by love of neighbor. He calls his hearers to trust enough in his previous testimony of what God has done in Christ and his current testimony about the end that, regardless of its arrival time, those in Christ live as if the end were here already.

To speak of and pray for Christ's imminent return is to give voice to the conviction that what God has begun in Christ's death and resurrection will, in fact and contrary to so many appearances, have cosmic consequences. It is to hope for more than most of us dare. A church formed by Paul's apocalyptic thought is neither preoccupied by timetables for the end and an eagerness for enemies to burn, nor is it puffed up by a sense of itself as a "dispenser of salvation" already achieved.[4] Instead, a church formed by Paul's apocalyptic gospel offers a patient yet intense witness to something not yet revealed. (*Apokalypsis*, after all, means "revelation.") We wait. We watch. We testify to our hope for the future both with prayers for Christ's return and with the practice of loving our neighbors as ourselves.

THE GOSPEL
MATTHEW 24:36-44 (RCL)
MATTHEW 24:37-44 (BCP, LFM)

The ultimate is bumping up against the everyday. The disciples have asked Jesus, "When?" (Matt. 24:3). When will it be that the Temple will come tumbling down? When will it be that "Heaven and earth will pass away" (Matt. 24:35)? The images in much of Matthew 24 are grand in scale and cosmic in scope. They evoke more than the mind's eye can take in. In a movie theatre, these images would fill the whole screen.

Then, at the end of the chapter, the images shrink. In today's Gospel reading, the subjects are individual human beings and their everyday lives. People are marrying and giving in marriage. They are working in the field. They are grinding meal outside the door of their home. Here, the cosmic intersects with the mundane.

It is common to say that apocalyptic imagery appeals most to communities experiencing persecution. According to this view, it is only when you have no hope of bringing about change by working within the system that you pin your hopes for vindication on a drastic intervention from outside that system. If a letter to your congressman or a little "sweat equity" will create the change you want to see in the world, you don't need stories about the sun darkened and the stars falling from heaven (cf. Matt. 24:29). When the system is working for you, you are not inclined to look with longing for a new heaven and a new earth. Thus, the conventional wisdom: apocalyptic imagery is for the disenfranchised. It gives oppressed people hope for real change precisely when that change is nothing they can effect on their own.

That is one theory. Yet in Matthew and Mark, Jesus seems to address apocalyptic imagery not to oppressed people but to sleepy people. "What I say to you I say to all: Keep awake!" (Mark 13:37). So ends Mark's "little apocalypse." Matthew echoes the same theme in today's Gospel reading. "Keep awake therefore, for you do not know on what day your Lord is coming" (Matt. 24:42) and "Therefore you also must be ready, for the Son of Man is coming at an unexpected hour" (24:44) are both part of today's text. Two chapters later in Matthew, Jesus asks the disciples to stay awake in Gethsemane while he prays. Twice he returns to find them sleeping. They have been neither watching nor praying as those who have arrived to arrest Jesus have moved into place.

Perhaps the problem anticipated by Jesus' words is not that people labor under a crushing reality of persecution, but that, whether they are persecuted or privileged, they no longer believe that anything will change. They imagine today and tomorrow looking exactly like yesterday, and after days, months, and years of such scaled-back expectations, they are getting . . . very . . . sleepy. In response, Jesus tells stories in which something drastic happens.

During college, I got up early one morning and headed toward breakfast. It could not have been much past 7:00 A.M. and hardly anyone was awake. As I turned the corner to the cafeteria, I saw a student lying on the sidewalk. I had no idea what had happened, but it looked as if she had fallen backwards and hit her head. She was breathing, but out cold. There was a little pool of blood at the back of her skull. Even as I ran up the stairs of the building to get help, I remember thinking those words, "a pool of blood," and thinking what a cliché they are—but true!

I swung open the door of the cafeteria, and inside I found people doing exactly what they did every morning. Some people were carrying trays to tables. Others were spreading peanut butter on English muffins. One woman with coffee seemed to be staring at the wall waiting for the caffeine to kick in. The contrast between the scene inside the cafeteria and the scene out on the sidewalk could not have been more dramatic. I got someone to call 911. Help arrived. It turned out that the girl who had fainted would be OK. But I remember that moment of entering the cafeteria, knowing there was an emergency outside and being stunned that everyone inside was simply beginning their day, as they did every morning. Of course, before I rounded the corner to the cafeteria and saw the collapsed student, I had been doing exactly the same thing.

Life happens that way. Daily life unfolds as one reasonably predictable thing after another—until it doesn't anymore. One minute you are fine, and then there is this odd sensation of pain running across your chest and down your arm. At 10:00 A.M., you have a job, and at 10:20, someone is walking with you to your desk to watch as you pack up your things. You are driving, not paying any more or less attention to the road than you ever do, and suddenly something happens: another car, or a deer, or a slippery spot, and everything changes in an instant.

In this text, all of the images that Jesus uses as analogies for the coming of the Son of man into everyday life are negative: normal life goes on until the flood, or until one person is snatched and another left, or until a thief breaks in. Earlier Jesus had used at least one positive image: in Matthew 13, Jesus compares the kingdom to someone finding treasure in a field. Everything changes there in the blink of an eye, too, but in that case, the change is welcome. In Matthew 25, bridesmaids await the arrival of the bridegroom and the start of a reception. In the story of the bridesmaids, as in today's Gospel, people are urged to stay awake, yet it is not so that they can stop their home from being broken into, but so they may be ready for a party.

Whether the analogies are negative or positive, the message is that the intervention of God into human affairs cannot be managed or scheduled the way many of the events of our days can be. Whether God's advent is as manageable as a heart attack, or as manageable as falling in love, either way, you know you are not in control, and you can be fairly sure the rest of your day will not go as planned.

As we journey down the long and seemingly endless path of discipleship, we never know when we may encounter the living God waiting for us around the next bend. Indeed, each unexpected meeting, each moment of holy surprise, is but an anticipation of the great climax of all human history and longing, when the world, seemingly spinning along in ceaseless tedium, will find itself gathered into the extravagant mercy of God.
—Thomas G. Long[5]

If God's intervention into human history is as unpredictable and unmanageable as all that, why bother to tell people to "keep awake" or "be ready" for it? What would a preacher want her sermon on this text to *do* in the lives of hearers? Surely the goal of a sermon on this text ought not be to inspire a lifetime of anxiety in one's hearers, so that whenever someone flips a light switch inside the front door at home, he expects either to see the place ransacked, or to watch a dozen people jump from behind the furniture and yell, "Surprise!"

The goal of a sermon on this text is to be able to imagine God at work in the world. It is to understand daily life as the arena for God's coming into the world, and so to see each day, each moment, as capable of bearing the infinitely valuable gift of God's own justice and mercy. The usual maxims of daily life that are contrary to God's justice and mercy (for instance, "The rich get richer, and the poor get poorer." "You get what you negotiate." "The more things change, the more they stay the same") may look like the truths to live by, but they are not. Watching them overturned is something worth staying awake for. The gift of another way is, for most of us, unexpected, but no less real for being a surprise.

Notes

1. Walter Brueggemann, *Isaiah 1–39,* Westminster Bible Companion (Louisville: Westminster John Knox Press, 1998), 24.

2. Christine Roy Yoder, "Hope That Walks: An Interpretation of Isaiah for Advent Preachers," *Journal for Preachers* 25, no. 1 (2001): 17.

3. N. T. Wright, "Romans," in *New Interpreter's Bible* (Nashville: Abingdon, 2002), 10:728. (Exact quote is "He expects them to be up. . . .")

4. J. Christiaan Beker, "The Promise of Paul's Apocalyptic for Our Times," in *The Future of Christology: Essays in Honor of Leander E. Keck,* ed. Abraham J. Malherbe and Wayne A. Meeks (Minneapolis: Fortress Press, 1993), fears that a church without Paul's apocalyptic eschatology "views itself no longer as a proleptic reality, but rather as a dispenser of salvation" (158).

5. Thomas G. Long, *Matthew,* Westminster Bible Companion (Louisville: Westminster John Knox Press, 1997), 276.

SECOND SUNDAY OF ADVENT

DECEMBER 9, 2007

REVISED COMMON	EPISCOPAL (BCP)	ROMAN CATHOLIC
Isa. 11:1–10	Isa. 11:1–10	Isa. 11:1–10
Ps. 72:1-7, 18–19	Psalm 72 or 72:1–8	Ps. 72:1-2, 7-8, 12-13, 17
Rom. 15:4–13	Rom. 15:4–13	Rom. 15:4–9
Matt. 3:1–12	Matt. 3:1–12	Matt. 3:1–12

KEY THEMES

• In Christ, God bridges long-standing divisions to create a holy and merciful community.

• In the reign of God, the most vulnerable are valued, protected, and welcomed.

• Those who announce God's reign offer both comfort and challenge.

FIRST READING
ISAIAH 11:1–10 (RCL, BCP, LFM)

Commenting on Isaiah 11:1–10, Ralph Klein calls Yahweh a woodsman, and David Carr quips, "Not only does this passage speak of a stump, but the passage itself is cut off in the lectionary!"[1] Both authors are referring to the fact that the stump in Isaiah 11:1 is the result of the Almighty's plan for clear-cutting, a plan reported just a few verses before the start of today's first reading. "Look, the Sovereign, the LORD of hosts, will lop the boughs with terrifying power; the tallest trees will be cut down, and the lofty will be brought low. He will hack down the thickets of the forest with an ax, and Lebanon with its majestic trees will fall" (Isa. 10:33-34).[2] It is another oracle of destruction from a prophet who is trying desperately to get people's attention.

The oracle of destruction is followed by a word of hope: a shoot will grow out of that stump. The Davidic monarchy, even though it is the target of much of Isaiah's judgment, will not be finished forever. Jesse was David's father. From the left-for-dead stump of Jesse will come a just, merciful ruler, with particular gifts

MARY HINKLE
SHORE

for governing God's people. With wisdom and understanding, the ruler will be a just judge. With counsel and might, he will be a competent commander-in-chief. With knowledge and the fear of the Lord, the ruler will have what is perhaps the most important characteristic a civil servant can possess: the recognition that he is not God, and that the One to whom he must give account never ceases to defend the widow and the orphan. The spirit of the Lord offers these gifts, and thus God creates a ruler who is gifted for the work of governing rather than one who merely inherits the task.[3]

The imagery changes halfway through the reading. The charismatic ruler creates an environment so void of wickedness that the animal kingdom is transformed. Those who used to be predator and prey coexist in mutual safety. The most vulnerable humans—tiny children—are safe as well. The nations beyond the borders governed by this ruler will come asking for counsel from one so wise.

For Christians, the One who actually comes as the clearest fulfillment of Isaiah's word decides that the only way to get to the peaceable kingdom is to live out its meekness here and now, no matter what. He does not breathe fire on anyone. He seeks out sinners. He is himself a lamb lying down in the midst of wolves. With his life, death, and resurrection, Jesus gave us a window on the peaceable kingdom.

In sum, Isa. 11:1-9 draws deeply on the various streams of ancient royal theology, but adapts each element to fit its particular focus on a just peace established by a wise, spirit-gifted king."
—David Carr[4]

RESPONSIVE READING
PSALM 72:1-7, 18-19 (RCL)
PSALM 72 or 72:1-8 (BCP)
PSALM 72:1-2, 7-8, 12-13, 17 (LFM)

Various verses of Psalm 72 are assigned for this Sunday. Perhaps because the psalm takes a nationalistic turn after verse 7, some lectionary options omit much of its second half. Also, while the psalm ends with doxology (vv. 18-20), these verses are omitted in some lectionaries as well. Rather than relating directly to Psalm 72, the verses of doxology actually close out the second book of the five books that make up the psalter, so the intent of the psalm itself may be better served when they are not read.

Like the first reading, the psalm describes a good king, but the psalm is a prayer offered on the occasion of such a king's coronation. While the psalm is traditionally tied to Solomon, its vision of justice and prosperity transcends a single monarch's reign. What do people need from their ruler? The answers given are just judgment (v. 2), prosperity (v. 3), and defense of the most vulnerable (v. 4).

ROMANS 15:4-13 (RCL, BCP)
ROMANS 15:4-9 (LFM)

A prospectus describing an investment opportunity will generally warn clients that "past performance does not predict future results." When it comes to whether God may be trusted to keep God's promises, however, the Apostle Paul is arguing exactly the opposite. Based on God's past performance, Paul proclaims that his readers have reason both for present kindness to one another across social divisions and for future hope of an even broader and more diverse community of those who recognize Jesus as Lord. Whether the epistle text for the day ends at verse 13 or earlier, at verse 9, the second reading offers another kind of peaceable kingdom to hearers. In the reading from Isaiah, animals were pictured as living in peace. Here it is humans. In the second reading, the ministry of Christ for both Jews and Gentiles points to a unified community that will "with one voice glorify the God and Father of our Lord Jesus Christ" (v. 6).

Romans 14 speaks of disagreements around observing certain holidays and eating meat offered to idols. Paul says, "If your brother or sister is being injured by what you eat, you are no longer walking in love. Do not let what you eat cause the ruin of one for whom Christ died" (Rom. 14:15). In 15:3, Paul uses Christ's service for others as a warrant for thinking of others before oneself: "Christ did not please himself; but, as it is written, 'The insults of those who insult you have fallen on me.'"

It seems to be that quotation about insults from Psalm 69:9 that leads to the observation at the beginning of today's second reading: "Whatever was written in former days was written for our instruction, so that by steadfastness and by the encouragement of the scriptures we might have hope" (Rom. 15:4). Both when the Scriptures talk about one who bears insults meant for another, and when they talk about the Gentiles joining God's people Israel in offering praise to God, the Scriptures are speaking truthfully. In Romans 15:9-12, Paul cites Old Testament passages one after another as a way of demonstrating that the diversity within the church to which he writes is not a human accident, but is rather part of God's plan from the former days, now brought into being among the Romans. Several of Paul's letters testify that the first Christian churches had as difficult a time as moderns do when it comes to forming genuine community across ethnic, social, and economic divisions. Even so, Paul sees that sort of community as evidence that God is keeping God's word.

> God's truth has as much to do with action as with speech. For Paul, to assert that God is truthful is to assert that God has always acted in a way consistent with God's speech. Christ is the ultimate proof that God tells the truth and does the truth, because Christ fulfills the promises made to Israel long ago.
> —Beverly Roberts Gaventa[5]

Paul prays that now, living in the same community, Jewish and Gentile Christians in Rome offer their common life as testimony to God's faithfulness. By being of one mind, they bear witness to their hope for the redemption of all creation. The phrase translated "to live in harmony" in Romans 15:5 is almost identical to that translated as "be of the same mind" in Philippians 2:2. One imagines a team working toward a common goal, or a pair of horses pulling in the same direction. The Roman church's shared work is to praise God together (v. 6) and to welcome one another (v. 7).

These things were written for our instruction. By praising God and showing hospitality toward each other, the church to which Paul first wrote—and the churches who hear his words as Scripture today—bear witness to the truth that Christ is the means and inspiration for both vertical reconciliation (between God and the humans who praise God) and horizontal reconciliation (among humans who welcome one another in spite of differences).

> God's radical acceptance of Gentiles, the outsiders, necessitates mutual recognition and respect within the community of faith.
> —Beverly Roberts Gaventa[6]

THE GOSPEL

MATTHEW 3:1-12 (RCL, BCP, LFM)

John the Baptist appears in all four Gospels at precisely the same moment: just before the adult Jesus enters the story. In all four Gospels, John prepares the way for Jesus. If we imagine ourselves standing with the crowds coming out for baptism, John prepares us for Jesus by directing our gaze (1) back to the record of Israel's hope for redemption and (2) back to evidence of our own broken relationship with God. John prepares us also by directing our gaze (3) forward to the One who is coming after him, with gifts of the Holy Spirit and fire.

Israel's Hope. John the Baptist is dressed like Elijah (cf. 2 Kings 1:8), and John recalls Israel's hope that God will send a prophet, perhaps Elijah himself, "before the great and terrible day of the LORD comes. He will turn the hearts of parents to their children, and the hearts of children to their parents" (Mal. 4:5-6). The prophecy is of a fire that burns like an oven and reduces the arrogant and evildoers to stubble (cf. Mal. 4:1). The Elijah figure will warn people and turn them back from arrogance and evil. Such a prophet's appearance is frightening, but also hopeful. It means that soon the wicked will no longer prosper at everyone else's expense. Instead, the meek shall inherit the earth (cf. Ps. 37:11; Isa. 11:4; and Matt. 5:5). Soon, God will establish a king for Israel like that one described in Isaiah 11 and Psalm 72. John the Baptist appears to do advance work for such a celebrity. He sees his work as preparing the way, turning the hearts of the people back to God.

John's Call for Repentance. John preaches a one-sentence sermon that Jesus will also preach (cf. Matt. 4:17): "Repent, for the kingdom of heaven has come near" (Matt. 3:2). About the phrase "kingdom of heaven," Robert Smith remarks, "To say that this kingdom or sovereign rule is 'of heaven' or 'of God' is not to locate it in the heavens above but to assert that it has its source in heaven or in God, that it comes as a gift from above, and that it is something wholly different from earthly kingdoms and sovereignties."[7] The "kingdom" is that time and place where God's name is properly hallowed, and God's will is perfectly done (cf. Matt. 6:9-11). It is that time and place where "the wolf shall dwell with the lamb, the leopard shall lie down with the kid, the calf and the young lion and the fatling together, and a little child shall lead them" (Isa. 11:6). Whatever else the kingdom is, it is the world turned upside down like that.

The arrival of such a time and place calls for repentance. The word connotes not a feeling of regret so much as an action, a change of direction, a turning around, or a turning back. "The crowds begin to own up to the fact that they have broken with God, broken faith with God, broken away from God, broken the bonds that tied them to God" and they receive baptism as a way of identifying with a widespread movement back to the covenant.[9]

Common wisdom has it that the three most important things in real estate are location, location, and location. The same is true for people. "Since the divorce she's been in a really bad place." "Our group just isn't there yet. We're stuck." . . . "Where are you on this decision?" . . . This richly textured passage not only helps us locate ourselves, it also challenges us to more forward into God's approaching reign.
—Raymond R. Roberts[8]

The movement is so widespread, it includes even Pharisees and Sadducees, religious leaders who would probably not be thought to *need* the sort of confession/repentance ritual over which John presides. John is skeptical of their motives, but skeptical or not, he apparently does not refuse their participation at the Jordan. The Pharisees and Sadducees, but also all the rest of those who appear for John's baptism, are religious people, looking for the redemption of Israel. This is an important point, especially for church people to hear. As Smith observes about John, "He summons not outsiders but insiders to radical reorientation, calling religious people in particular to stop insisting that they know best and to cease resisting God, God's judgment, God's sovereignty."[10] The text is humbling for religious people in this respect, first of all for those religious people who would preach it. The story of Jesus' ministry—and especially his rejection by the religious authorities who make their first appearance in the Gospel here—presses upon the preacher the question: What new thing God might be doing in our communities that we cannot recognize, as the Pharisees and Sadducees could finally not recognize God at work in Jesus? In what concrete ways have we and the communities of which we are a part "broken faith with God, broken away from God, broken the bonds that tied" us to God, and what would it look like to turn back, to repent?

Jesus' Gifts: The Holy Spirit and Fire. John the Baptist reminds his audience that the God who can bring a green shoot from a dead stump (cf. Isa. 11:1) can also raise up children for Abraham from stones. According to Isaiah, it is the Spirit of God who raises up a new king to judge the poor with righteousness and decide for the meek with equity. According to John the Baptist, the One coming after him will baptize with that Spirit and with fire.

The reference is curious. Sometimes commentators wonder aloud whether John got Jesus wrong. Was the Baptist expecting the king of Isaiah 11:4b ("He shall strike the earth with the rod of his mouth, and with the breath of his lips he shall kill the wicked"), when he should have been looking for the servant of Isaiah 42:3 ("A bruised reed he will not break, and a dimly burning wick he will not quench")? It is possible. Halfway through the Gospel, when Matthew wants to summarize Jesus' ministry, he chooses not a prophecy of destruction, but exactly that servant song of Isaiah 42 (cf. Matt. 12:18-21).

Yet there is another way to understand "the Holy Spirit and fire." In Matthew's Gospel, Jesus is explicitly referred to as "Emmanuel, which means God is with us" (Matt. 1:23). Jesus arrives at John's baptism, identifies with the turn his people are making back to God, and joins them. Recognizing that sin is not only an individual reality but also a communal one, he gives himself to a baptism of repentance for the forgiveness of sins, and then he gives himself to all those with whom he interacts. John's Gospel includes a narrator's note that Jesus would not entrust himself to some of the people who believed in him early as a result of miraculous signs (cf. John 2:24). No such note exists in the Synoptic Gospels.

To say that this kingdom or sovereign rule is "of heaven" or "of God" is not to locate it in the heavens above but to assert that it has its source in heaven or in God, that it comes as a gift from above, and that it is something wholly different from earthly kingdoms and sovereignties. —Robert H. Smith[11]

In Matthew, Mark, and Luke, Jesus gives the gift of the Spirit as he entrusts himself first to John, and then to all the sinners whom he befriends in the Gospel. To encounter Jesus is to know "God with us." It is also to receive the Spirit that the Father and the Son share. As Thomas Long writes, "The Holy Spirit is God, who gives the divine self to us as a gift. The Holy Spirit is given to us to teach wisdom, to guide us in the ways of mercy, to encourage our faith in a world where faith's vision seems foolish, to assure us that no matter how powerful evil may appear there is no lost good, and to confirm in our present ambiguous circumstances the bold promises of the gospel."[12] This list describes the work of Christ on both sides of the cross and resurrection. Jesus baptizes with the Holy Spirit by sharing himself and his spirit with humanity.

 As for fire, in almost every case in Matthew's Gospel, fire refers to an element of the last judgment. For instance, burning is what happens to the weeds that grow with the wheat until the harvest (cf. Matt. 13:30, 41-42). At their best, Christians have recognized that the image of a field in which both weeds and wheat grow

describes not only people outside the faith but also all of us within it, both individually and collectively. To pray for Christ's gift of fire, then, is to pray for the flame that incinerates everything within and around us that causes harm. We pray for such a flame, not so that the few righteous people left can congratulate themselves by firelight. We who take Paul at his word, "There is no one who is righteous, not even one" (Rom. 3:10), do not believe in "a few righteous people." We pray for an end to everything within and around us that causes harm so that lions, lambs, adders, humans, and the rest of creation may stop—once and for all—the predator/prey relationships and live in peace. Come, Lord Jesus.

Notes

1. Ralph W. Klein, "Isaiah for Advent," *Currents in Theology and Mission* 28, no. 6 (2001): 562, and David McLain Carr, "Light in the Darkness: Rediscovering Advent Hope in the Lectionary Texts from Isaiah," *Quarterly Review* 15 (Fall 1995): 301.

2. John the Baptist echoes similar sentiments when he says, centuries later, "Even now the ax is lying at the root of the trees; every tree therefore that does not bear good fruit is cut down and thrown into the fire" (Matt. 3:10).

3. Ralph Klein points out that only Saul and David were charismatic kings of Israel, while "Solomon and his descendants profited by dynastic inertia—Solomon and all his successors became king because their father was king before them." "Isaiah for Advent," 562.

4. Carr, "Light in the Darkness," 303.

5. Beverly Roberts Gaventa, "Homiletical Resources: Advent as Apocalypse," *Quarterly Review* 6, no. 3 (Fall 1986): 66.

6. Ibid., 63.

7. Robert H. Smith, *Matthew*, Augsburg Commentary on the New Testament (Minneapolis: Augsburg, 1989), 48.

8. Raymond R. Roberts, "Matthew 3:1-12," *Interpretation* 59, no. 4 (Oct. 2005): 396.

9. Ibid., 51.

10. Ibid., 49.

11. Smith, *Matthew*, 48.

12. Thomas G. Long, *Matthew*, Westminster Bible Companion (Louisville: Westminster John Knox Press, 1997), 31.

THIRD SUNDAY OF ADVENT

DECEMBER 16, 2007

REVISED COMMON	EPISCOPAL (BCP)	ROMAN CATHOLIC
Isa. 35:1-10	Isa. 35:1-10	Isa. 35:1-6a, 10
Ps. 146:5-10	Psalm 146	Ps. 146:6-7, 8-9a,
or Luke 1:46b-55	or 146:4-9	9b-10
James 5:7-10	James 5:7-10	James 5:7-10
Matt. 11:2-11	Matt. 11:2-11	Matt. 11:2-11

KEY THEMES

- God claims an exiled people and promises to redeem them.
- Christians anticipate the fullness of God's reign with a patient intensity that works for the good of others while waiting for God's redemption.
- Jesus inaugurates God's reign both with miraculous deeds of healing and by practicing suffering love.

FIRST READING

ISAIAH 35:1-10 (RCL, BCP)
ISAIAH 35:1-6a, 10 (LFM)

The cartoon shows a man and a woman in a restaurant booth. He is looking fondly into her eyes, and saying, "Your eyes are like . . . eyes. Your lips are like . . . lips." The caption to the cartoon is, "Why we need poets."

A people in exile need their poet-prophets more even than that man in the restaurant. In its canonical context, the message of redemption for Israel in Isaiah 35 stands in marked contrast to the oracle of judgment against the nations in Isaiah 34. These two chapters may belong to the preexilic time period usually associated with Isaiah 1–39, or they may have been written in the exile. Regardless of its date of origin, the first reading for this Sunday anticipates the redemption that sings in the poetry of so-called Second Isaiah (Isaiah 40–66). On the Second Sunday of Advent, the text from Isaiah offered a picture of the animal kingdom at peace, without predators and prey. This Sunday, tame lions appear again in the first reading, along with a description of a blooming desert and the news that God will be the redeemer of God's own.

Let's look first at the desert. Isaiah describes a desert that is blooming, and not just with a few little cactus flowers after a short rain. The news is climate change, and it means to give hope to people with a stretch of hostile environment between them and their home. "The desert shall rejoice and blossom" (Isa. 35:1). Imagine getting off the plane in Tel Aviv and being greeted with a lei. As with almost every image in this chapter, the image of water in the desert is introduced and then amplified. We hear not just of water in the desert, but of pools, swamps, and even springs of water. The water leaps with as much energy as the healed who are headed home.

There is a highway in this flowering former desert. Noted among this highway's characteristics is that one cannot get lost on it. Proverbs remarks that "the path of the upright is a level highway" (Prov. 15:19), yet on this level highway (cf. Isa. 40:3), even fools, about whom Proverbs has little good to say, will walk and not get lost. Neither will they get eaten: neither drought, nor disorientation, nor ravenous beasts will endanger those returning home.

Finally, this passage sees the goal of the divine-human encounter to be our sheer joy in God's presence. This is an Advent text for all those whose God is too small or whose view of the regenerate life is crimped and cramped. The gospel renews and empowers the church in its goal to transform society.
—Ralph W. Klein[1]

The people themselves need reassurance. Change—even a change from slavery into freedom, and from exile to homecoming—evokes fear, and so the poet says, "Be strong, do not fear!" (Isa. 35:4). It may also be that the people are not merely afraid of change, but honestly afraid of God's response to them. Do they need reassurance that God means to do good rather than harm to them? A colleague remarks that the preexilic prophets had a nearly impossible time convincing people that God would punish iniquity, while the postexilic prophets had an equally difficult time convincing people that God would restore a relationship with God's people. So here the prophet says, "Do not fear."

In this reading, God's restored relationship with the people begins with restored health. "Then the eyes of the blind shall be opened, and the ears of the deaf unstopped; then the lame shall leap like a deer, and the tongue of the speechless sing for joy" (Isa. 35:5-6a). People are healed and whole. Body parts fulfill their function, and then some. The tongue does not just speak, but rather sings for joy. People who could not walk are leaping like deer.

Many of us, much of the time, try to keep our expectations in check, because to dream too big is to court disappointment. From what we will receive for Christmas, to whether relationships or bodies might experience healing, to how our hearts' desires will be met, we scale back our hopes for fear of being let down. This is understandable. Certainly people who had lived a generation in exile would share such a fear of hope. Yet in response to that fear, Isaiah does not speak gently to them of incremental improvements or baby steps toward home. He tells a story not just of safe passage but of a blooming desert. He describes a way that will be not only predator free, but also fool friendly. He pictures the travelers not as tired slaves returning from exile, but freed prisoners, healthy and strong, and dancing their way home.

RESPONSIVE READING
PSALM 146:5-10 (RCL)
PSALM 146 or 146:4-9 (BCP)
PSALM 146:6-7, 8-9A, 9B-10 (LFM)
LUKE 1:46B-55 (RCL alt.)

Whether Psalm 146 or the Magnificat is chosen for the responsive reading, both texts show God to be the defender of the needy, offering justice as well as the more tangible gifts of food for the hungry, freedom for those imprisoned, and health for those who are ill.

The transformed land forms the backdrop to what God intends to do with his people who are transformed from the lost and forlorn into the "redeemed." Once known as the exiles who were forcefully taken from their own land, they are now the redeemed because God as their "kinsman/redeemer" comes and takes back his own: "He is our God" (v. 4).
—Scott L. Harris[2]

Is all of this only good poetry for a festive season? To ask the question another way, Is it true? Does God really intend to fill the hungry with good things, and send the rich away empty? Here we are close to John the Baptist's question to Jesus from the Gospel reading. Various responses to the question may be offered (some in the commentary on the Gospel below), but speaking in terms of the psalm for the day, Walter Brueggemann says that as we sing psalms of praise to God for such things, we "are drawn into a triangle with the God who cares powerfully and the neighbors who need desperately. The song is an act of strenuous, dangerous imagination."[3] What we sing we may be able to see. To sing is to admit that God may indeed change things—including us—in the way the song imagines.

SECOND READING
JAMES 5:7-10 (RCL, BCP, LFM)

At first, James makes it sound as if the judgment of the thoughtless rich is imminent. "Come now, you rich people, weep and wail for the miseries that are coming to you" (James 5:1). The rich have laid up treasures on earth, treasures that will do them little good in the last days. In fact, the wealth itself will stand as evidence of fraudulent business practices. Thus begins the chapter from which today's second reading comes.

After addressing *hoi plousioi* ("you rich") in 5:1, James turns in 5:7 to address *hoi adelphoi* ("brothers and sisters," or "beloved" in NRSV). The rich may not have long to enjoy their ill-gotten gain, but to the poor, the time will seem to pass more slowly. When James is addressing his brothers and sisters, he counsels patience even as he offers assurances of the Lord's return.

The reading and the material surrounding it give us two important bits of information about patience. First, patience is not resignation to evil or suffering. James is calling no one to suffer in silence or to suffer alone. In fact, the opposite is true. In the verses just after today's reading, James asks, "Are any among you suffering? They should pray. . . . Are any among you sick? They should call for the elders of the church and have them pray over them, anointing them with oil in the name of the Lord" (5:13-14). Believers do not prove their faithfulness by "settling in" to suffering and referring to that kind of resignation as "patience."

The second bit of news about patience comes from a closer examination of the two examples of patient people James offers. First are farmers, who plant and then wait for rain. Second are prophets, who speak God's word to the people and then wait for that word to have some effect. Neither of these groups is known for being resigned to injustice or lazy about their own work. Farmers study weather patterns, soils, and seeds; they maintain and improve their implements; they work as long as the sun will let them, and in modern times, even longer than that. Prophets stand between God and God's people and sometimes feel as if they do not quite belong in the company of either. They speak truth to power and often pay the price in terms of their freedom, comfort, and reputation. Neither farmers nor prophets shrink back from adversity. "Patience" is not "weak resignation to the evils we deplore."[4]

Save us from weak resignation to the evils
we deplore;
Let the gift of your salvation be our glory
evermore.
Grant us wisdom, grant us courage, serving you
whom we adore,
Serving you whom we adore.
—Harry Emerson Fosdick[5]

The common thread between prophets and farmers is clarity about what they control and what they do not. This clarity is the basis for the capacity to wait for the Lord. According to James, the rich lack any recognition of things beyond their control. The rich do not see the difference between human work and God's work (cf. James 4:13). Someone has told the rich that money is power—power even over the future—and they believe it. Being patient "until the coming of the Lord" (5:7) does not preclude hard work and fervent prayer that all injustice may soon come to an end. The patience that James commends only precludes thinking that such an outcome depends entirely on us.

MATTHEW 11:2-11 (RCL, BCP, LFM)

Sometimes in conversations about faith, unbelievers will explain themselves by telling Christian friends that they just do not believe in things they cannot see. Or they will wonder aloud about how any one religion could claim to be exclusively true when the earth includes so many cultures and religions, and good (and bad) people can be found in all of them. Other times, people will say, "How can you believe in a just, merciful, all-powerful God when the world is such a mess? If God exists, and if Jesus is as important as you claim, shouldn't things be better by now? Where is the peace on earth he was supposed to bring? Why are there still diseases, wars, earthquakes?"

These questions could be inspired by John the Baptist's circumstances in today's Gospel reading. John is in prison. Apparently Matthew's first readers knew enough of the circumstances of John's imprisonment that Matthew did not need to explain the facts of the case until later (cf. Matt. 14:1-12). It is enough here for Matthew to say, in almost an offhand way, that from prison John sent a message to Jesus. In Advent, John's imprisonment is a metaphor for all the ways that, even after the coming of Jesus as "God with us," injustice goes right on, unchecked. If God exists, and if Jesus is as important as we claim, shouldn't things be better by now?

So far in the Gospel, we know that John recognized Jesus as the One greater than himself, and consented to baptize Jesus only after Jesus insisted (Matt. 3:13-17). We also know that he expected that One who was to come to gather the wheat into his barn, and "burn the chaff with unquenchable fire" (Matt. 3:12). Finally and decisively, the wheat would be separated from the weeds. This is John's dream for the Messiah.

So far in a service for the Third Sunday of Advent, the congregation at worship will have heard the dream of exiles healthfully and joyfully making their way home along a highway where nothing can harm them. The congregation will have sung praises to God who "executes justice for the oppressed" (Psalm 146:7) or who "has brought down the powerful from their thrones, and lifted up the lowly" (Luke 1:52).

Now, in the Gospel for the day, the congregation hears a question from John the Baptist, the truest believer in Jesus whom Gospel readers have met so far. "Are you the one who is to come, or are we to wait for another?" (Matt. 11:3). Implied in that question are others: "If you are the one who is to come, when will you be starting to separate the wheat from the chaff? When, exactly, will the powerful Herod be brought down from his throne; when will release be proclaimed to the captive? If you, Jesus, are the one who is to come, what am I, John, doing in prison?"

Preachers can point out that those with questions like that one from John are in good company. If John could ask such things, we can too. "If you are the one

who is to come, why is my friend, Sarah, dying of cancer? Why does every generation seem to need to go to war? Why are so many kids abused? Why are there still
people around the world, like John the Baptist of old, unjustly held in prisons?"

In the text for the day, as well as the Gospel of Matthew as a whole, the
preacher can find at least two different responses to these questions. The first is
the answer that Jesus gives to John's disciples. Jesus documents the healing that
is happening as a result of his ministry. Isaiah had spoken of that time when "the
eyes of the blind shall be opened, and the ears of the deaf
unstopped; then the lame shall leap like a deer, and the
tongue of the speechless sing for joy" (Isa. 35:5-6). Jesus
says, "Go and tell John what you hear and see: the blind
receive their sight, the lame walk, the lepers are cleansed,
the deaf hear, the dead are raised, and the poor have good

> As we await the coming of Christ, what
> kind of person, what kind of ministry, what
> kind of relation to us are we anticipating?
> —Fred B. Craddock[6]

news brought to them. And blessed is anyone who takes no offense at me" (Matt.
11:5-6). The texts sound the same. Yes, John is still in prison. Yet Jesus' ministry is,
at least in part, enacting the hopes of the prophet Isaiah and others who spoke of
a time when physical healing and other kinds of liberation would come true.

The frontispiece for Frederick Buechner's autobiography, *Now and Then*, offers
this quotation from Paul Tillich's *The New Being*: "We want only to show you
something we have seen and to tell you something we have heard . . . that here and
there in the world and now and then in ourselves is seen a New Creation."[7] In his
introduction to the book, Buechner comments on the genre of autobiography by
saying, "If God speaks to us at all other than through such official channels as the
Bible and the church, then I think that he speaks to us largely through what happens
to us, so what I have done both in this book and in its predecessor is to listen back
over what has happened to me—as I hope my readers may be moved to listen back
over what has happened to them—for the sound, above all else, of his voice."[8]

Perhaps part of Jesus' message to John is that more is going on than John has
noticed. When Jesus reviews his ministry for John, he is saying to him, "Listen.
Look. God is at work here, maybe not with 'unquenchable fire,' but at work just
the same. Blessed is the one who takes no offense at me." Preachers today, then,
listening as Buechner encourages us, can help others point to the ways that "here
and there in the world, and now and then in ourselves is seen a New Creation."
To our non-Christian friends, we may say, "We are not claiming that everything
is 'all better' since the advent of Jesus as God with us, only that now we have a
clearer idea of how to spot the new creation, a concrete hope for its fulfillment,
and a fervent prayer for the present time: 'Come, Lord Jesus.'"

The second response to John's question has its beginning in the speech that
Jesus makes to the crowd after he has spoken to John's disciples. Jesus commends
John: "Among those born of women no one has arisen greater than John the

Baptist," and then Jesus speaks of the kingdom of heaven in terms that minimize even John's greatness: "Yet the least in the kingdom of heaven is greater than he" (Matt. 11:11). As important as John is, the kingdom is of a different order than John or John's ministry.

Something continuous with Israel's past and Israel's hopes is surely going on in the kingdom that Jesus enacts. Hence, Jesus' own use of Isaiah. Yet something discontinuous—at least with John's hopes and often with ours—is going on as well. When asked by his disciples who is greatest in the kingdom of heaven, Jesus introduces them to a child (Matt. 18:1-2). When being arrested in Gethsemane, Jesus does not appeal to his Father for "more than twelve legions of angels" (Matt. 26:53), but goes quietly with his accusers. The kingdom of heaven is the message and ministry of one who enacts God's will not by laying waste to his enemies, but by "giving his life, a ransom for many" (Matt. 20:28). To our friends who want to know why things are not better if God's Messiah has already come, we can say that God's Messiah chose to combat evil with his innocent suffering and death. This does not answer every question about persistent injustice, nor does it absolve Christians and others of working for the good of all their neighbors. Yet the choice Jesus made for the cross over those legions of angels is testimony that God's justice, mercy, and peace are probably not as likely to come by means of unquenchable fire as they are by means of suffering love.

Notes

1. Ralph W. Klein, "Isaiah for Advent," *Currents in Theology and Mission 28*, no. 6 (2001): 564.

2. Scott L. Harris, "Isaianic Texts in Advent, Christmas, and Epiphany." *Pro Ecclesia 7*, no. 4 (1998): 474.

3. Walter Brueggemann, "Praise and the Psalms: A Politics of Glad Abandonment," *The Hymn* 43 (1992): 16.

4. Harry Emerson Fosdick, "God of Grace and God of Glory," verse 4, *Evangelical Lutheran Worship* (Minneapolis: Augsburg Fortress, 2006), 705.

5. Ibid.

6. Fred B. Craddock, et al., *Preaching through the Christian Year A* (Philadelphia: Trinity Press International, 1992), 22.

7. Frederick Buechner, *Now and Then* (New York: Harper & Row, 1983). No page number is given for the quotation in Tillich.

8. Ibid., 3.

FOURTH SUNDAY OF ADVENT

DECEMBER 23, 2007

REVISED COMMON	EPISCOPAL (BCP)	ROMAN CATHOLIC
Isa. 7:10-16	Isa. 7:10-17	Isa. 7:10-14
Ps. 80:1-7, 17-19	Psalm 24 or 24:1-7	Ps. 24:1-2, 3-4, 5-6
Rom. 1:1-7	Rom. 1:1-7	Rom. 1:1-7
Matt. 1:18-25	Matt. 1:18-25	Matt. 1:18-24

KEY THEMES

- In his birth as a human child, as well as his ongoing presence in the lives of his followers, Jesus is "God with us."
- Everyday life is the realm in which God acts to inspire the obedience of faith.

FIRST READING

ISAIAH 7:10-16 (RCL)
ISAIAH 7:10-17 (BCP)
ISAIAH 7:10-14 (LFM)

King Ahaz is not in today's first reading as a model of royal wisdom. In his twenties when this scene takes place, the young king is afraid of the wrong people. His fear is the backdrop for a prophecy that, some seven centuries later, will come to be associated with Jesus.

Ahaz reigned in Judah in the eighth century B.C.E., during a time when the king of Israel and the king of Syria had joined forces. The coalition struck fear in the heart of Ahaz, but the Lord's spokesperson, Isaiah, sought to reassure Judah's king. The Lord gave this message to Isaiah for Ahaz: "Take heed, be quiet, do not fear, and do not let your heart be faint because of these two smoldering stumps of firebrands" (Isa. 7:4).

Unfortunately, the message did not have the desired effect. So, in Isaiah 7:10, the Lord himself speaks to Ahaz, rather than speaking through the prophet.[1] "Ask a sign of the Lord your God; let it be as deep as Sheol or high as heaven." Ahaz demurs, a divine-human social gaffe if ever there were one! Isaiah rolls his eyes ("Is it too little for you to weary mortals, that you weary my God also?"), and in spite of Ahaz's reply to the Lord, the prophet announces a sign. A young woman will bear a son, and by the time the child is old enough to know right from wrong, the kings whom Ahaz is worried about will no longer be a threat. It is as if the Lord were saying, through the sign, "Look, we're talking years, not decades, of threat here—and I am with you. Relax. Ride it out."

That is it for Isaiah 7:10-16. If the reading ends at verse 14 (as in the LFM), the only part of the sign hearers are introduced to is the birth of the baby and its name, Immanuel ("God with us"). When *God* is with us, two-bit kings like Rezin and Pekah (cf. Isa. 7:1) are inconsequential. If the reading goes on to verse 17 (as in the BCP lectionary), the word from Isaiah contains not just promise and reassurance, but also apparent threat. In verse 17, we hear that Ahaz has been afraid of the wrong powers, and that the Lord will use the king of the superpower, Assyria, to get Judah's attention.

This story would likely not be in the lectionary for Advent except that the prophecy from Isaiah 7:14 finds its way into Matthew's description of Jesus' birth. (For more on Matthew 1:23, see the commentary below on the Gospel for this Sunday.) Matthew, writing in Greek, read a Greek text of Isaiah, in which the Hebrew word *'almā* (which can mean either "young woman" or "virgin") had been translated into the Greek *parthenos* (which means "virgin"). With the help of a Greek translation that eliminated ambiguity in the word, Matthew found in the text a prophecy concerning Jesus' miraculous birth. The Hebrew text of Isaiah does not claim a virgin birth for the young woman about whom Isaiah speaks. Isaiah announces a birth by a young woman. It is something that happens regularly, but in the case Isaiah is talking about, the child born will be a sign of the protection God offers the admittedly tiresome King Ahaz.

> The church's subsequent development of the interpretation of the virgin, rich tradition as it is, cannot be said to be "wrong," but it can be said to go in a quite fresh direction, surely other than the Isaiah text itself.
> —Walter Brueggemann[2]

It is difficult to imagine how Christian preachers might appropriate the first reading as a sermon text for Advent worship if they did not want to connect Isaiah's prophecy to Matthew's reading of it. Perhaps one could use Ahaz as a negative example, someone who fears even when he has the voice of the Lord offering an assurance of protection. Such a sermon would eventually want to point out that the king and his fear are not at the center of this text: the focus of the text is God's care for Judah, and the sign of that care will be the regular, everyday life of a baby, who, as he grows into someone old enough to discern right from wrong, will be a daily reminder of "God with us."

PSALM 80:1-7, 17-19 (RCL)

Psalm 80 is a lament, offered not by an individual but by the congregation. The people address one they call "Shepherd," and whose glory and might they affirm. To this one, they speak frankly of their troubles. Their own tears, the scorn of neighbors, the laughter of enemies: they endure all these, and pray fervently, "Restore us, O God of hosts" (v. 7). Commenting on this psalm, Clinton McCann writes, "That we have to do with God in matters of suffering and death as well as in maters of prosperity and life is a remarkable affirmation, especially in a world where the most overtly religious folk are inclined to view suffering as evidence of alienation from God and where secular folk are inclined to locate the source of prosperity and life anywhere but in God."[3]

In short, we both celebrate and wait. To live in this paradox is to confront God in every circumstance and at every moment of our lives. It is, like the people in Psalm 80, to address God when God seems absent. It is to expect to see God in the most surprising places—in a manger—or the most God-forsaken places—on a cross.
—J. Clinton McCann, Jr.[4]

PSALM 24 or 24:1-7 (BCP)
PSALM 24:1-2, 3-4, 5-6 (LFM)

Christians hope that our way of life bears witness to our destination (that is, "God's holy place") and the identity of the one we seek. We hope that the true speech and faithful action described in Psalm 24:4 characterize us. Yet what we know for sure is not about us or our faithfulness, but rather about God: "The earth is the Lord's and all that is in it, the world, and those who live in it" (v. 1). "For those who see the world first and foremost as the sphere of God's reign, every human activity and ethical decision—personal, political, ecological, and otherwise—will be grounded in and result from unreserved trust in God and the desire to embody God's loving, life-giving purposes for 'the world, and all who live in it.'"[5] God reigns, and we belong to God. Everything follows from that.

SECOND READING

ROMANS 1:1-7 (RCL, BCP, LFM)

The second reading tells us much about several characters. About Paul, we learn that he is (1) a slave of Jesus Christ, (2) called to be an apostle to the Gentiles, (2) set apart for the proclamation of the gospel, and (4) aiming to bring about "the obedience of faith" in those to whom he has been sent. About the Romans, we learn that they are (1) called to belong to Jesus Christ (perhaps the belonging language about the Romans in verse 6 harkens back to the "slave" language about Paul in verse 1), and we learn that they are (2) called to be saints, or holy ones, sanctified, living out the very obedience of faith Paul saw as the goal of his preaching. Any of this material could be fodder for a fine sermon on topics from Christian identity (What does it mean today to be a slave of Christ?) to contemporary calls from God (How does God equip those who are "called to be saints"?). Yet on the Fourth Sunday of Advent, the preacher of this text will probably want to focus attention on what the introduction to Romans tells us about the Incarnate One.

Those of us whose work constantly involves us in preaching and studying Scripture must from time to time recognize and confess that we have handled these tasks lightly, that we have protected ourselves from their importance by treating them casually. Our close reading of the introduction to Paul's letter to Roman Christians reminds us that we deal with no small thing, but with the good news of the fulfillment of God's promises.
—Beverly Roberts Gaventa[6]

Information about Jesus abounds here. Although Paul does not organize it all like this in what he says about Jesus, we recognize One who bridges divides between:

• Israel and the nations
• Divine and human realms
• Death and life
• Paul and the Romans

Jesus was a Jew. That Jesus was "descended from David according to the flesh" (v. 3) is a statement about his humanity, but also about his Jewish identity. Even though Paul's primary "targets" for evangelism are Gentile, Paul cannot explain who Jesus is without naming him as a Jew. Contemporary marketing experts might argue that such identification with a tiny, apparently powerless ethnic group would hurt Paul's attempts to make Jesus a "universal" savior. Never mind that. Paul identifies Jesus as a Jew. At the same time, Jesus is also for "all the nations" (or "all the Gentiles," NRSV; v. 5). God's choice of Israel was always meant to have a ripple effect on the nations (cf. the detail about Abraham's call in Genesis 12:3b). In the Jewish man, Jesus of Nazareth, God is calling and empowering the nations for obedience.

Jesus, descended from David, is also "Son of God." It would take centuries after the time Paul wrote Romans for precise formulations about Jesus' humanity and divinity to be worked out.[7] Paul is not writing trinitarian doctrine here, but he is testifying to Jesus as both human, descended from David, and divine, declared Son of God, and risen from the dead. As the Incarnate One, Jesus bridges the divide between divine and human realms.

As the Risen One, Jesus bridges the divide between death and life, between mortality and immortality. Christians face death knowing that Jesus has preceded us there, and he is risen. To preach the gospel of which Paul speaks in these opening verses of Romans is to name Christ as crucified and risen.

Finally, Jesus connects the strangers to whom Paul writes (he has never been to Rome) with the apostle himself. Paul was called to be an apostle to the Gentiles, "including yourselves," he tells the Romans, "who are called to belong to Jesus Christ" (1:6). Paul tells the Romans that he hopes to visit them so that together they may strengthen one another in faith (1:12). The apostle and those to whom he has been sent are bound together in a common faith, the source and object of which are Jesus Christ.

In a Christmas poem by Wendell Berry, a farmer comments that the ground "wants the birth of a man to bring together sky and earth, like a stalk of corn."[8] As Paul describes Jesus in Romans 1, this One brings together sky and earth, reconciling humanity to God and creating community among peoples long divided.

It's the old ground trying it again.
Solstice, seeding and birth—it never
gets enough. It wants the birth of a man
to bring together sky and earth, like a stalk
of corn. It's not death that makes the dead
rise out of the ground, but something alive
straining up, rooted in darkness, like a vine.
That's what you heard. If you're in the right
mind
when it happens, it can come on you strong;
you might her music passing on the wind,
or see a light where there wasn't one before.
—Wendell Berry[9]

THE GOSPEL
MATTHEW 1:18-25 (RCL, BCP)
MATTHEW 1:18-24 (LFM)

Among the four Evangelists and Paul, only Matthew and Luke include virgin birth narratives. In the first verse of his Gospel, Mark calls Jesus "Son of God," but says nothing at all about his conception, birth, or childhood. John speaks of a miracle: the eternal Word "became flesh and lived among us" (John 1:14), but he does not add further specifics. Paul can describe Jesus by saying, "though he was in the form of God, did not regard equality with God as something to be exploited, but emptied himself, taking the form of a slave, being born in human likeness" (Phil. 2:6-7), but like John, Paul says nothing more about how such a thing would have happened.

Only Luke and Matthew report that Mary conceived Jesus by means of the Holy Spirit (cf. Matt. 1:18; Luke 1:35). Whatever else this variety across the earliest Christian witness means, it testifies to the fact that diverse communities of believers were able to preach and write about Jesus as uniquely related to God and humanity without making a virgin birth an article of faith about him.

Of course, the virgin birth is hardly the most "unbelievable" thing Christians are asked to believe in Advent. A mysterious conception seems like small potatoes next to other claims of Advent texts. From the First Sunday of Advent: "They shall beat their swords into plowshares, and their spears into pruning hooks; nation shall not lift up sword against nation, neither shall they learn war any more" (Isa. 2:4).

From the Second Sunday of Advent: "The kingdom of heaven has come near" (Matt. 3:2). From the Third Sunday of Advent: "He has brought down the powerful from their thrones, and lifted up the lowly; he has filled the hungry with good things, and sent the rich away empty" (Luke 1:52-53). So far, we have heard testimony of the nearness of (1) an end to war, (2) a time and place where God's will is done on earth as in heaven, and (3) the reality of hungry who have enough to eat while the rich stop getting richer. Surely none of these realities is easier to see in the natural world than is a virgin birth. All of them depend on God's intervention into the natural order of things. In Advent and Christmas, Christians testify that God is shaking up what we have come to think of as "natural."

For Joseph, such a shake-up must have felt seismic in proportion. The text says that he is a righteous man, which is high praise in Matthew's Gospel. This is the Gospel in which Jesus says that those who hunger and thirst *for righteousness* will be satisfied (Matt. 5:6; cf. Luke 6:21, where the blessing is for the hungry) and that his hearers should "strive first for the kingdom of God *and his righteousness*" (Matt. 6:33; cf. Luke 12:31, where the sentence lacks any reference to righteousness). In Matthew, Jesus convinces John to baptize him by saying, "It is proper for us in this way to fulfill all righteousness" (Matt. 3:15). Yet righteousness is not peevishness, or a slavish, inhumane attention to the letter of the law. To be righteous is simply to live with one's words and actions in sync and to have both focused on the values identified in the Beatitudes (cf. Matt. 5:1-12) and exemplified by Jesus in his ministry.

In Joseph's case, righteousness leads to mercy. Being a righteous man, he plans a merciful course of action toward the woman who is pregnant before their marriage: he will "dismiss her quietly" rather than insist on a more public disgrace than that which she has already endured, or will endure when her curiously timed pregnancy becomes common knowledge. He changes his mind about the dismissal because of a dream in which he hears that Mary's honor has not been harmed, that he need not fear, and that the child will "save his people from their sins."

Joseph is righteous, merciful, and courageous in the face of frightening circumstances. He is maybe just a kid,[10] yet "he did as the angel of the Lord commanded him" (Matt. 1:24). The contrast between the young king Ahaz's response to fear and a sign from God (cf. today's first reading) and Joseph's response is marked.

The Gospel reading for today gives the baby two names. The awkwardness of double naming is due at least in part to Matthew's use of Isaiah 7:14 to describe Jesus' conception and birth, and in fact, Mary's child is never called "Emmanuel." Even so, the explanations of both names have currency throughout the Gospel.

"Jesus" is a variation of Joshua, "Yahweh saves." The angel explains that salvation in terms of salvation from sin. In Matthew, as in Mark and Luke, Jesus forgives sin and makes enemies because of it. Additionally (and only in Matthew), as Jesus institutes the Lord's Supper, he says that his blood will be poured out for many "for the forgiveness of sins" (Matt. 26:28). Thus, at the beginning and the end of Jesus' life, Matthew tells his story in such a way as to remind us that Jesus means to bridge the gulf between humanity's brokenness and God's holiness. "He will save his people from their sins."

Although the name *Emmanuel* never appears again in Matthew, the news that Jesus is "God with us" is clarified throughout the Gospel, and the promise of Jesus' ongoing presence with the disciples gives the community that hears this Gospel hope and direction.[11] When Jesus finishes the Sermon on the Mount, the crowds marvel at his authority (7:28-29). When he rebukes a storm at sea, the disciples wonder, "What sort of man is this, that even the winds and the seas obey him?" (8:27). Jesus himself announces that in him something "greater than the temple" (12:6), "greater than Jonah" (12:41), and "greater than Solomon" (12:42) is here.

Gentiles recognize this as much as Jews. From the Magi who bring the child gifts (2:1-10), to the Canaanite woman who begs for healing for her daughter (15:21-28), to the centurion who witnesses an earthquake after Jesus' death and makes a terrified confession of faith (27:54), citizens of "the nations" recognize in Jesus someone worthy of worship. As the world meets Jesus, it is as if the Old Testament vision of the nations coming to know and worship the Lord, the God of Israel, is coming true.

Whether one chooses to focus a sermon on Joseph and his response to Mary's pregnancy and the angel's message, or on the identity of the baby as "Jesus" or "Emmanuel," it is fitting to give God some verbs here. God speaks to Joseph through an angel in a dream, and says, "Do not be afraid." Joseph responds faithfully and fearlessly, but it is God who is saving people from their sins, and it is God who allays Joseph's fears. Each of the lessons for this Sunday testifies to a God who faithfully comes to the aid of Israel and "all people according to their needs."[12]

Notes

1. It is uncommon, though not unheard of, for God to speak directly to kings, rather than to speak to them through a prophet. The most familiar examples of direct speech between God and a king of Israel come from God's interaction with Solomon (cf. 1 Kings 3:11 and 11:11).

2. Walter Brueggemann, *Isaiah 1–39*, Westminster Bible Companion (Louisville: Westminster John Knox Press, 1998), 70.

3. J. Clinton McCann, Jr., "Preaching on the Psalms for Advent," *Journal for Preachers* 16, no. 1 (1992): 16.

4. Ibid.

5. J. Clinton McCann, Jr. "The Book of Psalms," in *New Interpreter's Bible* (Nashville: Abingdon Press, 1996), 4:775.

6. Gaventa, "Homiletical Resources: Advent as Apocalypse," 80.

7. Noting that Paul's statement that Jesus was declared to be the Son of God sounds adoptionistic to some ears, Beverly Roberts Gaventa points out, "The fact that Paul can here employ a statement that reflects a 'low' christology and elsewhere employ statements with a 'high' christology (Phil. 2:5-11) indicates that he has not yet addressed the kinds of questions that later plagued the church's theology." "Homiletical Resources: Advent as Apocalypse," *Quarterly Review* 6, no. 3 (Fall 1986): 79.

8. Wendell Berry, "The Birth (Near Port William)," from *Collected Poems: 1957-1982*. Copyright © 1985 by Wendell Berry. Reprinted by permission of North Point Press, a division of Farrar, Straus and Giroux, LLC, 124–28. You can hear the poem read by the author on the National Public Radio news Web site at http://www.npr.org/templates/story/story.php?storyId=1032379 (accessed 1/1/07).

9. Berry, "The Birth (Near Port William)," *Collected Poems*, 127.

10. Tradition embellished the Gospel accounts by imagining Joseph as much older than Mary. Why? Joseph is not mentioned in Jesus' ministry and so is presumed to have died before Jesus reached his thirties. Yet from the evangelists themselves, we know nothing of Joseph's age. Based on the fact that he was engaged to Mary, a young woman, it is more likely (though not certain, of course) from that he, too, was young.

11. On the promise of Jesus' ongoing presence with his community, see Matt. 18:20 and Matt. 28:20. Note also Matt. 25:31-46 for the way Jesus intends to make incognito appearances to "the least of these" before he appears in a recognizable form.

12. The phrase is from the introduction to the prayers of the church in the Holy Communion liturgy of the *Lutheran Book of Worship* (Minneapolis: Augsburg Publishing House, 1978), in which the minister says, "Let us pray for the whole people of God in Christ Jesus, and for all people according to their needs" (p. 65).

THE SEASON
OF CHRISTMAS

MARY HINKLE
SHORE

The readings for Christmas testify to God's abiding, fervent love for humanity, and God's intention to reveal that love by becoming human. While this love is more sublime than any traditional Christmas gift, and probably for that reason ought not be compared to those gifts we exchange with each other during the Christmas season, a few similarities and differences present themselves. Recognizing the incarnation as gift highlights that it is free, that it is for everyone, and that it is not quite what we expected.

At their best, Christmas presents are gifts rather than payment for services rendered or part of an elaborate exchange of goods. Imagine a world in which no one is keeping score of who spent how much last year, or what is expected in order that no one feel shortchanged, left out, unappreciated, or overextended after decorations are taken down and the bills arrive. Preparing for Christmas celebrations with family and friends, most of us do not live in such a world. This is not to say that people who exchange gifts do not really love each other, but rather to lament that often Christmas heightens our need for tallying how much is enough rather than impressing upon us the reality of a free gift, with no tallying necessary or possible.

In the midst of this season characterized by running the numbers of checkbook balances and credit-card receipts and characterized further by achieving precise equity between presents bought for grandchildren, and other similar activities, we read texts in which God's move toward humanity in the person of Jesus just happens. It is beyond our calculating. Years later, the Gospel writers and Paul would read back through their Scriptures and be able to trace how God had calculated such a thing before it happened. Yet from our perspective the birth of Christ feels more like an unexpected gift—something not part of our prior calculations and offered freely, entering our world from above and beyond our numbers game. Writing about the prologue to John, Mark Stibbe notes, "The most startling thing about John's opening words, 'In the beginning was the Word', is that the Word comes on stage with a complete absence of preliminaries."[1] As Luke narrates the night of Jesus' birth, the angel just "stood before" shepherds keeping watch over their flocks by night. What had begun as a night like any other was transformed by the gift of "a Savior, who is the Messiah, the Lord" (Luke 2:11).

The gift of God with us is a particular gift, given to individuals, yet meant for every time and place. It is particular, like a wrapped package with one person's name on the tag. There were certain shepherds on a particular hillside during a specific night, and it was to these shepherds that an angel appeared. The incarnation is like that; indeed, it must be like that, with God becoming one particular flesh-and-blood person, part of a certain family, place, and time. Yet whenever the authors of Scripture describe this gift, they announce that it is for everyone. From that angel on that particular hillside, we hear that the message is "good news of great joy for all the people" (Luke 2:10). The psalms we read during Christmas delight in requesting praise from "all the peoples" (Ps. 67:5), even from "sea monsters and all deeps" (Ps. 148:7). The reach of God, when God becomes flesh, is universal as well as particular.

Finally, like other gifts of the season, the gift of the incarnation is not exactly what we expect it to be. Some of us are better than others at anticipating what gifts might be waiting for us as part of a Christmas celebration, but even the best at that game are sometimes surprised by something they had never thought to expect. The incarnation's surprise is that God's power is made perfect in weakness. The angel directs the shepherds to "a child wrapped in bands of cloth and lying in a manger" (Luke 2:12). Paul testifies that the Son "did not regard equality with God as something to be exploited, but emptied himself, taking the form of a slave" (Phil. 2:6-7). The author of Hebrews testifies that Christ's suffering is the way he redeemed humanity. In all of these texts, we witness the revelation of God into our world, yet that revelation is not of a God with power or force on display in intimidating proportions. It is the revelation of One who chooses the path of suffering and who sanctifies humanity by becoming "obedient to the point of death" (Phil. 2:8).

> The most startling thing about John's opening words, "In the beginning was the Word," is that the Word comes on stage with a complete absence of preliminaries. Who is the Word? What is the Word? Where does he hail from? How does he differ from other deities?
> —Mark W. G. Stibbe[2]

Notes

1. Mark W. G. Stibbe, *John's Gospel* (London: Routledge, 1994), 12.
2. Ibid., 12–-13.

NATIVITY OF THE LORD, PROPER I / CHRISTMAS EVE

DECEMBER 24, 2007

REVISED COMMON	EPISCOPAL (BCP)	ROMAN CATHOLIC MASS AT MIDNIGHT
Isa. 9:2-7	Isa. 9:2-4, 6-7	Isa. 9:1-6
Psalm 96	Psalm 96 or 96:1-4, 11-12	Ps. 96:1-2a, 2b-3, 11-12, 13
Titus 2:11-14	Titus 2:11-14	Titus 2:11-14
Luke 2:1-14 (15-20)	Luke 2:1-14 (15-20)	Luke 2:1-14

KEY THEMES

• In the midst of the circumstances of daily life, God is at work for good.
• All creation is invited to join in praise to God.
• Occurring in a stable, yet accompanied by an angel chorus, the birth of Jesus was at once humble and grand.

FIRST READING
ISAIAH 9:2-7 (RCL)
ISAIAH 9:2-4, 6-7 (BCP)
ISAIAH 9:1-6 (LFM)

"The people who walked in darkness . . . ." (Isa. 9:2). The darkness could be the weak rule of Judah's King Ahaz (cf. Isa. 7:1-17), the threatening maneuvers of Assyria into the northern areas of Israel (cf. Isa. 9:1), or the misguided spiritual practices of consulting the spirits of the dead (cf. Isa. 8:19-20). People depending on any of these were looking for light in all the wrong places.

Such was "the former time" (Isa. 9:1). Now, Isaiah says, "The people who walked in darkness have seen a great light" (v. 2). Before he describes the light or accounts for it, the prophet tells us the effect it has on people. The words are joy, rejoice, exult. The experience is celebration. Imagine the end of a growing season, at the harvest, with the crop safely gathered in. It is time to party. "Those who go out weeping, bearing the seed for sowing, shall come home with shouts of joy, carrying their sheaves" (Ps. 126:6). Or imagine the end of a war, with relief flooding the soldiers' veins where there had been only terror and adrenaline before. The BCP lectionary omits verse 5, recognizing that rejoicing in plunder is difficult to reconcile with the image of the good king as "Prince of Peace" later in the text, not to mention the counsel of Jesus not to take up arms and to love one's enemies (cf. Matt. 5:38-48). While verse 5 is admittedly difficult, the Isaiah text itself does not rejoice in battle, but rather in the end of battle. War clothes will be burned; there is no need for them anymore. This part of the image is close to that in the text for the First Sunday of Advent, "They shall beat their swords into plowshares, and their spears into pruning hooks; nation shall not lift up sword against nation, neither shall they learn war any more" (Isa. 2:4).

The reason for all this rejoicing is the birth of a child, an heir to the throne of David. He gets names that one commentator calls "ritualized hyperbole," and that others connect to Egyptian coronation ceremonies.

More important than the names are the characteristics imagined for his reign: peace, justice, and righteousness. In a time when religion is imagined to be a personal thing, and when many speak of their religious life in terms of their own search for meaning, inner peace, or positive feeling, the social and political themes in this text are striking. In this text, God's zeal is for lasting peace and a just society and the people's joy is life in such a society.

The birth and accession of this child is unlike any king before or after. He rules not for his own benefit but for the benefit and welfare of his people. It is no small matter that the child has been born "for us," "a son given to us" (Isa 9:6), thus giving fuller expression to his name, Immanuel, "God with us."
—Scott L. Harris[1]

RESPONSIVE READING

PSALM 96 (RCL, BCP)
PSALM 96:1-4, 11-12 (BCP alt.)
PSALM 96:1-2A, 2B-3, 11-12, 13 (LFM)

Psalm 96 is a call to praise issued to "all the earth" (vv. 1, 9). Everyone—and everything—is included. First, Israel is directed to declare God's praise among the nations (v. 3), and then the nations themselves are called to praise (v. 7). But there's more. Here, the din is even louder than that in Psalm 150, where "everything that breathes" is called to praise. By the last verses of Psalm 96, the nonhuman, nonbreathing creation is recruited (vv. 11-12). Let the heavens be glad, the earth rejoice, the sea roar, the field exult, the forest sing for joy. It is a joyful and lively picture of all creation praising God.

SECOND READING
TITUS 2:11-14 (RCL, BCP, LFM)

In Greek, the second reading is a single sentence whose main subject and verb are "grace appeared" (*epephanē charis*). Filling in around those words, we read that God's grace appeared for two purposes: saving all people (v. 11) and training readers of this letter (v. 12) for godly lives while we await a second epiphany of grace, namely "the manifestation of the glory of our great God and Savior, Jesus Christ" (v. 13). In this letter, good works are most certainly not a prerequisite to salvation (see, for example, 3:5). Yet they are central to the Christian life (see 2:7; 3:8, 14). Good works are the way that Christians bear witness both to that first epiphany of grace, the incarnation, and to their hope for Christ's second appearing.

The broader context of this reading names daily life as the realm of good works. Titus 2:1-10 is a series of exhortations to people on how to manage their daily social interaction with temperance and grace. Such behavior is commended as a means of evangelism. The grace that trains "us" (v. 12) to live godly lives is actually grace for "all people" (v. 11). The best way to proclaim that grace to others is to demonstrate it in our relationships. As James D. G. Dunn observes, "This is presumably why this final paragraph can function as the theological rationale for the seemingly mundane household rules of vv. 1-10. It is divine grace expressed in the quality of basic human relationships that will be the most effective witness to the character of God's saving purpose."[2]

> The appearance of three of the most highly prized virtues in Greek thought (piety, moderation, justice), following the classic Greek term for education, underlies the degree to which the Christianity of the Pastorals saw itself as complementary to the highest aspirations of Greek philosophical ethics.
> —James D. G. Dunn[3]

Part of the mystery of the incarnation is that "basic human relationships" are precisely where God wants to be involved. Jesus was a baby, dependent upon his parents for food, clothing, and shelter, two of which were reportedly difficult to come by on the night of his birth. The significance of his birth would be made known to regular people first: shepherds, then a couple of old people in the Temple (cf. Luke 2:25-40). In the incarnation, God is made manifest among regular people going about their everyday lives. What better place, then, for Christians to bear witness to the way we think God is working in the world than in our basic human relationships?

How might Christians bear witness to our deepest hopes for the reconciliation of all things to God in Christ in, say, our relationships at work or at home? The second reading's answer to that question is not uniquely Christian. The virtues of piety, moderation, and justice had as much currency in Greek philosophy as they did in Jewish and early Christian circles. Similar observations may be made today. In one of her time-management books, popular author Julie Morgenstern suggests, "Say 'Hello,' instead of asking 'Who made this mess?' when you first get home."[4] The advice is not "Christian ethics," except that Christians who behave this way are acting in accord with their belief that the person they greet at home is worthy of kindness and that the Christian love they show, like that shown to them, never appears "in general" but is always incarnate, real only when it is "made flesh" in interaction with other creatures, even creatures who are occasionally messy.

The Gospel
LUKE 2:1-14 (15-20) (RCL, BCP)
LUKE 2:1-14 (LFM)

If all of the Luke 2 pericope is read, the preacher may want to focus on the shepherds and their response to the word of the angels (vv. 15-20). For homiletical suggestions that focus on the last part of the chapter, see the Gospel commentary for Christmas Dawn, below.

Even though the contrasts in this story are familiar, cataloging them may spark the preacher's imagination to find a new sermon in the most well known of texts. There are contrasts in this story between great actors on the world stage and a baby in a stable, between rulers with the authority to move people and shepherds who are watching sheep, between a grand announcement for the whole world and its comparatively tiny target audience. Finally, there is the contrast between a gospel story that will take years to unfold in Jesus' life, and the news that today there is reason for great joy. The preacher could build a sermon around any of these contrasts and invite hearers to find themselves and their own joy in the reversal of fortune that the contrasts imply.

Not a palace, but a stable. When Luke introduces John the Baptist's ministry, he takes care to place John in the context of world history (cf. Luke 3:1-2). Similarly, Luke begins the story of Jesus' birth by speaking first of powers on the world stage. In one sense, Luke is just doing the work of a historian to give at least approximate dates for the events he narrates.[5] On the other hand, Luke is directing the reader to notice differences between the powers of the Roman world and the power of God. Luke begins with the widest possible angle of vision with Augustus in Rome and Quirinius as governor of Syria, and contrasts these grand men with their titles and residences with a young couple, on the road, lacking accommodations. Augustus is emperor, but is it the emperor in Rome or the child in Bethlehem who will bring peace? Whether Augustus can create peace or not, he can create difficulty in people's lives with only an edict and a messenger to deliver it, as Joseph's need to go from Galilee to Bethlehem illustrates. Yet the baby born on this road trip is really the one "destined for the falling and the rising of many in Israel" (Luke

2:34), and the fact that he is born in Bethlehem, the city of David, and is born in such humble circumstances actually functions as a sign that this one is "the Messiah, the Lord" (Luke 2:11). The contrast here is between greatness as the world would imagine it and greatness as the gospel proclaims it.

Not kings, but shepherds. We do not know whether Luke knew the story of Magi coming to visit the baby Jesus in Bethlehem (cf. Matt. 2:1-12), but in either case Luke's story has a very different focus. Luke begins with foreign dignitaries (Augustus and Quirinius), yet these men function more to set the stage for the story than to participate in it. There is no hint that they are aware of anything going on in Bethlehem.

In a surprising way, this ignorance and lack of involvement on the part of the most powerful is a sign of hope for the present time. Look how God was at work in a quiet corner of the provinces, on a night that was unremarkable to all except a couple of new parents and some shepherds outside a village in Judea! Since God was there, wouldn't it be in character for God to be present in uncelebrated or unexpected ways in other times and places too? Since at least the time of the Apostle Paul, the Christian church has confessed that God's power is "made perfect in weakness" (cf. 2 Cor. 12:9) and often hidden "under the form of the opposite." Augustus may have set Joseph and Mary's travel in motion, but he finally does not matter to this story. In the space of a few verses, Luke has taken us from Emperor Augustus to "shepherds living in the fields, keeping watch over their flock by night."

Not only tomorrow but already today. At several significant points in his Gospel, Luke either adds the word today or daily to a saying of Jesus we know from other sources, or he tells a story unique to his Gospel in which Jesus speaks of something happening "today." Jesus uses the word when he announces to the congregation at Nazareth the fulfillment of Isaiah 61 in his own ministry: "Today this scripture has been fulfilled in your hearing" (Luke 4:21). In Luke, Jesus says, "If any want to become my followers, let them deny themselves and take up their cross daily and follow me" (Luke 9:23). While other evangelists report the saying, they lack the idea of a daily experience of self-denial. Only in Luke do we meet Zacchaeus, to whom Jesus says, "I must stay at your house today" (Luke 19:5) and then later, "Today salvation has come to this house" (Luke 19:9). The repentant thief on the cross is another character unique to Luke's gospel, and to him Jesus says, "Truly I tell you, today you will be with me in Paradise" (Luke 23:43).

This proclamation of present-tense grace is also present in Luke's story of Jesus' birth. The angel says to the shepherds, "To you is born this day in the city of David

Luke lets the contrast stand between the glorious announcement and the humble sign. This again emphasizes that God's ways of ruling and bringing about the kingdom are not overt and coercive. . . . Jesus' identity and role are no secret in this story, but the participants in the story and the readers will be surprised and often perplexed by how Jesus will accomplish his mission.
—David L. Tiede[7]

a Savior, who is the Messiah" (2:11). It is not just that Jesus has been born "this day," but also that he is, already on the day of his birth, Savior, Messiah, and that he is a gift to the shepherds to whom the angel speaks. No one is denying that decades will intervene before Jesus begins his ministry, or that much is wrong that still needs to be set right, either in the first century or the twenty-first. Even so, with the angel's announcement a future hope breaks into the present time. In the response of the shepherds, we see that Jesus' birth matters, not just because of what he will do in the future but also because of who he is proclaimed to be in the present. About Advent, Guy Sayles writes, "We sense our destiny reaching out to us from the future."[6] The same could have been said on the night of Jesus' birth.

Notes

1. Scott L. Harris, "Isaianic Texts in Advent, Christmas, and Epiphany," Pro Ecclesia 7 (1998): 476.

2. James D. G. Dunn, "Titus," in New Interpreter's Bible (Nashville: Abingdon Press, 2000), 11:871. Emphasis added.

3. Ibid.

4. Julie Morgenstern, *Making Work Work: New Strategies for Surviving and Thriving at the Office* (New York: Fireside, 2004), 29.

5. The dating, from a historian's perspective, is puzzling since Augustus and Herod had both died by 4 c.e. and, according to Josephus, Quirinius did not become governor until 6 c.e. Josephus does report that early in his reign as governor, Quirinius was directed by Rome to conduct a census for tax purposes.

6. Guy Sayles, "Preaching Advent Hope While Millions Are Reading the Left Behind Series," *Journal for Preachers* 28 (2004): 13.

7. David L. Tiede, *Luke*, Augsburg Commentary on the New Testament (Minneapolis: Augsburg, 1988), 72.

NATIVITY OF THE LORD, PROPER II / CHRISTMAS DAWN

DECEMBER 25, 2007

REVISED COMMON	EPISCOPAL (BCP)	ROMAN CATHOLIC
Isa. 62:6-12	Isa. 62:6-7, 10-12	Isa. 62:11-12
	Psalm 97 or 97:1-4,	Ps. 97:1, 6, 11-12
Psalm 97	11-12	
Titus 3:4-7	Titus 3:4-7	Titus 3:4-7
Luke 2:(1-7) 8-20	Luke 2:(1-14) 15-20	Luke 2:15-20

KEY THEMES

- God's redemption is a free gift, initiated and brought to fulfillment by God's work on our behalf.
- When human beings recognize God's grace as a gift intended for them, the response is joy and praise.
- God's greatness is expressed chiefly in demonstrating goodness and mercy.

FIRST READING

ISAIAH 62:6-12 (RCL)
ISAIAH 62:6-7, 10-12 (BCP)
ISAIAH 62:11-12 (LFM)

The first lesson proclaims a city and a people redeemed. A destroyed and abandoned city would have no sentinels, no one watching to protect the city or announce its news. In this reading Jerusalem has sentinels calling out day and night, yet here they are not keeping watch or protecting the city from attack. They are there to make sure that the work to establish the city to its former greatness continues around the clock. They take no rest and they give the worker no rest either (62:6-7).

The text speaks urgency. The image of day-and-night work reminds one of workers logging hours of overtime to get a building project finished for the grand opening. Or perhaps one thinks of bleary-eyed students staying up all night to complete final papers at the end of a semester, or farmers on the plains working urgently to get a crop out of the field and into the barn before an early snowstorm. The rebuilder of Jerusalem is working that diligently, that quickly, that passionately to finish the task before him.

Who is this tireless builder of Jerusalem? It is the Lord himself. The Lord swears by symbols of God's own power—God's right hand and mighty arm—that the people will not again see the fruits of their labor go to their enemies. This promise is the opposite of an old curse used to announce that the one who worked for a harvest would not enjoy it: "You shall plant a vineyard, but not enjoy its fruit. Your ox shall be butchered before your eyes, but you shall not eat of it" (Deut. 28:30-31). Here the Lord pledges that such disenfranchisement will not happen again. "I will not again give your grain to be food for your enemies, and foreigners shall not drink the wine for which you have labored; but those who garner it shall eat it and praise the Lord, and those who gather it shall drink it in my holy courts" (Isa. 62:8-9). The people of Jerusalem will enjoy both the fruits of their labor and the safety of a city rebuilt.

Perhaps the best news of the text is that no one is minimizing the vast amount of work to be done. If the situation of the exiles is to improve, God must work vigorously on the people's behalf. There is much to be done, and as the work goes forward the people will need constant reassurance that the Lord is with them. In the context of a return from exile and the reality of devastation setting in, Isaiah cries out to God, "O that you would tear open the heavens and come down" (64:1) and the prophet laments, "Zion has become a wilderness, Jerusalem a desolation" (64:10). Such cries are the aftermath of war and exile. In the midst of this harsh reality, Isaiah proclaims that God will work tirelessly to give the people back their home. The text is a word of hope for anyone who has faced desolation, whether it be a natural disaster, a great personal loss, or the ravages of war. Finally, God is working day and night so that God's people will be called holy, redeemed, sought out, "A City Not Forsaken" (Isa. 62:12).

> In an age that awaits final redemption the sentinel's role is not so much that of defending the city as that of being prepared to make joyous acclamation of welcome to the conquering God. The remains of the city gates are not closed but flung open in a gesture of peace.
> —Scott L. Harris[1]

RESPONSIVE READING
PSALM 97 (RCL)
PSALM 97 or 97:1-4, 11-12 (BCP)
PSALM 97: 1, 6, 11-12 (LFM)

The themes of joy and justice are interwoven in each section of Psalm 97. In each section of the psalm, the connection between these concepts comes through. The psalm begins with an imperative, "Let the earth rejoice," and ends with a similar exhortation to the righteous, "Rejoice in the Lord." Near the center is the news that God's judgments inspires gladness and rejoicing in Zion (v. 8).

A psalm that includes images of the clouds and thick darkness surrounding the Lord, as well as the mountains melting like wax before God, might lead one to assume that God's greatness is the reason for worship. Yet this is not the case in Psalm 97. As great as God is ("His lightnings light up the world; the earth sees and trembles," v. 4), it is God's goodness that inspires the psalmist's song. God's just judgments and God's rescue of the righteous are the inspiration for praise and the cause for rejoicing.

SECOND READING

TITUS 3:4-7 (RCL, BCP, LFM)

A favorite Christmas carol proclaims, "How silently, how silently the wondrous gift is given! So God imparts to human hearts the blessings of his heav'n."[2] The second reading proclaims the wondrous gift of God's goodness and lovingkindness appearing in order to change the lives of those who were formerly "foolish, disobedient, led astray" and more (Titus 3:3).

The reading follows a description of believers' former lives as characterized by relationship-destroying vices. It is common in Pauline ethical discourse to contrast the former vicious behavior of Christians with their present potential for virtue (cf. 1 Cor. 6:9-11; Eph. 2:1-7; and Col. 3:5-8). Yet the emphasis in Titus is not on the before-and-after portraits, but rather on how to account for the change. The reading makes it clear that the change in the lives of readers is sheer grace. It is the result of God's goodness and lovingkindness, not of any works of righteousness on the part of human beings. Good works are fruit of a new life given "through the water of rebirth and renewal by the Holy Spirit" (v. 5) and such works are repeatedly commended (cf. 3:1, 8, 14). Yet good works are never meant to earn God's favor, for there is no need to earn something that has been freely given.

> [W]hen we are kind and gentle to people this itself is part of the "appearing" of God's kindness and loving goodness. God wants to continue the work of self-revelation he began in and through Jesus; and one of the primary ways he does this is by his followers acting in such a way that people will realize who God is and what he's like.
> —N. T. Wright[3]

Most Christians have probably heard this distinction between grace and works, and yet many of us find it difficult to trust. Is it really true that God is not keeping score of our accomplishments and sins in order to mete out rewards and punishments? James D. G. Dunn points out that reliance on good works as an avenue to divine favor "embraces a diverse spectrum of conditions and individuals," from the humble who fret that they will need "something to show for their life" at its end, to the arrogant who assume that their worldly success "must count for something in the heavenly account books."[4] Jokes about St. Peter granting or barring access to heaven based on the quality of the life of one standing before him would not have as much currency as they do if Christians did not at least flirt with the notion that human works can affect the dispensing of divine favor. The reading from Titus rejects such a relationship between the two.

The celebration of Christmas is a fitting time to proclaim God's favor as a gift, and not the result of any works of righteousness. The letter of 1 John reminds us, "We love because he first loved us" (4:19). In the context of Christmas we can say, "We give because he first gave to us." At their best, traditions of Christmas gift giving have at their heart an acknowledgment that before we were ever in a position to give anything, we had already received abundant grace from God in the gift of God's Son. In Christ, God shows us goodness, lovingkindness, and mercy. Finding our true lives in Christ means offering these gifts to others.

The Gospel
LUKE 2:(1-7) 8-20 (RCL)
LUKE 2:(1-14) 15-20 (BCP)
LUKE 2:15-20 (LFM)

Luke's narration of Jesus' birth can be divided into verses that offer background on the events (2:1-5), and then three scenes where various characters speak or actions unfold. In the first scene, Luke describes Jesus' birth (vv. 6-7). From the stable and the birth, the scene shifts to a hillside outside Bethlehem where an angel announces the birth to shepherds (vv. 8-14). In a third scene, the shepherds go to find the child, they report the angel's message to the parents, and then return to their flocks rejoicing (vv. 15-20). The Gospel reading for this worship service focuses not so much on the birth of Jesus as on the announcement by the angels and the shepherds' visit to the baby. (For commentary on the first half of the Luke 2 pericope, see the Gospel for Christmas Eve, above.)

Luke begins his Gospel with multiple angel appearances. The angel, Gabriel, visits Zechariah to announce the birth of John the Baptist (Luke 1:11-20). The same angel visits Mary to announce that she is to give birth to Jesus (Luke 1:26-38). In Luke 2, an unnamed angel brings the message of that birth to shepherds outside Bethlehem. In each case, early in the interaction with humans, the angel says, "Do not be afraid." This introductory line has led to much speculation on the appearance of such a messenger from God, with art and literature filling in detail unavailable to us from Scripture. In Luke 2 the appearance of the angel is accompanied by "the glory of the Lord" shining around the shepherds. This detail indicates that part of what may be so frightening about angels is the way they communicate the nearness of God as they announce God's word. An angel is a messenger, an envoy from one realm to another, and the messengers in Luke 2 carry not only a message but also the glory surrounding its sender.[5] The shepherds may be frightened because they recognize they are just one step removed from the court of the Most High.

The angel says, "Do not be afraid," and then goes on to announce the birth of "a Savior, who is the Messiah, the Lord" (Luke 2:11). It is just the sort of message one would expect from a ruler's envoy. Elsewhere in the ancient world, the titles "Savior" and "Lord" can be found applied to political rulers, and royal birth announcements were promoted as "good news." The difference in Luke's story is that here the words refer to one at a great distance from palaces and royal courts. Where the shepherds will go, they will not see tapestries or purple cloth. Instead, they will behold a child wrapped in bands of cloth and lying in a manger. The simplicity—even poverty—of the scene stands in starkest contrast to those places where any other newborn called "Savior" and "Lord" would be found.

Why do the angels speak to shepherds? Is it because Israel's King David was once a shepherd? It is true that shepherds remind us of David, yet at the time of Jesus they would have been the little people of the empire and possibly even outcast. R. Alan Culpepper puts it this way: "Shepherding was a despised occupation at the time. Although the reference to shepherds evokes a positive, pastoral image for the modern reader and underscores Jesus' association with the line of David (1 Sam 16:11; 17:15; Ps 78:80), in the first century, shepherds were scorned as shiftless, dishonest people who grazed their flocks on others' lands."[6] Perhaps the angel speaks to shepherds in order to demonstrate that already at his birth, Jesus is doing God's work of "lifting up the lowly" (Luke 1:52). As an adult, Jesus will be called a friend of sinners (Luke 7:34). Here at the beginning, the first to receive news of his birth are people far outside any structure of political power and without a particularly respectable social rank.

Shepherds may also be the first to receive the word of Jesus' birth simply because it is an urgent word to proclaim and they are outside and awake at a time of night when much of the rest of the countryside is asleep. To many of us who hear this story every year, the birth of Jesus is old news, but it was not always so. Imagine having such good news that it cannot wait until morning! You have good news of a great joy for all the people. With whom will you share it? The angel finds the only audience that is outdoors and more or less awake: shepherds, "living in the fields, keeping watch over their flock by night" (Luke 2:8), and the angel announces, "To you is born this day in the city of David a Savior, who is the Messiah, the Lord" (2:11).

Upon experiencing the angel visitation and the heavenly chorus, the shepherds do exactly what we imagine anyone would have done in their place: they go to find the family. Luke's comment that they went "with haste" implies that there was not much of a question about whether they would go or not. Preachers would do well to guard against making the shepherds' response the focus of the story, as if the subject of the sermon were the shepherds and not the child who is the Messiah, the Lord. Yes, the shepherds are model respondents, but after such an announcement, who would go back to dozing on the hillside? Who could go back to that? The shepherds do exactly what followers of Jesus will do throughout Luke and Acts: they get on the road. They start moving both so that they may see what God has done and so that they may tell others what they have experienced.

The shepherds find things as the angel had told them. They find Jesus, who is two contrasting things at once. He is a Savior whose birth is good news of a great joy for all the people, and he is a swaddled infant resting on a bed of hay. This combination of greatness and defenselessness will follow Jesus throughout his life as he performs deeds of power and yet is subject to arrest and vulnerable to death. In the incarnation, God chooses to move toward a broken humanity rather than away from it. A popular song asks, "What if God was one of us?"[8] In Christ, God becomes one of us, experiencing the weakness of infancy and the vulnerability of daily life. The shepherds outside Bethlehem are the first to hear this news, and the first to rejoice in it, but it is news for all the people. It is news of God's tireless work to heal and to save.

> *Shepherds, why this jubilee? Why your joyous strains prolong?*
> *What the gladsome tiding be which inspire your heav'nly song?*
> *Come to Bethlehem and see him whose birth the angels sing;*
> *Come, adore on bended knee Christ the Lord, the newborn king.*
> —"Angels We Have Heard on High"[7]

Notes

1. Scott L. Harris, "Isaianic Texts in Advent, Christmas, and Epiphany," *Pro Ecclesia* 7, no. 4 (1998): 476–77.

2. Phillips Brooks, "O Little Town of Bethlehem," in *Evangelical Lutheran Worship* (Minneapolis: Augsburg Fortress, 2006), 279.

3. N. T. Wright, *Paul for Everyone: The Pastoral Letters, 1 and 2 Timothy and Titus* (Louisville: Westminster John Knox Press, 2003), 162.

4. James D. G. Dunn, "Titus," in New Interpreter's Bible (Nashville: Abingdon Press, 2000), 11:879.

5. The idea that God's glory clings to one as a result of and encounter with the divine is present in other biblical stories. After his encounters with God, the altered appearance of Moses so frightens the Israelites that he veils his face (Exod. 34:29-35). At the Transfiguration, the face and clothes of Jesus change to reflect glory (Luke 9:29-32).

6. R. Alan Culpepper, *The Gospel and the Letters of John*, Interpreting Biblical Texts (Nashville: Abingdon Press, 1998), 116.

7. "Angels We Have Heard on High," French carol; trans. H. F. Hemy, The Crown of Jesus Music, 1864, in *Evangelical Lutheran Worship*, 289.

8. Eric Bazilian, "One of Us," *Relish*, 1995, Mercury 314 526 699-2.

NATIVITY OF THE LORD, PROPER III / CHRISTMAS DAY

DECEMBER 25, 2007

REVISED COMMON	EPISCOPAL (BCP)	ROMAN CATHOLIC
Isa. 52:7-10	Isa. 52:7-10	Isa. 52:7-10
Psalm 98	Psalm 98 or 98:1-6	Ps. 98:1, 2-3a, 3b-4, 5-6
Heb. 1:1-4 (5-12)	Heb. 1:1-12	Heb. 1:1-6
John 1:1-14	John 1:1-14	John 1:1-18 or 1:1-5, 9-14

KEY THEMES

• Throughout the history of Israel and the history of the church, God acts to redeem God's people.

• In God's own Son, Jesus Christ, we see the glory of God, and we receive grace and truth.

• The gift of Christ to humanity is "the power to become children of God."

FIRST READING

ISAIAH 52:7-10 (RCL, BCP, LFM)

Modern scholarship of Isaiah imagines that chapters 40–66, as well as some parts of chapters 1–39, were written after the Babylonian exile had ended. Thus, the work of two or even three prophets—one who was preexilic—has been combined into the biblical book of Isaiah. If we read with this reconstruction of history in mind, in Isaiah 52 a prophet still in Babylon with the exiles imagines the return to Jerusalem. The event combines realism about the difficulties of homecoming with eagerness and joy at the prospect of returning. The reading describes three homecoming scenes.

Scene One: The Messenger Appears. Imagine a runner bringing news of victory in battle. The modern distance-running event of the marathon has its roots in the run of a Greek messenger from Marathon to Athens to announce the victory of the Greeks over the Persians in battle. This is the image with which Isaiah begins. A lone runner appears, a speck in the distance, moving swiftly over the mountains. He arrives with good news. He announces peace (*shalom*) and salvation (*yeshuah*). Jerusalem's "warfare has ended" (Isa. 40:2; RSV).

The messenger announces to the city, "Your God reigns." Since the beginning of the monarchy the people had been ruled by many more corrupt or cowardly kings than just kings, ending finally with national defeat and exile. On one level, the message, "Your God reigns" proclaims that the people are free of their Babylonian rulers. On another level, the message reminds the people of the good news that no human king is their ultimate ruler. Instead, their God reigns.

Scene Two: The Sentinels Rejoice. Isaiah 52:7-10 contains the contrasting pictures of sentinels on top of city walls and the "ruins of Jerusalem" (v. 9). The images are difficult to reconcile with one another, and it may be well to remember here that we are reading poetry. Poetry allows the prophet to hold together the "already" and "not yet" realities of God's reign. Already a messenger brings news of peace and is hailed by sentinels, even when the walls have not yet been rebuilt and it is the ruins of Jerusalem that are exhorted to break forth in song.

Without mention of rubble, the scene of rejoicing could be read as nothing but the wishful thinking of a deluded prophet who refused to recognize the dire predicament of exiles returning to a burned-out city. Yet without the image of sentinels atop city walls catching that first glimpse of the one who brings good news, how would the people see how great were God's plans for their restoration? The prophet's call was to show them that God could inspire singing even from the ruins of Jerusalem so he combines images of the present and the future.

With the destruction and the Exile, Yahweh was believed to have abandoned the Holy City, and even the chosen people. With the release from captivity and the return, the divine presence comes back. The announcement in this passage, then, is addressed to persons who have experienced the absence of God.
—Gene Tucker[1]

Scene Three: Yahweh Returns. The sentinels rejoice, "for in plain sight they see the return of the Lord to Zion" (v. 8). We have moved from the image of the first lone runner's battlefield reports of victory to something like a tickertape parade as a triumphant commander returns home. Of course, the exile did not end with the parade of victorious troops back to a rejoicing city. The prophet wants to proclaim that God's favor has returned for the people. Speaking to a people who had felt the Lord's absence so dramatically in exile, the prophet borrows the most dramatic image he can find for Yahweh's strong, saving presence: the victorious king returns to the holy city. Yahweh saves and comforts in ways that are real and visible enough that "all the ends of the earth shall see the salvation of our God" (v. 10).

PSALM 98 (RCL, BCP)
PSALM 98:1-6 (BCP alt.)
PSALM 98:1, 2-3A, 3B-4, 5-6 (LFM)

Language from the first lesson is echoed in Psalm 98. The psalm proclaims the Lord's victory by "his holy arm," and announces that "all the ends of the earth have seen" that victory (cf. Isa. 52:10). As Ellen Davis observes, "Psalm 98 functions within the canon as a 'new song' (Isa. 42:10) celebrating the accomplishment of what the exilic prophet foretold."[2]

The psalm functions also to change humanity's perspective when we are tempted to imagine ourselves at the center of the universe, as if we had the starring role in the musical that offers praise to our Creator. It is true that the congregation of the faithful is exhorted to praise (v. 1), yet the human creation is only one of the stars of the show. "All the earth" is called to join the song (v. 4). Although readers of Psalm 98:1-6 might think "all the earth" refers only to all the people of the earth, verses 7-9 make it clear that human and nonhuman creation alike are in view. "Let the floods clap their hands; let the hills sing together for joy at the presence of the Lord" (vv. 8-9a). Together all the things that God has made rejoice at God's "passion for wholeness."[3]

The psalmist challenges us to see judgment, not as a matter for local or private celebration by the righteous and, correspondingly, dread for the wicked, but rather as the occasion of cosmic jubilation.
—Ellen Davis[4]

SECOND READING

HEBREWS 1:1-4 (5-12) (RCL)
HEBREWS 1:1-12 (BCP)
HEBREWS 1:1-6 (LFM)

Neither the recipients of Hebrews nor its author, nor even the genre of the writing can be clearly identified from the document itself. We call it a letter, but it has as many features of a sermon as a letter. It has been traditionally been associated with the Apostle Paul, but it does not claim to be authored by him and differences between the perspective of the letter and Pauline style and thought lead most scholars conclude that it is not Pauline.

In the midst of so many unanswered questions, we do know from its content that the author of Hebrews holds two different thoughts together at once. He deeply values Israel's Scripture and traditions, and he understands God to be speaking in a new way through Jesus Christ. Continuity and discontinuity with Israel's past are perhaps nowhere else in the canon held in such exquisite tension.

As Fred Craddock points out, "Hebrews is not only the most extended treatment of the Old Testament in the New, but is also, along with Luke, the most respectful of continuity. The Bible tells one story, not two, and it is the story of God's saving initiative toward humankind."[5] The second reading for today demonstrates the close weave of old and new in this author's proclamation.

Hebrews 1:1-4 sounds like a creed or a hymn describing Christ. With its declaration of Christ's role in creation and unity with God, it is fittingly paired in the lectionary with the prologue to the Gospel of John. Hebrews uses the roles of Israel's leaders of old to describe the Son. In ancient Israel, three different types of leaders were anointed: prophets, priests, and kings. In Hebrews 1:1-4, God's Son functions in the roles of prophet (speaking God's word to humanity), priest (making purification for sin and manifesting God's glory to the people), and king (seated at the right hand of Majesty).

Not only do all of Israel's roles for an "anointed one" come together in Christ, but creation and redemption come together in him as well. It is possible for Christians to observe Christmas with a degree of religious chauvinism, as if God's word, mercy, and glory, made known to us in Christ, are unlike any word that God spoke before Christ or any mercy or glory God made known to God's people of old. Christians sometimes speak as if the "God of the Old Testament" could be differentiated from the Father of our Lord Jesus Christ. The testimony of Scripture speaks against such a split personality for God. Hebrews 1:1-4 proclaims that in the person of Christ, God's past actions and God's present work on behalf of humanity come together. The same One through whom the worlds were created is the One who made purification for sin.

In verses 5-12 the author expands on the last comment in verse 4 regarding the Son's superiority to angels. Evidence is piled up from Scripture to argue that it is the Son, rather than the angels, who is truly the mediator between heaven and earth, and the Son is more excellent than the angels. The author leaves the topic of angels in 2:16 and does not return to it through the rest of the letter, but from this momentary preoccupation with the theme, we can make two observations, one about the continuity between time before and after Jesus, and another about its differences.

First, the Old Testament texts in Hebrews 1 argue for a longer-term plan of God now coming to fulfillment, rather than a change of direction on God's part. The difference between the Son and the angels has ever been in place. The Son has always been with the Father (cf. Hebrews 1:2) and the Son has always been different from the angels.

Yet there is something new here too. While the Son has always been closer to God than the angels, now God has done something new. In these last days, God might have sent a messenger from the holy court—the simplest meaning of "angel," after all, is "messenger"—but now, God chose neither a prophet from among the people, nor a messenger from among the heavenly host. "But in these last days, God has spoken to us by a Son" (Heb. 1:2). In the intertestamental period, when the traditional role of the prophet was being redefined, Hellenistic Jews increasingly saw angels as the bridge beings between a holy God and God's human subjects. Hebrews proclaims a holy God, to be sure, but God's holiness does not preclude God's presence with sinful humanity. In fact, in response to sin—and to redeem those lost in sin—God, in the person of the Son, comes closer to humanity rather than backing away.

THE GOSPEL
JOHN 1:1-14 (RCL, BCP)
JOHN 1:1-18 or 1-5, 9-14 (LFM)

The exegetical analysis here proceeds from the conclusion that the prologue to John's Gospel is a highly structured poem that begins at 1:1 and concludes at 1:18. At the center of the poem's chiastic structure is the news that "to all who received him, who believed in his name, he gave power to become children of God" (1:12). Many congregations will abbreviate the prologue, and although ending at 1:14 has the effect of putting the emphasis on verse 14 rather than verse 12, fine sermons may be preached on either collection of verses.

The Center of the Text: Relationship. R. Alan Culpepper describes a chiasm in the prologue:[6]

```
1-2   The Word with God
   3   What came through the Word
      4-5   What was received from the Word
         6-8   John announces the Word
            9-10   The Word enters the world
               11   The Word and his own people
                  12a   The Word is accepted
                     12b   The Word's gift to those who accepted him
                  12c   The Word is accepted
               13   The Word and his own people
            14   The Word enters the world
         15   John announces the Word
      16   What was received from the Word
   17   What came through the Word
18   The Word with God
```

The only place that one needs Greek to recognize this arrangement is at the center of the x-shaped structure, in verse 12. The order of phrases in Greek is

(a) to those who received him
(b) to them he gave power to become children of God
(a') to those who believed in his name

The pivot of the prologue, then, to borrow a phrase from Culpepper, is verse 12b, and the news of John's Gospel as a whole is that the Word became flesh in order to give those who received and believed in him a relationship with God like his own. The only Son, who is close to the Father's heart, makes the Father known. Why? The revelation is not so that humanity can have all our questions answered about religion, or so that we may admire the perfection, or the power, or some other attribute of God. The Son makes the Father known so that others may be related to God as he is—so that they may be children of God. The emphasis in the prologue is on relationship, just as it is later in the Gospel when the risen Jesus asks Mary Magdalene to tell his brothers, "I am ascending to my Father and your Father, to my God and your God" (John 20:17). In all the Gospels, Jesus redefines family relationships (see, for example, Mark 3:31-35 and its Synoptic parallels, as well as John 19:27). The prologue to John proclaims that Jesus is introducing God to humanity so that we may know God as intimately as he does.

All creation breathes with the life of the Logos, apart from whom there is no life (1:1-4). This conviction finds subliminal expression in John's masterful use of elemental, earthly symbols to articulate the Word: water, wine, bread, light, door, sheep, seed, vine, blood, fish. The truth of the Logos is manifest only in and through the medium of these symbols. No other New Testament writing so vividly visualizes the eternal in, with, and under the ordinary.
—Richard B. Hays[7]

Given that the Gospels are completely silent about what Jesus looked like, the scientists are guessing, of course. Yet they are making highly educated guesses, and the point with respect to the incarnation is that the effort reminds us of something implied in the prologue: Jesus had a particular face, stature, and eye color. The Word became flesh. We begin with a particular person who looked a certain way, and who experienced life as we do. As Gail O'Day reminds us, "to become flesh is to know joy, pain, suffering, and loss. It is to love, to grieve, and someday to die."[8] In John's Gospel, Jesus is thirsty, tired, angry, and weeping. He also claims to be one with the Father, and he uses the divine name, "I am," to describe himself. Charles Campbell notes the connection in verse 14 between divine glory in human flesh and observes, "The image challenges all abstract presuppositions about God's nature, both ancient and modern. To know God, we begin not with general definitions of the 'divine,' but with the particular person, Jesus of Nazareth."[9]

The Word also "lived among us." The vocabulary for the way the Word was among us is the same as the vocabulary used in the Septuagint to describe God's presence with the Israelites in the wilderness. God tented among them (the Greek verb is *skēnoō*). God was present in the tabernacle. Likewise, Jesus "pitched a tent," or "made his dwelling" (NIV) or "took up residence" (NET) among us. There is a transient quality about tenting. The image implies a willingness on the part of the divine to move toward humanity and to be on the move with them.

Creation and New Creation. The birth of the world (1:3) and its second birth (1:13) are both here. Whether the preacher chooses to focus on themes associated with the incarnation, or with the work of Christ to give his followers power to become children of God, or on something else within the reading, the prologue is proclamation about God's Son and God's creation coming together again, as at the first. As the Word was present in creation, so the Word becomes flesh in order to redeem God's people. As Genesis 1:1-4 had told the story of God's speaking creation into being "in the beginning" and separating light from darkness, so John 1:1-5 echoes the same themes and adds, "The light shines in the darkness, and the darkness did not overcome it." News of creation and of a restored creation mingle in the opening verses of John's Gospel, demonstrating (as in the reading from Hebrews) that the Bible really does tell one story. That story—which is still being written—is of God's self-revelation and God's self-giving love for humanity.

Notes

1. Fred B. Craddock, et al. *Preaching through the Christian Year, Year A* (Philadelphia: Trinity Press International, 1992), 41.

2. Ellen F. Davis, "Psalm 98," *Interpretation* 46 (1992): 172.

3. Ibid., 173.

4. Ibid., 171.

5. Fred B. Craddock, "Hebrews," in The New Interpreter's Bible (Nashville: Abingdon Press, 1998), 12:13.

6. R. Alan Culpepper, *The Gospel and the Letters of John*, Interpreting Biblical Texts (Nashville: Abingdon Press, 1998), 116.

7. Richard B. Hays, *The Moral Vision of the New Testament: Community, Cross, a New Creation*, A Contemporary Introduction to New Testament Ethics (San Francisco: HarperSanFrancisco, 1996), 156.

8. Gail R. O'Day, "John," in The New Interpreter's Bible (Nashville: Abingdon Press, 1995) 9:525–26.

9. Charles L. Campbell, "John 1:1-14," *Interpretation* 49 (1995): 396.

 FIRST SUNDAY AFTER
CHRISTMAS DAY /
THE HOLY FAMILY

DECEMBER 30, 2007

REVISED COMMON	EPISCOPAL (BCP)	ROMAN CATHOLIC
Isa. 63:7-9	Isa. 61:10—62:3	Sir. 3:2-6. 12-14
Psalm 148	Ps. 147 or 147:13-21	Ps. 128:1-2, 3, 4-5
Heb. 2:10-18	Gal. 3:23-25; 4:4-7	Col. 3:12-21
		or 3:12-17
Matt. 2:13-23	John 1:1-18	Matt. 2:13-15, 19-23

KEY THEMES

• In Christ, God shares the human experience of suffering in order to rescue, heal, and redeem.

• We demonstrate our love for God by showing kindness and love in our relationships with others.

• From the start of his life, Jesus represents a threat to established power structures who are willing to use violence to stop him.

FIRST READING

ISAIAH 63:7-9 (RCL)

The brief reading from Isaiah 63 is the opening stanza of a longer section of Isaiah (63:7—64:12) that has all the formal elements of a lament psalm. The lament opens with these verses of praise. In the context of great need and an aching sense of the absence of God (cf. Isa. 63:19), the prophet "recalls the gracious deeds of the Lord." The speaker is not simply looking on the bright side, however, or making the best of a bad situation. Setting a statement of need in the context of praise for one's deliverer has the effect of reminding God and oneself that the relationship is intact, even if the present time is grim.

A textual difficulty in Isaiah 63:8-9 leads to translations with two different senses of how God has been present to save God's people. Comparing the NRSV and the NIV illustrates the difficulty:

NRSV	NIV
8 For he said, "Surely they are my people, children who will not deal falsely"; and he became their savior 9 in all their distress. It was no messenger or angel but his presence that saved them. . . .	8 He said, "Surely they are my people, sons who will not be false to me"; and so he became their Savior. 9 In all their distress he too was distressed, and the angel of his presence saved them.

The difference between these translations is the difference in Hebrew between *lō'* (not) and *lô* (to him). The first yields the reading that it was not a messenger who saved the people, but rather God (NRSV). The second highlights the fact that the people's distress was distress also to God (NIV).

The end of verse 9 supports either reading almost equally: "In his love and his pity he redeemed them; he lifted them up and carried them all the days of old." On the one hand, the end of the verse pictures God as one who has pity for the people and so may in fact feel their pain as God's own ("in all their distress, he was distressed also"). On the other hand, the news that God "lifted them up and carried them" supports hearing in the previous phrase that God did not outsource the salvation of God's people, but lifted them up himself ("It was no messenger or angel but his presence that saved them").

For Christians, both readings find their deepest fulfillment in the work of Jesus Christ. God did not send an angel, but the Son. Nor did God only observe humanity's distress, but the divine self also felt it. About Christ, we confess, "Surely he has borne our infirmities and carried our diseases" (Isa. 53:4). With this christological reading of Isaiah in mind, David Read writes, "His way of salvation will be through his total immersion in the suffering that you and I must endure, and a total sharing of the consequences of our sins."[1]

ISAIAH 61:10—62:3 (BCP)

After the pain of exile, images of homecoming include travel on a safe highway through the desert, a parade of victorious troops returning to a fortified city, and now, a party—or better, a wedding—for which God outfits those who attend. "Returning exiles' wardrobe courtesy of Yahweh," says Isaiah 61:10, or words to that effect. The speaker of these verses is a single voice (notice the switch from God as speaker in 61:9), but probably one who stands for the whole people of God. For that one the Lord has provided salvation and righteousness. The speaker describes himself wrapped in these gifts of God, dressed up in them as a bride and bridegroom are joyfully overdressed for their own wedding.

Ralph Klein reminds us that in this context salvation is victory or deliverance from enemies and that righteousness is not a category of human behavior but a word for the faithfulness of God. "Righteousness means first of all God's faithfulness to his relationship to us, then all those actions which demonstrate his faithfulness—promise, incarnation, death and resurrection—and then the result of that faithfulness in our lives, our experience of salvation. . . . With a Gospel from John 1, his righteousness is the Word made flesh."[2] God gives signs of faithfulness to the people, steadfastly staying alongside them to sustain and deliver them.

SIRACH 3:2-6, 12-14 (LFM)

The First Epistle of John declares rather starkly, "Those who say, 'I love God,' and hate their brothers or sisters are liars; for those who do not love a brother or sister whom they have seen, cannot love God whom they have not seen" (1 John 4:20). As uncompromising as this language is, the verse is nonetheless a helpful reminder that we never love God "in general," apart from specific loving deeds toward fellow human beings and the rest of God's creation. Put positively, we could say that we demonstrate our love for God by honoring and seeking the best for others.

The reading from Sirach makes a similar point. In Sirach 2:15 we read that "Those who fear the Lord do not disobey his words, and those who love him keep his ways." We love God by obeying God's law, and God's law directs us toward loving actions on behalf of the neighbor. Loving the neighbor, whom we can see, is a way of loving God, whom we cannot see.

If "neighbor" is still too generic, what about loving father and mother? The poem in Sirach 1–16 directs the reader to precisely this specific action. The poem makes astonishing promises (cf. "those who honor their father atone for sins," v. 3) and it offers sweet, practical advice on kindness and generosity of spirit ("My child, help your father in his old age, and do not grieve him as long as he lives; even if his mind fails, be patient with him," vv. 12-13a). While the combination of material like these verses may seem odd at first, it points to something that experience also teaches: our closest relationships are at once the most rewarding and the most challenging realm within which we demonstrate our love for God.

RESPONSIVE READING
PSALM 148 (RCL)

"While the songs of praise generally push toward universality," J. Clinton McCann Jr. observes, "Psalm 148 takes inclusivity to the limit."[3] The call to praise goes out to everything in the biblical three-layer cosmos, from angels and celestial bodies who dwell above the earth, to the sea monsters and the deep waters under the earth, to humans and every other element of creation in between. The reference to "wild animals and all cattle, creeping things and flying birds" in verse 10 calls to mind Genesis 1:24. Indeed, the whole psalm is reminiscent of Genesis 1 and sounds like a roll call of all that God has made. Everything is called to praise God for creation (v. 5) and for God's faithfulness to God's people (v. 14).

PSALM 147 or 147:13-21 (BCP)

The psalter ends with four psalms that begin and end with the words, "Praise the Lord!" (hallelu-yah), and Psalm 147 is one of these. If only a portion of the psalm is used, it would be better to start at verse 12 than verse 13 since the last section or stanza of the psalm begins in verse 12.

Each section of the psalm combines praise for the God on account of creation with praise for God on account of God's deliverance for the chosen people. In verse 14, God gives peace to the people; in verses 15-18, God is commanding wind and weather. In verse 19, God is making God's law known to Israel. The One who creates also redeems and sustains. The God of Israel is the Lord of all creation.

PSALM 128:1, 2-3a, 3b-4, 5-6 (LFM)

All creatures, worship God most high!
Sound ev'ry voice in earth and sky: Alleluia!
*   Alleluia!*
Sing, brother sun, in splendor bright; sing, sister
*   moon and stars of night:*
Alleluia, Alleluia, alleluia, alleluia, alleluia!
—Francis of Assisi[4]

At the heart of the biblical faith is the astounding claim that the power that has strewn the stars into their courses (v. 4) is the same power that—or better, who—"heals the brokenhearted" (v. 3), "lifts up the downtrodden" (v. 6), and declares an intelligible, personal, life-giving word to Israel (vv. 19-20). In short, our trust—indeed, our only hope—is that the power behind the universe has a personal face that is turned toward us in "steadfast love" (v. 11b).
—J. Clinton McCann[5]

To those who fear the Lord, Psalm 128 announces blessings. It gives voice to the straightforward if naïve-sounding expectation that good will be rewarded or, one might say, that good things will happen to good people. The blessings named relate both to the home and to business: the recipient of God's favor will enjoy the fruits of his or her labor in the workplace and the blessing of children in his or her home. Lest this prayer lapse into a psalm for individual affluence, the last verses expand the realm of blessing in a way that guards against narrow, individualistic conclusions about God's favor. The psalm prays, "May you see the prosperity of Jerusalem" (v. 5), thus acknowledging that the community beyond the confines of the family unit needs God's blessing as well.

SECOND READING
HEBREWS 2:10-18 (RCL)

To speak of God, Christians must sooner or later tell the story of Jesus. We confess that the one whom our tradition calls the visible "image of the invisible God" (Col. 1:15) and the "Word made flesh" (John 1:14), Jesus of Nazareth, offers God's clearest self-revelation. We cannot talk for long about our view of God without speaking of Christ.

Likewise, if the authors of the New Testament are characteristic of Christians confessing their faith, we cannot explain much about our view of Christ without speaking of the cross. Even at this point in the church year, so close to Christmas, when one might expect the church to linger at least a week or two over the image of a baby "asleep on the hay," such is not the case. Instead, the lectionary directs our eye to a picture of Jesus as One who suffered for the sake of those he called brothers and sisters, in order to free them from bondage to the fear of death (Heb. 2:15).

Jesus is an older brother to humanity, which means he is an example, an intercessor, and a trustworthy guardian.[6] He is also One who was made perfect through sufferings (v. 10) and who, through death, destroyed the power of death (v. 14). Piling multiple descriptions of Jesus, the author of Hebrews shows us One who is brother, high priest, and something more. He is, in the words of Dietrich Bonhoeffer, "the suffering God." As Christ became like us in every respect, he revealed a God who identifies with human anguish in order to transform it.

> The Bible directs man to God's powerlessness and suffering; only the suffering God can help.
> —Dietrich Bonhoeffer[7]

As we consider the Gospel reading for this Sunday, with its all-too-believable portrait of violence against innocents and of the grief-stricken for whom there is no consolation, this view of Christ is especially important. Christ not only suffers with his brothers and sisters but he does so in order to bring healing. This portrait takes seriously the desperate situation of humanity and the reality of unjust suffering, and it proclaims that that is precisely where God is working most fervently to bring healing and transformation.

GALATIANS 3:23-25; 4:4-7 (BCP)

See the comments on Galatians 4:4-7 on the Holy Name of Jesus (January 1), below.

COLOSSIANS 3:12-21 or 3:12-17 (LFM)

The reading from Sirach counsels love for parents as a way of keeping God's law and so honoring God. The second reading expands on the theme of sanctification lived out in our closest relationships. The author of Colossians begins this part of his argument saying, "So if you have been raised with Christ, seek the things that are above, where Christ is, seated at the right hand of God. Set your minds on things that are above, not on things that are on the earth, for you have died, and your life is hidden with Christ in God" (Col. 3:1-3). In John, Jesus had said to Pilate, "My kingdom is not from this world" (John 18:36). Here a different New Testament author can confirm that insight. His readers do not belong to this world. Their life is hidden with Christ in God and their minds are to be set on things above.

Just when readers may be led to think that such a lofty mind-set means that they cannot or need not attend to the most basic of human relationships, however, the author of the letter provides instruction in those relationships. "As God's chosen ones, holy and beloved, clothe yourselves with compassion, kindness, humility, meekness, and patience" (Col. 3:12). Christians confess that we love God best, and we have our minds set most firmly on "things above" when kindness, forgiveness, and love toward one another characterize our everyday lives. This insight is a corollary of the incarnation. God honored human life with God's very self: "the Word became flesh" (John 1:14). As God chose the arena of human life to reveal the divine self most clearly, so that same arena is the one in which we return our thanks to God and show God our love. Throughout the history of the church, our understanding about the specifics of "clothing yourselves with compassion" have changed, as is evidenced by many modern readers' ambivalence about much of the household code in Colossians 3:18—4:2. Yet the commendation of virtue remains instructive for us, as does the insight that the way to set one's mind on things above is to put on love in our everyday life.

THE GOSPEL
MATTHEW 2:13-23 (RCL)
MATTHEW 2:13-15, 19-23 (LFM)

In his commentary on Matthew, Warren Carter titles his analysis of Matthew 2 "The Empire Strikes Back."[8] As Carter reads this chapter, the contrast is not between Jews who reject Jesus and Gentile Magi who honor him but, rather, between established imperial power in the person of the Idumean, Herod, who actively, brutally works to destroy the child and itinerant outsiders to that established order—both his parents who are Jews and the visitors who are Gentiles—who honor and protect Jesus. "The division consists of a sociopolitical dynamic between the powerful settled center (Herod, the religious elite) and the apparently powerless, insignificant, and mobile margins (magi, Joseph and Mary)."[9] From beginning to end, Matthew tells the story of Jesus in a way that distrusts established authority and imagines discipleship as an itinerant existence on the edges of the empire. This Gospel ends with Jesus' commission to the Eleven to make disciples "as you go" (cf. Matt. 28:19). The commission's language implies itinerancy for the church rather than stability. Matthew also includes the strongest language of any of the Gospels against clerical offices and titles (cf. 23:8-12). Such values—and reasons for them—are in evidence as the Magi leave the holy family and the family must flee the dangers of established power.

As the reading begins, Herod is about to "search for the child, to destroy him" (Matt. 2:13). The Magi find out in a dream that they are to avoid Herod on their way home. Joseph learns of Herod's plans in a dream as well, one that is vivid enough for him to pack up the family immediately and leave by night.

The horror that unfolds may be even greater than either set of travelers imagined. In the film *Schindler's List*, there is a scene in which Nazi troops raid a Jewish neighborhood, searching for those in hiding, detaining everyone they can, and killing any who resist. Children as well as adults are targets. The horrible sense of inevitability one feels watching that scene, as little ones try to hide from the troops and are discovered, is like the experience of reading this text. Matthew does not describe the bloodshed. He does not write about swords, or tiny corpses, or soldiers prying crying babies from their screaming mothers' arms. Matthew does not need to write about these things because with only the simplest allusion to the terror, we can imagine it well enough. This world's tyrants rage, and the little people suffer.[10]

Matthew does write the story in such a way that it recalls highly significant moments in Israel's history. Mary's husband, Joseph, dreams and rightly interprets those dreams, just as the patriarch, Joseph, had done before him (Gen. 37:5-11). Baby Jesus is under the threat of death, thanks to government-sanctioned murder of baby boys, just as baby Moses had been (Exod. 2:1-10), who was destined, like Jesus, to liberate God's people and teach them the way of covenant faithfulness. The families in and around Bethlehem grieve their lost infants, and Matthew describes the lament with words spoken by Jeremiah about the wailing of the people at the time of the Northern tribes' exile to Assyria: "Rachel weeping for her children; she refused to be consoled, because they are no more" (Jer. 31:15). This short story of Jesus' infancy calls to mind the time of the patriarchs, the exodus, and the exile. For those who know Israel's story, Matthew's opening chapters have a familiar ring to them.

Whether one knows Israel's story or not, this reading from Matthew also has the familiar ring of a story about how power corrupts. Herod's title, issued from Rome, was "King of the Jews." When the Magi come looking for an heir to that designation, he is frightened (v. 3), and then infuriated (v. 16). Matthew 2 documents the familiar tale of humans wreaking havoc in direct proportion to their access to power. In this way, the slaughter of the innocents is the opposite of the gospel. The gospel of Jesus Christ is the story of the One who freely renounces power over others and freely chooses suffering for the good of the many. Matthew 2 is the story of the many forced into suffering for the sake of the one desperately trying to keep his position of power over others. Children die; families grieve; soldiers live with the horror of their own actions. The many suffer so that the one—Herod—may feel momentarily more secure.

About Jesus, the angel had told Joseph, "He will save his people from their sins" (Matt. 1:21). This story illustrates sin at its most insistent and dangerous, inspiring the hope and prayer that Jesus will indeed save from sin, both the sins we commit and those of others that threaten to devastate our lives.

The empire strikes back as Herod, Rome's vassal king, and Jerusalem's settled elite of chief priests and scribes respond negatively. Herod employs military, religious, and social resources and strategies to thwart God's work. His murderous actions, allied with the inaction of the religious elite, demonstrate the oppressive structures from which Jesus is to save the world.
—Warren Carter[11]

Sermon preparation on this text could fruitfully include reading it with those who share the deeply emotional experiences described in it. For instance, how hard would it be for you to find someone in your neighborhood who has hidden or fled in fear for their lives? If you are not sure whether you know such a person already, try calling a refugee resettlement agency like Lutheran Social Services. Such a call would probably put you in touch with people who could tell you from firsthand experience what it is like to get up, pack, and flee in the middle of the night. A call to the local shelter for victims of domestic violence would likely do the same. Ask to meet someone with a story like this, and ask them to listen to the Gospel text with you. Read it with them. What do they hear in it?

Or call someone whose sorrow is so deep that they "refuse to be consoled." This call may be harder than the first one, especially if you are their pastor and they do not seem to be "making progress" through the stages of grief, or if you are their pastor and the depth of their sorrow has made it increasingly tempting for you to avoid them. Don't worry about facilitating their grief in this visit. Just ask them to listen to the story with you and to tell you what they hear in it. Where is God in the story? Who will comfort the afflicted?

From Matthew we learn that before Jesus is old enough to walk, he is going toe-to-toe with the rulers of this age. From infancy, Jesus' own life is at risk as a result of tyranny that masks itself as a concern for national or personal security. As an adult, Jesus teaches a prayer that includes the petitions, "Thy kingdom come; thy will be done" (cf. Matt. 6:9-13). The prayer still offers a direct and courageous response to Herod and his offspring, for as we pray it we testify that God's rule and God's will, as they are made manifest among us, signal an end to such tyranny.

JOHN 1:1-18 (BCP)

See the comments on the Gospel for the Nativity of our Lord III (Christmas Day), above.

Notes

1. David H. C. Read, "Journey to Jordan." Expository Times 98 (1986): 80.

2. Ralph W. Klein, "Preaching Helps," *Currents in Mission and Theology* 12 (1985): 72.

3. J. Clinton McCann, Jr. "Psalms," in The New Interpreter's Bible (Nashville: Abingdon Press, 1996), 4:1272.

4. Francis of Assisi, "All Creatures, Worship God Most High," trans. composite, *Evangelical Lutheran Worship* (Minneapolis: Augsburg Fortress, 2006), 835.

5. McCann, "Psalms," 1269.

6. Patrick Gray, "Brotherly Love and the Christology of Hebrews," *Journal of Biblical Literature* 122, no. 2 (2003): 335–51, reads Hebrews alongside Plutarch's essay, "On Brotherly Love," demonstrating that Plutarch's description of the ideal brother has much in common with the description of an ideal high priest in Hebrews. The ideal older brother intercedes with parents when necessary, guards and passes on an inheritance in some circumstances, is a trustworthy guardian and "forerunner" in various household and civic responsibilities, and so on.

7. Dietrich Bonhoeffer, *Letters and Papers from Prison*, ed. Eberhard Bethge (New York: Macmillan, 1971), 361.

8. Warren Carter, *Matthew and the Margins* (Sheffield, Eng.: Sheffield Academic Press, 2000), 73–89.

9. Ibid., 73.

10. W. D. Davies and Dale C. Allison, Jr., *Matthew* (Sheffield, Eng.: T & T Clark, 1988), 1:264–65, note the reports from Josephus of Herod's tyranny and review other Jewish traditions that make use of the story of Moses' dangerous infancy to describe the dangers that tyrants present to the faithful in every age. Although we have no external evidence of this particular massacre, historians agree that "Herod's reign was marked by the slaughter of many innocents," and it would have been in character for him to order such a thing (164).

11. Carter, *Matthew and the Margins*, 84.

HOLY NAME OF JESUS / MARY, MOTHER OF GOD

January 1, 2008

Revised Common	Episcopal (BCP)	Roman Catholic
Num. 6:22-27	Exod. 34:1-8	Num. 6:22-27
Psalm 8	Psalm 8	Ps. 67:2-3, 5, 6-8
Gal. 4:4-7	Rom. 1:1-7	Gal 4:4-7
or Phil. 2:5-11	or Phil. 2:9-13	
Luke 2:15-21	Luke 2:15-21	Luke 2:16 -21

KEY THEMES

- To receive God's blessing is to be reminded of God's work to provide everything needed for daily life.
- Love motivates God's mercy toward the Israelites in the wilderness.
- Love motivates Christ's self-emptying life, ministry, and death on behalf of humanity.

FIRST READING
NUMBERS 6:22-21 (RCL, LFM)

Because Martin Luther incorporated the benediction in Numbers 6 into his German Mass, generations of Protestants know these words well even if they do not recognize them as biblical. In the context of the canon, the threefold benediction is introduced during the time Israel spends in the wilderness. The prophets and historians of Israel would remember the wilderness period as that time when the Israelites had the fewest illusions of self-sufficiency. There in the desert, without God's daily provision, they would die. While their daily need of God would not diminish in later years and other contexts, the wilderness was the place where their needs—and God's work to meet those needs—were clearest to everyone.

In the wilderness, God directs Moses to tell Aaron and his sons to bless the Israelites. The blessing is carefully structured liturgical material. Both the verb forms ("May God bless ...") and the repeated use of the divine name as the subject of each sentence make it clear that God is doing the actual blessing. The priests will speak the blessing and God will do it (cf. 6:27). The object of the blessing is in the singular, making it direct address to individuals, though from the use of plural objects in both verse 23 ("the Israelites") and verse 27 ("them") we know that the words are for the gathered assembly as much as for individual blessing.

Thanks to the work of Claus Westermann and others, we understand blessing to be provision for daily life.[1] It is not equivalent to salvation or deliverance, but neither is it just a pat on the back, a supportive exhortation from God to "break a leg" or "go get 'em, slugger," as we exit worship and return to daily life. Vernon Kleinig draws a helpful parallel between blessing and providence. Kleinig writes, "All this is no pious wish, but a richly-effective divine action. The beneficial nearness of our Lord accompanies us into our week of work. Since our identity often gets blurred there, this blessing reminds us who we are."[2]

These are the actions of God that we take into our work-week: (1) God's keeping: the Hebrew word for keep is the same used to describe what the first human is to do in Eden, where God directs him to till and keep the garden (cf. Gen. 2:15). For God to offer God's keeping is to promise regular care and attention. (2) God's showing and shining God's face: Psalm 30 helps us define this blessing by showing it to us alongside its opposite. The psalmist admits, "While I felt secure, I said, 'I shall never be disturbed. You, Lord, with your favor, made me as strong as the mountains.' Then you hid your face, and I was filled with fear" (Ps. 30:6-7).[4] As quickly as it takes God to hide God's face—in the blink of an eye—the speaker reports having gone from confidence to being "filled with fear." To put to rest all fears of abandonment, God lifts up God's face and looks upon God's people with favor. (3) God's giving peace: Peace is shalom, translated variously as "good, welfare, well-being, security, prosperity, harmony, unity, concord, rest ease, completeness, and contentment."[5] God grants peace to each person, for the well-being of individual and community.

> A blessing is the kind of statement that determines and settles something, a clinching statement or verdict. Such power is surely something great, for it really brings and grants physical goods for the household, temporal goods for the government, and spiritual goods for the priesthood.
> —Martin Luther[3]

EXODUS 34:1-8 (BCP)

Exodus 32–34 narrates the story of the golden calf incident and its aftermath. During Moses' absence from them, both the people and their leadership (in the person of Aaron) break their covenant with God. The reading from Exodus 34 appears in the context of a story about Israel's rejection of God, and the question answered by the text is, "What now?" What will God do? Will God punish the people in anger and then make a great nation of Moses alone (Exod. 32:10)? Will God send Moses and the people on their way but not accompany them (Exod.

33:3)? God considers both of these options and rejects them. Exodus 34 is the story of what God chooses to do instead.

God chooses to renew the covenant, and in order to explain why God will stay faithful to the people when they have been unfaithful, God reveals the divine name again (God's speech begins with "The Lord, the Lord") and then exegetes that name, as it were, using nine terms to describe the nature of "the Lord." Sometimes when the authors of Israel's Scripture want to describe God, they speak of God's actions: "The Lord brought us up out of Egypt with a mighty hand and an outstretched arm" (Deut. 26:8). Other times, the authors of Scripture describe God not with actions but with adjectives. Such is the case in Exodus 34:6-7. If its language sounds familiar, it may be because forms of this description for God show up more than twenty times in the Old Testament.

According to Exodus 34:6-7, God's decision to continue on with the people is not based on Moses' intercession for the people, though Moses has interceded for the people (Exod. 32:11-14). God's decision is not based on a conclusion that adequate punishment has been meted out, though the people have been punished with a plague (32:35). God's decision is not based on the people's earnest repentance, though they have repented (cf. 33:4-6).

> Mercy is not indulgence, saying, well, you really shouldn't do that but if you do I probably won't do anything about it. Mercy is not something that can be claimed, as if the standards were faulty or impossibly high, and God really owes us leniency. Mercy finds us condemned, and then for some reason we do not know, set free.
> —Donald E. Gowan[6]

God's decision to continue on with the people and to stay faithful to the covenant is based on God's character. Exodus 34:6-7 is a statement of God's nature. It is in the nature of God to abound in steadfast love and faithfulness. It is also in the nature of God to show restraint with respect to punishment, without ignoring sin or its consequences. Seven adjectives describe God's graciousness; two report God's refusal to ignore actions that ravage others.

The close proximity here of abounding graciousness and God's steadfast refusal to overlook sin is the topic of much scholarly conversation. "When the two elements are combined, forgiveness is not mistaken as being just divine leniency," writes Thomas Raitt. "God's right to express unmerited love is the only thing strong enough to counterbalance God's right to punish covenant violations. It is a complex and intimidating balance, but a balance nonetheless."[7]

Like other complex personalities, God's personality includes some elements that exist in tension with each other. On the one hand, how can God abound in mercy and still punish sin? On the other hand, how can God require justice and then forgive sin? The text raises these questions without resolving them. Even without resolution, however, the text reports that God is still present with the people. Maybe the "answers," if there are any, come only as we live in relationship with this God. As for the people of Israel, the God whom one commentator on this text calls "interesting, credible, and dangerous"[8] is still present and in relationship with the people. The pillars of cloud and fire continue to lead them and give them visible signs of God's presence, even in the aftermath of sin and with much ground to cover on the way toward the promised land.

RESPONSIVE READING

PSALM 8 (RCL, BCP)

References to human dominion over creation have rightly received an ambivalent reception in recent biblical scholarship, even though words for the concept are used in the Genesis account of creation (Gen. 1:26, 28) and here in Psalm 8. Scholars are right to point out that the words for humanity's relation to the rest of the created order were never meant to communicate domination, much less a careless consumption of creation's bounty to satisfy our own desires. Psalm 8 speaks of humanity's rule over creation, but it does not celebrate that rule. It celebrates the majesty of God. "O Lord, our Sovereign, how majestic is your name in all the earth!" (8:1, 9). Notice all the verbs used in the psalm to describe God's action. Above all, Psalm 8 celebrates God's name and God's work on behalf of the whole creation.

What would our world, our attitudes, our practices, and even our political policies look like if we began to see and value God, the environment, all creatures, and human beings in mutually beneficial and covenantal relationship? Psalm 8 is a good beginning point for reflection on these questions.
—Elizabeth Hinson-Hasty[9]

PSALM 67:2-3, 5, 6-8 (LFM)

Psalm 67 is structured around a statement of God's blessing of all nations, rather than God's favor shown exclusively to Israel. Verse 4 states, "Let the nations be glad and sing for joy, for you judge the people with equity and guide the nations upon earth." On each side of this verse is the refrain, "Let the peoples praise you, O God; let all the peoples praise you." The call for praise is to everyone, both those in Israel and those beyond the usual boundaries of the chosen people. The Scriptures of the Old and New Testament agree: from the call of Abraham in Genesis 12, to the call of Paul in Acts 9, we hear that God means to work through particular people in order to bless all humanity. This psalm is a call for all the peoples to recognize God's blessing upon them and respond with praise.

GALATIANS 4:4-7 (RCL, LFM)

For a few weeks, as one year turns into another, we live with a heightened sense of time. We read or watch reports documenting the "top ten" news stories of the year just past. We listen to predictions about how the real estate market or stock market will do in the next year. We look back and forward, thinking about what has changed since this time last year, and what we can expect from this point forward.

Paul is doing the same sort of thing with the Galatians. At two different points in chapters 3 and 4 he gives his readers a kind of "before and after" picture of their lives. In chapter 3, he writes, "Now before faith came, we were imprisoned and guarded under the law until faith would be revealed" (Gal. 3:23). He goes on to talk about the law as a "disciplinarian" (v. 24). The role of the law before faith is like the role of someone keeping an eye on things in the kitchen before dinner guests arrive—to make sure no one raids the refrigerator before the party. By definition, the role is an interim one. It would be all wrong to guard a refrigerator after the party has begun, when everyone for whom the food was intended is present.

The difference between the era "before faith came" (3:23) and "the fullness of time" (4:4) is the presence of Christ to redeem and to give "adoption as children" (4:5). Paul uses two different metaphors to speak of Christ's work. Christ redeems those under the law, meaning that he buys their freedom as one buys the freedom of a slave. Christ is not content, however, with conferring the status of freed slaves; he changes the relationship to the household altogether by making everyone he has freed, "no longer a slave but a child, and if a child then also an heir" (4:7).

> The task for the preacher working with this text is to reflect deeply on the ways in which our congregations today unaccountably reject God's gift of adoption and liberation, choosing instead familiar destructive patterns of life and religiosity. Then, after identifying such analogies and patterns, our next task is to reproclaim the good news of 4:3-7: God has sent the Son to set us free and has given us the Spirit as a sign that we are children and heirs of God.
> —Richard B. Hays[10]

By limiting the law's role like this, Paul is not here making an argument for moral carelessness or for license that cannot be bothered to show love for God and neighbor (cf. 5:14). He is saying only—but amazingly!—that God has acted, in Christ, to welcome Jews and Gentiles into the same family, to invite them sit down to meals together, and to give them all the inheritance due sons and daughters.

The current time, Paul writes, is as different from the past as the dinner hour is different from that time just before the doorbell has rung to signal the first guest's arrival. "When the fullness of time had come, God sent his Son . . ." (4:4). For Gentiles to seek to keep the law—that is, for them to become Jews in order to confess Jesus as Messiah and Lord—is to act if God had not sent his Son. It is to look at a dining room full of guests and not see that the time has come to open the refrigerator and get on with the party!

ROMANS 1:1-7 (BCP)

See the comments on the second reading for the Fourth Sunday in Advent.

PHILIPPIANS 2:5-11 (RCL alt.)
PHILIPPIANS 2:9-13 (BCP alt.)

In the status-conscious Roman colony of Philippi, Paul urges the Philippians to relate to each other with the mind of Christ. Paul describes that mind or mind-set as voluntary denial of status in relationship with others. Paul is not encouraging the Philippians in a thought experiment but toward a way of life, and it is one that Paul himself has already taken up. Paul begins his letter by referring to himself and Timothy as slaves (1:1). Aware that his current incarceration may be an embarrassment to his friends, Paul has to explain how his further degraded status—from slave to prisoner—is turning out for good (1:12-14). Recognizing that the Philippians may be imagining those who keep the law as having a status to which to aspire, Paul boasts about his own reasons for confidence in the flesh and then says decisively, "Whatever gains I had, these I have come to regard as loss because of Christ" (cf. 3:2-11).

English translations note a difficulty in 2:5. Is Paul commending the imitation of Christ (the mind-set about to be described "was in Christ Jesus"), or is Paul proclaiming a gift given by the reality of his readers having been united with Christ (the mind-set is theirs "in Christ Jesus")? The Greek of Philippians 2:5 supports either of these translations. Elsewhere in Paul's letters, we can find both an ethic of the imitation of Christ and an ethic based on union with Christ. Whichever way one translates verse 5, Paul is commending a deeper and more profound ethic than can be summarized with the question, "What would Jesus do?" as he tells the story of Christ's self-emptying, incarnation, obedience to death, and exaltation by God. Paul makes this clear when he says later in Philippians that he presses on toward the goal of knowing Christ and sharing fellowship in his sufferings "because Christ Jesus has made me his own" (cf. 3:10-12). As it had been in Christ's initial self-emptying move toward humanity, the initiative is always with Jesus. Any imitation of Christ reflects the prior reality of union with Christ.

In preparation for preaching this text, the preacher will benefit from recalling one of Søren Kierkegaard's parables. It posits love as the motivation for Christ's self-emptying. It is the story of a king, in love with a humble maiden. The king wants to love and be loved by the woman, but he cannot make this known to her as long as he stays in the role of king, for then at best he would win not her love but only her gratitude for lifting her from her low estate. How may they love one another? The king makes his way down the social ladder, not "in costume" or by means of a deception, which is the way of fairy tales, but really, truly by becoming a servant. "This servant-form is no mere outer garment, like the king's beggar-cloak, which therefore flutters loosely about him and betrays the king. . . . It is his true form and figure. For this is the unfathomable nature of love, that it desires equality with the beloved, not in jest merely, but in earnest and truth."[11]

That is kind of love Christ was showing by the activities Paul describes in Philippians 2:6-8. Recognizing such love, God joyfully approved, exalting him and giving him the name above every other name.

Since we bear that name, how might Christians share Christ's kind of love within our congregations and beyond them? Without trivializing the sacrifice of Christ, preaching on Philippians 2:6-8 may bring into focus how our own interest in status actually thwarts our best efforts to love one another and how Christ has acted to love us truly and so free us from such interests.

Nobody knew his secret ambition,
Nobody knew his claim to fame.
He broke the old rules steeped in tradition;
He tore the holy veil away,
Questioning those in powerful position
Running to those who called his name,
[but] nobody knew his secret ambition
Was to give his life away
—Michael W. Smith[12]

The Gospel
LUKE 2:15-21 (RCL, BCP)
LUKE 2:16-21 (LFM)

See the commentary for the Nativity of Our Lord, Proper II, for remarks on Luke 2:15-20. Today's reading includes one extra verse. In the context of the Gospel, Luke 2:21 fits with what follows it rather than what comes before, namely the story of Joseph and Mary's pilgrimage to the Temple for Mary's rite of purification, and the responses of Anna and Simeon to the holy family. In the context of the lectionary, Luke 2:21 is an appropriate reading for the Holy Name of Jesus since it reports the child's naming along with his circumcision.

The verse suggests at least two directions for preaching. First, the name is the one given by the angel to Mary at the annunciation (Luke 1:31). The note about this in Luke 2:21 reminds us (if we needed reminding) that an epic is unfolding. All along the way, astonishing things like angel visitations and other powerful indications of God's presence and plan have occurred. Such things will continue to occur alongside the most mundane happenings in a small family's life. Here a couple is naming a baby. Such an event is completely common, inevitable, and at the same time sublime: "Jesus" is the baby's given (as in, "inspired") name, and it means "Yahweh saves."

The second direction preachers might take from this verse would be to point out how the practice of religious rituals is an occasion for blessing. In the story of Jesus' first few weeks, there is no such thing as "empty ritual." About the visit of the holy family to the Temple in Luke 2:21-40, Alan Culpepper comments, "The ceremony was not a foreign intrusion into their lives but an expression of their deepest awarenesses and commitments. Joseph and Mary saw God at work in the events they had experienced. They lived within a covenant community, and they sought to fulfill vows they had made as well as to introduce their son into that covenant community."[13] The family and the people they meet in the Temple (Anna and Simeon) are a blessing to each other. May it be so for us as well. Whether we begin a Sunday morning thinking we will "go through the motions" or anticipating an encounter with the divine, may the rituals of corporate worship of God and fellowship with one another be an arena for blessing.

Notes

1. Claus Westermann, *Blessing in the Bible and the Life of the Church*, trans. Keith Crim (Philadelphia: Fortress Press, 1978).

2. Vernon P. Kleinig, "Providence and Worship—the Aaronic Blessing: Numbers 6:22-27," *Lutheran Theological Journal* 19 (1985): 123.

3. Martin Luther, *Lectures on Genesis Chapters 26–30*, vol. 5 in Luther's Works, ed. Jaroslav Pelikan (Saint Louis: Concordia Publishing House, 1968), 141.

4. Translation from *Evangelical Lutheran Worship* (Minneapolis: Augsburg Fortress, 2006).

5. Kleinig, "Providence and Worship," 123.

6. Donald E. Gowan, *Theology in Exodus: Biblical Theology in the Form of a Commentary* (Louisville: Westminster John Knox Press, 1994), 237.

7. Thomas M. Raitt, "Why Does God Forgive?" *Horizons in Biblical Theology* 13 (1991): 47.

8. Walter Brueggemann, "Exodus," in The New Interpreter's Bible (Nashville: Abingdon, 1994), 947.

9. Elizabeth Hinson-Hasty, "Psalm 8," *Interpretation* 59 (2005): 394.

10. Richard B. Hays, "Galatians," in The New Interpreter's Bible (Nashville: Abingdon Press, 2000), 11:292.

11. *The Parables of Kierkegaard*, ed. Thomas C. Oden (Princeton, N.J.: Princeton University Press, 1978), 44–45.

12. "Secret Ambition" by Wayne Kirkpatrick, Michael W. Smith and Amy Grant, © careers-BMG Music Publishing / O'Ryan Music, Inc / Riverstone Music Inc. All rights reserved. Used by permission of Music Services.

13. R. Alan Culpepper, "Luke" in The New Interpreter's Bible (Nashville: Abingdon Press, 1995), 9:75.

THE SEASON OF EPIPHANY

HERMAN C. WAETJEN

THE APPEARANCE OF THE STAR OF JACOB AND THE DAWN OF A NEW AGE

Epiphany, derived from the Greek word *epiphaneia*, means "appearing" or "manifestation" and celebrates the showing, the "being seen" of Christ, the Son of God, at his birth, at his baptism, and at his transfiguration. All are events of disclosure!

In the early fourth century, before Jesus' birth was celebrated on December 25, Eastern Christianity began to celebrate his birth in the night from the 5th to the 6th of January. This is Epiphany! This is the first of many divine manifestations that Epiphany combines: Jesus' birth as the private manifestation of God's light, Jesus' baptism as the public manifestation of God's light, and Jesus' transfiguration as the manifestation of his authentic identity as the Son of God and "the Son of Man."

An Egyptian papyrus from the beginning of the fourth century has preserved a liturgical formula for a church choir that was sung at the festival of Epiphany on the 5th to the 6th of January. It is the oldest Christmas liturgy that celebrates the Nativity on this particular night in January. The choir responds to the Gospel lections of Jesus' birth in Bethlehem, the flight into Egypt, and the return that led to settlement in Nazareth by singing, "Born in Bethlehem, raised in Nazareth, lived in Galilee!" After the priest reads the story of the Magi, the choir responds with the words, "We have seen a sign from heaven, the shining star." A reading of the Christmas story from Luke 2 follows, to which the choir answers, "Shepherds pasturing in the fields, amazed, fell to their knees and sang honor to the Father. Hallelujah! Honor to the Son and to the Holy Spirit! Hallelujah, Hallelujah, Hallelujah!"

The fourth-century church father Ephrem characterized Epiphany as the loftiest of the Christian festivals and described the manner in which it was celebrated. On January 5/6 every Christian house was decorated with wreaths, perhaps the very beginning of Christmas decorations. On the night of January 5, Jesus' birth, the adoration of the shepherds and the appearance of the star were celebrated. The next day, January 6, was dedicated to the adoration of the Magi and the baptism of Jesus.[1]

Like December 25, the celebration of Epiphany on January 5/6 is not the celebration of a datum or fact. It is the memorialization of the manifestation of God's light, the light of a new day, the light of God's truth, that was incarnate in Jesus Christ and that has confronted humanity ever since with the truth of being human in a fallen creation and the possibilities of transformation and the recovery of God's image and likeness for both the individual and the entire community of humankind.

Ironically, in the darkness of the winter solstice the light of the sun begins to grow in strength. Correspondingly, in the darkness of war, terrorism, fear, and alienation that has enveloped our planetary society, the texts of Epiphany announce the appearance of a star as the divine signal of the beginning of a new creation and a new humanity. Jesus is the Star of Jacob, the dawning light of a new day, and the prophet who stands in the tradition of Isaiah issues the rousing call, "Arise, *shine*; for your light as come!" If the light has come, those who have been seated in darkness awaiting its arrival are exhorted to greet that light and the new age that it inaugurates by *shining* in order to reflect its glory in all the activities and relationships of everyday life. Like Jesus, the Star of Jacob, they are mandated to be "the light of the world."

The season of Epiphany is that time in the church year to ponder and meditate on the eschatological fulfillment of the prophetic texts that anticipate the dawning of a new day at the appearance of God's Son, Jesus the Christ. It is also the season to renew the call that he, in an echo of the prophets, issued to his disciples to continue the presence of that Light in the darkness of today's world by "laying aside the works of darkness and putting on the armor of light," indeed, "by putting on the Lord Jesus Christ" (Rom. 13:12-14). The words that W. H. Auden has placed on the lips of the Magi can also be our words: "To discover how to be human now / Is the reason we follow this star."[2]

Notes

1. Some of this material has been drawn from Hermann Usener, *Das Weih-nachtsfest* (Bonn: Bouvier Verlag, 1969 [3rd ed.], originally published in 1888) and Oscar Cullmann, *Der Ursprung des Weihnachtsfestes* (Zürich/Stuttgart: Zwingli Verlag, 1960). It should also be noted that many, if not most, of the quotations of both Old and New Testament texts are presented as my own translations.

2. The words that the Magi speak in W. H. Auden's poem come from "For the Time Being: A Christmas Oratorio," in *Collected Longer Poems* (New York: Random House/Vintage Books, 1975), 159.

EPIPHANY OF THE LORD

THE STAR AND THE DAWN OF A NEW CREATION

JANUARY 6, 2008

REVISED COMMON	EPISCOPAL (BCP)	ROMAN CATHOLIC
Isa. 60:1-6	Isa. 60:1-6, 9	Isa. 60:1-6
Ps. 72:1-7, 10-14	Psalm 72 or 72:1-2, 10-17	Ps. 72:1-2, 7-8, 10-11, 12-13
Eph. 3:1-12	Eph. 3:1-12	Eph. 3:2-3a, 5-6
Matt. 2:1-12	Matt. 2:1-12	Matt. 2:1-12

KEY THEMES

- God is coming, and through the ministry of God's Son, Jesus the Christ, God's people will begin to experience a new self-worth through a new self-understanding.
- The history of Israel has reached its goal: the promised and long-awaited Messiah King has come to inaugurate God's reign and its new moral order.
- The Holy Spirit that Jesus received at his baptism and that empowered his ministry is the heritage that he wills for his disciples.
- Commissioned to continue his work and empowered by the Holy Spirit, his disciples as the Body of Christ are called to collaborate in the work of transforming the powers and the principalities.

FIRST READING

ISAIAH 60:1-6 (RCL, LFM)
ISAIAH 60:1-6, 9 (BCP)

The Dawning of a New Day

For the first time in Israel's history a prophet in the tradition of Isaiah voices the expectation of God's direct intervention in history in order to establish a new moral order. As Paul D. Hanson rightly contends in his book, *The Dawn of Apocalyptic*, this is the beginning of apocalyptic eschatology.[1] Isaiah 60–62 especially announce the salvation that will imminently be actualized for God's people.

A dramatic reversal is about to occur: "For darkness shall cover the earth and thick darkness the peoples; but the Lord will rise upon you and his glory will appear over you." God is coming, and God's people will begin to experience a new self-worth. Fallen Zion, specifically the marginalized community of Levitical priests, has been dispossessed of its service in the priesthood by the Zadokite priests. The latter, after their return from Babylonian exile, have taken control of the Temple cult and reject the Levitical priests as associates in the priesthood and members of God's people Israel.

On behalf of God, the prophet specifically addresses them. Although they have been repudiated, they will rise and shine, like the sun at the dawn of a new day. They will reflect God's glory, and the light of that glory will attract nations: "Kings will come to the brightness of your rising." The call, therefore, is to shine like the very Light that will inaugurate a new day and, by their shining, God's glory will be manifested in the world! This is the vocation to which God is summoning them.

God's theophany of light that illuminates God's people and draws the nations to its Source has multiple meanings. It is the light that guided Israel to the promised land. It is the light of the new age that the Messiah inaugurates (Num. 24:17). It is the light of a new creation that Third Isaiah anticipates (65:17). It is the very light that God generated on the first day of creation, the light that God separated from the darkness. This primordial light, the light of truth, the light of God's glory, the light that Jesus the Christ will disclose, will shine upon God's people. To accentuate the discontinuity between the past and the new future that will dawn for Israel, the prophet bestows the new name of "Hephzibah" upon these repudiated members of God's people and the new name "Beulah" on their land (62:4). In this new age justice will finally be established in the world (65:21-25), and "Hephzibah," the new Israel, will begin to experience a new self-worth. "The abundance of the sea will be turned to you, the wealth of nations will come to you" (60:5). Trade and commerce will begin to flourish. Caravans carrying goods will come from other parts of the world: "A multitude of camels shall cover you. . . . All those from Sheba shall come. They shall bring gold and frankincense" (v. 6). Peoples and nations who are drawn to the light of God's truth will share their wealth with them. According to verse 9, ships will come from as far as Spain bringing returning members of God's people, along with their wealth of silver and gold, because "God has glorified you." This is the vision of the restoration that Second Isaiah had previewed in Babylonian exile, and Third Isaiah is announcing its imminent fulfillment.

This vision of restoration, however, was not fulfilled until Jesus the Christ was born. The epiphany of God's light drew the Magi from the east, and they followed the star in its rising until it reached its zenith and stood over the place where the child Jesus lived. At that moment, when the star and Jesus the Christ became

HERMAN C.
WAETJEN

identified, they "rejoiced with exceeding great joy" (Matt. 2:10) and presented to him their gifts of "gold, frankincense, and myrrh" (Matt. 2:11). Jesus will reflect the light of God's glory, and the truth that he will unconceal will draw people from the east and west. In addition, as Jesus says in Matthew 8:11-12, they will recline at table with Abraham and Sarah, Isaac and Rebecca, Jacob and his wives in the reign of God. Moreover, by sharing this messianic banquet with God's people around the world, they will be motivated to share their material blessings with those who are poor, dispossessed, and marginalized. They will feed the hungry, clothe the naked, look after the sick, offer hospitality to strangers, and visit those in prison. They will not separate themselves from the world, but in their covenant with Jesus, the Light of the world, they will commit themselves to the reign of God and pledge themselves to the work of justice and peace. In that way they will shine and manifest the Light that has illuminated their lives.

In Walker Percy's novel, *The Second Coming*, the major character, Will Barrett, finally realizes that the name of the real enemy in American society is death, "not the death of dying but the living death. The name of this century is the Century of the Love of Death. Death in this century is not the death people die but the death people live."[2] Barrett's marriage to Allie, after his experience of resurrection, marks an entry into a new beginning of a life dedicated to justice and peace.

Everybody thinks that there are only two things: war which is a kind of life in death, and peace which is a kind of death in life. But what if there should be a third thing, life?
—Walker Percy[3]

RESPONSIVE READING

PSALM 72:1–7, 10–14 (RCL)
PSALM 72 or 72:1–2, 10–17 (BCP)
PSALM 72:1–2, 7–8, 10–11 (LFM)

The Light of God's Justice

This is a psalm ascribed to Solomon that petitions God to give the king and the king's son God's own justice as judgments for the exercise of divinely acceptable government, indeed, for the actualization of God's reign on earth. In his emulation of God's righteousness the king must serve as a defender of the poor and as a redeemer who delivers his people from oppression and whose blood, or life, is precious in his sight. The peace and security that such a government will establish will in turn generate reverence and love for the king by his subjects.

The psalm expresses the Hebraic ideal of kingship that is oriented to and manifests God's justice, a justice that is responsible to all members of society and is solicitous for the welfare of all, regardless of the realities of status and class. Such a rule that constitutes God's reign is destined to be extended to the ends of the earth. It is particularly this feature of the universality of the king's rule that led Jewish tradition to interpret this psalm messianically. The Talmud identifies specifically verse 17 with the Messiah.

SECOND READING

EPHESIANS 3:1-12 (RCL, BCP)
EPHESIANS 3:2-3a, 5-6 (LFM)

The Grace of Being Co-heirs of God's Reign

In the light of both Isaiah 60:1-6 and Psalm 72, which anticipate the universal inclusiveness of God's reign, this text appropriately expounds "the mystery of the Christ, unknown to human beings of previous generations but now unconcealed . . . by the Spirit" (3:4-5). The Gentiles, the non-Jewish people of the world, have been drawn into the reign of God, become fellow heirs, members of the Body of Christ, and partakers of the promise in Christ Jesus through the proclamation of the Gospel.

The ultimate objective of this mystery is to fulfill God's plan to unite heaven and earth by the Church's continuation of Jesus' ministry and its collaboration in communicating God's wisdom "to the principalities and powers in the heavenly places" (v. 10). These are the systemic structures of society that are invisible and yet profoundly affect the lives of all who participate in them. They constitute the domination systems of the world. They are the invisible forces of institutions and organizations that engender class structures and erect political, economic, and social boundary lines that advance the interests of the rich and the powerful and at the same time disinherit the masses. The reign of God cannot become a universal reality, and heaven and earth cannot be united until these powers and the principalities have been transformed.[4] The Apostle Paul voices the same eschatology in 1 Corinthians 15:24-28, but in order to appreciate its relevance, it is necessary to read the Pauline phrases, "Christ" or "Christ Jesus," according to 1 Corinthians 12:12, as the Body of Christ. The Church as the Body of Christ is joined to the Head, the Lord Jesus Christ. Here "Head" is not to be interpreted hierarchically as a chief or boss, but as the One who in his co-enthronement with God is simultaneously united with his Body, the Body of Christ, and draws that Body into his co-enthronement. Consequently, in view of its empowerment by

> Part of the church's evangelistic task is proclaiming to the Principalities and Powers in the heavenly places the manifold wisdom of God (Eph. 3:10). And that means addressing the spirituality of actual institutions that have rebelled against their divine vocations and made themselves gods.
> —Walter Wink[5]

the Holy Spirit, the Body of Christ is called to collaborate in this work of transforming the powers and the principalities.

THE GOSPEL
MATTHEW 2:1-12 (RCL, BCP, LFM)

The Light of the New Human Being, Jesus Christ

Among the Gentiles in Matthew's narrative world are the Magi. They are astrologers "from the east" who observed "his star in the rising" and came in search of the newborn king of the Jews in order to worship him. The two prepositional phrases of verses 1-2, *apo anatolōn* and *en tē anatolē*, which employ the same noun, should be carefully differentiated. The former, which is in the plural, is a geographical expression and is appropriately translated "from the east," while the latter, which is in the singular, denotes astronomical movement and means "in the rising." The reaction that their announcement of the newborn king evokes—"Herod was agitated and all Jerusalem with him . . ." (v. 3)—is curiously similar to that of Belshazzar and his court in Daniel 5:9 when they saw the divine sign of a hand writing on the plaster wall of the king's palace and discovered that the Magi were unable to interpret its words. In that context Daniel is introduced by the queen and proceeds to interpret the writing for the king. In Matthew's Gospel the situation is ironically reversed. The Magi, who once appeared inferior to Daniel, have interpreted the meaning of the star, and they announce it upon their arrival in Jerusalem to a community that is not yet aware of its appearance.

Herod's turmoil is not caused by his inability to grasp the meaning of the sign. For him the star "in the rising" can only point to a fulfillment of Numbers 24:17-18 and accordingly his own dispossession as an Edomite by the newborn Messiah. In reply to Herod's inquiry on behalf of the Magi, the chief priests and the scribes of the people cite Scripture to support their identification of Bethlehem as the birthplace of the Messiah. The text that they cite in 2:6 has a composite character, combining a clause from 2 Samuel 5:2 with Micah 5:2: "For out of you [Bethlehem] will come forth the ruling one who will shepherd my people Israel."

After a briefing from Herod, the Magi set out for Bethlehem. As soon as they leave Jerusalem they rediscover the star which they saw "in the rising" and are guided by it to their desired destination: "It led them until coming it stood over where the child was" (v. 9). The star continues to ascend until it reaches its zenith in the sky; and that is when it stands directly over the house in which Jesus lives. Precisely at that moment, when the star is identifiable with Jesus, "They rejoiced with exceeding great joy" (v. 10). This is eschatological joy! According to the significance that the ancient world attached to a star reaching its zenith in the heavens, the king, whom the star represents, has begun his rule. That is what the astrologers acknowledge when they offer Jesus their worship and their gifts: "Opening their treasures, they present to him . . . gold, frankincense, and myrrh" (v. 11). This is the fulfillment of Isaiah 60:6 intimated by the Evangelist. The Magi are outsiders, foreigners, yet they are the first and the only ones who pay homage to Jesus, the Son of David, the Messiah, at the beginning of his reign. In the persons of these astrologers the nations are being drawn to the light of God, the star that was previewed by Balaam, who after an encounter with "the angel of the Lord" pronounces blessing on Israel three times, and in a fourth oracle prophesies the future rising of "a star of Jacob." Eduard Schweizer cites the Damascus Document 7:19, which refers to the Teacher of Righteousness as a star and the Testament of Levi 18:3 in which the Messiah's "star will rise in the heavens."[6] But the brightness of the star's glory at its zenith is climactically transferred to Jesus who becomes the embodiment of the Epiphany, the manifestation of the light and glory of God.

Herod and Jerusalem pose a stark contrast. The Magi's announcement does not precipitate the anticipated response of celebration and festivity. The history of Israel has reached its goal: the promised and long-awaited Messiah King has come to inaugurate God's reign and its new moral order. But his presence goes unacknowledged by those who know the Old Testament prophecies. The Magi, warned in a dream not to return to Herod, journey to their homeland by another route.

"To discover how to be human now / is the reason we follow this star."[7] May that also draw us into a journey, a journey into an open-ended future that culminates in our being with God forever in everlasting life. The ancient pledge still holds true, "The eternal God is our dwelling place, and underneath are the everlasting arms." But now, because we are following the star to Bethlehem, we are being drawn into a new future, a new destiny.

Notes

1. Paul D. Hanson, *The Dawn of Apocalyptic* (Philadelphia: Fortress Press, 1975).

2. Walker Percy, *The Second Coming* (New York: Washington Square Press, 1980), 311–12.

3. Ibid.

4. For further insights into the principalities and powers, see Walter Wink, *Engaging the Powers: Discernment and Resistance in a World of Domination* (Minneapolis: Fortress Press, 1992).

5. Ibid., 84–85.

6. Eduard Schweizer, *The Good News according to Matthew* (Atlanta: John Knox Press, 1975), 38.

7. W. H. Auden, "For the Time Being: A Christmas Oratorio," in *Collected Longer Poems* (New York: Random House/Vintage Books, 1975), 159.

BAPTISM OF THE LORD / FIRST SUNDAY AFTER THE EPIPHANY / FIRST SUNDAY IN ORDINARY TIME

THE EPIPHANY OF GOD'S VALIDATION OF JESUS TO ISRAEL

JANUARY 13, 2008

REVISED COMMON	EPISCOPAL (BCP)	ROMAN CATHOLIC
Isa. 42:1-9	Isa. 42:1-9	Isa. 42:1-4, 6-7
Psalm 29	Ps. 89:1-29 or	Ps. 29:1-2, 3-4,
	89:20-29	3b–9b–10
Acts 10:34-43	Acts 10:34-38	Acts 10:34-38
Matt. 3:13-17	Matt. 3:13-1	Matt. 3:13-17

KEY THEMES

• The Servant of the Lord may have been an individual, but he is also representative of the people of God, and that has significant consequences for the Many who follow the Servant and become bearers of God's Spirit.

• Peter's sermon is another Epiphany, a manifestation of God's salvation to the nations of the world following its disclosure to the Jewish people.

• Jesus insists on expressing solidarity with all those of the land of Israel who have come to John for a baptism of repentance. What implications does this solidarity have those who follow him?

FIRST READING

ISAIAH 42:1-9 (RCL, BCP)
ISAIAH 42:1-4, 6-7 (LFM)

The First Servant Song of Second Isaiah

This is the first of four Servant Songs embedded in the prophetic utterances of Isaiah 40–55, which are commonly attributed to an anonymous exilic prophet who carried on the visionary tradition of Isaiah and accordingly is referred to as Second Isaiah. God is the speaker addressing an individual who is the bearer of what appears to be a title, "Servant." Who he or she is has been in dispute down through the centuries. In the past Christian interpreters have considered the Servant to be an ideal individual eschatologically prefiguring Jesus the Christ who, therefore, is to be regarded as the fulfillment of all four Songs: 49:1-6; 50:4-9; 52:13—53:12; and 42:1-9. Jewish interpreters, on the other hand, have identified the Servant as the Jewish nation or, more precisely, as the people of God in Babylonian captivity. More recently, subsequent to the development of historical-critical scholarship, Christian interpreters have begun to affirm the Jewish perspective on these Songs.

The 'Ebed Yahweh or Servant of the Lord may have been an individual, as the fourth Servant Song seems to indicate, but he is also representative of the people of God. Analogous to Uncle Sam as the personification of the American people, he is the embodiment of the One and the Many. In his individuality he serves as the prototype of the Many. In this respect the Servant is like Daniel's "son of a human being" (7:13), who is acknowledged in 7:27 as the community of the saints of the Most High. He is like "the Son of Man" in the four Gospels, a corporate figure that includes both Jesus and his followers. He is also like "the Body of Christ" in 1 Corinthians 12:12. As the embodiment of the One and the Many, the Servant does not belong to a dualistic world of "the clean" and "the unclean." It is noteworthy that there is no indication in Second Isaiah that the Jewish people were expected to live within a pollution system according to the Levitical purity code in their Babylonian exile. The Servant embodies the future of an inclusive humanity and consequently the gender of the Servant can be both Jew and Gentile, both male and female. Validated by God as "my Chosen, in whom my soul delights" and empowered by God's Spirit, the Servant works quietly and unobtrusively to fulfill God's will, while he/she is held and kept by God's hand. As God's surrogate, the Servant will raise up the tribes of Jacob and be a light to the nations so that God's salvation may reach to the end

> The Servant is like a new element, a new physics, because he is in fact a new anthropology. He is a covenant of people, a breakthrough that enables a new union based on the overturning of universal victim-making into love. Alongside him the sense of God is changed from warrior to mother-in-labor.
> —Anthony Bartlett[1]

of the earth (49:6). The Servant will establish God's justice in the earth. The Servant will open the eyes of the blind in order to perceive God's truth and walk accordingly in society; he or she will liberate those in prison. As God has fulfilled the former prophecies, God will also actualize these new things that God declares.

Matthew is the only evangelist who cites this Song, or at least a part of it. The Septuagint translation of Isaiah 42:1-4 has been incorporated into a context of controversy and conflict in 12:18-21 in order to present Jesus as the fulfillment of the Servant and, therefore, also as the one through whom God is doing a new thing. His act of healing a human being with a withered hand on the Sabbath has alienated the Pharisees, who, for the first time in Matthew's narrative world, express their wish for his destruction. In the face of this threat Jesus withdraws, and the narrator interrupts the story momentarily in order to introduce the opening four verses of this Servant Song to show that

Jesus' retreat corresponds to the character of the Servant who "...will not contend nor cry out, neither will anyone hear his voice in the streets" (Isa. 42:2; Matt. 12:19). Verse 20, which corresponds to Isaiah 42:3, calls to mind the works of restoration that Jesus has performed, while verse 21, citing 42:4, functions as an anticipation of the universalism that will culminate the Gospel in 28:16-20. It is in this final narrative of Matthew's Gospel that Jesus, the Servant as well as the Son of the Human Being and therefore the embodiment of the One and the Many, joins the group of his eleven disciples on the mountain in Galilee in order to become the twelfth and so to constitute a new Israel with whom he shares "all authority in heaven and on earth."

RESPONSIVE READING
PSALM 29 (RCL)
PSALM 29:1-2, 3-4, 3b + 9b-10 (LFM)

God's Majestic Voice in Nature as Attestation to Enact
"the New Things"

In the Hebrew Scriptures Yahweh is sometimes characterized as a storm God. In this psalm specifically, as also in Psalm 18:14, the thunderclaps of the storm are metaphorically identified as Yahweh's voice: "The voice of Yahweh is upon the waters; the God of glory thunders" (29:3). Verses 3-9 characterize the voice of Yahweh in seven different ways, perhaps linking them to each of the seven days of the week. Yahweh's voice is the storm that blows in from the Mediterranean; it is the voice that breaks the mighty cedars of Lebanon. Yahweh's voice is the lightning of the storm; it makes the mountains shudder in terror. It is the sandstorm that blows in from the desert; it is the terror of the storm that causes animals to give birth prematurely. It is the voice that strips the forest. God, however, is enthroned above the storm and "gives strength to his people" and, perhaps, with this seventh voice God "blesses his people on the Sabbath with peace." According to *Berachoth* 29a of the Talmud, the seven Sabbath benedictions correspond to the seven voices of Yahweh in this psalm. These benedictions assure the people that the God whom they worship, who speaks through the mighty forces of nature, magisterially speaks words of blessing and peace to them, particularly on the Sabbath after they have experienced the storms of life during the week that lies behind them.

God's voice will be heard in the Gospel lesson for this Sunday that celebrates the baptism of the Lord. It will be an epiphany, like the thunderclaps of Psalm 29. But it will not be a thunderclap; it will be an intelligible voice from heaven presenting Jesus as God's Son to the Jewish crowd, assembled under John's baptism to inaugurate "the new things."

PSALM 89:1-29 or 89:20-29 (BCP)

God's Endorsement of David

The theme of this psalm is announced in its opening verse: "the mercies of Yahweh." The poet has reflected on the history of Israel and therefore is constrained to emphasize God's mercy and faithfulness. These qualities are manifested in the stability of the heavens and in the covenant with David who is designated as "my servant" (v. 3). These two themes are elaborated in the two major sections of the psalm, verses 6-15 and 20-38.

Verses 6-15 recount God's wonders in heaven and on earth. The members of the divine council over which God presides fear God. God is sovereign over the chaos of the sea and stills the waves. God crushed the sea monster Rahab in delivering Israel from Egyptian enslavement. Verses 16-19 recount Israel's response as God's people to God's faithfulness. God is Israel's glory, Israel's shield, and Israel's king.

The remaining verses of the psalm (20-38) accentuate the royal ideology of God's covenant with David, as set forth in 2 Samuel 7. God's faithfulness and mercy will remain with David, and the blowing of David's horn will be exalted through all that God's name represents. If his descendents disobey God's law, they will be punished, but God's covenant with David will not be terminated. God's faithfulness to David is ultimately fulfilled in the epiphany that occurs at Jesus' baptism. Adopted by Joseph and therefore bearing the identity of David's son, Jesus is presented by God to the readers of Matthew's Gospel as well as to the Jews of the narrative world as they are gathered at the Jordan River under John's baptism. Together they will hear God's own endorsement, "This is my beloved Son in whom I took pleasure!"

SECOND READING
ACTS 10:34-43 (RCL)
ACTS 10:34-38 (BCP, LFM)

No More Purity Codes That Separate the Unclean from the Clean!

Up to this point in the narrative world of the Acts of the Apostles the mission activity of the early Jewish Christians, particularly that of the apostles, has been limited to Jews. Even the remarkable story of Pentecost in chapter 2, which intimates the reversal of the confusion of languages at Babel in Genesis 11, should be restricted to the Jewish Diaspora that had gathered in Jerusalem for the festival of the First Fruits.

In the narrative world of Acts it is Peter who inaugurates the evangelization of the Jews in Acts 2 and eventually also the Christian mission to the nations, the

Gentiles. He is portrayed as a Jew who lives according to the purity code and therefore lives in the dualistic world of "the clean" and "the unclean." His trance-like experience of a descending sheet containing all kinds of animals, reptiles, and birds is his personal entry into a reorientation to universalism: "What God has cleansed, you must not call defiled" (10:15). Immediately following this vision he is summoned to the home of Cornelius, a centurion of the Roman Cohort who has been directed by a divine messenger to send for Peter in order to hear what he has to say.

The text for this First Sunday after Epiphany is the tradition of Peter's sermon addressed to Cornelius. It is a very apposite transition from Ephesians 3:1-12, the second reading of Epiphany Sunday, in which the Holy Spirit revealed the mystery of God's revelation to the apostles and prophets that the Gentiles are fellow heirs, members, and partakers of the Body of Christ.

This is another Epiphany, a manifestation of God's salvation to the nations following its disclosure to the Jews. As Beverly Roberts Gaventa states in her commentary on Acts, "Here, as in other early Christian literature, impartiality becomes a fundamental theological claim (as also in Rom 2:11)."[2] In his sermon Peter announces that he has learned that God is no "face-receiver" (v. 34), a word that in Greek is limited to the Christian tradition. God does not look upon the face and all that it may reflect; God looks upon the heart. The noun that is used in the Greek text is usually translated as though it were a verb, "shows no partiality." Peter proceeds to give Cornelius a synopsis of Jesus' ministry, stressing his own involvement as an eyewitness of "all that he [Jesus] did" in order to validate the climactic events of Jesus' career, his death and his resurrection. He concludes with the additional witness of the prophets that calls Cornelius—and, of course, all Jews and Gentiles—"to believe into him and to receive the forgiveness of sins through his name" (v. 43). It is this call to repentance that Peter issues to Cornelius, as he also issued it to the Jews in Acts 2:38 and 3:19, that leads directly into the Gospel lesson for this Sunday of the Baptism of the Lord.

As an illustration for this text, preachers may want to turn to Flannery O'Connor's story, "Revelation," which dramatizes the experience of Mrs. Turpin, who transcends her racism when she experiences an epiphany not unlike that described in the biblical text.

A visionary light settled in her eyes. She saw the streak as a vast swinging bridge extending upward from the earth through a field of living fire. Upon it a vast horde of souls were rumbling toward heaven.

—Flannery O'Connor[3]

THE GOSPEL
MATTHEW 3:13-17 (RCL, BCP, LFM)

God's Endorsement of Jesus

John the Baptizer has announced that one is coming "who is stronger than I, whose sandals I am not worthy to carry. He will baptize you with the Holy Spirit and with fire" (3:11). In accordance with the apocalyptic expectation of Judaism, God is coming to render judgment, and the great anticipated separation will take place. The grain will be gathered into God's barn, and the chaff will be burned with inextinguishable fire.

Now, under John's ministry, all Israel is gathered and waiting at the Jordan River. But it is not the Lord God who appears. Jesus, having crossed the Jordan, arrives from Galilee. In Matthew's narrative world it is his second return to his own country, "the land of Israel." Like all the other Jews he comes to be baptized by John. Evidently he, too, wishes to participate in this eschatological act of repentance expressed in baptism; his own words in verse 15b make that explicit. But John objects to baptizing Jesus, "I have need to be baptized by you and you come to me?" (v. 14). Such an admission indicates that John recognizes who Jesus is.

Jesus' surprising reply, "Let it be so now, for it is fitting for us to fulfill all righteousness!" (v. 15) is at once an acknowledgment of the validity of John's objection and at the same time a disclosure of Jesus' self-understanding. He is the One whom John has heralded, and, although there is no instance in the Gospel in which Jesus baptizes with the Holy Spirit, he, as the Son of God, the New Adam, and therefore the founder of a New Humanity, should be baptizing him. In spite of his superiority Jesus refuses to show any elitism. For the moment he insists on expressing solidarity with all those of the land of Israel who have come to John for a baptism of repentance. He is like Moses, who in Exodus 34:9 identifies himself with the iniquity and sin of his people. Nothing less can be involved in the meaning of his determination "to fulfill all righteousness." Through the peculiar use of the first-person plural pronoun *us* in verse 15b, the addressees of Matthew's Gospel are drawn into Jesus' identification with his fellow Jews and his submission to John's baptism. Here is a notable instance of Jesus' embodiment of the Servant, the One and the Many of Isaiah 42:1-9. As the One who is in solidarity with the Many, his baptism is his experience of "doing all that God requires" and "fulfilling all righteousness," as

---

Today we should recall that baptism is both adoption into the very life of God and a mission to proclaim justice in the land, to be a light for the nations, open the eyes of the blind and free prisoners from their dungeons (Is. 42:7). What an awesome task for a little baby. But it is not really for him or her; it is rather for those who bring the child to baptism and are commissioned to renew their life of faith and form their "beloved" son and daughter, so that they too may work to bring justice to its fullness.

—John R. Donahue[4]

Eduard Schweizer writes.[5] At his "coming up from the water" (v. 16), "the heavens are opened" and God's Spirit descends upon him. Having been generated by the Holy Spirit, according to 1:18, Jesus is now the bearer of the Holy Spirit and therefore empowered to fulfill his divinely appointed role of "Emmanuel, God with us." At that moment of the Spirit's descent upon him, a voice sounds from heaven. According to Mark 1:11, Jesus alone was addressed. Matthew, however, has substituted a demonstrative pronoun, "*This* is my beloved Son in whom I took pleasure" (v. 17). God has come, as John the Baptizer promised, and God introduces Jesus to all of Israel assembled at the Jordan River as well as to the readers of Matthew's Gospel and endorses him as God's own offspring. Empowered by the Holy Spirit, he, as the Servant will begin to act on God's behalf and inaugurate the long-awaited Reign of God.

Notes

1. Anthony Bartlett, commentary on Isaiah 42:1-17, at the "Preaching Peace" Web site, http://www.preachingpeace.org/biblestudies.htm (accessed 1/08/07).

2. Beverly Roberts Gaventa, *The Acts of the Apostles,* Abingdon New Testament Commentaries (Nashville: Abingdon, 2003), 169.

3. Flannery O'Connor, "Revelation," in *The Complete Stories of Flannery O'Connor* (New York: Farrar, Straus & Giroux, 1978), 508.

4. John R. Donahue, "The Beginning Holds the Future I," meditation on the Web site of *America: The National Catholic Weekly*, http://www.americamagazine.org/SundayScripture.cfm?articletypeid=40&textID=1377&issueID=357 (accessed 1/08/07).

5. Eduard Schweizer, *The Good News according to Matthew* (Atlanta: John Knox Press, 1975), 56.

6. Frederick Houk Borsch, "The Baptism of Our Lord/The First Sunday after the Epiphany," in *Epiphany, Year A, Proclamation 4: Aids for Interpreting the Lessons of the Church Year* (Minneapolis: Fortress Press, 1989), 10–11.

SECOND SUNDAY AFTER THE EPIPHANY / SECOND SUNDAY IN ORDINARY TIME

THE EPIPHANY OF JESUS AS THE "LAMB OF GOD" AT THE COMMENCEMENT OF HIS MINISTRY

JANUARY 20, 2008

REVISED COMMON	EPISCOPAL (BCP)	ROMAN CATHOLIC
Isa. 49:1-7	Isa. 49:1-7	Isa. 49:3, 5-6
Ps. 40:1-11	Ps. 40:1-10	Ps. 40:2, 4, 7-8, 8-9, 10
1 Cor. 1:1-9	1 Cor. 1:1-9	1 Cor. 1:1-3
John 1:29-42	John 1:29-41	John 1:29-34

KEY THEMES

• We, like the Israel of Second Isaiah, are in exile as we continue to live in a world that is dominated by the powers and principalities of evil.

• Whether actual or potential, the grace of God that has been given to the Corinthians—and to us—by virtue of membership in the Body of Christ is at work in both them and us. What are the manifestations of God's grace as the Body of Christ participates in the reign of God?

• For the Second Sunday after Epiphany all of these texts acknowledge the realities of deliverance that are only beginning to take place.

FIRST READING
ISAIAH 49:1-7 (RCL, BCP)
ISAIAH 49:3, 5-6 (LFM)

The Second Servant Song of Second Isaiah

Jerusalem has been destroyed (587–586 B.C.E.), and Israel is in exile, living as displaced people in the Babylonian Captivity. In this historical context of his prophetic utterances Second Isaiah inserts four Servant Songs in order to inspire and motivate the dispirited people of God. Isaiah 49:1-7, the second Servant Song, features a dialogue between the Servant and Yahweh. It is the Servant, the personification of the One and the Many, possibly an individual representing ideal Israel, who speaks first and summons people from near and far to hear what he has to say. Having been endowed with God's Spirit, according to God's own declaration in the first Servant Song of 42:1-7, he now acknowledges both his commission and his empowerment. Yahweh named him, and thereby called him into being while still a fetus in his mother's uterus. Correspondingly, he claims two correlate realities for himself in his relationship to Yahweh: (1) his mouth, the organ of speech, as a weapon of empowerment, "He made my mouth like a sharp sword"; and (2) his protective concealment by God: "in the shadow of his hand he hid me" (49:2).

Yahweh answers him in verse 3 by addressing him as Israel, affirming him in his personification as the people of God and confirming him in his identity and role as "my servant, Israel, in whom I will be glorified."

In response, however, the Servant acknowledges his failure in fulfilling God's call, a commission that evidently applied to preexilic Israel. The efforts he had expended in a prophetic ministry to "bring back Jacob and to prevent Israel from being swept away" have been futile. The Hebrew verb of verse 5c, *yeaseph*, which is preceded by the negative particle *lō'*, meaning "not," should be translated together as "not swept away." The NRSV's rendering, "that Israel might be gathered to him," incorrectly translates *lō'* as a preposition that includes the masculine pronoun "to him." The Northern Kingdom was destroyed before it could be reincorporated into a united kingdom, and the surviving kingdom of Judah that had appropriated the name *Israel* to itself was swept into Babylonian captivity. Yet, in spite of having labored in vain, the Servant is convinced that his rectitude, his right, is secure with God and his reward is ensured by God.

Now, however, Yahweh confronts the Servant with a new commission, the resurrection of Israel. But as vital as it is to serve Yahweh by restoring the tribes of Israel, it is an undertaking that earlier prophets had already invoked. Now, in Babylonian exile, a new and more formidable assignment is imposed on God's people. In view of the capacity and capability of the Servant, endowed by the Spirit of God and equipped with a mouth whose words will be like a sharp sword, the commission is expanded into a worldwide mission to serve Yahweh as "a light to the nations." Ironically, it is in the Babylonian Captivity that Israel is confronted with this new and greater response-ability: communicating by means of the sharp sword of the mouth the light of the first day of creation, namely the truth of God to all the peoples of the world, so that God's salvation may reach to the end of the earth. And, according to the reversal that God promises in verse 7—a reversal that Third Isaiah also will envision—Israel's servanthood among the rulers of the world will be altered: "Kings shall see and arise; princes shall prostrate themselves before Israel, because of Yahweh who is faithful."

According to the witness of Matthew, kings did prostrate themselves before Jesus, the embodiment of a New Israel. Moreover, Jesus, as he enters into his ministry, will fulfill both of these commissions that the Servant of the Lord has received: restoring Israel and being "a light to the nations." In the fulfillment quotation of Matthew 8:17 and 12:17-21 Jesus is intimated to be the Servant of the Lord. In Matthew 10:6 he charges his disciples to go rather "to the lost sheep of the house of Israel," but in the great commission of 28:16-20 he commands them to proceed into the world to make disciples of all nations.

How can the disciples of Jesus, continuing this role of the Servant of the Lord, fulfill this twofold commission today? To be a light to the nations is an undertaking in which the Church as the Body of Christ has been engaged for many centuries and, according to Isaiah 49:6, it might be concluded that "it is too light a thing." But can the Church, in view of all the evil that has been perpetrated against the Jewish people, become a light to the Jewish people of the world by acknowledging that they continue to be God's elect people and by working with them to eliminate anti-Semitism from our society and from the world?

Like Israel in Babylonian exile, the Church as the New Israel of God is living in the same world of darkness and evil. But can the Church embrace the self-understanding that the Apostle Paul voices in Philippians 3:20, the self-understanding that "our citizenship is in heaven"? That implies that we, like the Israel of Second Isaiah, are in exile as we continue to live in a world that is dominated by the powers and principalities of evil. Consequently, we also must be reminded of the heritage we have received in and through the great ancestors that we share with Israel, Abraham and Sarah. As Second Isaiah exhorts in 51:1-2, "Look to the rock from which you were hewn, and to the quarry from which you were dug." Abraham and Sarah, after leaving Ur, lived as nomads journeying from place to place "looking for a city whose architect and builder is God." Like them, we are journeying into an open future, and in our vulnerability we are called to be the embodiment of God's light to all the people we meet along the way, regardless of nationality, religion, class, and race. Like Israel in exile, we as the members of the New Israel are appointed to follow Jesus into the fulfillment of this Servant Song in all the concrete circumstances of our everyday life.

Following Jesus requires the integrity of discipleship, as Jesus' parable of "The Ten Virgins" discloses. The number ten represents the *minyan*, the required number of males to establish a synagogue, a mini-community of Israel; but Jesus iconoclastically substitutes women. To be a bearer of light requires the integration of identity and activity. Only those women who had enough oil in their lamps to provide light for the bridegroom and his party are admitted to the wedding feast, the banquet of God's reign.

PSALM 40:1-11 (RCL)
PSALM 40:1-10 (BCP)
PSALM 40:2, 4, 7-8, 8-9, 10 (LFM)

Praise for Past Deliverance, Petition for New Deliverance

The first part of this psalm, verses 1-11, is a hymn of praise for the deliverance that the poet has experienced in the past. The second half, verses 13-17, petitions God for a new act of deliverance. Verse 12 serves as the transition from the past to the present by its pronouncement of the present condition: "Evils have encompassed me without number," and a desperate appeal for deliverance, "O Yahweh, make haste to help me." It is noteworthy that verses 13-17 appear as a separate psalm in Psalm 70.

Two attitudes arising out of the experience of the past are expressed at the very beginning of the psalm: petitioning Yahweh for help in time of trouble and waiting patiently for God's rescue. The deliverance that the poet experienced engendered a new sense of security: "[God] set my feet upon a rock making my steps secure" (v. 2). It also evoked "a new song" and therefore a new response of praise to Yahweh. The witness that the psalmist faithfully offers, according to verse 5, will enable others to "see and fear and trust in Yahweh" (v. 3). A beatitude expresses the poet's resulting conviction in universal terms: "Happy is the human being who has made Yahweh his/her trust" (v. 4).

Attendantly, the psalmist acknowledges that God has opened his ears so that he is able to hear God's word, specifically the word that has also been spoken by various prophets, "Sacrifice and meal-offering you do not desire, burnt-offering and sin-offering you do not require" (v. 6). Instead, he holds God's law in his very guts or bowels (v. 8) and acts in accordance with it. Consequently, what he brings to his worship in the Temple is a scroll that pays tribute to Yahweh for the salvation that he has experienced, salvation that he has proclaimed as a witness to God's justice and faithfulness. It is "the glad news" or *gospel* of deliverance.

The psalmist, like the Servant of Isaiah 49:1-7, believes that his rectitude or right is secure with God. The new appeal that he makes for help in verses 13-17 is readily transferable to the fulfillment of the new commission that Yahweh imposes on the Servant "to raise up the tribes of Jacob" and "to be a light to the nations." It is also transferable to the Apostle Paul's charge to the Corinthian Christians in 2 Corinthians 3:2-3 that they live as personifications of such a scroll that pays tribute to God for the salvation that has been experienced by becoming "a letter from Christ" "to be known and read by all human beings."

All of Psalm 40 should be prayed by Christians today! Verses 1-12 would be an acknowledgment of all the manifestations of God's grace in our lives; and verses 13-17 would be our recognition of "evils that have encompassed [us] without number" as we confront the terrorism of those who engage in retaliation for the terrorism that they themselves have suffered through the injustices of economic globalization.

SECOND READING
1 CORINTHIANS 1:1-9 (RCL, BCP)
1 CORINTHIANS 1:1-3 (LFM)

Commissioned and Empowered—Like the Servant

Paul, the author of this letter, refers to himself as" an apostle of *Christ Jesus*." His reversal of the name "Jesus Christ" and his attendant use of "the Christ" throughout his letters is noteworthy because, as 1 Corinthians 12:12 indicates, it designates the "Body of Christ," the community of the One and the Many. The One of course is Jesus Christ and the Many are the members of his Body. "Christ Jesus" is the communion of saints on earth who are represented by the *Lord Jesus Christ* in his co-enthronement with God. As an apostle, Paul is a representative of Second Isaiah's Servant of Yahweh who has committed himself to the fulfillment of Isaiah 49:6b, "to be a light to the nations so that God's salvation may reach to the end of the earth."

In his prescript and salutation, verses 1-3, Paul addresses the Corinthian congregation as a community of individuals who are "consecrated in *Christ Jesus*" and who therefore are *"called holy."* What is presupposed in this acknowledgment is their participation in the new creation, as he will stipulate later in 2 Corinthians 5:17. Also presupposed is their membership in the new humanity of the "Last Adam," Jesus Christ, who is the founder of a new people of God, as Paul indicates in 1 Corinthians 15:45.

The epiphany or manifestation of God's light among the Corinthian Christians, "and all who call upon the name of our *Lord Jesus Christ*," particularly those who are Gentiles, establishes the fulfillment of Isaiah 49:6b. After pronouncing a benediction upon these Corinthians, Paul proceeds to give thanks for them on the grounds that the grace of God has been given to them *in Christ Jesus*, that is, on the basis of their membership in the Body of Christ. As a result of their participation in this new moral order of the new humanity, their lives have been enormously enriched. They have been aggrandized in their Greek heritage "with all speech and with all knowledge" (v. 5). Speaking and knowledge were gifts most prized in Greek Corinth, as the letter indicates. *Gnōsis* (knowledge) is used sixteen times in 1 and 2 Corinthians. Their pursuit of wisdom, which has undergone a reorientation in their discernment of all things, has continued to mature. Their witness of Christ confirms that they are not lacking in any gift.

By borrowing from Hellenistic rhetoric in his expression of thanksgiving, Paul is affirming these Christians in their consecration to Jesus Christ. Not all of them, as the subsequent content of the letter indicates can legitimately be affirmed in this manner. But whether actual or potential, the grace of God that has been given to them in their membership in the Body of Christ is at work in their lives.

Their participation in the new creation, established by God's raising Jesus from the dead, has a divinely appointed goal: "the disclosure of our *Lord Jesus Christ.*" While they grow into exercising the reign of God on behalf of God here and now, they are engaged in the activity of transforming the powers and principalities, that is, those systemic structures and institutions of society that oppress, dispossess, marginalize, and dehumanize those who participate in them. When that commission has been fulfilled, when, as Paul states in 1 Corinthians 15:24-28, every rule, authority, and power has been rendered ineffective by *the Christ* in collaboration with God, then *the Christ* will hand over the reign to God, death will finally be abolished forever, and God will be all things in all things. As the Corinthian Christians eagerly await that consummation and its epiphany of the "second coming" of the *Lord Jesus Christ,* they will be confirmed blameless by God to the very end as they follow *our Lord Jesus Christ* in fulfilling the role of servant in their discipleship.

> Even though the traditional faith, hope, and love do not appear in this thanksgiving, the corrections that Paul makes in the Corinthians' understanding of speech, knowledge, and spiritual gifts show that faith, hope, and love are at stake in this letter.
> —Pheme Perkins[1]

The Gospel

JOHN 1:29-42 (RCL)
JOHN 1:29-41 (BCP)
JOHN 1:29-34 (LFM)

The Epiphany of the Beginning of Jesus' Ministry

Matthew 2:1-12 presents the epiphany of Jesus as the star of Jacob at his birth. John 1:29-42 introduces the epiphany of Jesus as "the Lamb of God" at the beginning of his ministry.

Four days are differentiated by the Greek word *epaurion* ("the next day") in John 1:19-51. Its first occurrence is in verse 29, and it announces an event of day two that will intimate the beginning of the fulfillment of the Servant Song of Isaiah 49:6. Throughout the Fourth Gospel Jesus is engaged in "restoring the survivors of Israel." John 12:20-24 foreshadows the inclusion of the Gentiles after "the seed falls into the ground and dies and consequently bears much fruit."

Jesus appears on day two of chapter one, and it is his epiphany to Israel. John, the great witness of the Word and the Word made flesh, who also baptizes, observes Jesus coming toward him and identifies his epiphany to the readers of the Gospel as "the Lamb of God who removes the sin of the world." Jesus, who has been named only once prior to this moment, namely in the prologue of verse 17, appears as an unannounced stranger. This distinctive epiphany, as Raymond E. Brown acknowledges, may have been derived from "an apocalyptic strain of messianic expectation where the Messiah's presence on earth would be hidden until suddenly he would be shown to his people."[2] In the course of the Gospel story Jesus will be identified paradoxically as the one whose origin is known (7:27) and as the one whose origin is unknown (8:14). In his first appearance in the Gospel he apparently is coming to John for baptism, but, in contrast to the Synoptic Gospels, the act of baptism is presupposed to have already taken place. His identification by John as "the Lamb of God" precedes all other christological epithets that are encountered in the Gospel and bears a significance that will not be clarified until 19:28-30. During his crucifixion, in response to his cry of thirst, a sponge will be filled with wine vinegar, placed on a branch of hyssop, in fulfillment of Exodus 12:21-27 and Psalm 69:21, and raised to his lips. Jesus, after partaking of it, will announce, "It has been accomplished!" He has drunk the wine of the wrath of God, in fulfillment of Psalm 75:8, while at the same time he, after having identified himself in 10:7 and 9 as the Door, will symbolically fulfill the ritual of the Passover and become "the Lamb of God who removes the sin of the world."

John repeats the words he had spoken earlier in verse 15 as a witness to Jesus as the incarnate Word, "This is the one on behalf of whom I said, 'There comes a man after me who has happened before me because he was my First.'" The words "my First" translate the Greek adjective *prōtos* ("first") accompanied by the personal pronoun "of me" or "my"; and they refer back to the Septuagint translation of Isaiah 44:6 and 48:12, where Yahweh declares, "I AM the First!"[3] Jesus, as the incarnation of the preexistent Word, happened before John because in his union with God he is John's "First." John acknowledges that he did not know Jesus as the incarnation of the preexistent Word, but God, who sent him to baptize, had disclosed to him that "The one upon whom you see the Spirit descending and remaining, this is the one who baptizes with the Holy Spirit" (v. 33). He concludes this introduction of Jesus to the readers of the Gospel by declaring that Jesus is "the Son of God." It is the title that Jesus will continually presuppose when he speaks of "the Father" and refers to himself as "the Son."

A third day is introduced by the same word, *epaurion* ("next day"), in verse 35. John again identifies Jesus as "the Lamb of God" and thereby accentuates the fundamental significance of this epithet for the Fourth Gospel. Two of John's disciples hear his witness and begin to attach themselves to Jesus. When Jesus perceives them following him, he inquires, "What are you seeking?" They reply, however, with their own question, "Rabbi, where do you remain?" (v. 38). In response Jesus invites them with a present imperative, "Keep on coming and you will see!" This is, of course, an invitation to the two, but more especially to the readers of the Gospel who are summoned to continue to read and interact with the story in order to *see*. If they comply, they will experience the epiphany of God's glory, as it will be manifested throughout the Gospel, but above all in Jesus' death and resurrection.

The two not only remain with Jesus that day, but they continue to follow him as disciples. One of them is identified as Andrew, whose immediate inclination expresses his discipleship: "He first finds his own brother Simon and says to him, 'We have found the Messiah!'" (v. 41). Andrew, in beginning to follow Jesus, has experienced the epiphany of Jesus' messiahship. This christological identification of Jesus should be a stunning surprise to the readers of the Gospel. John had identified him as "the Lamb of God." On what basis can Jesus' messiahship be deduced from this title? There is no historical connection in the Old Testament that might have intimated to Andrew that the Lamb of God is also the Messiah. Here is a conundrum that the readers must take with them as they continue to read the Gospel in order to arrive at the relationship between the two christological titles, "Lamb of God" and "Messiah." It will be disclosed to them in the crucifixion.

As Jesus confronts Simon, he bestows on him a new name, a name that carries the significance of a title, *Cephas*, the Aramaic word for "rock," which the narrator translates as *Petros*. The readers will be required to determine whether Simon Peter will fulfill the meaning of that name as they move forward in their interaction with the narrative world of the Gospel.

[Mrs. McIntyre] had given [Mr. Guizac] a job. She didn't know if he was grateful or not. She didn't know anything about him except that he did the work. The trust was that he was not very real to her yet. He was a kind of miracle that she had seen happen and that she talked about but that she still didn't believe.
—Flannery O'Connor[4]

The other disciple, who also left John and attached himself to Jesus is unnamed. Who he is remains a matter of conjecture. Some commentators are inclined to identify him as "the Beloved Disciple" who will begin to play a major role in the Gospel in 11:1-44; 13:23; 18:15; 19:26; 20:1-8; and 21:7, 20-24.

For the Second Sunday after Epiphany all of these texts acknowledge the realities of deliverance that are only beginning to take place. The Star of Bethlehem affirms God's faithfulness to the prophetic promises of the Old Testament. The sign of Epiphany signifies that we will be drawn up from "the desolate pit." Like the Corinthian Christians, we have begun to be enriched in Christ, and all the spiritual gifts are at our disposal for our own and each other's growth into the full stature of Jesus Christ. But these texts also look forward to the actualization of the deliverance that will be disclosed as we move toward the crucifixion in the Gospel according to John when the work of Jesus as "the Lamb of God who removes the sin of the world" and Jesus' identity as the Messiah will be fulfilled in relation to each other in his death on the cross.

Analogous to Jesus' entry into the saving work of his ministry, Flannery O'Connor's story "The Displaced Person" recounts the ugly racist reaction that Mr. Guizac, a Polish refugee, experiences when he begins to work on Mrs. McIntyre's farm. Because he engages in "saving work," he is soon treated as the "outsider," someone who doesn't fit in, someone who upsets the balance of the community. Innocent as a lamb, he is killed, and his death, like the death of Jesus, terminates the little farm community with its dehumanizing moral order. Mr. Shortley, the racist who deliberately set the farm tractor on a course that would kill the Polish man, is compelled to move out into the world and in his new vulnerability to find a future for himself and his family elsewhere.[5]

Notes

1. Pheme Perkins, "The Second Sunday after the Epiphany," in *Epiphany, Year A, Proclamation 5: Interpreting the Lessons of the Church Year* (Minneapolis: Fortress Press, 1992), 19.

2. Raymond E. Brown, *The Gospel according to John,* The Anchor Bible (Garden City, N.Y.: Doubleday, 1966), 53.

3. For a more thorough analysis, see Herman Waetjen, *The Gospel of the Beloved Disciple: A Work in Two Editions* (New York: T & T Clark, 2005), 92–102.

4. "The Displaced Person," in *The Complete Stories of Flannery O'Connor* (New York: Farrar, Straus & Giroux, 1978), 225–34.

5. Ibid.

THIRD SUNDAY AFTER THE EPIPHANY / THIRD SUNDAY IN ORDINARY TIME

THE DAWNING OF LIGHT IN GALILEE
JANUARY 27, 2008

REVISED COMMON	EPISCOPAL (BCP)	ROMAN CATHOLIC
Isa. 9:1-4	Amos 3:1-8	Isa. 8:23b—9:3
Ps. 27:1, 4-9	Ps. 139:1-17 or 139:1-11	Ps. 27:1, 4, 13-14
1 Cor. 1:10-18	1 Cor. 1:10-17	1 Cor. 1:10-13, 17
Matt. 4:12-23	Matt. 4:12-23	Matt. 4:12-23 or 4:12-17

KEY THEMES

• The dawning of a new day and its new moral order that Christmas and Epiphany celebrate should evoke great joy and renewed hope.

• Jesus Christ, "the power and wisdom of God," is continuing to conduct his ministry of resurrection in us and among us. How does it affect our lives?

• As disciples of Jesus the Christ, we are living in a new day; we are participants in a new creation that we are commissioned to actualize.

FIRST READING

ISAIAH 9:1-4 (RCL)
ISAIAH 8:23b—9:3 (LFM)

From Contempt to Glory

Isaiah 9:2-7 conveys a double measure of good news. The enemy that threatened the invasion and conquest of the little kingdom of Judah has been defeated, and a royal child, probably Hezekiah, has been born who, as a descendent of David, is proclaimed by the prophet as "Wonderful in counsel is God the mighty, the Everlasting Father, the Prince of Peace" (9:6). It is he who will establish the throne of David through justice and righteousness in order to bring about an endless peace.

A part of this text has already recently served as the lection for the Christmas Eve celebration of the Nativity of the Lord. This shorter reading for the Third Sunday after the Epiphany focuses on the first half of the good news: deliverance from the enemy and the joy that attends the resulting liberation from oppression and exploitation. Whether the defeat of the Syro-Ephraimite coalition or the failure of the Assyrian siege is the cause of the great festivity remains ambiguous. Whatever the resolution might be, it has no immediate significance for Epiphany.

The central issue of this text is the manifestation of "a great light" (v. 2). The sun has risen, and a new day has dawned. The defeat of the enemy of God's people marks the beginning of a new time, a new era, a new moral order. What has been excluded from this reading is the vision of the destruction of the equipment used to wage war, clothing as well as shoes, which, according to verse 5, will be burned as fuel for the fire. This, of course, corresponds to the eschatological vision of the abolition of all warfare in 2:4, a part of the lection for the First Sunday of Advent. Both Christmas and Epiphany celebrate the commencement of that new moral order that Isaiah envisaged, and it deserves to be accentuated repeatedly, precisely because the vision of 9:4-5 and 2:4 appears to be light years away from fulfillment. Nevertheless, the dawning of a new day and its new moral order that Christmas and Epiphany celebrate should evoke great joy and renewed hope. Indeed, the scope of the celebration, along with the hope that it renews, is tantamount to the ecstasy that a harvest of grain, vegetables, and fruit arouses for hungry human beings who have suffered famine as the result of a lengthy period of drought. The joy, and the hope, arising from "the dividing of spoils" (v. 3) would relate to the materiel: food, clothing, and equipment that a colonial power left behind as it withdrew from an occupied territory. In our own society it is comparable to a student from a poor marginalized background winning a scholarship under an affirmative-action program that actualizes the long-dreamed-of possibility of an education for a future vocation.

The Roman Catholic lection omits v. 4 and concentrates on the dawning of a new day and the joy that it elicits. At the same time it includes the final verse of chapter 8 in the Hebrew text of the Jewish Scriptures, namely verse 23. The NRSV and many of the English translations place 8:23 at the beginning of chapter 9 as its initial verse. The New American Bible, the translation used by the Roman Catholic lectionary, follows the numbering of the Vulgate that corresponds to the Hebrew text. The Hebrew text is problematic, and its translation as well as its placement, either at the end of chapter 8 or at the beginning of chapter 9, determines its interpretation. The NRSV reads, "But there will be no gloom for those who were in anguish. In the former time he brought into contempt the land of Zebulon and the land of Naphtali, but in the latter time he will make glorious the way of the sea, the land between Jordan, Galilee of the nations." In this rendition God is the acting subject, and the positive eschatological perspective that it conveys would validate its placement at the beginning of chapter 9 and the prophet's announcement of the dawning of a new day.

On the other hand, the Hebrew text of 8:23 may be translated: "For there is no gloom to him who brings stress to her. The former [referring here to an individual instead of time] has lightly afflicted the land of Zebulon and the land of Naphtali, but the latter [here also referring to an individual instead of time] has dealt a more grievous blow by the way of the sea, beyond Jordan, Galilee of the nations." The one who is responsible for "lightly afflicting" Israel is generally considered to be Tiglath Pileser III, who had deprived the Northern Kingdom of Zebulon and Naphtali, the territory of what later was called Galilee. Sargon probably is the latter who will relentlessly complete the work at a later time, probably 722 B.C.E. It will not be a dark time for the Assyrians, but Israel's oppression will continue unabated.

Either rendition of the text, whether that of 9:1 or that of 8:23, is meaningfully appropriate to this Epiphany lection. While 8:23 accentuates the desolation Israel has continued to suffer at the hand of the Assyrian conquerors, 9:1 of the Hebrew text and the New American Bible enunciate the appearance of "a great light" and the dawning of a new day without any reference to a corresponding acting subject. The dramatic address in the form of the second-person pronoun of the verse that follows, "You have multiplied the nation . . ." refers, of course, to God, who is intimated to be the Creator of that "great light" and the new day that it inaugurates.

On the other hand, the version of 9:1, as it appears in many, if not most, of the English translations introduces an eschatological change in Israel's future with an implied identification of the Inaugurator of this new age: "There will be no gloom for those who were in anguish" for "in the latter time *he* will make glorious the way of the sea, the land beyond the Jordan, Galilee of the nations." God is the innovator of this change! God is the originator of this new age and the dispenser of all the marvelous changes that 9:3 enunciates.

Matthew will announce the fulfillment of this prophecy when Jesus takes up his residence in "Capernaum by the sea in the land of Zebulon and Naphtali" and proceeds to inaugurate his messianic ministry. Galilee of the Gentiles, and therefore, to some extent, a land of contempt, a land despised by the Pharisees because it is the home of the *am haaretz*, the vulgar masses who do not observe the Law, will be made glorious through the ministry of Jesus who is intimated to be "Wonderful in counsel is God the mighty, the Everlasting Father, the Prince of Peace."

Isaiah's promissory utterances . . . revolve around the artifacts of the Jerusalem establishment, to which Yahweh will remain faithful. The promises of [Isaiah 9] are Davidic in substance, so that Yahweh's future, as anticipated in this tradition, is a royally shaped future, in which "a proper king" will do the work of monarchy in order to bring the world right.
—Walter Brueggemann[1]

AMOS 3:1-8 (BCP)

God's Appointment with Us

This lection is an unexpected and disconcerting departure from the festival of Epiphany, but it can be given a stunning twist that would transform it into an effective memorialization of Epiphany. It consists of nine questions, arising out of the introductory acknowledgment, "You only have I known of all the families of the earth" (v. 2), and ending with the culminating query, "Yahweh God has spoken, who will not prophesy?" (v. 8). A lion does not roar unless it has a prey. A bird is not captured unless a lure has been set. A snare does not spring up unless it has caught something. People in a city do not tremble unless a horn is blown that signals impending danger. A city does not fall if God does not will it. Should not the children of Israel, the people of the Northern Kingdom, tremble because the prophet is unable to refrain from prophesying no more than a lion roars over its prey, or a bird is captured unless a trap has been set, or a snare springs up without having caught something? Amos's prophecy is directed toward the people of God to warn them of the impending doom that awaits them: "You only of all the families of the earth I have known. Therefore I will visit upon you all your iniquities."

In the context of Epiphany, the Amos text confronts the preacher with the possibility of a new—indeed, opposite—perspective: not doom but deliverance! God has visited the families of the earth with deliverance and salvation, deliverance from alienation and salvation for the healing of brokenness. If the lion roars, who will not fear? If Yahweh God has spoken through the manifestation of light, who will not celebrate and give thanks? "Do two walk together unless they have made an appointment?" (v. 3) Epiphany and its manifestation of Light discloses that God has made an appointment with us by giving us God's very self in the person of Jesus, the Messiah, God's Son. Will we keep that appointment by opening our lives, our hearts, and our minds to all that the Light communicates to us?

RESPONSIVE READING
PSALM 27:1, 4-9 (RCL)
PSALM 27:1, 4, 13-14 (LFM)

The Light of God's Truth Displaces Fear

The Septuagint translation of this psalm adds, "before he was anointed" to its heading, "a psalm of David." Evidently the translator assumed that David's persecution by Saul was the original context of the hymn. Whether that is true or not, the psalm expresses a profound confidence in Yahweh in the midst of desperate circumstances, for example, in verse 2, "When evildoers pressed upon me to eat up my flesh," and in verse 12b, "For false witnesses are risen up against me."

As in the context of Isaiah 9:1-4, the poet acknowledges the presence of God in his experience of "light" and "salvation." Yahweh's identification with light echoes the primordial light of the first day of creation, the light of truth. The presence of that light of truth belongs to the realized eschatology that the text of Isaiah 9 projects into the celebration of Christmas and Easter as the dawning of a new day. Verse 4 expresses the supreme desire of the poet: "to dwell in the house of Yahweh." His aspiration is not to be interpreted as a literal residence in the Jerusalem Temple but as a profound longing to live in God's presence always.

The desperate circumstances, which the psalmist confronts, evoke a call for help in verses 7-14, but in and with the confidence that was voiced at the very beginning. In the concluding verses of the psalm the poet confronts himself with the conditional sentence of verse 13 that is left incomplete. The NRSV translates, "I believe that I shall see the goodness of the LORD in the land of the living." But the Hebrew text reads, "If I had not believed to look upon the goodness of Yahweh in the land of the living . . ." The reader is compelled to add the apodosis, "what hope would I have?" Embracing the confidence that was expressed in verse 1, the poet summons himself and his readers, "Wait for Yahweh, . . . be strong, . . . take courage!"

> Not to know the name of the enemy is already to have been killed by him. . . . The name of the enemy is death. . . . To know the many names of death is also to know, there is life. I choose life. . . . Death in none of its guises shall prevail over me because I know all the names of death.
> —Walker Percy[2]

In Walker Percy's novel *The Second Coming*, Will Barrett discovers the truth of things and at the same time also that the meaning of salvation is Christ. Discipleship is not simply being destined to everlasting life. More immediately, it is the fullness of life in the here and now. Barrett's response to his discovery is made in the form of a lengthy litany that serves as an attestation of his identification of the enemy in our society.

PSALM 139:1-17 or 139:1-11 (BCP)

The Wonderful Abiding Presence of God

This must be the sublimest of all the psalms in its acknowledgment of the profound personal experience of the awareness of God. Not merely the poet's awareness of God, but God's awareness of the poet who in all the circumstances of life is enclosed by the presence of God! God knows the psalmist intimately: what he/she thinks, what she/he does. There is nothing that is hidden from God's critical eye. God knows what is consciously communicated in speech, but also what may be intended unconsciously by the words that are used.

Verses 1-6 center on Yahweh's omniscience, verses 7-12 on Yahweh's omnipresence. It is impossible to remove oneself from God's all-knowing and ever-abiding presence. God has known the poet already as an embryo in his mother's womb. The wonder of God's work in human creation culminates in an expression of awe at the unfathomability of God. Theology in its reflections will never exhaust the richness and the immeasurability of God's being: "they are more in number than the sand." And even "were I to come to the end of them"—what ultimately matters to the poet is the certainty, "I would still be with you."

SECOND READING
1 CORINTHIANS 1:10-18 (RCL)
1 CORINTHIANS 1:10-17 (BCP)
1 CORINTHIANS 1:10-13, 17 (RC)

An Entreaty for Solidarity

In this text the Apostle Paul formulates his thesis statement or "prothesis." It is the starting point of his argumentation to unify. The verb he uses at the outset, *parakalō* ("I request"), initiates the transition from the thanksgiving of verses 4-9 through the "prothesis" into the body of the letter. It is an entreaty based on the reality that unites Paul and the Corinthian Christians, "the name of our Lord Jesus Christ." The "name," of course, represents the totality of the person and work of Jesus Christ, more specifically all that his death and resurrection have achieved for the salvation of human beings.

From the people of Chloe's household Paul has learned that there are splits or factions among these Christians. Chloe herself may be an upper-class woman whose home is the meeting place of a group of these Corinthians. According to the report of her people that Paul has received in Ephesus, four contentious groups have emerged, and they identify themselves with specific individuals whom they revere and to whom they may have attached themselves as disciples: "I am for Paul," "I am for Apollos," "I am for Cephas," "I am for Christ" (v. 12). The first two have been present in Corinth, preaching and teaching, and therefore are known by these Christians. There is no evidence of a visit by Cephas

> What makes the 1 Corinthians letter exciting are the fragmentary reflections of a growing church struggling with new ideas, willing to speak theologically, impassioned for the faith, uncertain of what form of ecclesiology fits them. Paul's own problematic tone may be adopted, or his text may be preached as a reflection of a concerned pastor willing to engage those struggling to make sense of the power of Jesus Christ and his cross.
> —Susan K. Hedahl[3]

(Peter), but some have aligned themselves with him. The last group, if it does not represent an ironic twist to show the absurdity of these cliques, may refer to those who, according to 12:1-3, curse Jesus and praise Christ and therefore express an early form of Gnostic dualism. They may be identifiable with those who aggrandize themselves by the practice of glossolalia.

Paul's objective in writing this letter is to enable these factious Christians to undertake a process of mending and recovering their solidarity. He calls all of them into question by rhetorically posing the fundamental absurdity: Has Christ been chopped into parts to accommodate the perspective of each group? Paul then uses himself to accentuate the senselessness of such an apportionment: "Was Paul crucified on your behalf? Were you baptized into the name of Paul?" (v. 13). How then can the Corinthians split themselves into factions, if the unity of Christ and his work cannot be partitioned into separate features or facets of faith?

Paul acknowledges that he conducted a few baptisms: Crispus, Gaius, and the household of Stephanas. He was not commissioned to baptize but to evangelize, however, and his preaching and teaching are oriented to "the word of the cross" and not to "the wisdom of speech." The latter is manipulative rhetoric by which an audience is argued into an acknowledgment of the speaker's perspective. It is "the wisdom of the world." In contrast, "the wisdom of God" is the "foolishness of the proclamation" of a crucified Savior, a scandal to the Jews (on the basis of Deuteronomy 21:23) and foolishness to the Gentiles. But to those who are "called," both Jews and Greeks, "Christ is the power of God and the wisdom of God" (v. 24). In spite of how the world may evaluate "the word of the cross," it conveys the Good News of the fulfillment of Isaiah 9:1-4 and therefore the dawning of a new day and the epiphany of the one who is "Wonderful in counsel is God the mighty, the Everlasting Father, the Prince of Peace." At a time, like that of Amos, when "a trumpet is being blown in a city" or when "the lion is roaring," and war and terrorism arouse fear throughout our nation, Jesus Christ, "the power and wisdom of God," is continuing to conduct his ministry of resurrection in us and among us.

The Gospel
MATTHEW 4:12-23 (RCL, BCP)
MATTHEW 4:12-23 or 4:12-17 (LFM)

From Darkness into Light

When the news of John the Baptizer's imprisonment reaches Jesus, he withdraws from Judea once more. The use of the verb *anechōrēsen* ("he withdrew") in verse 12 intimates that the delivering up of the one poses danger to the other.

Jesus and John are linked to each other eschatologically, and therefore what happens to the one has consequences for the other. John in his Elijah role as the forerunner prepares the way of the Lord by calling Israel to repentance and baptizing all the people in the Jordan River. He also prepares the way of the Lord by going before him into rejection and death in Judea. As for Jesus, this is his third retreat from Judea, the land of his messianic inheritance.

He returns to Galilee, and according to the distinctively Matthean tradition of verse 13, "he took up residence in Capernaum." This, as 9:1 indicates, becomes "his own city"; and the edited verses of 9:10, 28; 13:1, 36; and 17:25 show that he had a dwelling there. As the Messiah, the Son of David, Jesus lives among his people. In 9:10 "tax collectors and sinners" join him "in his house" in order to recline at table and share a meal with him as the host. Later, in 9:28, he is followed "into his house" by two blind men whose sight he restores. Jesus leaves "his house" in 13:1 in order to teach the crowd of people by the sea; he reenters "his house" in order to impart special instruction to his disciples alone. Jesus' reprimand of Simon Peter's all-too-quick response to the tax collectors in 17:24 occurs privately after having gone "into his house."

Residence in Capernaum is as irregular for Jesus, the messianic Son of David, as it was in Nazareth (2:23). His country is Judea, named "the land of Israel" in 2:20-21, and, according to 2:11, he lived in a house in Bethlehem. Nevertheless, compelled to withdraw this third time, he chooses to move into Capernaum "by the sea" (4:13). For, in as far as it belongs to the territory of the tribes of Zebulon and Naphtali, it will enable him, according to 2:6, to function as "the one who will shepherd my people Israel." For Matthew this incongruity is confirmed by the prophecy of Isaiah, "The land of Zebulon and the land of Naphtali, the way by the sea, across the Jordan, Galilee of the Gentiles. The people who sat in darkness began to see a great light, and to those seated in the country and shadow of death light began to dawn" (vv. 15-16). The Evangelist is quoting a part of Isaiah 9:1-2 in order to express divine fulfillment in the ministry of Jesus. A star arose over Judea until it reached its zenith in Bethlehem over where the child Jesus lived, but only the Magi saw it and followed it. Now, as Jesus commences his messianic ministry in Galilee, the land of contempt, light begins to dawn in the territory of Zebulon and Naphtali, and its inhabitants begin to be illuminated by it.

"From then Jesus began to preach and to say, 'Repent, for the reign of God has drawn near'" (v. 17). This moment of transition is underlined by the unusual combination of a preposition, *apo* ("from") and an adverb, *tote* ("then"). It calls the reader's attention to this historic moment of the commencement of Jesus' career. The eschatological proclamation that John the Baptizer originated, and to which Jesus himself responded (3:13), is now adopted and introduced by him in Capernaum and Galilee. Jesus will traverse the cities and villages of this province, proclaiming the Good News of God's reign and curing every sickness and disease. He especially has compassion for the crowds, because they are harassed and helpless, like sheep without a shepherd. Soon he will send his disciples to expand his mission to these lost sheep of Israel (10:6f.).

Matthew discloses the immediate success of Jesus' Galilean ministry by the discipleship of two pairs of brothers who immediately respond to his message and follow him: "Simon, the one called Peter and Andrew his brother" and "James the son of Zebedee and John his brother." Both pairs are fishers. The first two are poor. Having only hand casting-nets, they must wade into the water and concentrate on fishing around the shore of the lake. The other two are moderately affluent. James and John are in business with their father, who owns a boat, and therefore can fish in the deep waters of the lake, and who also has hired hands to help with the larger nets and the greater quantity of fish that will be caught. Called to become "fishers of human beings," the four enter into the discipleship of Jesus.

The narrative of Book One ends with a summary statement of Jesus' activity "in all of Galilee," accentuating his teaching, his proclamation of the Good News, and his healing "of every kind of sickness and malady among the people" (v. 23).

Epiphany for us, in the light of this Matthean text, affirms us as those who once sat in darkness but now have seen "a great light." As disciples of Jesus the Christ, we are living in a new day; we are participants in a new creation. But the only evidence of this reality that our society will experience must be be actualized by us. By incarnating this season of Epiphany, the manifestation of God's light, in our daily life and conduct our society will be confronted with empirical evidence of the reality of a new creation.

> We are here because we are in need. We are here because we are hungry. I am always being told how nice it is that we feed them; but I know in my heart that we are being fed all the time, and if it is hard to explain that to others, then we have to keep trying, because Christ asked it of us—the recognition that He is part of suffering, wherever it takes place, and of course, so are we.
> —Dorothy Day[4]

It is in servanthood that all of Jesus' disciples can be "the greatest" (Matt. 18:1-3). There are many such examples in our own time. Dorothy Day, a genuine embodiment of "the servant," is distinguished by Robert Coles in his book *Harvard Diary* as he alludes to the change that took place in his life through his encounter with her in her ministry to the poor, the vulnerable, the marginalized, the sick of mind, and the sick of heart at her "hospitality house" in Manhattan.

Notes

1. Walter Brueggemann, *Theology of the Old Testament: Testimony, Dispute, Advocacy* (Minneapolis: Fortress Press, 1997), 647.

2. Walker Percy, *The Second Coming* (New York: Washington Square Press, 1980), 312–13.

3. Susan K. Hedahl, "Third Sunday after the Epiphany," in *Epiphany, Year A, Proclamation 6: Interpreting the Lessons of the Church Year* (Minneapolis: Fortress Press, 1995).

4. Dorothy Day, to Robert Coles, quoted in a sermon preached by the Rev. Senter Crook at Grace-St. Luke's Episcopal Church, Memphis, Tenn., April 23, 2006 (http://www.gslparish.org/serApr23-2006.htm; accessed 1/08/07).

TRANSFIGURATION OF OUR LORD / LAST SUNDAY AFTER THE EPIPHANY / FOURTH SUNDAY IN ORDINARY TIME

JESUS' TRANSFIGURATION AS A FORESHADOWING
OF PRESENT AND FUTURE GLORY
FEBRUARY 3, 2008

REVISED COMMON	EPISCOPAL (BCP)	ROMAN CATHOLIC
Exod. 24:12-18	Exod. 24:12 (13-14) 15-18	Zeph. 2:3; 3:12-13
Psalm 2 or Psalm 99	Psalm 99	Ps. 146:6-7, 8-9a, 9b-10
2 Peter 1:16-21	Phil. 3:7-14	1 Cor. 1:26-31
Matt. 17:1-9	Matt. 17:1-9	Matt. 5:1-12a

KEY THEMES

• Mount Sinai is the navel of the world where Israel is born as the people of God.

• Jesus is God's agent and surrogate who inaugurates the reign of God.

• Jesus' transfiguration on a Sinai-like navel is an eschatological anticipation of the dissolution of the old creation and its history that he will inaugurate by his death and the new creation that he will establish by his resurrection from the dead.

FIRST READING

EXODUS 24:12-18 (RCL)
EXODUS 24:12 (13-14) 15-18 (BCP)

God's Epiphany and God's Covenant with Israel

The Exodus has begun! Israel under the leadership of Moses has arrived at Mt. Sinai. A Covenant Code (Exod. 20:22—23:31) is being transacted between Yahweh and Israel, with Moses serving as the mediator at the request of the people who fear that they will die if God speaks to them directly.

A ceremony for the ratification of the covenant is enacted. The Israelites must give their consent and bind themselves to this covenant. When, therefore, Moses informs the people of all the words and ordinances of Yahweh, they respond unhesitatingly with one voice, "All the words that Yahweh has spoken we will do" (24:3). On the following morning, therefore, Moses builds an altar at the foot of the mountain and sets up twelve pillars, symbolically signifying the participation of the twelve tribes in the covenant. Sacrifices of oxen are offered up as burnt offerings to Yahweh as an atonement for Israel. As a culmination to the ritual of ratification, the blood of the oxen is then dashed against the altar and against the people to express the finalization of the union between God and Israel.

Moses and Aaron, Nadab and Abihu, two of Aaron's sons, and seventy elders of Israel ascend the mountain at the command of God in order to celebrate the enactment of the covenant with a meal: "and they saw the God of Israel. Under his feet there was something like a pavement of sapphire stone, like the very heaven for clearness. God did not lay his hand on the chief men of the people of Israel, but they beheld God and they ate and drank" (vv. 10-11).

But only Moses is permitted to approach Yahweh and experience a greater fullness of God's glory. He climbs further to the summit in order to receive the gift of the tablets of stone on which God has written the commandments of the covenant. A cloud covers the mountain as the glory of Yahweh settles upon it, and "it was like a devouring fire on top of the mountain" (v. 17). The people of Israel witness this awesome epiphany, but Moses alone enters the cloud and experiences the presence of God for forty days and forty nights.

Mount Sinai becomes the architectonic center of the world, the navel at which Israel was born as the people of God. But only their representative, Moses, the covenant mediator, is given the immense prerogative and prestige to experience the glory of God for a circumscribed period of time.

Matthew's Gospel intimates that Jesus is a New Moses. Even as the Pharaoh of Egypt attempted to end the life of Moses at his birth, Herod the Great sought to have Jesus killed soon after he was born. In fulfillment of Deuteronomy 18:15 Jesus delivers a new law on the mountain in Galilee (5:1). Should Jesus be identified as "the New Moses?" Or is he superior to Moses?

> This testimony about this singular encounter at Sinai makes clear that it is a one-time encounter to which only the leadership is invited. It is nonetheless clear that this encounter obligates Israel not only to do justice for the neighbor, but also to be in the presence of God, to see God, to submit to the unutterable overwhelmingness that is the very character of God. . . . The encounter is conducted in an environment of beauty, which makes the communion possible and which is reflective of Yahweh's own character.
> —Walter Brueggemann[1]

The Summons for the Integrity of Identity and Activity

Prophesying during the early period of Josiah's reign (639–608 B.C.E.) and therefore before the discovery of the book of Deuteronomy and the reformation that it inaugurated, Zephaniah warned Israel of the punishment that awaited those who embraced foreign values and practiced idolatry (1:4-5, 8, 11-13). The officials of Jerusalem are roaring lions, the judges are evening wolves that leave nothing until the morning, the prophets are reckless, and the priests have profaned what is sacred" (3:3-4). They have not accepted correction; they have not drawn near to God. "But they were more eager to make all their deeds corrupt" (3:7). Consequently, the day of the Lord that is coming is a day of ruin and devastation, a day of darkness and gloom. "The great day of Yahweh is near; it is near and it hurries greatly. It is a day of trouble and distress" (1:14-15).

In view of the approaching disaster, Zephaniah exhorts the faithful few, "the humble of the earth," to seek both justice and humility. "It may be that you will be hidden in the day of Yahweh's anger" (2:3). Because they will be protected, a remnant will survive. That is the promise of 3:12-13. They will be "the afflicted and poor people who will take refuge in the name of Yahweh." "They shall do no wrong, nor shall they tell lies, nor shall there be found in their mouths a deceitful tongue." Those who constitute the remnant are committed to their covenantal relationship to God and the ethical integrity that it requires. Their well-being is characterized metaphorically in 3:13b in the language of Psalm 23, "They shall feed and lie down with none to disturb them."

This first reading for the Fourth Sunday after the Epiphany is directed toward a characterization of integrity that circumscribes those who identify themselves as the people of God. Accordingly, if Christian identity signifies bearing witness to Epiphany by confessing Jesus as the Light of the world, the integrity of discipleship requires activity that corresponds to identity (5:14). It is fulfilling what God wills for the entire creation: "to seek first the reign of God and its righteousness," and then "all these things shall be added to you" (Matt. 6:33).

RESPONSIVE READING

PSALM 2 (RCL)

The Enthronement of God's Messiah

Psalm 2 affirms that God is the Lord of history who exercises sovereignty over the nations and kingdoms of the earth. It is a royal psalm that probably was composed for the enthronement of a Davidic king of Judah and acknowledges him as "Yahweh's anointed" or, literally according to the Hebrew, *meshiah*, "Yahweh's messiah."

The psalm has a four-part structure that consists of a dialogue of voices evoked by the design of the nations surrounding Judah to attack God's anointed, the king who has been enthroned over God's people. Verses 4-6 convey God's response to the planned revolt: "He who sits in the heavens laughs." They will know God's wrath and fury when their impudence will be confronted with God's pronouncement, "I, indeed, I have anointed my king in Zion, my holy hill." Their audacity to conspire against the king God has installed will have its consequences.

In verses 7-9 God's anointed, the king, speaks and declares that he holds his office by divine decree, "Yahweh said to me, 'You are my son! Today I have begotten you!'" The enthronement of the king is a begetting of the king as God's offspring, and that status imposes divine sovereignty and power upon him to rule God's people as God's surrogate. Therefore God will not hesitate to give his son, the anointed king, the ends of the earth for his possession. By his divine empowerment he will break these attacking nations with a rod of iron. Verses 10-12 conclude the psalm with an exhortation to these kings in revolt, "Serve Yahweh with fear, and rejoice in the enthronement of his messianic son."

The evangelist Matthew develops the christological identity of Jesus in the contrasting pair of titles: (1) Messiah and therefore the descendent of King David and (2) "the Son of Man" as the One who embodies the community of the Many who are and who will become his disciples. Jesus' Son of David messiahship culminates on the cross when he "gives his life as a ransom for many" (20:28). In his resurrection from the dead he as "the Son of Man," in fulfillment of Daniel 7:14, has received all authority in heaven and on earth, and joins his eleven disciples as the twelfth to reconstitute Israel as the new people of God, "*I* with you *AM* all the days even to the consummation of the age."

This psalm became an intertextual source of christological reflection in the early church, as Luke 3:22, Acts 13:33, and Hebrews 1:5, 5:5 witness. If it is to be related to Matthew's account of Jesus' transfiguration, it should be kept in mind that, in view of Jesus' self-identification as "the Son of Man" in 17:9 and 12, God's acknowledgment of Jesus as "My Son" is not to be construed in terms of a hierarchical kingship. "The Son of Man," as is indicated by Daniel 7:13 and its interpretation in 7:27, is a community, indeed, the community of the One and the Many. According to Paul in Romans 8:29, "He is the firstborn among many brothers and sisters."

As the fierce dark teaching of his childhood had never sunk into his heart, so that first article in his code of morals was, that he must begin, in practical humility, with looking well to his feet on Earth, and that he could never mount on wings of words to Heaven. Duty on earth, restitution on earth, action on earth; these first, as the first steps upward. Strait was the gate and narrow the way; far straiter and narrower than the broad high road paved with vain professions and vain repetitions, motes from other men's eyes and liberal delivery of others to judgment—all cheap materials costing absolutely nothing.
—Charles Dickens, *Little Dorrit*

The Paradox of God's Justice and Forgiveness

In this psalm God, and not the Davidic king of Judah, is celebrated as king: "Yahweh reigns!" or, according to the Hebrew text, "Yahweh has become king." God's enthronement is such an awesome reality that the people of God should tremble, and the earth should respond with a quake. Why? Because God is holy! But more significantly, because God's power, unlike that of the kings of the earth, is controlled by God's justice! As the poet says, "You have established equity, you have executed justice" (v. 4).

Because God's rule is just, the people of God are urged to worship God with praise and exaltation at the place of Yahweh's presence on earth. For to prostrate oneself "at his footstool," that is, at the Ark of the Covenant, is to acknowledge God's enthronement and God's rule.

Moses, Aaron, and Samuel are cited as priests who kept God's decrees and who called upon God and, therefore, as the psalmist declares, "O Yahweh our God, you answered them!" They are models of doing justice, loving mercy and walking humbly with God, but they also stumbled and sinned. "You were a forgiving God to them, but you did take vengeance for their sins" (v. 8). The consequences for doing wrong are not necessarily cancelled by the grace of forgiveness. As the Apostle Paul states in Romans 6:1-2a, "What then shall we say, 'Let us continue in sin so that grace may abound?' By no means!"

PSALM 146:6-7, 8-9a, 9b-10 (LFM)

God's Integrity and Therefore God's Dependability

In this psalm the poet looks to the ultimate trustworthy and reliable Ruler, the Creator "who made heaven and earth, the sea, and all that is in them" (v. 6). Yet it is not power alone but the "truth"—the Hebrew word *'emeth* means "truth," not "faith"—that the Creator "keeps forever." And God's truth is the foundation of the trust to which Israel is summoned. The beatitude of verse 5 enunciates the well-being of those put their trust in the God of Zion. God alone, therefore, is the unfailing source of the restoration and renewal that humanity hopes for, as specifically verses 7-9 affirm. God will reign forever, as verse 10 states, because "his" dependability and integrity are manifested in his activity but also because they will be manifested in the lives of those who will become God's mouth, hands, and feet in order to serve as God's surrogates in fulfilling the work of restoration and renewal. The appropriate response, therefore, is "Hallelujah," the opening summons of Psalm 146.

SECOND READING
2 PETER 1:16-21 (RCL)

Guaranteeing the Truth of the Scriptures

Second Peter presents itself as a testament or a farewell address of Peter (1:13-14) and attests to the prominence and the authority of his person in the early second century. Probably written in Asia Minor, it was addressed to Gentile Christians who had received 1 Peter, as 3:1 suggests. Its earliest attestation occurs in the writings of Origen, who observes that it was contested as a genuine letter of the disciple and apostle Peter.

To certify his self-identification as Peter, the author states that he was among the eyewitnesses of Jesus' transfiguration on the holy mountain. He and his fellow disciples heard the words spoken by the heavenly voice, "This is my Son, my Beloved, into whom I began to take pleasure" (vv. 17-18). This eyewitness event guarantees the reliability of the prophetic word, and therefore the addressees of 2 Peter are urged to attend to their message as "a lamp shining in a dark place" (v. 19). The metaphor of the Scriptures as a lamp may have been derived from Psalm 119:105, "Thy word is a lamp to my feet and a light to my path." Because these Scriptures of the Old Testament are God's Word, ". . . no prophecy of scripture is a matter of one's own interpretation, because no prophecy ever came by the impulse of human beings, but individuals moved by the Holy Spirit spoke from God" (vv. 20-21). This hermeneutical principle was verbalized specifically to refute the false teaching of Christian Gnostic groups.

PHILIPPIANS 3:7-14 (BCP)

The Spirituality of Participating in Jesus' Death and Resurrection

In 3:2-14 Paul is attacking those Christians in the Philippian congregation who are perverting the gospel by incorporating the legalistic observances of circumcision and the purity code into Christian spirituality. His refutation is determined by an autobiographical account of his own movement from obedience to the law into the salvation of Christ Jesus. In verses 7-14 he imparts the spirituality that he is pursuing as a participant in the new creation, which he acknowledges in other contexts as the canonical reality of the Christian faith (Gal. 6:16).

His earlier pursuit of righteousness under the law and all the benefits he derived from it are now regarded as rubbish in order to gain Christ. For him that means "the righteousness of God through the trust of Christ" (v. 9). The inheritance of all that belongs to the salvation that God has established through Jesus Christ cannot be received on the basis of the law, for the law in its function as a mirror discloses the condition of sin and therefore engenders alienation and death (Rom. 3:20). All that belongs to God's salvation is based on faith and is inherited through the "trust" that God constituted though Jesus Christ. Paul's desire to gain Christ involves him in the quest of "knowing him and the power of his resurrection and the fellowship of his sufferings by being conformed to his death, if somehow I might attain to the resurrection from the dead" (vv. 10-11). This is the core of Paul's spirituality. He readily acknowledges that he has not attained it yet. He is not complete; he is not whole. But in order to gain this completeness, this wholeness, he allows himself to be seized by Christ Jesus. His goal is that transcendence in his historical existence that will enable him to achieve the fullness of the stature of Jesus Christ.

1 CORINTHIANS 1:26-31 (LFM)

The Weakness and the Foolishness of God

Paul begins 1 Corinthians from the perspective of "the cross of Christ" and culminates his letter in chapter 15 with the resurrection of Christ. That corresponds to the movement of his thought in Romans 5. Good Friday establishes reconciliation: "peace towards God through our Lord Jesus Christ." Easter inaugurates a new creation and with it "the abundance of grace and the legacy of justice" in order to enable those who have died and risen with Christ to exercise God's reign and therefore "to rule in life" (Rom. 5:17).

But to the Greeks the cross is foolishness because of its shame and its powerlessness. Consequently, many of the Corinthian Christians have replaced the cross with socially acknowledged forms of power, the power of wisdom and the power of rhetoric. Paul contends, however, that the proclamation of Christ crucified is actually the power of God and the wisdom of God. It opens up a new way of being in the world because it confronts human beings with their arrival at the crossroads of history. Not only does it offer them the forgiveness of sins. More significantly, the proclamation of Christ crucified summons them to end their participation in the old moral order that is dominated by the power of evil and the power of death and to be resurrected from the dead by the power of the Holy Spirit.

Ironically, therefore, as Paul continues in verse 25, the foolishness of God is beyond human wisdom and the weakness of God is beyond human strength. That, as he points out, is evident in their calling. For there are not many among them who are influential and powerful because of their social status, their wisdom, or their wealth. Their own lower-class status in Corinthian society establishes the reality that the prophet Zephaniah already recognized. God chooses the foolish, the weak, the socially insignificant, indeed, the nobodies of the world, in order to put to shame those who are powerful and influential because of their wealth, their status, and their education. Within the ironic reality of God's foolishness and weakness, boasting about human wisdom and human strength is no longer justifiable. By being in Christ Jesus, the Corinthian Christians participate in the righteousness, the holiness, and the redemption that the Lord Jesus Christ imparts to all who are members of his Body, the New Humanity of the Last Adam.

THE GOSPEL
MATTHEW 17:1-9 (RCL, BCP)

Foreshadowing the Present and the Future Glory of the New Humanity

The story of Jesus' transfiguration is found toward the end of the narrative of Book Four. It not only climaxes Jesus' ministry in Galilee, especially his training of his disciples for future ministry; it offers the reader a glimpse of the final outcome of Jesus' career and by inference the identical glory that awaits his disciples. The incident is introduced by a significant time reference, "And after six days . . ." Jesus' transfiguration will occur on the seventh day of the week, the Sabbath. It is a symbolic representation not only of his own consummation but of the culminating Sabbath of history, that time in the future when Jesus, as the founder of a new humanity—that is the meaning of the christological designation, "the Son of Man," that he employs throughout the Gospel—will be transfigured with all the members of his New Israel. (*For more information on the Transfiguration festival tradition, see below, "Second Sunday in Lent," by Richard Eslinger.*)

Jesus leads Peter, James, and John "into a high mountain, by themselves" (v. 1). These three disciples did not form an inner circle among the larger group of twelve male disciples who in the Gospel tradition represented the patriarchs of the New Israel. Historically speaking, they are present because this unit of tradition probably originated in the early Jerusalem church when they, according to Galatians 2:9, constituted the leadership of the Mother Church. A mountain is the site of this incident. It is another architectonic center or navel of the earth. But here the mountain is not preceded by a definite article. Within the narrative world of Matthew's Gospel it poses a contrast to "a very high mountain" of the wilderness of Judea (4:8) on which Jesus was tempted to worship Satan in order to receive "all the kingdoms of the world." The kingdoms of the world, however, will enter into a new moral order of justice and peace, not by worshiping Satan, but by following Jesus into the reign of God that his death and resurrection constitute. The transfiguration "on a high mountain" in Galilee adumbrates Jesus' apotheosis by his resurrection from the dead and with it the reign of God that he will receive as a result of his co-enthronement with God, according to his testimony at his trial before the Sanhedrin (26:64).

In place of Mark's description of Jesus' metamorphosis, "And his garments became very shining white such as a bleacher on earth is unable to whiten," Matthew has substituted the language of an apocalyptic theophany, "His face shone as the sun and his garments became as white as the light" (v. 2). In this transformation Jesus, "the Son of Man," is being disclosed to his disciples as the Son of God (17:9)! Moses and Elijah, the Old Testament representatives of the Law and the Prophets, both of whom are associated with the Old Testament architectonic center of Mount Sinai, suddenly appear and Jesus begins to give them an audience: "They were seen speaking with him" (v. 3). The content of their dialogue is not revealed, but the sight of the three engaged in discourse evokes from Peter the christological identification of Jesus as the last prophet of history. He must be ranked with Moses and Elijah. He is the prophet Moses predicted in Deuteronomy 18:15; he must be the final prophet of the old moral order. In contrast to Mark's version of this incident, Peter expresses his willingness to construct three tabernacles, but only "if you wish." Matthew has deleted Mark's comment on Peter's ignorance and fear. His proposal, however, is embarrassingly interrupted by the heavenly voice speaking out of the cloud, "This is my beloved Son in whom I began to take pleasure. Keep on listening to him!" (v. 5). The significance of Jesus' metamorphosis is validated by God. Jesus is more than a new Moses! He is more than the final prophet of the old moral order! As God's Son he is superior to both representatives of the Old Testament. He is God's agent and surrogate who inaugurates the reign of God! In a reaction typical of theophanies the disciples fall on their faces in great fear. Jesus reaches out to them with a calming and reassuring touch, bidding them to "Be raised up and stop being afraid!" (v. 7). The first of his two imperatives employs the resurrection verb, *egeirō,* and could also be rendered as "Be resurrected." In the light of their experience on this very high mountain the disciples are to begin to participate in the destiny that this transfiguration foreshadows. By following Jesus into death and resurrection and engaging in the work that he has inaugurated, namely the reign of God, they will eventually have a share in the reality of his apotheosis that this metamorphosis anticipates. As Jesus states at the end of his interpretation of his parable of "The Wheat and the Darnels" in 13:43, "Then the righteous will shine as the sun in the reign of their Father."

The epiphany of the transfiguration, as Jesus instructs his disciples, is not to be communicated to anyone until after "the Son of Man" has been resurrected from the dead. That is the time when "the Son of Man" or the New Human Being will come into his reign, but a reign that he will share with his disciples. Jesus' transfiguration is an eschatological anticipation of the new creation that he will inaugurate after his death and its attendant dissolution of the old creation and its history. Matthew 27:52-53 bears witness to this cataclysmic event, "And the earth was shaken and the rocks were split apart." At the death of Jesus the old creation collapses into primordial chaos in fulfillment of apocalyptic prophecy. A new creation is constituted as the Old Testament saints are resurrected: "The tombs were opened and many bodies of the holy ones being asleep were resurrected [*egeirō*]." The long-awaited new creation dawns but is not established until Jesus leads these resurrected saints out of their tombs on Easter morning (27:53).

At the Great Commissioning of 28:16-20, Jesus joins the eleven disciples who have encountered him *on the mountain* in Galilee, and by attaching himself to them as they go forth to fulfill his final command, he becomes the twelfth and thereby establishes a New Israel. He not only shares with them "All authority in heaven and on earth," but he incorporates them into his divine I AM. As the Greek word order of 28:20 reads, "See, *I* with you *AM* all the days even to the consummation of the age."

Hester Prynne is transfigured in Nathaniel Hawthorne's novel, *The Scarlet Letter*, as she emerges from prison carrying her baby and wearing on the breast of her gown the letter A, elaborately embroidered and finished with a fantastic flourish of golden thread. She is a sinner, and the letter A, of course, stands for adulteress.

> In such emergencies, Hester's nature showed itself warm and rich; a well-spring of human tenderness, unfailing to every real demand, and inexhaustible by the largest. Her breast with its badge of shame, was but the softer pillow for the head that needed one. . . . Such helpfulness was found in her,—so much power to do, and power to sympathize,— that many people refused to interpret the scarlet A by its original signification. They said that it meant Able; so strong was Hester Prynne, with a woman's strength.
>
> —Nathaniel Hawthorne, *The Scarlet Letter*

But in the course of time, as she becomes a "self-ordained Sister of Mercy" and the letter serves as a symbol of her calling, her fellow citizens begin to think that the A signifies "Able"; and there are some who believe it means "Angel." Hawthorne has apprehended the paradoxical character of Christian identity. Today we could substitute the big letter S, Saint and Sinner. Although we remain sinners, even in our best discipleship, we are transfigured, like Hester Prynne, as we make the S the letter of our calling and enter into a ministry of servanthood in our society. That is our glory, as we are being metamorphosed, transfigured, into the image of Jesus Christ, from one degree of glory to another (2 Cor. 3:18).

MATTHEW 5:1-12a (LFM)

Pronouncing Blessedness on Certain Conditions and Activities

The Beatitudes constitute the introduction to Jesus' ethical teaching of the Sermon on the Mount. As a part of the entire so-called Sermon, they are spoken on a mountain, indeed, a particular mountain because the narrator of the Gospel has employed the definite article in front of the word *mountain*. (In Greek the phrase is *eis to oros* ("into the mountain"). The mountain, however, is not identified by name because it is intended to symbolize an architectonic center, an umbilicus or navel that represents the birthplace of a new people of God—like Mount Sinai, the sacred *axis mundi* at which Israel came into being as the elect people of God. Jesus seats himself on the mountain in order to convey a posture of authority. He is a New Moses, the fulfillment of Deuteronomy 18:15, and he will hand down a new Torah, a new teaching, which, while affirming Moses' Law, will also revise it in order to make it conform more perfectly to the will of God.

This becomes more evident in 5:17-48. Jesus will introduce six interpretations of various commandments by declaring in verses 17-20 that he did not come to tear down the Law and the Prophets but to fulfill them. The key word is the verb "to fulfill." Jesus will not hesitate to cancel a piece of Mosaic legislation if it does not conform to the will of God. In 5:21-30 he will uphold but at the same time radicalize two commandments of the Decalogue, but in 5:31-47 he will abolish four laws because they prohibit human beings from realizing their divinely willed wholeness and integrity, the kind that Jesus stresses in 5:48, "You therefore will be whole/complete even as your heavenly Father is whole/complete." The Greek word that is translated "whole/complete" is *teleios*, and it means "perfect," in the sense of being whole or sound. It occurs in only one other context in Matthew's Gospel, in 19:21, where Jesus informs the rich man that his desire for everlasting life can only be fulfilled by ceasing to be torn between his wealth and the authentic life that God willed for him. "If you want to be *whole*, go sell your possessions and give to the destitute, and you will have treasure in heaven and come and follow me." Jesus' ethical teaching is about the achievement of wholeness, integrity, and maturity in the relationship one has to others and to oneself.

But before Jesus delivers his ethical teaching to his disciples—and ultimately to the crowds (7:28)—he pronounces blessedness on certain conditions and activities, introducing each one by the adjective *makarios* ("fortunate"). Three, possibly four, appear to have been adopted from the Q Source (Luke 6:20-22); five are uniquely Matthean. Each is accompanied by an eschatologically focused promise, which is introduced by the causal conjunction *hoti* ("because"). This forms a pronouncement of blessedness followed by a guarantee that has no parallels in the Old Testament.

The first is an expanded version of Luke 6:20. Matthew has added the phrase "with reference to the spirit" to the pronouncement: "Blessed are the destitute with respect to the spirit, for theirs is the reign of God" (v. 3). It is poverty with reference to the human, not the divine Spirit that Jesus is blessing here. This is psychological or spiritual impoverishment that results from social, economic, or political oppression and/or depression. It may refer to destitution of the human spirit caused by a lack of self-esteem, which in turn effects a loss of "heart."

The reign of God belongs to those who find themselves in this *condition*, and it belongs to them *here and now*.

Only the eighth beatitude (v. 10), in addition to the first, enunciates such an eschatological actuality: "Fortunate are those who are persecuted on account of justice, for theirs *is* the reign of God." Neither 5:3 nor 5:10 offers a promise or a reward. Both sayings pronounce a *present* blessedness on specific *circumstances*: poverty of spirit and persecution, but on the basis of the present possession of the sovereignty of God's reign.

Between these two benedictions, 5:3 and 10, Jesus declares a series of six affirmations of certain *activities* and *attitudes* that he upholds by promises of *future fulfillment*. These are no entrance requirements into the reign of God, for it is already a present possession. Neither are they simply a set of virtues or moral ideals that characterize the Christian life. They are rather dispositions of character, pursuits of certain activities that bear promises of gratification. They are postures of authentic human existence because they have a future.

The blessings of the first stanza [5:3-6] may be construed as reversals and those of the second [5:7-10] as rewards, but in either case these blessings reflect the intrinsic effects of God's rule being established. . . . God's rule sets things right. Those for whom things have not been right are blessed by the changes it brings and those who have been seeking to set things right are blessed by the accomplishment of what they have sought.
—Mark Allan Powell[2]

"Blessed are those who grieve, for they will be comforted" (v. 4). Jesus speaks a benediction on the act of sorrowing and promises consolation and encouragement. "Blessed are the unassuming, for they will inherit the earth" (v. 5). Not the pushy, aggressive people, but the modest, the unpretentious, will fulfill themselves by finding the treasure and the pearl of Matthew 13:44-46. "Blessed are those who hunger and thirst for justice, for they will be satisfied" (v. 6). Engaging in activities of social, economic, and political justice with the same kind of craving that the human body has for food bears the promise of ultimate satisfaction. "Blessed are the merciful, for they will be mercied" (v. 7). Showing compassion to others, especially enemies, and exercising forbearance toward those who offend are dispositions that will result in experiencing compassion and forbearance in return. "Blessed are the pure with reference to the heart, for they will see God" (v. 8). The heart was considered to be the seat of motivation. Accordingly, those who have pure motives in their relationships and activities will experience the ultimate fulfillment. They will see God! "Blessed are the peacemakers, for they will be called God's offspring" (v. 9). Those who work for peace wherever possible will be disclosed as God's true daughters and sons, for they will be acting on behalf of God whose will is *shalom* for the whole world.

The final beatitude is spoken in the second-person plural. Here Matthew presents Jesus speaking directly to his disciples, who represent the addressees of Matthew's Gospel. They are the members of Matthew's church who are being persecuted by those who are reconstituting Judaism after 70 C.E. on the basis of both the written and oral Law and requiring conformity in order to continue to maintain their ethnic identity. "For so they persecuted the prophets before you" (v. 12). Matthew's Christian Jews are thereby certified to be the true people of God because, on the basis of the persecution they are suffering, they stand in the historic progression of Israel's prophets. They are the true Israel!

Notes

1. Walter Brueggemann, *Theology of the Old Testament: Testimony, Dispute, Advocacy* (Minneapolis: Fortress Press, 1997), 425.

2. Mark Allan Powell, *God With Us: A Pastoral Theology of Matthew's Gospel* (Minneapolis: Fortress Press, 1995), 138.

THE SEASON
OF LENT

RICHARD L. ESLINGER

THE JOURNEY TO EASTER:
AN INVITATION

The conventional interpretation of the season of Lent is penitential—almost exclusively so. Certainly, there is an authentic penitence that the liturgy of Ash Wednesday invites, expressed most profoundly, perhaps, as we pray Psalm 51, "Create in me a clean heart." Yet the origins of Lent were not in the church's decision to establish a season of sorrow and penance. Rather, Lent emerged in early Christianity as the final, intensive time of preparation—of instruction and formation—for the catechumens. These catechumens had already come a good way from the darkness of the world toward their baptism at the Great Vigil of Easter. By turning to the biblical type of forty days, this emerging season was designed to lead these candidates to their baptismal waters.

The earliest form of Lent, then, is a time of baptismal preparation. And as the season takes shape, a three-Sunday sequence can be discerned, including distinctive Gospel lessons, a sequence that has been recovered in the three-year lectionaries of the Western church (the Roman Catholic Lectionary and the Revised Common Lectionary). In Year A—the year that recovers this earliest baptismal Lent—the third, fourth, and fifth Sundays echo the early church's wisdom for making new Christians. The catechumens journeyed toward the waters of their salvation by way of Jacob's Well ("The Woman at the Well," John 4:1-42), the Pool of Siloam ("The Man Born Blind," John 9:1-41), and the burial cave at Bethany ("The Raising of Lazarus," John 11:1-44). The church regarded each of these lessons as having profound baptismal significance. The church further shaped the baptismal character of these three Sundays by placing distinctive "scrutinies" at each, related to the imagery and themes of the respective Gospel lessons. The catechumens were examined as to their growing faith and formation in rites that invited them to enter into each of these narratives and to renew and deepen their commitment to be baptized into Jesus Christ.

The recovery of this baptismal character of the season of Lent has come in a most providential manner. We Western Christians are increasingly aware that Christendom is dead and gone; American Christians now live in what law professor and columnist Stephen Carter has termed "a culture of disbelief." With the demise of Christendom, however, has come a most wonderful opportunity and challenge for the church. We will need to learn once again how to make Christians, that is, to recover the adult catechumenate. Notice that apart from this evangelical and formational character of Lent, the lectionary's texts do not really make any sense. (Their primary task and reason for selection are not to drive home sin and guilt!) Similarly, the lessons of the Easter Vigil only can be understood if their profoundly baptismal quality is perceived. In fact, observing the Easter Vigil without reference to baptism into Christ, his death and rising would be a liturgical oxymoron.

ASH WEDNESDAY

REVISED COMMON	EPISCOPAL (BCP)	ROMAN CATHOLIC
Joel 2:1-2, 12-17 or	Joel 2:1-2, 12-17 or	Joel 2:12-18
Isa. 58:1-12	Isa. 58:1-12	
Ps. 51:1-17	Ps. 103 or 103:8-14	Ps. 51:3-4, 5-6ab,
		12-13, 14, 17
2 Cor. 5:20b—6:10	2 Cor. 5:20b—6:10	2 Cor. 5:20—6:2
Matt. 6:1-6, 16-21	Matt. 6:1-6, 16-21	Matt. 6:1-6, 16-18

KEY THEMES

- Lent is the season designed to form and inform those seeking faith in Christ and membership in the Body of Christ.
- Lent is also the season for the baptized to grow more fully in personal and social holiness.
- What are the personal and communal virtues necessary for the journey through Lent? And what disciplines are we and the assembly being asked to assume in this season (if any)?
- Shall we be in denial about the "locust plagues" afflicting church and culture, or with Joel "blow the trumpet" and name them?
- The seriousness of our Lenten fast will be measured by the degree to which any in the world benefit from our self-denial and by the ways in which it exercises our capacity of heart.

FIRST READING
JOEL 2:1-2, 12-17 (RCL, BCP)
JOEL 2:12-18 (LFM)

The traditional Old Testament lesson for Ash Wednesday, its call for repentance, and the liturgical language of that call (2:12-13) have served to shape the piety and worship not only for this opening occasion of Lent, but for the entire season. Here is an instance of Scripture's "vested interest" in creating a community capable of the life and work and worship befitting a biblical people.[1] It is interesting, therefore, to note that the various interpretations of this text vary widely and advocates of these positions remain in contentious debate with each other. Before focusing on the specific text for Ash Wednesday, then, it is wise to look both to the context for the lection within the book of Joel and to touch briefly on some of the major points of disagreement among scholars. I will begin, therefore, by considering the context of the lection within the book.

In the first chapter of Joel, at least several realities are abundantly clear. God's people are in the midst of a locust plague unique in its devastation and duration. No locust infestation in the past has come close to what is now being experienced (1:2). It is the Hurricane Katrina of locust plagues! Moreover, it will remain singular in its magnitude—something to tell your children and your children's children (1:3). By way of a terrible, poetic, drumbeat-like meter, the locusts are depicted as the invincible army they are:

> What the cutting locust left,
> the swarming locust has eaten.
> What the swarming locust left,
>   the hopping locust has eaten,
> and what the hopping locust left,
>   the destroying locust has eaten. (1:4)

These small insects are imaged as an invading nation, "powerful and invincible," with teeth like lions and with fangs like the lioness (1:6). Everything has been consumed before them. The people lament, but they do not only lament the devastation of the locusts. The locusts have even devoured the foodstuffs used for offerings of sacrifice to God. In a diminishing series of metric phrases, the lament focuses on this lost hope:

> [F]or the grain is destroyed,
>   the wine dries up,
>   the oil fails. (1:10)

In response to the question in the psalm and in the gospel song, "What shall I render unto the Lord?" Joel would respond for the people, "Nothing. We have nothing to render, nothing to offer to petition the Lord to come to help us." The locust plague has taken everything away, especially hope.

Now, listen to the opening call of the first lesson for Ash Wednesday: "Blow the trumpet in Zion; sound the alarm on my holy mountain!" (2:1). The alarm cry continues and announces that "the day of the LORD [*Yom Yahweh*] is coming, it is near" (2:1b). There follows a quartet of descriptors: it is "a day of darkness and gloom, a day of clouds and thick darkness." The quartet of images actually has a chiastic pattern with darkness surrounding the gloom and clouds on all sides. The very structure of the alarm cry leaves no escape! And what's more, as with spreading darkness, "a great and powerful army comes" (2:2b). Never has there been an army like this, nor will their like ever be seen "in ages to come" (2:2c). Both the imagery itself and the close parallels in poetic meter and point of view (nothing like this in the past or the future) with the description of the locust plague in the first chapter are striking. Hence, the challenge for all of us who read this text and for God's people who hear it is, simply put, What is going on here in chapter 2? More specifically, as Old Testament scholar Willem Prinsloo notes, problems abound when considering this pericope, "the chief one being whether it is a description of an actual locust plague or an apocalyptic army."[2] In spite of interpreters who opt for the former position, Prinsloo and others are convinced that what has occurred between the first and second chapters is a sudden shift from the immediate crisis at hand (the locust plague) to the ultimate Crisis of the impending day of the Lord.

Concurring that we have a shift in scale of dramatic proportions between the locust plague and the coming day of Yahweh, Hans Walter Wolff writes that the sequence from chapter 1 to 2:1-17 "is irreversible. We have here not a parallel to the temporary distress, but an intensification of it into the ultimate one."[3] But the rest of our pericope shows that there is in fact a parallel between the crisis and the Crisis.

In the material beginning in verse 12, the God of the covenant offers a grace note, in spite of the earlier dire depiction of the coming "day of darkness." An invitation is extended to the people by God to repent: "return to me with all your heart . . . ; rend your hearts and not your clothing" (vv. 12b, 13). The Hebrew word for "return," Wolff remarks, means "total reorientation toward Yahweh."[4] And if this return is "heart-felt," the Lord, who is "gracious and merciful, slow to anger, and abounding in steadfast love" (v. 13), may "turn and relent" (v. 14a). The parallelism is interesting: the people are called to return and repent while Yahweh may turn and relent. But the divine grace does not stop at the possibility of turning and relenting. "Who knows," the prophet ponders, whether God will not also "leave a blessing behind him, a grain offering and a drink offering for the LORD, your God?" (v. 14b). And not only is such a grace-filled prospect proposed by the prophet, the liturgical expression of the return is spelled out in detail (2:15-17). That this liturgical section is begun with the same call that began the apocalyptic cry in 2:1—"Blow the trumpet"—emphasizes the relationship between the alarm and call to repentance on one hand and the possible return and restoration on the other.

But as to possible parallels between the locust plague in chapter 1 and the nearing day of Yahweh in chapter 2, two recurring images should be noted. First, in both cases, the people have no resources with which to feed themselves or their livestock. (The situation at the beginning of the second chapter assumes that the devastation of the locust plague still obtains.) And in both contexts, the prophet Joel directs the people to "sanctify a fast" (1:14a; 2:15). The shift in condition between "forsaken-people-starving" and "God's people-fasting" is profound. The former involves victimization and passivity; the latter reflects faithfulness and agency. Sometimes, all we have to offer is a fast! Second, both the sequence related to the locusts and the sequence dealing with the day of Yahweh have embedded within them this quandary regarding the lack of provisions to offer to God in sacrifice. In both

---

I invite you, therefore, in the name of the church, to observe a holy Lent: by self-examination and repentance; by prayer, fasting, and self-denial; and by reading and meditating on God's Holy Word.
—"Invitation to the Observance of Lenten Discipline"[5]

---

contexts, "Grain offering and drink offering are withheld from the house of your God" (1:13c). However, when the people hear this alarm about a coming day of darkness, the trumpet also plays that grace note: "Who knows?" Yahweh may turn if the people repent and God may provide the offering! So the answer to the question from Psalm 116—"What shall I render?"—is once again heard as of old: "The Lord will provide" (Gen. 22:14).

ISAIAH 58:1-12 (RCL alt., BCP alt.)

The Isaiah pericope is offered as an alternative to the Joel passage in both the RCL and BCP. Both options deal with fasting, although Joel's context is a unique occasion—on the microscale of a locust plague while on the macroscale, the Day of the Lord. The context for the issues related to fasting in the Isaiah text appear to have more ritualized, cultic observances in mind, fasts that continued for some time after the exile in remembrance of the sequence of disasters that befell Judah, its leaders, and the Temple. This Isaiah lesson especially commends itself if the preacher is called to focus on the hypocrisy of fasting as public show in Matthew 6:16-18.

This lesson begins with a formula well known to Israel. A prophet is being called by the Lord to "shout out" (lit., "with the throat") and "lift up your voice like a trumpet!" (58:1a). The "trumpet" invoked here is "the šōpār, a musical instrument made from a ram's horn, [which] was the primary device used to gain community-wide attention in ancient Israel, whether for alarm (18:3) or for communal activity (27:3)."[6] This announcement links the subsequent proclamation with prophetic oracles in Israel's past and thereby authorizes the one who proclaims the message as one of God's prophets. The divine word continues beyond this opening formula. The Lord God notes to the prophet that the people "seek me and delight to know my ways," adding, "as if they were a nation that practiced righteousness"(v. 2b). It is this "as if" that adds the heavy irony to the prophet's burden. On one hand, the people piously keep the rituals especially designed to secure God's favor and blessing. They fast, and apparently do so with remarkable dedication (see v. 5). Yet the intended outcome of this religious self-abnegation is withheld from the fasting ones. From their perspective, they are fully justified in coming before God and asking, "Why do we fast, but you do not see?" (v. 3a). But what they do not see is that these days of fasting "had become occasions for pursuing the people's own interests (Zech 7:5-6, they fast only for themselves)."[7] Even more than the self-centeredness of this fasting, however, was that overt violation of Torah that accompanied the ritual piety. Days of fasting can become days of evil if workers are oppressed and even quarreling and violence marks the holy day (see vv. 3b-4a). No matter what excesses of public display accompany the fasting, the actions are cruel hypocrisy before the righteous God of the covenant. "Will you call this a fast, a day acceptable to the LORD?" (v. 5c). The answer is obvious, and is completely in the negative!

The implied answer to the question regarding a fast acceptable to the Lord is provided in a new section of the pericope beginning in verse 6. Such an acceptable fast will bring freedom to those in any form of bondage (v. 6b); it requires that one share bread with all who hunger (v. 7a), cover the naked (v. 7b), and "not hide yourself from your own kin" (v. 7c).[8] Most commentators are agreed that this depiction of a true fast does not imply a repudiation of this act of piety in general (as is also the consensus related to Matt. 6:16-18). Claus Westermann accordingly notes that the prophet's "meaning can only be that the actions towards men and women now detailed have some connection with fasting, and that they may be designated as a mode of fasting."[9]

Beginning in verse 8, the oracle or sermon shifts to a proleptic vision of the conditions that will obtain consequent upon this acceptable form of fasting. The imagery in this section of the pericope is especially rich and connects by reversal with the negative images of unrighteous fasting chronicled earlier and by a positive resonance with Israel's exodus experience. Upon such fasting as detailed in verses 7-8, "your light shall break forth like the dawn" (v. 8a). Here, we encounter language quite similar to "the beginning of the eschatological core of Isa. 56–66 addressed to Jerusalem. . . ."[10] Here, however, the force of the statement is more personal in its appeal. A second image is now added to that of light; the new situation of the righteous fast-keeper will be like a sudden healing of an old wound. The Hebrew term, 'arūkā, means a new layer of skin that "will stretch itself rapidly over wounds that had been suppurating and infected."[11] The imagery contrasts vigorously with the naked who need to be covered in v. 7b. Their condition is the real wound afflicting God's people! And just as the nakedness of the poor needs to be addressed with immediate action, so this blessing of a righteous one who fasts will come rapidly or "quickly" (NRSV). Then, invoking the imagery of God's redemption of Israel at the exodus, "your vindicator shall go before you, the glory of the LORD shall be your rear guard" (v. 8c). God's light will not only come quickly as the dawn, but go before and follow the righteous one as the pillar of fire guarded the people from Pharaoh's hosts, both in front and behind. If any fasts in this way, declares the Lord, there will be a rapid response from Yahweh. "You shall cry for help, and he will say, Here I am" (v. 9a).

The final section of the pericope offers a poetic expression of this wholeness (the "covering of new skin") God will bring to the people. A series of "if, then" statements set up the promises. *If* the people fast by liberating those in bondage, by refusing to speak evil of others, by feeding the hungry, and by satisfying "the needs of the afflicted" (v. 10b), *then* "your light shall rise in the darkness and your gloom be like the noonday" (v. 10c). The promises now continue and the images of healing and wholeness tumble over each other. God will guide the people (here, perhaps another allusion to the exodus), satisfying their needs "in parched places" (another exodus theme), and "make your bones strong" (v. 10b). And by way of transforming those "parched places," those who fast in righteousness "shall be like a watered garden, like a spring of water, whose waters never fail" (v. 11c). Claus Westermann notes regarding this imagery,

> The words that follow are reminiscent of Ps. 23. Their metaphors of making the bones young again, of the watered garden, the spring of water, and the waters that fail not, employ the language used in the blessing.[12]

The final image of restoration and wholeness both serves to reintroduce a strongly communal context and to underline the eschatological weight of these latter metaphors of healing. In this time of blessing, consequent upon fasting acceptable to the Lord, "your ancient ruins shall be rebuilt" (v. 12a). What had been destroyed as a result of the people's sin and rebellion against God will be rebuilt through their righteousness and the grace of God.[14]

> By almsgiving and fasting we add wings of fervor to our prayers so that they may more easily fly up and reach God . . .
> —Augustine of Hippo[13]

Responsive Reading

PSALM 51:1-17 (RCL)
PSALM 51:3-4, 5-6ab, 12-13, 14, 17 (LFM)

The paradigmatic psalm of penitence is appropriately located within the broader liturgical context of Ash Wednesday and the specific context of response to the first lesson from Joel. This penitent's prayer is a most fitting response to the prophet's call to "rend your hearts and not your clothing" (Joel 2:13a).

The alternate specified in the Episcopal lectionary invites the assembly to respond to the Joel lection with deep gratitude for God's "compassion and mercy" (v. 8a). Psalm 103 functions more as an extended "Word of Assurance" more than the penitential rite itself.

Second Reading
2 CORINTHIANS 5:20b—6:10 (RCL, BCP)
2 CORINTHIANS 5:20—6:2 (LFM)

This pericope serves the liturgical and formational purposes of Ash Wednesday by way of two major trajectories in the Pauline text. First, this passage serves as a summarizing statement with regard to Paul's appeal to the Corinthians to live lives that befit the gospel. The opening appeal of the lection sets the context for the Lenten journey of both the baptized faithful and for those who now enter this final stage of catechesis on their way to baptism at the Easter Vigil—"Be reconciled to God" (5:20b). Then, a second trajectory of the passage deals with Paul's self-presentation, his sufferings and the virtues in Christ needed to face such opposition and adversity. Even as the lengthy list proceeds, his rhetorical "we" eventually becomes an ecclesial "we." That is, as the apostle speaks of his own hardships and of the virtues that were tried and tested in this crucible, the intention is that believers will begin to see such challenges, and the character necessary to overcome them, as their own. Paul's self-referential "we" is intended rhetorically to become owned by the community of faith in Christ (as well as those seeking faith in Christ). The two main movements of the text dovetail completely. It is only because of the reconciliation with God made possible in Christ that such endurance can prevail and such character be formed.

The pericope begins in the middle of verse 20 of chapter 5: "we entreat you on behalf of Christ, be reconciled to God." The verb translated "entreat" (*deomai*) Paul also uses in this epistle in 8:4 and 10:2. In the former of these instances, the NRSV quite appropriately interprets the term as having the sense "to beg." (The Macedonians were "begging us" for the privilege of sharing in the ministry to those churches even more impoverished than they.) In 10:2, the NRSV less vigorously translates the term simply as "ask." Alternative translations with more vigor include reading *deomai* as "implore." (So the NAB reads 5:20b, "We implore you on behalf of Christ, be reconciled to God.") Then Paul proclaims one of the mysteries of the Incarnation: "For our sake he made him to be sin who knew no sin, so that in him we might become the righteousness of God" (v. 21). In affirming the sinlessness of Jesus Christ, Paul here in 2 Corinthians joins with a number of other New Testament texts: Matthew 27:4; Luke 23:47; John 8:46; Hebrews 4:15; and 1 Peter 1:19, 2:22.[15]

At the outset of chapter 6, Paul addresses the Corinthians on the basis of his apostleship. The NRSV translates *parakaloumen* as "urge," while other scholars prefer "appeal."[16] The exhortation continues that the Corinthians "not accept the grace of God in vain." The literal meaning of *kenon* is "empty," although in this context, "in vain" is the appropriate reading. (We note the alternative meaning of the term in the hymn in Philippians 2:7, "but emptied [*ekenōse*] himself . . .") Now the apostle provides a quote from Isaiah 49:8 and concludes, "See [*idou*], now is the acceptable time [*kairos*]; see, now is the day of salvation!" (6:2b). The eschatological day has in Christ become every "now," both for believers and nonbelievers. The *kairos* has come in Christ's work of justifying and reconciling love, and the *kairos* comes to all who respond in faith upon hearing this good news.

The verse that follows this ringing good news serves as a transition bridging the proclamation with a section of more personal testimony by the apostle. No obstacle is placed in the way of any and therefore no fault may be found in Paul's ministry. The term "obstacle" (*proskopē*) literally means "stumbling block," and New Testament scholar William Baker suggests that "Paul presumes that there are those who are out to get him . . . , since the word suggests someone who is looking for something at which to take offense."[17] Given this sense of some who may be in his audience at Corinth, Paul adopts an interesting rhetorical strategy. He develops a classic pathos system (a series of negative events that he has experienced on behalf of the gospel) and then shifts to an ethos system that catalogues the virtues essential to any believer who, like Paul, will receive opposition and not approbation in the world. The movement, then, is from a catalogue of Paul's "great endurance" to a catalogue of virtues any Christian needs in order to endure. We may sketch out the two systems as follows:

Appeal to Pathos (6:4b-5)

". . . through great endurance,
in afflictions,
hardships,
calamities,
beatings,
imprisonments,
riots,
labors,
sleepless nights,
hunger" (or, better, "fasts" [NAB])

Appeal to Ethos (6:6-7)

"by purity,
knowledge,
patience,
kindness,
holiness of spirit,
genuine love,
truthful speech, and
the power of God."

The dialectic of the gospel continues: "treated as imposters and yet are true; as unknown, and yet we are known; as dying, and see—we are alive; as punished, and yet not killed; as sorrowful, yet always rejoicing; as poor, yet making many rich; as having nothing, and yet possessing everything" (6:8b-10). In this summarizing statement, Paul speaks on behalf of himself and all faithful; ethos and pathos have now come together in the mystery of the gospel.

The Gospel

MATTHEW 6:1-6, 16-21 (RCL, BCP)
MATTHEW 6:1-6, 16-18 (LFM)

In this final section of the Sermon on the Mount, a series of oppositions are offered with regard to true righteousness that befits followers of Jesus Christ. The issue here is not merely "piety," as important as the three cornerstones of Jewish piety remain: prayer, fasting, and almsgiving. In fact, the three aspects of Jewish (and Christian) piety organize the entire passage, although Matthew shifts the sequence in order to begin with almsgiving. The NRSV use of "piety" to translate *tēn eleēmosynēn* is weak. A more literal translation would be "merciful deeds," although many versions of the text employ "righteousness."[19]

> He, our Lord Jesus, fulfilled all your will and won for you a holy people; he stretched out his hands in suffering in order to free from suffering those who trust you.
> —Eucharistic prayer, *Evangelical Lutheran Worship*[18]

While the three issues before us are aspects of piety, something deeper is at stake here in this final section of the Sermon. Structurally, each of the elements of righteousness is developed with regard to oppositions that call for a decision by the Matthean community. In the words of the old freedom song, the question presented to the church is, Which side are you on . . . ?

Several rhetorical strategies are employed to heighten this alternative and mutually exclusive approach to these "merciful deeds." First, the distorted expression of righteousness is seen in the actions and motivations of "the hypocrites" (*hypokritai*), while those of true righteousness will possess both a different heart and model different actions. The use of "hypocrites" is deeply polemical in this context, derived as it is from the Greek term for "actor." These actors wear masks to cover their true identity and project another. Another rhetorical strategy in the passage pertains to the consistent use of the plural for the hypocrites, while those who are truly righteous are addressed in the singular. That is, this issue of hypocrisy or righteousness is deeply personal and the latter is so countercultural as to prevent a collective depiction. Another rhetorical strategy helps structure the oppositions. On one hand, the hypocrites parade their actions openly—"before others" (6:1). On the other hand, the truly righteous practice these "merciful deeds" in secret (*en tō kryptō*). A final aspect of each opposition deals with the outcome of the motivations and actions in each case. New Testament scholar Daniel Patte observes that "divine rewards are contrasted with human rewards."[20] With these oppositions in place, structured by a series of rhetorical strategies, Matthew now invites us into these oppositions at the center of the Sermon on the Mount.

The first opposition deals with almsgiving. It is first important to acknowledge that these are not oppositions that reject the expression of righteousness out of hand. Each is of God and those honoring each will receive their reward. However, there are ways in which almsgiving can be so distorted that is ceases to be a blessing in the eyes of God. "So whenever you give alms," Jesus begins, "do not sound a trumpet before you" (v. 2). It is probably not the case that Jesus is speaking of a literal sound of a brass choir. In fact, our culture uses the term in a very similar metaphorical way—regarding someone who "trumpets" their own importance (a metaphor possibly derived from this text). The hypocrites do such things "in the synagogues and in the streets" (v. 2b). Their motive is quite transparent; they do these merciful acts "so that they may be praised by others" (v. 2c). With a solemn preface to this declaration, "Truly, I tell you," Jesus continues, "they have received their reward" (v. 2d). The force of the statement is that they have received their reward "in full."[21] No further reward should be expected from God! On the other hand, "when you [singular] give alms, do not let your left hand know what your right hand is doing" (v. 3). Various commentators go to some length to spell out the dynamics of this left- and right-hand reference. So, for example, Matthean scholar Robert Gundry comments that "the expression should be understood literally: a gift should be slipped unobtrusively to the receiver with the right hand alone, not offered with both hands in a fashion designed to attract the attention of others nearby."[22] Patte offers a simpler explanation: it is "a metaphorical expression of the unselfconscious character of the action."[23] The first unit concludes with a refrain that will close each of three: "and your Father who sees in secret will reward you" (v. 4b). The reward of the Father must not become the new motive for the acts of justice, however, or the process collapses and the almsgiver becomes yet another one of the hypocrites. "By leaving the question of reward to God, one is set free for the concerns of others."[24]

> Giving alms seems, I think, to imply more than merely writing out a check to a favorite charity. It means adopting a conscientious way of life that expresses a caring relationship with the whole of God's creation.
> —Nancy Mairs[25]

The second subsection of the pericope deals with prayer, and our expectations are that the unit will proceed by way of opposition between the hypocrites and the righteous, employing the same familiar rhetorical strategies. We will not be disappointed. Here, instead of the image of sounding a trumpet before giving alms, the issue is a fondness for standing at prayer "in the synagogues and at the street corners" (v. 5b). The issue is not the traditional Jewish stance for prayer (standing); the issue is their motive—"so that they may be seen by others" (v. 5c). Notice, moreover, that the hypocrites "love" (*philousin*) this habit of standing and praying public, thereby receiving public adulation. This "delight in seeking public approval,"[26] Matthean scholar Warren Carter notes, serves to intensify the polemic. He adds, "[l]ove for public approval means that prayer ceases to express love for God (the first commandment; cf. 22:37), but like almsgiving, serves the one praying."[27] Once again the refrain is heard: "Truly I tell you, they have received their reward." And once again, the term translated "reward" means a receipt for complete and full payment.

Now the stance of justice is stated in opposition to that of the hypocrites. When a righteous person prays (again the shift to the singular), "go into your room and shut the door and pray to your Father who is in secret" (v. 6a). Again, commentators take different approaches to this dominical injunction. Some interpret the room as the storeroom, because in most houses "only the storeroom has a door."[28] Others, however, again see a metaphor at work in the text. What is most important in every case is that the place for prayer is "out of the public gaze and space, and in the presence of God."[29] The prayer to the Father by the just is therefore "in secret" (again, *en tō kryptō*), and God "who sees in secret

> Prayer should never have another purpose than to speak with God.
> —Ulrich Luz[30]

will reward you" (v. 6b). The Greek verb here is completely different from that dealing with the full and complete payment to the hypocrites. It has a literal meaning of "will repay." Once again, the paradox is lurking in the text. Anyone who would go into that storeroom, pray in secret, but with a motive of becoming rewarded by God has already joined the ranks of the hypocrites. The righteous will not pray with any thought of reward, but will pray out of their love for God.

The third of the subsections deals with fasting. By now we anticipate Jesus' depiction of the hypocrites' actions and motivations and are not disappointed. They look dismal while they fast and "they disfigure their faces so as to show others that they are fasting" (6:16a). Once again, they are looking dismal for public show—a hollow show of fasting repudiated by the prophets (see Isa. 58:3-9). But there is a deeper irony lurking in the text. Gundry notes that the verb literally means "they cause to vanish" and adds that "the hypocrites made themselves unrecognizable . . . in trying to be recognized."[31] Their overdone self-anointed ashes worn in public ironically rendered them anonymous! Such a display has its own rewards, perhaps including ridicule rather than public praise.

The righteous when fasting are not to call attention to their act of piety. The means of keeping secret such fasting is not to hide away in one's storeroom, but to hide the action in a very public way. Jesus tells the righteous, "put oil on your head and wash your face" (v. 17). In other words, in place of a dismal look and a disfigured face, the dominical command is to fast with every appearance of being on the way to a wedding banquet! With such a clean and oil-anointed face, the act of fasting is totally in secret even as the disciple is in public. In fact, the fast is not merely hidden, but a washed and anointed face conveys to all the signs of rejoicing and of feasting. That way, the righteous can fast in secret openly and convey kingdom joy even as they fast. Only the Father will see what is in secret and will reward such a righteous one. But the righteous will not hide their fasting, we recall, in order to achieve any future reward from God. If such a motive obtained, this disciple would tragically become numbered among the hypocrites.

HOMILETICAL STRATEGIES

Matthew the Evangelist has a fondness for triplets. Things come in threes throughout his Gospel. We sing of the "gold, frankincense, and myrrh" offered to Emmanuel; we will soon hear of the three temptations Jesus faced in the wilderness; and have heard (in LFM, will hear) Peter's suggestion to Jesus on the Mount about building those three dwellings. But here, the triplet has to do with the three cornerstones of Jewish and Christian piety: prayer, almsgiving, and fasting. To be sure, the preacher could organize a sermon that deals in sequence with each of the three activities, thereby providing a reworking of the "three-point" sermon of a previous era. However, the liturgical context for these lessons is Ash Wednesday and the sermon will both provide some important teaching regarding the Lenten fast and, more specifically, invite the listeners to receive the imposition of ashes with faith and with humility. With each of the three acts of piety providing ample material for proclamation, the liturgical context argues for the choice of the last of the three—the Lord's teaching regarding the act of fasting in verses 16 to 18. This choice is especially to be commended since many of those who assemble for this liturgy find the words of Jesus somewhat at odds with the rite of the imposition of ashes. (Are they being like the hypocrites?) Since this question is a perennial one at this worship service, we are drawn to Eugene Lowry's homiletical plot, a sequence that famously "loops" from an opening conflict to a concluding unfolding by intermediate steps of complication and a sudden shift.[33] We will shape our Ash Wednesday sermonic plot, then, by way of such a narrative sequence.

1. *Conflict.* The immediate conflict is obvious to worshipers who assemble for an Ash Wednesday service: "Here we are, preparing for the rite of the imposition of ashes and yet cautioned by our Lord not to show our fasting to anyone." The only way around the quandary, it would seem, is to go back to the days when an Ash Wednesday service ironically had no ashes in sight, anywhere. (Or perhaps a deacon could pass out those handy-wipe make-up removers to each worshiper as he or she turns from receiving the imposition of ashes!) Our dilemma, it would

> The Father "sees" all things done in secret, not in a "Big Brother is watching you" way, but in the sense that disciples live out their lives in conscious awareness of the presence of God with whom they have an intimate filial relationship.
> —Brendan Byrne[32]

seem, is sort of a reverse image of that of the "hypocrites" to which Jesus referred in the text. They were so eager to show off their fasting in public that they hid themselves behind masks of ashes and solemn frowns, becoming invisible in the process. What an irony! But this is more than a humorous incident. The larger question is how to live a disciplined Christian life in faith and with passion while not being seduced into that reward-seeking business. Just how do we negotiate between what we do "in public" and behind the door of our closet?

2. *Complication.* The issues that complicate the opening conflict are numerous and will need to be evaluated with regard to their theological and pastoral appropriateness. For example, one complication is a growing "culture of disbelief"[34] in North America. We live in the midst of a culture that generally reacts negatively to most any signs of Christian piety. So, shall we delete most every symbol and liturgical rite of the tradition in order to attract "seekers" from our world? On the other hand, a serious complication has resulted from the very public nature of our in-church battles and from clergy sexual misconduct. A sad procession of ecclesial hypocrites have been paraded in public because their private sins have not remained in some closet or other. This ongoing scandal affects both liberals and evangelicals, whether regarding sexual misconduct or sermon plagiarism or financial misdoings. A further, and even more ironic, complication relates to our Lord's admonition in the text. We are to appear before people as if we are off to a wedding banquet even when we are fasting. No solemn, sorrowful expressions that say, "Hey, look, I'm being pious!" When a visitor first joins in worship when the Eucharist is celebrated, however, how often the parishioners look for all the world like they are attending a wake or funeral for a departed friend! Here is the mirror image of the text. At the church's "feast of joy," our appearance conveys that we are showing off our fasting! The "reward" for all of this sad hypocrisy is an even more entrenched cynicism in the culture regarding the integrity of the faith and the faithful.

> *Each new-born servant of the Crucified bears on the brow the seal of him who died.*
> —"Lift High the Cross"[35]

3. *Sudden Shift.* The "torque" that provides for the homiletical plot's sudden turn always will be derived from the gospel. In this sermon, the preacher has led the listeners from an opening problem—the quandary regarding appropriate piety—to a serious complication regarding the church's public face of hypocrisy. Now, it is time for the sermon's sudden shift. One strategy is to reframe the imagery of this service. One can invite the assembly to recall that these ashes about to be blessed were previously blessed at last year's Palm/Passion Sunday service when they joined in procession to sing "Hosanna" to great David's greater Son. Probing the imagery more deeply, the preacher can affirm that this sign of our dust and ashes is always a partial sign. Our ashes are given life by the Spirit of the living God, whose same Spirit also enlivens the Body of Christ. And the dust and ashes of our

mortality, worn on our brow as we leave this liturgy, are temporarily smeared over the "the seal of him who died."[36] But that baptismal seal is indelible and eternal; Christ's name will forever be upon the foreheads of the faithful (see Rev. 22:4). The sudden shift is the good news of our new life in Christ.

4. *Unfolding.* Could we imagine a sermon on Ash Wednesday whose unfolding is one of celebration, with images of joy-filled fasting and growing holiness? Certainly at the heart of this sermon's unfolding is the anticipation of the terminus of these forty days of fasting in the great feast of Easter. But during these forty days, while we fast and pray and give alms, we will do so without thought of reward and we will live lives that befit the gospel . . . that the world may believe.

Notes

1. Walter Brueggemann, "The Social Nature of the Biblical Text for Preaching," in *Preaching as a Social Act: Theology and Practice*, ed. Art Van Seters (Nashville: Abingdon Press, 1988), 130. Brueggemann notes that "there is no textual activity that is not linked with a vested interest."

2. Willem S. Prinsloo, *The Theology of the Book of Joel* (Berlin and New York: Walter de Gruyter, 1985), 39.

3. Hans Walter Wolff, *Joel and Amos*, Hermeneia, trans. Waldemar Janzen, S. Dean McBride, Jr., and Charles A. Muenchow; ed. S. Dean McBride Jr. (Philadelphia: Fortress Press, 1977), 42.

4. Ibid., 49.

5. "Invitation to the Observance of Lenten Discipline" in *The United Methodist Book of Worship* (Nashville: The United Methodist Publishing House, 1992), 322.

6. John N. Oswalt, *The Book of Isaiah: Chapters 40–66* (Grand Rapids, Mich.: Wm. B. Eerdmans, 1998), 495.

7. Joseph Blenkinsopp, *Isaiah 56–66,* The Anchor Bible 19B (New York: Doubleday, 2003), 178.

8. Oswalt notes that the Hebrew term translated "your kin" or "your relatives" (lit., "your flesh") "can also refer to people in general . . . , and it seems that the more general reference might be more appropriate here." *The Book of Isaiah*, 504.

9. Claus Westermann, *Isaiah 40–66: A Commentary* (Philadelphia: The Westminster Press, 1969), 336.

10. Blenkinsopp, *Isaiah 56–66,* 180. ("Arise, shine, for your light has come" [Isa. 60:1a]).

11. Oswalt, *The Book of Isaiah*, 504.

12. Westermann, *Isaiah 40–66,* 399.

13. Augustine of Hippo, "Sermon 206, 2," quoted in Adrian Nocent, *The Liturgical Year, Vol. 2: Lent* (Collegeville, Minn.: The Liturgical Press, 1977), 20.

14. Oswalt adds that "God always gives us the dignity of being involved in putting back together what we have broken." *The Book of Isaiah*, 507.

15. Cited from William R. Baker, *2 Corinthians: The College Press NIV Commentary* (Joplin, Mo.: College Press, 1999), 240.

16. Victor Paul Furnish, *II Corinthians,* The Anchor Bible (New York: Doubleday, 1984), 341.

17. Baker, *2 Corinthians,* 246.

18. "Eucharistic Prayer: Setting One, XI," *Evangelical Lutheran Worship, Leader's Edition* (Minneapolis: Augsburg Fortress, 2006), 205.

19. So, for example, Warren Carter translates the term *justice/righteousness.* Warren Carter, *Matthew and the Margins: A Socio-Political and Religious Reading* (Sheffield, Eng.: Sheffield Academic Press, 2000), 158.

20. Daniel Patte, *The Gospel According to Matthew: A Structural Commentary on Matthew's Faith* (Philadelphia: Fortress Press, 1987), 85.

21. Robert Gundry comments that the Greek word translated "received" "appears in commercial language and on receipts for completion of payment." Robert H. Gundry, *Matthew: A Commentary on His Handbook for a Mixed Church under Persecution,* 2nd ed. (Grand Rapids, Mich.: Wm. B. Eerdmans, 1994), 102.

22. Ibid.

23. Patte, *The Gospel According to Matthew,* 86.

24. John P. Meier, *Matthew,* Lex Orandi (Wilmington, Del.: Michael Glazier, 1980), 58.

25. Nancy Mairs, "In the Garden," in *The Upper Room Disciplines* (Nashville: Upper Room Books, 2005), 54.

26. Carter, *Matthew and the Margins,* 161.

27. Ibid., 162.

28. Gundry, *Matthew,* 103.

29. Carter, *Matthew and the Margins.* 162.

30. Ulrich Luz, *Matthew 1–7: A Commentary,* trans. Wilhelm C. Linss (Minneapolis: Augsburg, 1989), 360.

31. Gundry, *Matthew,* 111.

32. Brendan Byrne, *Lifting the Burden: Reading Matthew's Gospel in the Church Today* (Collegeville, Minn.: Liturgical Press, 2004), 63–64.

33. See Eugene L. Lowry, *The Sermon: Dancing the Edge of Mystery* (Nashville: Abingdon Press, 1997). Also see my *The Web of Preaching: New Options in Homiletic Method* (Nashville: Abingdon Press, 2002), 33–56.

34. See Stephen L. Carter, *The Culture of Disbelief: How American Law and Politics Trivialize Religious Devotion* (New York: Knopf, 1994).

35. A reference to our baptismal sealing with the Spirit. See the hymn "Lift High the Cross," v. 2, George Willam Kitchin and Michael Robert Newbolt, 1916, alt., in *The United Methodist Hymnal* (Nashville: The United Methodist Publishing House, 1989), 159.

36. Ibid.

FIRST SUNDAY OF LENT

FEBRUARY 10, 2008

REVISED COMMON	EPISCOPAL (BCP)	ROMAN CATHOLIC
Gen. 2:15-17; 3:1-7	Gen. 2:4b-9, 15-17,	Gen. 2:7-9; 3:1-7
Psalm 32	25—3:7	
	Psalm 51 or 51:1-13	Ps. 51:3-4, 5-6,
		12-13, 14, 17
Rom. 5:12-19	Rom. 5:12-19	Rom. 5:12-19 or
	(20-21)	5:12, 17-19
Matt. 4:1-11	Matt. 4:1-11	Matt. 4:1-11

KEY THEMES

• The issue for this First Sunday in Lent is temptation. But the challenge is to uproot a pietistic understanding of this reality of life and replace it with the biblical witness to the subtlety and perniciousness of our temptations and their consequences.

• Sin and death have spread like an infectious disease across the generations. As Lent begins, we acknowledge this "curse in the texture of earthly life" (Ernst Käsemann) and stand amazed at God's free gift of life.

• On the Sunday, the "elect" (catechumens) begin their Lenten journey toward baptism at Easter. This ministry of making new Christians will infuse our preaching during the entire Forty Days.

• The Eucharist on this First Sunday in Lent contrasts our Lord's refusal to turn stones into bread for himself with his gracious gift to us of loaves that are the Bread of Life.

GENESIS 2:15-17; 3:1-7 (RCL)
GENESIS 2:4b-9, 15-17, 25—3:7 (BCP)
GENESIS 2:7-9; 3:1-7 (LFM)

The distinction between the creation account in Genesis 1:1—2:4a and that in the rest of chapter 2 and all of chapter 3 is widely known and acknowledged. The Old Testament lesson for the First Sunday in Lent is taken from the latter narrative and it is also widely acknowledged to be composed of groupings of earlier oral traditions. One thesis—the creation story continues to elicit unending possible interpretations—is that the present text is largely derived from two collections of oral tradition. Claus Westermann proposes that "one group was concerned with the actual creation of human beings, the other with the meaning of human existence, what characterizes it, the fact that it is a created state, and consequently with its limitations."[1] Moreover, Westermann suggests that the two verses from chapter 2 that begin the pericope are most closely linked to the latter grouping found in chapter 3 (or possibly "inserted" into the "A" collection by the Yahwist).[2] Whatever the redaction situation, the lesson smoothly flows from the account in 2:15-17 to the story in the "B" account of 3:1-7. Another perspective on the structure of the second creation account is offered by Walter Brueggemann, who labels it a "drama in four scenes."[3] The four scenes as proposed by Brueggemann are as follows:

   I. 2:4b-17 (omitting vv. 10-14)—the placement of the man in the garden
  II. 2:18-25—the formation of a "helper"
 III. 3:1-7—the disruption of the garden
 IV. 3:8-24—judgment and expulsion[4]

The Old Testament lesson for the First Sunday in Lent, then, includes the latter portion of scene I and all of scene III.

The pericope begins, "The LORD God took the man [*ha'adam*][5] and put him in the garden of Eden to till it and keep it" (2:15). What may be surprising to the "conventional listener" to this lesson is that we do not have a vision of Paradise here! Upon being placed in the garden by the Lord God, the fullness of human existence includes labor. "Work is a part of human existence because the living space which the creator has assigned to his people demands this work."[6] (Again, the "conventional reading" of the creation story is that work is one of the curses of God on the human family after the garden's disruption.) After the Lord God put the man in the garden with this distinctive role, there follows a command: "You may freely eat of every tree of the garden; but of the tree of the knowledge of good and evil you shall not eat, for in the day that you eat of it you shall die" (2:16b–17). Although the literal Hebrew states, "on the day," the phrase need not be construed to mean "the instant." Rather, what is introduced into human existence "on that day" is our mortality. Brueggemann is helpful in identifying three warrants for the garden's existence and the place of human beings in it:

a. "There is a *vocation*." (Humanity is created to share in the work of the Creator.)
b. "There is a *permit*." (All that is needed for human life is permitted.)
c. "There is a *prohibition*."[7] (With no interest in explanation, the Yahwist simply indicates this exception to what is permitted.)

Each of these will be in play—and subject to distortion in the temptation scene. However, it will remain the case for human beings as God's creation that life as intended will involve vocation, permit, and prohibition.

Now, in 3:1, the serpent (*hannakhash*) is introduced—a creature "more crafty than any other wild animal that the LORD God had made."[8] Now a dialogue develops that is unique to the garden, especially in the awareness that God is not an immediate partner to the conversation. First, the serpent speaks, then the woman, and then the serpent again. Each of these three speeches involves distortion and/or falsehood. The serpent asks, "Did God say, 'You shall not eat from any tree in the garden'?" (v. 1b). The serpent is quite wily, and attempts to depict God as prohibiting more than permitting. The woman's response is mostly correct: "We may eat of the fruit of the trees in the garden; but God said, 'You shall not eat of the fruit of the tree that is in the middle of the garden, nor shall you touch it, or you shall die'" (v. 2). The woman makes a "slight refinement" to the divine prohibition, by adding the business about not touching the tree. The serpent then responds, "You will not die . . ." and continues by suggesting that once eaten, the fruit will make humans like God, "knowing good and evil" (v. 5). So two lies are uttered by the serpent. God has already stated the punishment for this crime—death, and a temptation to be like God will become such a tragic condition for humanity east of Eden.[10]

In creating this human community, God gave the woman and the man senses with which to experience the world, feelings to enjoy it and each other and their Creator, and a capacity for reason. All of these are now distorted, including the human community God has intended. The woman "saw that the tree was good for food" (thereby putting aside God's prohibition and ignoring all of the provisions in the garden that are permitted), "and that it was a delight [*ta'avah*] to the eyes" (thereby turning from all the delights God had placed in the garden), "and that the

Guide these catechumens in the days and weeks ahead:
strengthen them in their vocation,
build them into the kingdom of your Son,
and seal them with the Spirit of your promise.
We ask this through Christ our Lord. Amen.
—"Prayer over the Catechumens"[9]

142

THE SEASON OF LENT

RICHARD L. ESLINGER

tree was to be desired to make one wise" (thereby attempting to rise above the human condition and overstepping the limits place on it), "she took of its fruit and ate; and she also gave some to her husband, who was with her, and he ate" (v. 6). The rhetoric of fidelity has given way to analysis and calculation. The givenness of God's rule is no longer the boundary of a safe place. God is now a barrier to be circumvented. The scene moves quickly to its sorry resolution. The *prohibition* of 2:17 is violated. The *permission* of verse 16 is perverted. The *vocation* of verse 15 is neglected. What had been a story of trust and obedience (chapter 2) now becomes an account of *crime and punishment* (3:1-7).[11] With eyes now open, knowing they were naked, "they sewed fig leaves together and made loincloths for themselves" (v. 7). At this moment, and in all these ways, they now are subjected to the power of death.

RESPONSIVE READING
PSALM 32 (RCL)

The Thirty-second Psalm responds to the Garden of Eden narrative by inviting the assembly to give thanks to God for the forgiveness that is granted following upon true repentance. The psalmist acknowledges sin and iniquity and confesses transgressions to the Lord (v. 5). The psalm praises the God who forgives the sinners and invites them to "Be glad in the LORD . . ." (v. 11).

PSALM 51 or 51:1-13 (BCP)
PSALM 51:3-4, 5-6, 12-13, 14, 17 (LFM)

See the responsive reading for Ash Wednesday (RCL, LFM), above.

SECOND READING
ROMANS 5:12-19 (RCL, LFM)
ROMANS 5:12-19 (20-21) (BCP)
ROMANS 5:12, 17-19 (LFM alt.)

The epistle lesson in all three lectionaries is some version of the material in Romans 5:12-19 in which Paul develops his typology regarding Christ as the new (and abundantly graced) Adam. Liturgically, all lectionary citations have this pericope serve as a theological commentary on the sin of Adam and Eve in the Garden of Eden—the first lesson for this First Sunday in Lent. With respect to Paul's Letter to the Romans, the text is developed as a culmination of the witness to Christ provided in 5:1-11. Emphasizing this sequential logic, Paul begins the new section, "Therefore . . ." (*dia touto*), and immediately begins to establish the typological relationship between Adam and Christ. Sin came into the world through Adam, and because of sin, death also afflicted the human condition. In his testimony that sin along with death originated with Adam and thereafter enslaved all humanity to both sin and death, Paul is arguing on at least two levels. First, there is an argument at work here that is in solidarity with frequent prior and contemporary Jewish writings, namely, "that Adam's sin brought death on all his descendants."[12] Second, it is also clear that Paul argues that the consequences of Adam (and Eve's) sin extend to the whole human race, Jews and Gentiles alike. "Death," Paul remarks, "spread [literally, "to pass through"] to all because all have sinned" (v. 12b). Such a "passing through," Ernst Käsemann comments, "allows death to spread across the generations like an infectious disease. It is a curse in the texture of earthly life which ineluctably affects every individual."[13]

Did all sin because of Adam's sin? interpreters have asked from the ancient church. The answers have varied from the hearty affirmative response of those holding the doctrine of original sin (which is not Paul's chief concern here) to those who maintain as many origins to sin and death as there are human beings (a doctrine termed "polygenism" as opposed to the "monogenism" of the original-sin doctrine).[14] The doctrine of original sin aside, however, it is clear that Paul intends to specify Adam as the author of sin and death just as he will proclaim Christ the author of life.[15]

In the following two verses (13–14), Paul briefly follows up on his assertion that Jews and Gentiles all have become bondservants to sin and death. Waiting for further development, however, is this typological relationship between Adam and Christ. The apostle to the Gentiles does not want the equation flattened out to the extent that Christ simply undoes what Adam has done, the former erasing the condition the latter has introduced. "But the free gift is not like the trespass," Paul announces (v. 15). There is an immeasurable "much more" (*pollō mallon*) to the grace of Christ as opposed to the sin of Adam. So Paul articulates this point precisely: "And the free gift is not like the effect of the one man's sin" (v. 16). Now Paul expands on this dialectic between Adam and Christ, all the while reminding the reader of the "much

Adam	Christ
sin (v. 16a)	(who is sinless)
judgment (v. 16b)	grace (v. 15b)
condemnation (v. 16c)	justification (v. 16b)
death (v. 17a)	abundance of grace (v. 17b), the free gift of righteousness, and life (v. 17c)

more" of Christ. The sequence in verses 16-19 may be sketched as follows:

For those in Christ, there is this "abundance of grace" and the gift of life that more than restores what Adam and all humanity lost. These "free gifts" are offered to Jew and Gentile alike and are manifestations of the sheer grace of God.

The last section of the pericope, verses 18-19, serve as a summary of this dialectical relationship between Adam and Christ. Christ is the anti-type to Adam, but "much more." Then, picking up the thread he had left back in the opening section of the text, Paul returns to the significance of the gift of the law. Ironically, sin did not diminish with Moses, but as God's law was violated, it grew exponentially, "the trespass multiplied" (v. 20a). Paul then adds, "but where sin increased, grace abounded all the more" (v. 20b). The "much more" that is Christ's abundant grace offers not only the free gifts of forgiveness and the rest, but eternal life as well (v. 21b).

Preachers who responsibly interpret Paul's letters will be invited and challenged to proclaim a gospel with relevance for communal as well as individual existence.
—Brad R. Braxton[16]

THE GOSPEL
MATTHEW 4:1-11 (RCL, BCP, LFM)

Matthew's temptation story is not that of Mark's Gospel. There are no intimations of Eden—with the wild beasts near Jesus at the close of the forty days and angels doing him table service (Mark 1:13). Jesus is not here presented, therefore, as the new Adam. Rather, with such elaboration of the testing there in the wilderness, Matthew and Luke share a common tradition that draws strong parallels between Israel in the wilderness (where they failed the time of testing) and Jesus in this wilderness (where he gloriously passed the test). Moreover, as Robert Gundry comments, "Matthew shows a special interest . . . in a comparison between Jesus and Moses, a comparison already introduced in 2:13, 16, 20-21."[17] And contrary to any ecclesial temptation toward antinomianism, Gundry adds that "Moses stands for law."[18] So laying aside frequent references to the Markan tradition, it will be important to keep Luke's rendition of this tripartite temptation narrative in mind. Differences between the two are both major and obvious—the very order of the three tests—as well as not so obvious, yet in some cases also important. The former issue, though, calls for our initial attention. The Gospel of Luke orders the three temptations in the following sequence: (1) the stone into bread temptation, (2) the offer of the glory and authority of all the world's kingdoms, and (3) the testing of God by Jesus' throwing himself from the Temple pinnacle (Luke 4:5-13). Most scholars believe Matthew's ordering, however, to represent the early tradition more carefully. Jesus is tempted to alleviate his hunger by turning the stones into bread, he is tempted to throw himself down from the pinnacle of the Temple, and he is finally offered all the kingdoms of the world in exchange for the worship of the devil. This Matthean sequence radiates outward from a personal temptation in the wilderness to one that plays to all of Israel, and finally, to a gambit involving all the kingdoms of the world and their splendor. Meanwhile, a number of less noticeable features are significant within Matthew's version of the narrative, and the preacher will want to take note of these distinctions.

Matthew begins by indicating that it was through the Spirit's leading that Jesus come into the wilderness. This forty-day season is of God and not of the devil. However, he was led there by the Spirit "to be tempted by the devil" (4:1). Right from the start, we see that the story will entail a cosmic struggle between Jesus, the Son of God, and the tempter, the devil. "The passage is almost entirely involved in narrative oppositions," Daniel Patte notes, "each polemical exchange forming an opposition."[19] But even before the first exchange, the Evangelist develops a deep tension. Jesus "fasted forty days and forty nights, and afterwards he was famished" (v. 2). Matthew first draws our attention to Jesus' wilderness action—he fasts.[20] The tension begun here will be a thread in the warp of the entire Gospel; there are times for feasting and times for fasting (see especially 9:14-15). Then, the narrator intensifies the reader's sense of the duration of the fast by expanding the time in the wilderness to "forty days and forty nights," thereby also aligning the passage more closely to Deuteronomy 9:9-18.[21] At the end of the forty days and forty nights of fasting, "he was famished." Now the devil attempts to exploit this situation. What ensues, then, is a conflict with no higher stakes imaginable.

The first and second temptations begin with "the tempter" (*ho peirazōn*) addressing Jesus, "If you are the Son of God ..." Commentators are divided on the intention of the devil's opening address. Is the tempter attempting to create doubt in Jesus' understanding (a knowledge of himself revealed at his baptism) or to transform his will (those convictions that shape Jesus' life and work)? On one hand, some scholars interpret the conditional, "If you are ..." as an attempt by the devil to cast doubt. Hence, Warren Carter maintains that "[t]he use of 'if' questions whether God's declaration about Jesus as God's Son (3:17) is either adequate or truthful." Carter adds that the tempter "suggests its veracity requires proof."[22] On the other hand, other interpreters see the devil's causing a turn in Jesus' will as the ultimate goal. The devil's intent may be that of causing Jesus to doubt the truth of God's revelation at his baptism or to change his will. Perhaps both are at stake when the tempter begins with these "if" questions!

The first "if" in the tempter's arsenal is quite personal and immediate to one

Convincing someone to do something is not forcing the person to do something against his or her will (this would be coercion), but leading the person *to want to do something* (something not previously envisioned, or something else than what one is doing). . . . A temptation is the attempt to change a person's will from good to bad, and thus it aims at causing the person to want to do something wrong. —Daniel Patte[23] who is famished: "command these stones to become loaves of bread" (v. 3). Immediately, we are struck by the use of the plural "stones" and "loaves" as opposed to the singular in Luke's rendition. We recall that Matthew has related the Baptist's stern message about God's being able to raise up children of Abraham "from these stones" (3:9). Moreover, there may well be operating here a subtle allusion to the devil "as a type of the Jewish leaders who opposed Jesus."[24] Jesus responds to the devil, "It is written . . . ," and he delivers the longer quote from Deuteronomy 8:3. The temptation involves the use of God's power to satisfy the hunger brought on by Jesus' fasting. To be sure, he needs bread—as do so many hungry people—and he will multiply the loaves (note the plural) in the feeding of the five thousand (14:13-21). The issue here in this first temptation, however, "resides in causing Jesus to act at the devil's behest."[25] Such action would, of course, render Jesus incapable of acting on God's behalf. Warren Carter uncovers another layer of importance to Jesus' response to this first temptation:

> If Jesus supplies his own bread at the devil's command, he acts for his own benefit as the elite do. He ceases to trust and obey God, contrary to his own subsequent teaching (6:25-35). In not trusting God, he yields to the devil's directives.[26]

Of course, not trusting in God's gracious provision was Israel's failure in their testing in the wilderness. Their attempted hoarding of the manna revealed a deeper failure. God's Son, then, is being tempted by the devil to imitate God's people in their tragic testing in the wilderness. The subsequent issue in Deuteronomy is also at stake here. Following the quote Jesus chose in reply to the tempter, there is this injunction: "Therefore keep the commandments of the LORD your God, by walking in his ways and fearing him" (Deut. 8:6). Jesus will keep these commandments; he will trust and obey.

Now, Jesus is taken to "the holy city" (tēn hagian polin) by the tempter, not "Jerusalem" as in Luke. The devil "took him" and "placed him on the pinnacle of the temple" (4:5). Now follows the second of the "if" questions. "If you are the Son of God, throw yourself down . . ." (v. 5a). The devil by now has caught on that this will be a duel of holy texts and so the tempter mimics Jesus, "for it is written." Now follows the citation from Psalm 91:11-12. However, the devil "omits the phrase 'in all your ways' because the deliberate throwing of oneself from a high perch does not correspond to accidental stumbling over a stone in one's path (as in the psalm)."[27] By way of this removal of Jesus to the Temple's pinnacle, the holy city and the Jewish people are now in play as witnesses and as potential subjects. Jesus stands high above the center of religious and political power, placed there by the tempter, and all that previously was so elevated in the holy city would be under his domination. Simply "throw yourself down." Jesus' response is prefaced by "Again it is written," and he returns to Deuteronomy for his citation: "Do not put the Lord your God to the test" (v. 7, quoting Deut. 6:16b). Of course, as Daniel Patte notes, this is precisely what the devil is attempting with Jesus, "namely, [to] try to cause God to do something by manipulating his will."[28] It is to be emphasized once more that the Deuteronomic context for these citations by Jesus is the exodus. In this case, the context for the quote includes the remembrance of the promise of "the good land that the LORD swore to your ancestors to give you" (Deut. 6:18). Ironically, the tempter has placed Jesus high above this land that God has given to Israel, given in spite of their failure in the time of testing.

Once again expanding the horizon of temptation, the devil now takes Jesus to "a very high mountain." Amy-Jill Levine observes that "Satan symbolically attempts to replace the traditional religious and political center, the Temple, with a new center under his own authority."[29] However, the precedent high mountains of Israel's story are numerous: from Abraham to Moses and Elijah. Carter reminds us that "the gods were thought to reside on Mt. Olympus."[30] And by way of anticipation, Matthew will narrate Jesus' gathering of the eleven on a mountain at the time of his ascension where he sends them to all nations. However, here the tempter has taken Jesus to this high mountain and shows him "all the kingdoms of the world [*tas basileias tou kosmou*] and their splendor [*doxan*]" (v. 8b). The devil adds, "All these I will give you . . ." (v. 9). "The offer," Carter remarks, "is staggering."[31] He adds,

> The devil claims to control the world's *empires/kingdoms* including Rome, the chief empire. . . . Here Rome is shown to be allied with the devil's reign. The devil's claim discloses the hidden power manifested in the external actions of the empire and vassals such as Herod (ch. 2).[32]

Interestingly, the tempter did not preface this strategy with an "if" question regarding Jesus' Sonship. However, the "if" does come in a most brutal and cynical invitation: "if you will worship me [*kynēsēs moi*]" (4:9). The verb for "worship"

The "testing" episode thus makes a theological as well as a Christological statement. Jesus will place his cause in the Father's hands right up to the obedience of the cross, because the Father he reveals and whose mission he serves is worthy of such trust.
—Brendan Byrne[33]

here has already appeared in one other brutal and cynical context in Matthew; Herod employs it while telling the Magi to return and tell him of the Christ Child's location. Then, as if to redeem the term, the Wise Men do find the Child and fall down and worship. It is such an act of adoration and awe seen in the action of the Magi that Herod and the devil—already well aligned in this passage—cynically distort. Jesus' response is immediate and decisive: "Away with you, Satan!" (v. 10a). There is no such command in Luke's version of the temptations, this being the second in that Evangelist's sequence of the three encounters. One other novelty is present, though, in the Matthean text: finally, the tempter is named "Satan." The devil is the adversary, not of God, but against God and God's beloved Son. Moreover, by providing the tempter with the name "Satan," there is now a most powerful template in place when Jesus turns to rebuke Peter. Refusing to be taken aside and instructed as to his vocation by the apostle, Jesus exclaims, "Get behind me, Satan!" (16:23). Of course, with regard to the devil, there is no need to add "*opisō mou*" ("behind me"). For some indeterminate season, Satan is banished from the presence of the Son of God, but not before Scripture is once again brought to bear against the tempter. "For it is written," Jesus begins, "Worship the Lord your God, and serve only him" (v. 10). Deuteronomy is again quoted, but with two changes. First, the "fear" of God is transformed to the "worship" of God, a shift that is made because of the issue of false worship brought by Satan. Second, from Jesus' mouth the injunction adds "only," thereby intensifying the singularity of the worship and service of the living God. Once again, the context of the Deuteronomic quote is important. "Moses'

> Human everyday experiences are not dealt with in our narrative, but it is the question of who has power in the world, the devil whom Jesus does not serve and who has to quit the field, or God who sends his angels.
> —Ulrich Luz[34]

address to Israel reminds the Israelites not to forget God's liberating action in the exodus and to reject idolatry."[35] Jesus' word of rebuke to Satan even intensifies this commandment. "Then the devil left him" (v. 11a); Satan is dismissed.

In an instant, Jesus is apparently back in the wilderness rather than up on the very high mountain. A Markan tagline completes the narrative: "Suddenly, angels came and waited on him" (4:11b). The term "waited upon" does suggest the diaconal "doing table service." But in this Matthean context an even richer meaning possibly overlay the tale service.

> The ministering of angels to Jesus includes the serving of food, but in Matthew it also becomes an example for the ministry of "the sheep" to Jesus, through their kindness to the least of his brothers (25:44, unique to Matthew), and for the ministry to Jesus of "many women" who followed him as disciples (27:55).[36]

The ministry of the angels, which appears so suddenly following the ordeal, signifies that Jesus' fasting is completed and the bridegroom is about to begin his own ministry. This table service also is a foretaste of the ministry of many in the Gospel who will follow Jesus and even minister to him. God's new reign in Christ is already becoming clear and present.

Homiletical Strategies

I have already noted Matthew's fondness for triplet rhetoric systems. In this pericope, the tripartite scheme deals with the three temptations of Jesus in the wilderness, all at the hand of the devil. Each is certainly rich enough in meaning to be preached on its own (an approach I proposed for preaching from the triplet system for Ash Wednesday). However, the liturgical context of the First Sunday in Lent does not so clearly favor one element in the pericope as compared to Ash Wednesday. For parishes that are beginning the Lenten catechumenate on this day—either by a rite of enrollment or of sending[37]—the three particular temptations all relate to their Lenten journey toward baptism at the Great Vigil. Therefore, the approach I offer will be to explore each temptation in sequence for homiletical possibilities. One of the three could be explored in a homily in depth or all three could be more briefly examined. One must be careful, though, to keep the primary focus on the person of Jesus Christ who was tempted and who triumphed. There is a temptation for preachers to transform such a distinctive witness to the identity of Jesus Christ into a cipher representing the ways in which we encounter temptations in life.

- *"Command these stones to become loaves of bread."* Several issues commend themselves homiletically. I begin, however, by noting once more that the Matthean version of the temptations tradition offers Jesus "stones" rather than the Lukan "stone." This seemingly innocuous shift from the singular in Luke to the plural in Matthew has important consequences for the preacher. The singular—providing us with "a loaf of bread" in Luke 4:3—invites the analogy of the eucharistic loaf of bread (see Luke 22:19 and 24:30). On the other hand, the plural ("stones" to become "loaves") offers more resonance with the stories of the miraculous feedings (Matt. 14:17, 19 and 15:34, 36). Two further issues could be explored dealing with the image of the loaves and the identity of Jesus. On one hand, liturgical scholars have noted that while the Sacrament of Holy Baptism involves water, a sheer gift of God's gracious creation, the Sacrament of the Table involves bread and wine, both a product of the creation and of human agency. The issue for Jesus seen in this light, then, is the devil's enticement to bypass the human labor and careful tending that result in loaves of bread. The Son of God will not dehumanize the loaves that he will later divide to feed the multitudes! A second issue has appeared in the exegetical commentary above, but it bears repeating:

> If Jesus supplies his own bread at the devil's command, he acts for his own benefit as the elite do. He ceases to trust and obey God, contrary to his own subsequent teaching (6:25-35). In not trusting God, he yields to the devil's directives.[38]

The homiletical implications of this insight are manifold and immediate for the American church.

• *"Throw yourself down."* The temptation obtains both for the Son of God and for members of his church. For both, the devil invites some very risky behavior with a distorted promise that God will save us from the consequences. Especially for those ordained to the ministry of Word and Sacrament, there appears to be a growing softness with regard to this temptation. One physician recently commented that forty years ago, the clergy were among the healthiest groups in American society. Now, he added, the clergy as a group have some of the poorest health, due

mainly to stress, lifestyle choices, and addictive behavior. It would appear, then, that the clergy have succumbed to the devil's temptation to "throw yourself down." Of course, this issue of wellness and lifestyle choices afflicts many laity as well. The same (il)logic applies to all: we pray for those who have become ill due to addictions to food, alcohol, or tobacco. Will we also name the addictions themselves that are examples of testing God?

The Son of God, however, resists this temptation and will not throw himself from the Temple pinnacle. He will not put the Lord God to the test. It was noted in the commentary that the devil has taken Jesus to a place high above not only the Temple in the holy city, but also a pinnacle that towers over the Promised Land. As David's Son, the one "who is to shepherd my people Israel" (2:6), Jesus is already the ruler of this land. He has no need to be on a Temple pinnacle to achieve that status. He is already Emmanuel.

Jesus' first temptation is to "command these stones to become bread," a curious echo of God's first task to humans in Genesis, namely, to create nourishments by tilling the soil. Jesus responds, "One does not live by bread alone." One of my favorite cartoons has a character standing in front of a huge ice cream sundae saying exactly those words. Even Scripture can be quoted to fulfill our own desires rather than point us to living and acting for others so that all can have bread. —Glen Nengson[39]

• *"Fall down and worship me."* This last temptation is the most direct and the most obscene. Satan now plays his biggest card—taking Jesus to "a very high mountain." Again, the ironies heap up. Jesus will reveal his glory upon a very high mountain when he is transfigured before the disciples. But that vision on the mountain of transfiguration will be bracketed both before and after by clear predictions of his passion, death, and resurrection (16:21; 17:22-23). But as for "the kingdoms of the world and their splendor," they already belong to God who has given all authority to Jesus (28:18). Herod and Satan both speak of "worship" that is idolatrous and ultimately evil. Jesus insists that only the Lord God is worthy of such homage and praise.

For God's people in Christ, this temptation falls into its two component idolatries. On one hand, we are tempted to ascend to some privileged pinnacle in this post-Christendom world. Of course, such a prospect is a delusion. The era of the church's privileged status in North America is now well behind us and we cannot return to that "pinnacle." On the other hand, the temptation comes with a built-in idolatry. Whenever we are tempted to worship anything or anyone other that the Triune God, we have yet again succumbed to this temptation. The alert preacher will provide specific examples of such idolatrous temptations as this sermon is being preached.

Notes

1. Claus Westermann, *Genesis 1–11: A Commentary*, trans. John J. Scullion (Minneapolis: Augsburg, 1984), 196.

2. Ibid., 223.

3. Walter Brueggemann, *Genesis,* Interpretation: A Bible Commentary for Teaching and Preaching (Atlanta: John Knox Press, 1982), 44.

4. Ibid., 44–45.

5. Commentators frequently note the interplay between *ādām* ("man") and *ādām* ("soil"). See, for example, E. A. Speiser, *Genesis,* The Anchor Bible (Garden City, N.Y.: Doubleday, 1964), 16.

6. Westermann, *Genesis 1–11,* 222.

7. Brueggemann, *Genesis,* 46.

8. Brueggemann notes that the serpent functions as "a device to introduce the new agenda." He adds, "The serpent has been excessively interpreted" (p. 47).

9. "Prayer over the Catechumens," in *Rite of Christian Initiation of Adults, Study Edition* (Chicago: Liturgy Training Publications, 1988), 59.

10. See Westermann, *Genesis 1–11,* 240–45, for an in-depth analysis of the motif of knowing good and evil.

11. Brueggemann, *Genesis,* 48.

12. Thomas H. Tobin, *Paul's Rhetoric in Its Contexts: The Argument of Romans* (Peabody, Mass.: Hendrickson Publishers, 2004), 180.

13. Ernst Käsemann, *Commentary on Romans,* trans. and ed. Geoffrey W. Bromiley (Grand Rapids, Mich.: Wm. B. Eerdmans, 1980), 147.

14. See Joseph A. Fitzmyer, *Romans,* The Anchor Bible (New York: Doubleday, 1993), 405–10.

15. Tobin notes that this Adamic typology serves Paul well regarding his ongoing concern for the Gentiles and their relationship to the covenant. "Because [Adam] stands at the ultimate origin of both Jews and Gentiles, he serves as an apt foil to Christ, who for Paul unites both Jews and Gentiles." Tobin, *Paul's Rhetoric in Its Contexts,* 181.

16. Brad R. Braxton, *Preaching Paul* (Nashville: Abingdon Press, 2004), 16.

17. Robert H. Gundry, *Matthew: A Commentary on His Handbook for a Mixed Church under Persecution.* 2nd ed. (Grand Rapids, Mich.: Wm. B. Eerdmans, 1994), 54.

18. Ibid.

19. Daniel Patte, *The Gospel according to Matthew: A Structural Commentary on Matthew's Faith* (Philadelphia: Fortress Press, 1987), 51.

20. Gundry notes that only Matthew "uses the word for fasting." He adds that Jesus then commends this distinctive activity to the disciples in 6:16-18. Gundry, *Matthew*, 55.

21. Ibid., 54.

22. Warren Carter, *Matthew: Storyteller, Interpreter, Evangelist*, rev. ed. (Peabody, Mass.: Hendrickson, 2004), 127.

23. Patte, *The Gospel according to Matthew*, 52.

24. Gundry, *Matthew*, 55.

25. Warren Carter, *Matthew and the Margins: A Socio-Political and Religious Reading* (Sheffield, Eng.: Sheffield Academic Press, 2000), 108.

26. Ibid.

27. Gundry, *Matthew*, 57.

28. Patte, *The Gospel according to Matthew*, 53. Patte offers a cogent distinction between viewing Scripture as promise and conceiving it as a means of testing the faithfulness of God (or Jesus). See pp. 54–55.

29. Amy-Jill Levine, *The Social and Ethnic Dimensions of Matthean Social History* (Lewiston, N.Y.: Edwin Mellen Press, 1988), 200.

30. Carter, *Matthew and the Margins*, 110.

31. Ibid.

32. Ibid.

33. Brendan Byrne, *Lifting the Burden: Reading Matthew's Gospel in the Church Today* (Collegeville, Minn.: Liturgical Press, 2004),

34. Ulrich Luz, *Matthew 1–7: A Commentary*, trans. Wilhelm C. Linss (Minneapolis: Augsburg, 1989), 191.

35. Ibid., 112.

36. Gundry, *Matthew*, 55.

37. In the Roman Catholic Rite of Christian Initiation of Adults (RCIA), this First Sunday in Lent at the parish level may involve a liturgy for sending in which the inquirers are named and blessed as they are sent to the episcopal liturgy later in the day where they will be enrolled as catechumens. See *Rite of Christian Initiation of Adults, Study Edition* (Chicago: Liturgy Training Publication, 1988), 305–13.

38. Carter, *Matthew and the Margins*, 108.

39. Glen Nengson, "First Sunday of Lent," in *Hunger for the Word: Lectionary Reflections on Food and Justice, Year A*, ed. Larry Hollar (Collegeville, Minn.: Liturgical Press, 2004), 62.

SECOND SUNDAY OF LENT

FEBRUARY 17, 2008

REVISED COMMON	EPISCOPAL (BCP)	ROMAN CATHOLIC
Gen. 12:1-4a	Gen. 12:1-8	Gen. 12:1-4a
Psalm 121	Ps. 33:12-22	Ps. 33:4-5, 18-19, 20, 22
Rom. 4:1-5, 13-17	Rom. 4:1-5 (6-12) 13-17	2 Tim. 1:8b-10
John 3:1-17 or Matt. 17:1-9	John 3:1-17	Matt. 17:1-9

KEY THEMES

• On this Second Sunday in Lent we join either with Nicodemus in the dark or with Peter, James, and John in mountaintop brilliance. Both locations restate the Prologue of John: "the light shines in the darkness. . ."
• Birth from above may be rapid or prolonged. It is always a work of the Spirit and it always tears the fabric of normalcy.
• Some scholars propose that the Transfiguration is an out-of-place resurrection account. But while Moses and Elijah talk with Jesus about his "exodus" (Luke) on the mountain, only the Lord makes his passover from death to new life on the First Day.
• Of all the scandals of the faith, the claim that we are a people of God with Abraham as our ancestor is one of the most contrary to the spirit of the age.

TRANSFIGURATION: A MULTIPLE FEAST

The Festival of the Transfiguration may hold the record for frequency of observance within any given liturgical year.[1] For those observing the calendar of saints, Transfiguration has long been celebrated on August 6, while within the temporal calendar, Roman Catholic faithful also meet the Feast on the Second Sunday in Lent. Those within Episcopal and Protestant Communions that follow some version of the three-year lectionary and calendar observe Transfiguration on the last Sunday after the Epiphany (the Sunday immediately before Lent begins on Ash

Wednesday). Although these arrangements may seem rather scattershot, two themes are constants with regard to all three calendar locations. On one hand, each of the dates for the festival follows the precedent of the Gospel lessons with regard to Jesus' journey from the mount to the cross. That is, all of the Transfiguration festivals take the passion predictions surrounding the vision quite seriously; Jesus "must go to Jerusalem and undergo great suffering . . . and be killed, and on the third day be raised" (Matt. 16:21). On the other hand, the Transfiguration pericope itself invites the faithful to an almost Easter-like joy as the glory of the Lord is revealed to the disciples and to the church. How we arrived at our present situation of these multiple feasts of the Transfiguration, though, is an interesting story in itself.

Prior to the late twentieth-century revision of the calendar, the Transfiguration was celebrated in the West on the Second Sunday in Lent. This was occasioned by the fact that the day before was Ember Saturday, a time for ordinations.[2] The Gospel for that day was the Transfiguration narrative in Matthew, and because Lent II had been an "open" Sunday, Saturday's Gospel was repeated. (It is interesting to note that the Ember Saturday liturgy was particularly special in that it had four sets of collects and lessons preceding the epistle and Gospel, an indication of its use for ordination. These lessons continued to be used at ordinations on that Saturday up until the modern Roman revision of the Calendar.)

The Orthodox Church did not observe the Transfiguration on Lent II, but it is worth noting that it dedicated that Sunday to St. Gregory Palamas, whose writings make much of the uncreated light, and so the theme of light is maintained in a different way. The Orthodox have since the late fourth century celebrated the Transfiguration on August 6. Again, attention should be called to the fact that this is forty days before September 14, the Exaltation of the Cross, thus keeping a connection between Transfiguration and Calvary.

The icon for the Feast of the Transfiguration, according to its canon, always has a steep, pointed mountain. Christ stands on the summit, clothes in white, with halos of many colors surrounding him. Moses and Elijah appear in the upper corners of the icon, Moses holding the tablets of the Law and Elijah in his fiery chariot, both speaking to the Lord. And then there are the three chosen disciples: Peter, James, and John. They are sprawled in different directions with sandals flying.
—M. Basil Pennington[3]

There was a shared practice in the West of observing August 6 in honor of the Transfiguration, probably because of Eastern influence, but it was not until 1457 that Pope Callistus III extended it as a required observance in the West to commemorate the victory of John Hunyady over the Turks in a battle near Belgrade the previous year and which was announced at Rome on August 6.

The work of calendar and lectionary revision in the United States in the 1960s resulted in a reconsideration of the place of the Transfiguration in the Sunday cycle by non-Roman Catholic traditions. Transfiguration was placed on the Sunday before Lent, thus representing the last of the epiphanies prior to the resurrection.

It thus sums up the previous weeks and it becomes a hinge opening the way to Calvary. This dating of the festival was offered as an option as early as the 1958 Lutheran *Service Book and Hymnal,* although wider acceptance of this calendar location had to wait upon the reforms mandated at the Second Vatican Council of the Roman Catholic Church and the emergence of Episcopal and Protestant variants of the three-year lectionary. The Episcopal Church's *Services for Trial Use,* published in 1971, introduced this use of the last Sunday after Epiphany within the context of the new lectionary, and it was quickly adopted by others.

FIRST READING
GENESIS 12:1-4a (RCL, LFM)
GENESIS 12:1-8 (BCP)

The Old Testament lesson for the Second Sunday in Lent provides the assembly with nothing less than a new creation account following on the heels of the Edenic narrative of Lent 1. If the backdrop of the story of the first humans in the garden is that "God made the earth and the heavens" (2:4b), the force of the story in Genesis 12:1ff. is that God made a new people in the promise to Abram. In the former, the creation of the heavens and the earth are out of nothing (*ex nihilo*), while in the latter, God creates a people and their posterity out of barrenness. The beginning of chapter 12, then, represents a new beginning for the narrative begun in the Garden. "Indeed, it is perhaps the most important structural break in the Old Testament and certainly in Genesis."[4] Other parallels come to mind between the two creation stories. In the Garden there is disobedience, while with Abram there is obedience. The man and the woman leave the Garden in shame; Abram with Sarai begin their sojourn as the recipients of a divine promise. The Edenic creation story initiates a history of curse; the new creation narrative begins a history of blessing.[5] Covenant history, too, is begun at this new creation.

The pericope begins with God saying to Abram, "Go from your country and your kindred and your father's house to the land that I will show you" (12:1).[6] Now follows a series of five statements made by the Lord God to Abram (vv. 2-3a):

1. I will make of you,
2. I will bless you (*'aberekah*),
3. I will magnify your name,
4. I will bless those who bless you,
5. I will curse those who curse you.[7]

These five first-person statements of Yahweh make a series of promises to Abram, none of them based on any merit or virtue possessed by the patriarch. The sovereignty of God is exercised in the sheer grace of these promises. (One notation should be made regarding the NRSV translation of *mishppekhot* as "families" in verse 3: E. A. Speiser notes that the term is best understood as "communities" rather than "familes."[8]) These promises, we recall, are addressed by God to one whose wife "was barren; she had no child" (11:30). The One who speaks to Abram makes promises that are both sheer gift and sheer folly. Moreover, no signs or portents accompany them, only the Word of God.

In accord with the commands/promises, Abram begins his sojourn, taking with him Lot, Sarai, "the persons whom they had acquired in Haran; and they set forth to go to the land of Canaan" (v. 5). While earlier commentators were fond of speaking of this journey as that typical to desert nomads, something far more profound is at work here. "This text introduces the metaphor of journey as

a way of characterizing the life of faith."[9] After passing through Shechem and moving on to the oak[10] of Moreh, the narrator notes almost in passing, "At that time the Canaanites were in the land" (v. 6b). The comment is especially interesting in its matter-of-fact simplicity; the Canaanites are depicted neither as enemies or oppressors. Abram and his extended family are called to sojourn through their land. However, a further promise is made by Yahweh as Abram moves through Canaan: "To your offspring ["seed," *lezar'aka*] I will give this land" (12:7a). Therefore, Abram builds an altar "to the LORD, who had appeared to him" (12:7b). Now, a second metaphor is added to the earlier one of "journey." "Promised land" will from henceforth reside within the communal heart of the biblical people alongside the motif of "journey."

God loves this world. God loves the people within it. Though we have been tragically separated from God by sin, God's love has never been conditional. When we do not know that we are out of order, God loves us. When we do not want God to interrupt the selfish flow of our lives, God loves us. When we do not love ourselves (or anyone else), God loves us. God loves us individually; God loves humankind collectively. We are part of creation created in God's image—and God loves us!
—Abena Safiyah Fosua[11]

The two will have an enduring relationship, denoted by tension and by the periodic dominance of one over the other. Yet the paradoxical relationship remains. On one hand, as sojourners, God's people remain "strangers and foreigners on the earth," while on the other hand "seeking a homeland" (Heb. 11:13b-14a). The paradoxical tension is embodied in the last verse of the pericope; both journey and a deep sense of place are in play—both a gift of this God who promises such grace. Abram "moved on . . ." (the journey continues to the hill country east of Bethel) and there Abram "built an altar to the LORD and invoked the name of the LORD" (12:8). The altar is built on the promised "homeland" by Abram who sojourns as a "stranger and foreigner" on the earth.

RESPONSIVE READING
PSALM 121 (RCL)

The selection of Psalm 121 in response to the Old Testament narrative of the call of Abram and Sarai serves to emphasize the trustworthiness of God's providence. The word to our ancestors, Abram and Sarai, and to us is, "The LORD will keep your going out and your coming in from this time on and forevermore" (v. 8).

PSALM 33:12-22 (BCP)
PSALM 33:4-5, 18-19, 20, 22 (LFM)

The LFM begins the responsory psalm with the witness to God's righteousness and justice in verses 4-5. This lectionary then bypasses the well-known material in verses 12-17 and picks up the concluding verse in which the psalmist again witnesses to the faithfulness of God and the blessings of those who are faithful and who hope in God's love. Verse 21 is also omitted in the LFM ("For in God our hearts rejoice; in your holy name we trust," NAB). The BCP provides a more continuous reading, beginning with "Happy is the nation whose God is the LORD" (v. 12a), while omitting the LFM's interest in verses 4 and 5.

SECOND READING
ROMANS 4:1-5, 13-17 (RCL)
ROMANS 4:1-5 (6-12) 13-17 (BCP)

Paul offers the example of Abraham in response to his rhetorical questions and his affirmation in 3:27 and by way of an answer to the related issues in 3:31. In the former citation, boasting is excluded based not on law, but by "the law of faith"; in the latter (3:31), while holding to righteousness through faith, Paul affirms that the law is not overthrown. He now turns to Abraham and argues several points in verses 1-5. First, Paul acknowledges that the patriarch is "our ancestor according to the flesh [kata sarka]" (4:1). Thereby, Paul aligns himself with his Jewish tradition and community. Paul then moves on to raise the question of the source of Abraham's righteousness. If the patriarch had been made upright by virtue of his works—in obedience to the law—then Abraham would remain solely "our ancestor according to the flesh." Paul quotes Scripture, however, which states that "Abraham believed God, and it was reckoned to him as righteousness" (4:3, quoting Gen. 15:6 in the LXX). The Greek word translated "reckoned" (elogisthē) may also mean "credited," and is "a bookkeeping term figuratively applied to human conduct."[12] Joseph Fitzmyer expands on the term's implications for Paul's argument: "Abraham's faith was counted *by God* as uprightness, because God sees things as they are. Hence, this manifestation of Abraham's faith was *de se* justifying."[13]

The grace of God by which Abraham was counted as righteous is now interpreted in a figure containing contrasting systems of "reckoning." On one hand, one who works receives wages not as a gift, "but as something due" (v. 4). On the other hand, if one lacking any works trusts the God "who justifies the ungodly, such faith is reckoned as righteousness [*dikaiosynēn*]" (v. 5). Abraham did precisely this, and righteousness, therefore, comes only by such faith and trust rather than by works.

In the latter section of the lesson (vv. 13-17), Paul again picks up his argument for righteousness by faith with regard to Abraham. The apostle now brings the promises of God made to Abraham into the conversation. Those promises—including the promise that he would "inherit the world!"—did not come by the law. The argument that follows proceeds as follows:

1. The promises of God came to Abraham through faith and not the law.
2. If only adherents of the law can inherit the promises, (4:14a) then
3. "Faith is null and the promise is void" (v. 14b).

Left unspoken for the moment is Paul's final assertion: "Since this cannot be so, the promise must be mediated through faith."[14] However, Paul immediately follows through on his argument's implications. The promises of God depend on faith, and upon this foundation, they (the promises) are guaranteed "to all his descendants, not only to the adherents of the law but also to those who share the faith of Abraham (for he is the father of all of us" (v. 16b). Abraham's "seed" (*spermati*) therefore includes Jews and Gentiles—a radical claim of the gospel! Paul once again quotes Scripture (Gen. 17:5) in support of his argument: "I have made you the father of many nations." Commentators note that the Greek, *ethnōn*, can be rendered as "nations" or as "Gentiles." Once again, an unstated conclusion is unavoidable. Only if this Scripture is in error could Abraham's seed be limited only to those of the flesh. But the God to whom Scripture attests "gives life to the dead and calls into existence the things that do not exist" (v. 17b). Such gracious acts of creation were manifest to Abraham and Sarah (both quite "dead" with regard to heirs) and to all Abraham's seed. The promises come by "the righteousness of faith" (v. 13).

2 TIMOTHY 1:8b-10 (LFM)

The brief epistle lesson in the Roman Catholic lectionary corresponding to the Transfiguration Gospel text resonates most fully with that event as it closes with the witness to the grace that "has now been revealed through the appearing [*epiphaneias*] of our Savior [*sōtēros*] Jesus Christ" (v. 10a). This "epiphany" is seen most fully within the ministry of Jesus at his transfiguration; his glory is revealed on the high mountain. However, this short lection is making other claims as well. Oddly omitting the beginning of the pericope (8a: "Do not be ashamed, then, of the testimony about our Lord or of me his prisoner"), the latter portion of the verse deals with Paul's invitation to Timothy to join with him in suffering for the gospel, "relying on the power [*dynamin*] of God" (v. 8b). With regard to the material between this opening and the closing reference to the epiphany of this grace in Christ, verse 9 contains several weighty themes. Our God "saved us and called us with a holy calling" (v. 9). These profound mysteries of the gospel are located in the past, yet are made "a present reality in the liturgical recitation and preaching."[15] To become ashamed of the gospel, therefore, is to leave our salvation and calling only in the past. Yet through the liturgy and preaching of the church, our salvation is always made contemporaneous through the power of God, most centrally in the sacrament of the Holy Eucharist. Moreover, this grace "was given to us in Christ Jesus before the ages began [literally, "before eternal times"]" (v. 9b). Such a glorious heritage for those saved and called! But the epiphany "has now been revealed " (v. 10a). Celebrating the Transfiguration, up on the mountain with Jesus, beholding his glory, will we be ashamed of the gospel and will we shirk from our calling? This epistle urges readers—and worshipers—to hold fast to the power of God that is in Christ Jesus.

> Many texts claim that Abraham is the ancestor of particular Gentile peoples. . . . Paul, however, shows no interest in Abraham as a culture bringer or as the ancestor of any particular Gentile people or group of peoples. His interest is in the more general notion that Abraham was the father of many nations and that these nations would prosper or be blessed because of him.
> —Thomas H. Tobin[16]

THE GOSPEL
JOHN 3:1-17 (RCL, BCP)

The appearance of this "leader of the Jews" is timed to put Nicodemus in the very worst light. First, we have just heard of Jesus' actions in the Temple and his response to those who sought a sign from him (2:18-19). That many were believing because of the signs he was doing was not regarded by Jesus as a glorious movement of faith. So he "would not entrust himself to them, because he knew all people and needed no one to testify about anyone; for he himself knew what was in everyone" (2:24-25). So now, Nicodemus enters the story, coming at night. Here is "strike one." In the Gospel of John, "[d]arkness and night symbolize the realm of evil, untruth, and ignorance."[17] Just which of these unsavory qualities this leader possesses is a matter yet to be determined. But he already does not stand in the best light! Then, to make matters worse, Nicodemus blurts out a rather pompous introduction, beginning, "Rabbi, we know . . ." (3:2). He acts both as a spokesperson for the power elite and also sounds like a junior-grade prophet (who discerns the inner state of Jesus that allows for such signs). Now, Jesus has just challenged this power elite in Jerusalem in the Temple action and has expressed distrust of anyone who bases their faith solely in his signs. Moreover, as the narrator just informed us, Jesus himself "knew what was in everyone" (2:25b). Now, Nicodemus comes to Jesus by night and proceeds to claim knowledge of what is in Jesus! Wes Howard-Brook captures this mood of suspicion the Evangelist has evoked in the readers. "Before [Nicodemus] can open his mouth, careful readers of the fourth gospel will likely distrust him deeply."[18] Then when Nicodemus opens his mouth, he speaks with the plural "we," blithely enthuses about the signs that Jesus has performed, and assumes prophetlike insight into Jesus' inner self. In just this brief time, Nicodemus has ratified our suspicions that he is in the dark.

Jesus' response is interesting in that he does not respond directly to any of these opening problematics by Nicodemus. Rather, he begins with a most grave statement, "Very truly, I tell you . . . ," continuing, "no one can see the kingdom of God without being born from above" (3:3). We note first that the term, "kingdom of God," which is so prevalent in the Synoptics (along with the Matthean equivalent, "kingdom of heaven), is extremely rare in the Fourth Gospel, appearing only here and then two verses later.[19] But most of the attention of commentators is drawn to the Greek term, *anōthen*, a double-meaning word equally translated as "again" and "from above." In a response that will become a familiar motif to the reader, Nicodemus seizes on the "earthly" meaning of the term, which then provides Jesus with the opportunity to unveil the "heavenly" meaning. So, Nicodemus takes the meaning of "born again" to its most literal and absurd extreme. He asks how anyone can reenter his or her mother's womb and be born again. Jesus' response once more begins most solemnly: "Very truly, I tell you . . . ," adding, "no one can enter the kingdom of God [here, the only other use of the term in John's Gospel] without being born of water and Spirit" (v. 5).[21] Now, Jesus adds the duality of "flesh" and "spirit." "What is born of the flesh is flesh, and what is born of the Spirit is spirit" (v. 6). An important caution is worth noting at this point. We are not being presented with a Hellenistic dualism of flesh and spirit, especially since Jesus refers to the entirety of a person prior to birth from above as being of the flesh and, likewise, the whole being of anyone born from above is of the spirit. Raymond Brown helpfully adds that for the Gospel of John, "'flesh' emphasizes the weakness and mortality of the creature (not the sinfulness as in Paul); Spirit, as opposed to flesh, is the principle of divine power and life operating in the human sphere."[22]

The flesh-spirit duality is amplified by Jesus, reemphasizing the necessity of birth "from above" (v. 7). At this point, this "Rabbi" makes a statement that com-

> While natural birth is contrasted to divine birth and flesh to spirit, flesh in and of itself is not condemned—but neither can it effect new birth.
> —Marianne Meye Thompson[20]

162

THE SEASON
OF LENT
―――――
RICHARD L.
ESLINGER

pletely befuddles and amazes Nicodemus. The meanings layer upon each other as Jesus employs double-meaning words at two critical locations. "The wind," Jesus begins (which is one possible translation of *pneuma* along with "the Spirit") "blows where it chooses" (v. 8a). Now a second double-meaning term is added to confound Nicodemus even further: "and you hear the sound of it" (with *phōnēn* being rendered equally as "sound" and as "voice"). In either case, "you do not know where it comes from or where it goes" (v. 8b). It is also this way, Jesus adds, for everyone born of the Spirit. Remaining in the dark, Nicodemus weakly answers, "How can these things be?" (v. 9). He will now fade away from the scene after hearing Jesus' chastisement: "Are you a teacher of Israel, and yet you do not understand these things?" (v. 10). At least in this opening dialogue near the first Passover in the Gospel, the clear answer is "No." Nicodemus does not understand these things; he is not ready to be born from above.

As if to underline the Cheshire Cat-like disappearance of Nicodemus, Jesus' pronouncement alters its direction, signaled by the shift from the first-person singular "you" in verse 11 to the plural thereafter. Jesus tells these others (John's church/the perennial readers?) of the descent and ascent of the Son of man, to and from heaven. Then, an image is borrowed from the exodus narrative, one that will become intimately associated with the Johannine motif of Jesus' "hour." Referring to the lifting up of the serpent by Moses in the wilderness, "so must the Son of Man be lifted up, that whoever believes in him may have eternal life" (v. 15). Although the verb in Numbers 21:9 speaks of the serpent being "placed" rather than "lifted up," the Evangelist accomplishes several tasks by means of the new perspective on the sign[23] of the serpent. The imagery of this "lifting up" of the Son of Man effectively weaves the crucifixion, the resurrection, and the ascension of the Lord into one seamless garment. Moreover, the alignment with Moses also brings with it a profound contrast. "If Moses' 'raising up' of the serpent gave 'life' (Num. 21:9), the 'raising up' of the Human One gives '*eternal* life'."[24]

> In the death of his Son the Father offers life *to his enemies*. This is the "ultimate insanity" of the revelation that this narrator is trying to convey to his readers. To believe in that insanity is what requires a rebirth through the Spirit.
> —Paul S. Minear[25]

For the first time in the Gospel, eternal life (*zōēn aiōnion*) has been brought into play. It functions as a climax to the words regarding the lifting up of the Son of man (in verse 15) and now will serve the same role in 3:16. However, the spatial imagery is reversed. In 3:15, the imagery is shaped by the vertical movement of ascent—of Jesus raised on a cross, raised from the dead, and raised to glory. But in the next verse, there is a vertical descent as God gives the Son to the world. The profound warrant for such a gift is that God loved (*ēgapēsen*) the world. Therefore, "everyone who believes in him may not perish but may have eternal life" (v. 16b). This love is manifest at the sign of the loaves and fishes (6:1-15) where Jesus directs the disciples to gather the fragments "so that nothing may be lost [literally, 'perish']" (6:12). The theme of divine condescension continues in the next statement: "Indeed, God did not send the Son into the world to condemn the world, but in order that the world might be saved through him" (3:17). Those who refuse this love and insist on darkness will judge themselves. But the Word becomes flesh and lives among us as an expression of the love (*agapē*) of the Father. Paul Minear adds,

> For us to read this episode as an encounter between Jesus and Nicodemus is entirely natural. I am convinced, however, that this episode becomes much more illuminating when read as a major segment of John's conversation with his readers.... He is looking back on the story he is telling (God *gave*, God *sent*, the light *has come*) and he is looking at a present period in which crucial decisions are being made, choices of believing and hating and loving and living.[26]

MATTHEW 17:1-9 (LFM, RCL alt.)

The story of the transfiguration follows immediately upon Peter's confession (Matt. 16:13-20), Jesus' passion prediction (vv. 21-23), an invitation to discipleship and the way of the cross (vv. 24-26), and the promise of the glorious return of the Son of man (vv. 27-28). The context is significant for Matthew as the "vision" (17:9) will touch upon each of these themes. Moreover, the temporal placement of the event "Six days later . . ." (17:1) directly connects the vision with the prior narrative sequence.[27] As the narrative opens, Jesus "took with him Peter and James and his brother John and led them up a high mountain, by themselves" (17:1). Once more, Matthew provides a high mountain for a profound and revealing event, consistent with the Markan account. The transfiguration itself is announced and described in highly poetic strophes:

> and he was transfigured before them,
> and his face shone like the sun,
> and his clothes became dazzling white.[28]

The opening line speaks of Jesus' "metamorphosis." The verb points to a visible change or transformation and is a term familiar to both Jewish and Gentile auditors.[29] The second line regarding the effect of this transformation on Jesus' face is absent in Mark's rendition. Clearly, if Matthew's christological intent is to present Jesus as the new Moses, such a shining face will serve as a significant pointer. The description of Jesus' dazzling white clothes returns to follow the Markan text, though the comparison to any earthly bleaching is omitted. The clothing of dazzling white in both

Gospels evokes images of the resurrection and the parousia. Warren Carter adds that white garments "can also indicate martyrdom (Rev. 3:5, 18; 4:4; 6:11; 7:9, 13)."[30]

There is now a sudden appearance of Moses and Elijah, "talking with him." Matthew prefaces the statement with *idou* (the RSV and NAB, "Behold!"). We also note that Matthew has reordered the Markan sequence of these figures. No longer does "Elijah with Moses" appear, but the more traditional "law and prophets" sequence is followed. Also of importance is the address Peter uses in making his "constructive" suggestion to Jesus. In Mark, Peter begins, "Rabbi," while in Matthew, the recurring title "Lord" (*kyrie*) is used. (This may also reflect Mark's more negative assessment of the faith of the Twelve.) Peter continues by saying, "it is good for us to be here" (v. 4). However, the apostle shifts from the plural to the singular as he proposes building the three dwellings or tents.[31] At this point also, there may not be for Matthew as negative a judgment on Peter's proposal as in Mark; the former deletes entirely Mark's comment about Peter not knowing what to say and ascribing fear as the motive. However, the proposal is rendered obsolete while Peter is still describing his project. "While he was still speaking, suddenly a bright cloud overshadowed them" (v. 5). Only Matthew provides the descriptor, "bright" (*phōteinē*), an image that links this new appearance with Jesus' brightly shining face. The "overshadowing" of the cloud certainly evokes the scene on Sinai where Moses was greeted with the presence of God, establishing yet another parallel between Moses and Jesus.[32] Once again, the NRSV employs "suddenly" to translate *idou*. The NAB, however, retains "behold" in both verses 3 and 5. (While somewhat archaic, the use of "behold" in the NAB retains the visual quality of *idou*, lost completely in the NRSV's "suddenly.") Now, from the cloud a voice announces, "This is my Son, the Beloved; with him I am well pleased" (v. 5b). The heavenly voice repeats the words that were heard at Jesus' baptism (3:17), although the audience on the high mountain is restricted to the three disciples, perhaps Moses and Elijah, and, of course, the Beloved Son. The voice from the cloud adds one command not heard at the Jordan: "listen to him!" (*akouete*). The ending in the Greek is emphatic and is rather puzzling in a vision with all its "beholds." That is, within the scope of the pericope, while Jesus was discovered speaking to Moses and Elijah, the disciples were not a party to that conversation. If the disciples are to obey the voice from the overshadowing cloud, they will need to recall the words of the Lord spoken to Peter and the others before he led the three up the mountain and be attentive in the future.

The voice from the cloud now brings the response Mark had ascribed to the disciples at an earlier location in the narrative. Not only are the disciples stricken with fear (NAB: "very much afraid"), but Matthew also adds that upon hearing the voice, "they fell to the ground" (17:6). Ironically, as Daniel Patte notes, "Instead of being put in relationship with heaven by this direct revelation from heaven, they fall on their faces. . . ; they turn away from heaven."[33] Overcome by fear, they fall to the ground.[34] The story has now gained a strong auditory quality. Immediately after the voice announces, "*akouete!*" ("listen!") the disciples "*akousantes*" ("heard"). It is at this critical location in the story that Matthew now focuses our attention on the agency of Jesus. Three actions mark the Lord's response to this scene of his fallen, fear-ridden followers. He *came* to them, *touched* them, and *speaks* to them. Each of the actions merits attention. In most other stories in the Gospel, as Robert Gundry notes, "others approach Jesus." He adds: "Here he has to approach them because fear took hold of them when they heard the affirmation of his divine sonship and the command to hear him."[35] Second, Jesus touches them. This intimate gesture both reassures and also invites recall; Jesus has healed the sick with such a touch. Finally, Jesus speaks to them. He announces, "Get up [NAB: "Rise"] and do not be afraid" (v. 7). We wonder, Will these three be able to hear and obey? They look up to Jesus—being still in a prone position—and "they saw no one except Jesus himself alone" (17:8). Patte comments insightfully:

> Note that in 19:9 the disciples see Jesus alone. It is Jesus in his human form, no longer Jesus transfigured in the company of Moses and Elijah, who can alone be seen without fear by the disciples. As long as the disciples have a human perspective (17:4), they can receive the revelation from the Father (as Peter did, 16:17) only because they have an intimate, physical relationship with Jesus (the touch, the I-you direct relationship expressed by his words . . .).[36]

The scene concludes with their coming down the mountain. "Jesus ordered them, "Tell no one about the vision until after the Son of Man has been raised from the dead" (v. 9). Only when these disciples have been transformed by the resurrection will their testimony be both true and devoid of fear.

O God, who before the passion of your only-begotten Son revealed his glory upon the holy mountain: Grant that I, beholding by faith the light of his countenance, may be strengthened to bear my cross, and be changed into his likeness from glory to glory . . .[37]

HOMILETICAL STRATEGIES

John 3:1-17

The Gospel lesson for this Second Sunday in Lent (from the Revised Common Lectionary and the Book of Common Prayer lectionary) presents a challenge to the preacher while offering at the same time a feast of Johannine theology and rhetorical brilliance. The challenge brought by the text derives from the Evangelist's abundance of literary motifs (double-meaning words especially) and multiplicity of literary forms. Regarding the latter challenge, we note that the pericope begins by providing every evidence to the reader that what follows will consist of an extended narrative, rich in character, plot, and intention. However, what begins in a narrative mode soon becomes a monological discourse by Jesus to the reader (or, better, the listeners within the church). Moreover, by the end of the lesson, it is not clear who is speaking to the church, Jesus or the narrator. (Perhaps this really matters only to editors of "red-letter" editions of the Bible. In the Fourth Gospel, Jesus and the narrator share the same ideological perspective.) At any rate, a narrative approach to this lesson will restrict the preacher to those portions of the text in which Nicodemus is an active partner in the dialogue. After verse 10, Nicodemus exits, stage right! A similar challenge obtains for preachers familiar with sermons in David Buttrick's mode of immediacy. Following Nicodemus's exit, the text spirals around images and testimonies that offer anything but a linear, plottable sequence for the sermon. However, this lesson would appear to be tailor-made for Buttrick's mode of reflectivity. Here, the preacher remains nearby the text while assembling a sermonic plot that will invite the listeners to reflection on issues presented in the text and contemporary context.[38] Contrary to preaching in the mode of immediacy, where the movement and structure of the sermon tracks closely with the biblical text, the mode of reflectivity offers numerous approaches to the sermon's movement and intention. One possible sermon in the reflective mode might be shaped with the following moves:

Move 1. "Born again" is having quite a rebirth in our world. Seems that almost everyone in public life has a story about their being born again. Especially for anyone who is caught in scandal or criminal behavior, we have grown used to next hearing from that person that they have now been born again. What a success for our beleaguered churches! At least when it comes to the possibility of new birth, we seem to have carried the day out there in the world.

Imagery: Perhaps an example system that invites the congregation to bring to consciousness several arenas within which "born again" thrives.

T.V. evangelists. Here, invite the listeners to channel-surf over to a religion network on cable. What is the preacher talking about? Being born again.

Celebrities. Among the 69,500,000 entries that pop up when you type "born again" on a Google search, some of the most interesting are those that keep score of the celebrities who confess to being born again. The lists go on and on, with some very surprising names.

"Born again" is now part of American vernacular. There is even a California company called "Born Again Boards," a maker of upscale surfboards.

Move 2. Problem is, for so many on these "born again" lists, it looks for all the world as if their lives remain "of the flesh" rather than "of the Spirit." Ask yourself, Where are the fruits of these born-again ones? Or wonder, What about the communities of faith where they have become members? And recall the scandals, too, where it was discovered that it was all talk and no walk.

Imagery: Here, an illustration from recent news of someone who talked of being born again, but whose actions were exposed by the light to be of the flesh. (If the preacher decides to deploy a story here, please provide only one. Multiple story-illustrations compete against one another and may produce confusion rather than clarity in the congregational hearing.)

Move 3. But what if we took our baptism seriously? I mean, many of us have been born through water and the Spirit; we have gone down into the waters of our salvation and we have been anointed with the Holy Spirit. Remember how we renounced Satan and all the spiritual forces of evil? Recall how we affirmed our faith in Christ? (The specific renunciations and confessions of faith should be taken from the baptismal liturgies of the parish's communion.)

Imagery: For those parishes devoting themselves in these Lenten days to the forming of catechumens who will be baptized at Easter, specific rites of renunciation and confession of faith may be brought as examples.

Move 4. And here is such great good news. Eternal life is at the heart of this gift of birth from above. Not only that, for those born of water and the Spirit, eternal life is a gift that begins now. Even in the midst of the present darkness, God loves the world so much that all who believe in his Son will have eternal life.

Imagery: Here is the opportunity for celebration. Since the move deals with eternal life as a present gift as well as a future promise, the preacher will need to offer examples that are communal rather than remain with only the individual and bring both contemporary as well as heavenly images to consciousness. Who are examples of eternal life lived in the present? Ask what people come to mind who are living the Johannine virtues of witness, hospitality, and *agape* love.

Matthew 17:1-9

Matthew's account of the transfiguration is so richly detailed and powerful that it calls for some sort of narrative telling. That is, one would not want to deprive the assembly of the gift of being located within this story and being a party to this journey with Jesus up the high mountain. Since the pericope is not that long, even a homily at Mass on this Second Sunday in Lent can "run the story" rather than simply extract a theme or two. In this approach to method, the plot of the homily is basically that of the biblical story and the dominant point of view will be from the perspective of the disciples. With regard to the question of contemporizing the story, the preacher will decide upon a number of locations in the narrative where the story may be paused and contemporary analogies developed out of the lived experience of the listeners. With such a strategy in mind, I will leave the enjoyment of shaping the storytelling itself to the preacher and identify several locations along the way where these contemporary excursuses might be located. I will also suggest possible strategies for imaging those locations out of the assembly's lived experience. A second strategy will be employed along the way—that is, providing "contemporary cues." Here, I will not develop a full-blown illustration of example as I pause the narrative. Rather, I will simply "salt" the storytelling with brief cues out of contemporary experience. We may identify these excursuses and contemporary cues as follows:

• *Jesus leads the disciples up this high mountain.* As a contemporary cue, one could bring to communal consciousness the sensory experiences of climbing such a mountain—especially for the disciples grown accustomed to life at sea level! The sound of sandals on gravel and shale, the thinning air and out-of-breath puffing, the feeling of the cool but thinner air, the wish that Jesus would pull up for a break in the ascent—the list of possible images goes on. Since one will certainly want to image the bodily experience later of laying flat on the stone knoll and of being touched by Jesus, it is valuable to orient the assembly to bodily feelings at this early juncture.

• *Jesus is transfigured.* In this excursus, one will want to achieve two goals: (1) provide some analogy to Matthew's portrayal of the transfigured Jesus and (2) sense some of the wonder and glory of that vision. Many contemporary experiences of "transfigured" bright figures abound in our culture. They have become common fare in all sorts of films thanks to digital technology. Some of these may seem to "fit" as examples of a transfiguration. The preacher will need to exercise extreme care here, however. "Close" may be alright in horseshoes, but not in developing analogies to biblical imagery! For example, a striking scene in Harry Potter may come to mind: *Harry is alone at a pond deep in a nighttime woods. He lies at the water's edge, water becoming ice. Those awful dementers gather about him, like so many vultures. They swoop down, attacking and sucking his very life-force from him. Suddenly* (idou) *from across the pond, a bright and shining figure appears and its light grows and expands to surround Harry with brightness. The dementers break off their attack and flee away.* In this image, several elements seem to dovetail with the transfiguration account: the bright, mysterious light and the white radiance of the figure. On the other hand, too many elements in this image fail to provide analogy, or even openly conflict with the biblical story. First, there is a low-lying pond in the Potter example and a high mountain in Matthew. Second, while a dementer may serve as some kind of analogy to Satan, the tempter is not depicted as being anywhere near this mountain with Christ's glory being revealed. Third, Harry is prone on the ground while the disciples have not yet "hit the dirt," and finally, the ideological foundations of the two narratives differ widely and wildly. The preacher will need to leave this "close, but not fitting" image for perhaps some other time.

One way to approach imaging such a transcendent scene is to provide less exalted imagery but add that the reality is "so much more" or "even more glorious." Each of the three lines of the hymnic description can find some more mundane example that will need a tagline as to Jesus' transfiguration being "even more glorious." First, the line that speaks of transfiguration itself could pick up an image system derived from Natalie Sleeth's song, "Hymn of Promise."[39] Second, the line that describes Jesus' face as shining like the sun could be imaged in the radiant faces of the couple who, after making solemn vows and giving and receiving of rings, are proclaimed husband and wife "in the name of the Father and the Son and the Holy Spirit" by the priest/minister. Finally, the dazzling white of Jesus' garments especially lend themselves to being imaged by the albs that will garb the catechumens after they come up from the waters of their saving at the Easter Vigil. (This image would be pastorally appropriate to the class of catechumens listening to the homily before being dismissed later in the liturgy.) In every case, we are reminded, the tagline would need to reemphasize the "how much more" of Jesus' transfiguration.

• *Moses and Elijah appear, talking with Jesus.* Since we have deployed a three-example system in the previous excursus, we will want to shape a different type of illustrative strategy at this point. Since the narrative is a vision, imaging this scene perhaps in the striking stained-glass window at The Church of the Transfiguration in Ironwood, Michigan, would be effective. Here, Christ is centered and in his stance of dominical instruction with Moses lower on the left and Elijah lower on the right. The former clutches his tablets of the Law while the latter holds the wheel. Both are completely attentive to what their Lord is speaking.[40]

> *Jesus, on the mountain peak,*
> *stands alone in glory blazing.*
> *Let us, if we dare to speak,*
> *join the saints and angels praising:*
> *Alleluia!*
> —Brian Wren[41]

• *Peter blurts out the scheme about the three dwellings.* He wishes that this moment could be enshrined here for all time. One possible example: in Gatlinburg, Tennessee, there is a tourist attraction called "Christus Gardens." The white building enshrines great moments in the Bible, including the transfiguration of the Lord. Peter would have been thrilled!

•*The bright cloud overshadows them all.* Here, the assembly could be invited to be up on a mountain overlook—where will depend on the congregation—with other members of a group (family, church visit, and so forth). The view is stunning and is in all directions. With no warning, a cloud sweeps up a ravine and over the mountaintop. All of a sudden, you have been "overshadowed." The feeling is strange—nothing can be seen, and the voices of the others are strangely muffled. You are isolated and detached from "earthly things." This was the experience of Peter and the others, with one thing more. The cloud was thick with the presence of the Holy God.

• *The voice from the cloud announces the Beloved Son and directs, "Listen to him."* Here again, for parishes conducting the Rite of Christian Initiation of Adults, the baptismal connection of this scene should not be lost. At the Jordan, on the mountain, and at our baptistery, these words continue to echo: "This is my Beloved Son."

• *The fearful disciples fall to the ground.* Perhaps a contemporary cue related to soldiers falling down and hugging the earth. Except on the mountain, there is not violence coming at these three; their Lord moves toward them in compassion.

• *Jesus touches the prone disciples and invites them to arise.* The touch is important to image. One possibility: A child cries out in the night. The darkness has become filled with fear. The child's mother hears, comes to the bedside, and touches her child. "It is alright, my love, I am here." The child looks up and is reassured. The fear is gone.

• *Following Jesus, the disciples stumble back down the mountain.* "Listen to him," they voice said. The assembly is invited to listen to Jesus' words from 8:24-25.

Clearly, not every step along the way will be developed into a full excursus. The preacher brings theological reflection, a pastoral heart, and homiletical savvy to these decisions. However, at every location along the journey with Jesus first up and then down the mountain, analogies will need to be developed that are concrete, vivid, and fitting.

Notes

1. I am indebted to my colleague, Professor Kendall McCabe, for his essential contributions to this analysis of the origins of the multiple feasts of the Transfiguration.

2. For an analysis of the origins of Ember Days and their relation to ordination, see Josef A. Jungmann, *The Early Liturgy to the Time of Gregory the Great*, trans. Francis A. Brunner (Notre Dame, Ind.: University of Notre Dame Press, 1959), 269–72.

3. M. Basil Pennington, "Tabor: Icon of Contemplation," *Weavings* 16, no. 4 (July/August 2001): 33–34.

4. Walter Brueggemann, *Genesis*, Interpretation: A Bible Commentary for Teaching and Preaching (Atlanta: John Knox Press, 1982), 116.

5. Ibid.

6. Literally, "from your land and your birthplace." E. A. Speiser, *Genesis,* The Anchor Bible (Garden City, N.Y.: Doubleday, 1964), 86.

7. Brueggemann, *Genesis*, 118. Brueggemann adds parenthetically, "The self-assertion of Yahweh here is nicely contrasted to the destructive self-assertion of the first man and woman in Gen. 3:10-13."

8. Speiser, *Genesis*, 86.

9. Brueggemann, *Genesis*, 121.

10. Speiser notes that the best textual evidence favors *terebinth* rather than "oaks." This would give the location a significance as a "high place" or shrine." Speiser, *Genesis*, 86.

11. Abena Safiyah Fosua, "Yes, Jesus Loves Me," *Mother Wit: 365 Meditations for African-American Women* (Nashville: Abingdon Press, 1996), 307.

12. Joseph F. Fitzmyer, *Romans,* The Anchor Bible (New York: Doubleday, 1992), 373.

13. Ibid.

14. Thomas H. Tobin, *Paul's Rhetoric in Its Contents: The Argument of Romans* (Peabody, Mass.: Hendrickson, 2004), 150.

15. Martin Dibelius and Hans Conzelmann, *The Pastoral Epistles,* Hermeneia, trans. Philip Buttolph and Adela Yarbro, ed. Helmut Koester (Philadelphia: Fortress Press, 1972), 99.

16. Thomas H. Tobin, *Paul's Rhetoric in Its Contexts: The Argument of Romans* (Peabody, Mass.: Hendrickson Publishers, 2004), 150 n. 60.

17. Raymond E. Brown, *The Gospel According to John,* vol. 1, The Anchor Bible (Garden City, N.Y.: Doubleday, 1966), 130.

18. Wes Howard-Brook, *Becoming Children of God: John's Gospel and Radical Discipleship* (Maryknoll, N.Y.: Orbis Books, 1994), 87.

19. Brown, *The Gospel According to John,* vol. 1, 130.

20. Marianne Meye Thompson, *The Humanity of Jesus in the Fourth Gospel* (Philadelphia: Fortress Press, 1988), 43.

21. The baptismal implications of the phrase, "by water and Spirit," have been an on-going topic of conversation within the history of interpretation. Many would agree with Raymond Brown that "the baptismal motif that is woven into the text of the whole scene is secondary" (ibid., 143). See Brown's extended discussion of this motif in ibid.,141–44. On the other hand, it is possible that the community of the Beloved Disciple would accord this baptismal motif a primary status rather than a secondary one.

22. Ibid., 131.

23. Brown notes that in the Septuagint, the word for the distinctive pole "is literally the word for 'sign'." Brown continues with a reflection on this insight: "Could this be one of the factors that led to the Johannine use of 'sign' for the miracles of Jesus?" Ibid., 133.

24. Howard-Brook, *Becoming Children of God,* 91.

25. Paul S. Minear, *John: The Martyr's Gospel* (New York: The Pilgrim Press, 1984), 41.

26. Ibid., 40.

27. John P. Meier notes that "[s]uch precise time-indications are rare outside the passion narrative"; *Matthew,* Lex Orandi (Wilmington, Del.: Michael Glazier, 1980), 189. Meier adds that attempts to link the temporal marker to such precedents as the Feast of Tabernacles or the ascent of Moses on Sinai "are questionable."

28. Robert H. Gundry provides this rhetorical insight; *Matthew: A Commen-

tary on His Handbook for a Mixed Church under Persecution. 2nd ed. (Grand Rapids, Mich.: Wm. B. Eerdmans, 1994), 343.

29. Warren Carter, *Matthew and the Margins: A Socio-Political and Religious Reading* (Sheffield, England: Sheffield Academic Press, Ltd., 2000), 349.

30. Ibid., 350.

31. Commentators and translators now are less interested in reading *skēnas* as "booths" (which had been used, for example, in the RSV), thereby diminishing the interplay of this narrative with the Feast of Tabernacles. On the other hand, "tents" especially evokes the God's holy presence with Israel in the exodus.

32. Gundry, *Matthew*, 344.

33. Daniel Patte, *The Gospel according to Matthew: A Structural Commentary on Matthew's Faith* (Philadelphia: Fortress Press, 1987), 237.

34. Commentators note other scriptural references to this response of the disciples as they are filled with fear and fall on their faces in the presence of the divine. See, for example, Meier, 191.

35. Gundry, *Matthew*, 345.

36. Patte, *The Gospel according to Matthew*, 238.

37. "The Prayer Appointed for the Week," *The Divine Hours: Prayers for Springtime: A Manual for Prayer*, ed. Phyllis Tickle (New York: Doubleday, 2001), 149.

38. See my *The Web of Preaching: New Options in Homiletic Method* (Nashville: Abingdon Press, 2002), 161–63.

39. Natalie Sleeth, "Hymn of Promise." See, for example, *The United Methodist Hymnal* (Nashville: The United Methodist Publishing House, 1989), 707.

40. See this window online at http://museum.msu.edu/museum/msgc/oct03.html. Accessed 12/15/06.

41. Taken from "Jesus on the Mountain Peak" by Brian Wren © 1977, 1995 Hope Publishing Co., Carol Stream, IL 60188. All rights reserved. Used by permission.

THIRD SUNDAY OF LENT

FEBRUARY 24, 2008

REVISED COMMON	EPISCOPAL (BCP)	ROMAN CATHOLIC
Exod. 17:1-7	Exod. 17:1-7	Exod. 17:3-7
Psalm 95	Psalm 95 or 95:6-11	Ps. 95:1-2, 6-7, 8-9
Rom. 5:1-11	Rom. 5:1-11	Rom. 5:1-2, 5-8
John 4:5-42	John 4:5-26 (27-38)	John 4:5-42 or
	39-42	4:5-15, 19b-26,
		39a, 40-42

KEY THEMES

- The Third Sunday in Lent is the first of the "scrutiny" Sundays for the catechumens. These "elect" are a unique group within the congregation as we preach.
- The Woman at the Well has become a popular lesson among both women and men in the "college of preachers." However, the homiletical theme of boundary crossing is aligned in the text with this woman's reception of the gift of living water, her discovery of the Messiah, and her testimony to her townspeople.
- The rebellion and murmuring themes are enduring elements within the Exodus saga. Just as the Exodus typology will reverberate throughout the liturgical year, so, too, the memory of rebellion and murmuring will echo with disturbing persistence.

FIRST READING

EXODUS 17:1-7 (RCL, BCP)
EXODUS 17:3-7 (LFM)

The incident in which Israel murmured in the wilderness against Moses and the Lord resonates through Scripture and becomes a significant motif within baptismal imagery in the early church. The place of rebellion and murmuring— Meribah and/or Massah—is referenced in Deuteronomy 6:16; 9:22; and Psalm 95:8-9 in the Old Testament and figures significantly along with the manna story in the Bread of Life discourse in John 6. Jewish and Christian piety and worship are deeply rooted in this Exodus narrative. Within Lenten spirituality and catechesis the church continues to reserve a privileged place for this narrative with its baptismal imagery and its cautions against murmuring against God.

Exodus 17:1-7 continues the wilderness wanderings and are journeying by stages from the wilderness of Sin, camping at Rephidim (17:1). This segment of the wilderness journey continues the sequence mentioned in 16:1—it was in the wilderness of Sin where the Israelites murmured about the lack of bread and were blessed with manna from the Lord. In our pericope, verses 2 and 3 have been interpreted as being essentially related to the same incident, but perhaps from differing traditions. These interpreters see "the redundancy of the people's complaint in vv 2–3" as evidence of parallel accounts being conflated at a later stage of redaction.[1] The alternate position is that the pericope represents mostly one source and the question regarding the supposed redundancy of verses 2-3 disappears upon a closer reading. From this latter perspective, the two accounts are not parallel but represent "two successive stages in the growth of tradition"[2] and in the text become an important sequential movement of the plot. That is, when the people camped at Rephidim and discovered there was no water to drink, they anticipate a crisis and demand that Moses give them water to drink.[3] Moses' response to this "sea-lawyer" demand by the people repeats his frustration with them during the manna episode: "Why do you quarrel with me? Why do you test [*mah-tenassun*] the Lord?" (17:2b). But the crisis that was anticipated in the first complaint by the people has now in fact become their condition. The initial sequence was *anticipation of thirst* leading to *complaint*. Now, in this second stage of the crisis, the sequence becomes *experience of dire thirst* leading to *complaint* yet again. Now, they add: "Why did you bring us out of Egypt, to kill us and our children and livestock with thirst?" (v. 3). The indictment is clearly twofold; it was the Lord God who brought them out of Egypt. Both Moses and the Lord are the objects of the objections! How serious this complaint has become is disclosed in Moses' address to the Lord: "What shall I do with this people? They are almost ready to stone me" (v. 4). By way of this address to God, it is disclosed that the complaining has become rebellion. And since the rebellion is directed against both Moses and the Lord, it is clear "that Israel suffers a marked lack of faith."[5]

The Lord now speaks to Moses and in a sequence of statements, outlines the actions that are to take place:

a. Go on ahead of the people,
b. Take some of the elders of Israel with you,
c. Take in your hand the staff with which you struck the Nile,
d. And go. (v. 5)

That while awaiting the gift of God, they may long with all their hearts for the living water that brings eternal life, let us pray to the Lord.
—"Intercessions for the Elect, First Scrutiny"[4]

Even though Moses is directed to move away from the people, the presence of the elders will stand for a witness that Moses did not simply find an oasis up ahead![6] Yahweh adds, "I will be standing there in front of you on the rock at Horeb. Strike the rock, and water will come out of it, so that the people may drink" (v. 6). Moses strikes the rock, using the staff (*matteka*) with which he struck the Nile. "The implement that rendered the Nile undrinkable (7:15-18) now produces water."[7] The elders (*zaqne*) stand as a witness to the miracle of deliverance. But Moses "named the place Mas'sah and Mer-i-bah, because the Israelites quarreled and tested the LORD, saying, 'Is the LORD among us or not'?" (v. 7). Brevard Childs offers one way to construe this ending of the pericope:

> Although it is possible that the names Massah and Meribah may once have denoted a place of legal decision, the names have entered the tradition in relation to the murmuring motif. God provided water for a contentious people who challenged his presence among them. Ps. 95 speaks of Israel's hardness of heart when putting God to the test, even though they had repeatedly seen his great work.[8]

RESPONSIVE READING

PSALM 95 (RCL, BCP)
PSALM 95:6-11 (BCP alt.)
PSALM 95:1-2, 6-7, 8-9 (LFM)

In the midst of this psalm of praise to Israel's God, there is a caution that links this liturgically to the first lesson. The people of the covenant are admonished: "Do not harden your hearts, as at Meribah, as on the day at Massah in the wilderness" (v. 8). The alternatives are clear. God's people will either murmur or offer joyful praise.

SECOND READING

ROMANS 5:1-11 (RCL, BCP)
ROMANS 5:1-2, 5-8 (LFM)

It is clear that Paul is beginning some significant new rhetorical move in Romans 5:1-11. "Therefore," he begins, "since we are justified by faith, we have peace with God through our Lord Jesus Christ . . ." (5:1). But precisely what rhetorical objectives are being achieved is a topic of keen dispute among Pauline scholars. One contributing factor to these disagreements is the multiplicity of themes and metaphors crammed into these eleven verses. In fact, those interpreters who like to reduce the purposes of the pericope to one overriding topic are then faced with the text's other images and topics that refuse to be collected nicely under one dominating main idea. Rather than attempting such a reductionist approach, it may well be more wholesome—and fruitful—to identify these rhetorical moves and their corresponding images and themes. The pericope is incredibly rich and laden with multiple meanings. Some of the major components to the text include the following:

• To be sure, Paul continues to employ his forensic, judicial metaphor by way of interpreting justification. The opening phrase of the section again picks up this theme and much of the material in verses 6-10 provides another argument for the metaphor. From this point of view, the pericope could be best construed as Paul's summary of material whose center of gravity was in 3:21-26.

• However, a new note is sounded before Paul completes the opening statement of the passage. "We have peace with God through our Lord Jesus Christ," he proclaims. In fact, this note of reconciliation gradually overshadows the theme of justification, the concluding word being the Christian's boast that in our Lord Jesus Christ, "we have now received reconciliation" (5:11b). Given this newly emergent and dominant theme, the consensus of a number of scholars is that 5:1-11 represents a new section of the epistle now dealing with reconciliation.

• In the opening section of the pericope, after gesturing toward the previously developed theme of justification and then introducing the motif of Christ's gift of peace, Paul then shifts to material that deals with ethos and the virtues of the Christian life. This material is both unexpected and rhetorically powerful, beginning with Paul's motif of "boasting" and turning its focus from the previous law/gospel dialectic to that of the virtues of the community in Christ. The shift is so sudden and surprising that at least one commentator simply deletes this material from consideration![9] On the other hand, others regard this ethos material as providing a crucial insight into the function of the entire pericope.

With this analysis in mind, we will briefly review the attention Paul devotes to justification while turning to assess his fresh metaphor of reconciliation along with his dealings with ethos and Christian virtue. It is interesting that with regard to the sequence of the passage, Paul only resumes his treatment of justification after bringing reconciliation into the discussion. Moreover, the rhetorical sense of his dealing with reconciliation and ethos is much less that of argument and more that of exhortation. Here, "Paul's purpose is to emphasize from the start that his viewpoint about being made righteous by grace is not devoid of ethical consequences but, rather, is fraught with them."[10] The apostle introduces this ethical exhortation by way of a typical dialectical movement. Previously in the epistle

(3:27-31; 4:2), Paul has employed the motif of "boasting" (*kauchēsis*). No longer boasting in the law or in works, by the end of chapter 4 we are brought to a place of being able to boast only in Jesus Christ. But now, Paul adds that we may boast, moreover, in our hope (5:2b) and in our *sufferings* (5:3a)! There ensues a sequence of related virtues that tumble out in succession: "knowing that suffering produces endurance, and endurance produces character, and character produces hope . . ." (vv. 3b–4). Thomas Tobin comments,

> [Paul] emphasizes the reality and significance of afflictions and encourages the practice of the virtues of patience, character, and hope. . . . The fact that Romans 5 begins with a short ethical exhortation and that this exhortation contains the point that Paul wants to develop in the rest of the chapter is not at all accidental. The issue at stake is the ethical seriousness of Paul's gospel.[11]

That Paul has called the Christians at Rome away from any boasting in the law or in works does not mean that the gospel is devoid of ethical implications.

In the following section, Paul brings Christ's death into alignment with the gift of peace and the capacity for a moral life. "For [*gar*] while we were still weak, at the right time Christ died for the ungodly" (v. 6). This weakness of ours relates to our unjustified existence with its sin as well as our ongoing afflictions. Simply put, we are unable to save ourselves or heal ourselves. The response of God "at the right time" is the kerygma: "Christ died for our sins " (see 1 Corinthians 15:3). At this point, Paul provides a "how much more" argument with reference to the death of Christ. He argues, (1) no one would die for an unrighteous person (this thesis is implied in the argument); (2) rarely would anyone die for a righteous person, adding, "though perhaps for a good person someone might actually dare to die" (5:7b); (3) but Christ died for us while we were yet sinners; and (4) by this "God proves his love [*agapēn*] for us" (v. 8).[13] Now Paul brings a further dialectic into play. While we were sinners ("weak"), we were the enemies of God and subject to divine wrath. But Christ died for us while we were still sinners, manifesting God's love and reconciling us to God. Moreover, we are saved by his life (his resurrection). Tobin concludes, "The emphasis shifts from what God has done in Christ's death to the consequences, for believers, of his resurrection."[14] Now we can also boast "in God through our Lord Jesus Christ, through whom we have received reconciliation" (v. 11).

> If God would not try us by tribulation, it would be impossible for us to be saved.
> —Martin Luther[12]

THE GOSPEL
JOHN 4:5-42 (RCL, LFM)
JOHN 4:5-26 (27-38) 39-42 (BCP)
JOHN 4:5-15, 19b-26, 39a, 40-42 (LFM alt.)

This profound and detailed story follows upon a sequence of events that function in differing ways to shape the reader's expectations as the Samaritan journey is undertaken. Jesus' first sign in Cana of Galilee (John 2:1-11) is followed by three Judean-based events: the incident in the Temple (2:13-22), the visit by Nicodemus (3:1-21), and a brief narrative relating the ministries of the Baptist and Jesus at the Jordan (3:22-36). Thus, as the Fourth Evangelist brings us along as Jesus enters Samaria, we bring with us questions regarding the sign of water become wine, the Temple cult, new birth, baptism, and, underlying all of these, the identity and work of Jesus. The Samaritan journey's motivation is somewhat vague, although the Evangelist implies that there is some connection with baptismal activity at the Jordan—"although it was not Jesus himself but his disciples who baptized" (4:2). Perhaps the impending arrest of the Baptist was a factor (in 3:24, we are told that "John, of course, had not been thrown into prison"). At any rate, Jesus now was leaving Jerusalem and Judea and returning to Galilee.

Regarding this return trip, a certain tension is introduced as John mentions that Jesus "had to" (*dei*) go through Samaria on the way down to Galilee. Some commentators interpret the force of the term to indicate that Samaria lay between Judea and Galilee and that the narrator is telling us of a geographical necessity. Other interpreters refer to pious Jews who "must not" go through Samaria on such a journey, crossing and recrossing the Jordan in order to avoid the hated Samaritans. However, these arguments speak only to an "earthly" aspect of the issue. A "heavenly" meaning of *dei* stresses that this course is of divine intent; Jesus "had to" go through Samaria for purposes related to his mission. Something of great import for God's reign is about to come to light. Immediately, the plot thickens. Coming to the Samaritan city of Sychar,[15] Jesus sits by the well Jacob had given to his son Joseph. He is tired from the journey and it is about noon. And there, in the heat of the day, a Samaritan woman comes to draw water. Jesus asks the woman for a drink. John notes that "his disciples had gone to the city to buy food" (v. 8). Gail O'Day notes that this verse "informs the reader that the actions of the Samaritan woman and the disciples are never completely independent of one another."[16] Now, under "normal" circumstances, such an encounter with the woman at the well triggers all of our type-scene memories as a biblical people. Whether in the case of Isaac and Rebekah, Jacob and Rachel, or Moses and Zipporah, the dynamics are remarkable similar:

A man comes to a well, finds a maiden there, asks her for a drink; they converse; she runs home to tell her people what has happened; they return with her to the well and approve the man; he returns to their home and marries the maiden.[17]

Also added to that list, we might suggest to Wes Howard-Brook, is one final item: in every case, the resulting marriage alters the course of history for the covenant people!

Of course, such a possibility is subverted by all of the social and religious barriers that have preceded Jesus and the woman to the well. These are well known by now within the college of preachers and were well known to the woman of Samaria as well. "How is it that you, a Jew, ask a drink of me, a woman of Samaria?" (v. 9b). In case any of John's readers were not equally in the know, he adds: "Jews do not share things in common with Samaritans" (v. 9c). By the mid-60s of the first century, this custom had become Jewish regulation; Samaritan women were ritually unclean and nothing could be shared in common. However, the force of the ritual impurity was clear enough to the woman. If Jesus drank from her water jar, he would impose on himself a status of outcast even more severe than what she experienced coming in the noonday heat to draw water instead of with the other women either early or late in the day. At any rate, a serious "breach of conduct" has just transpired![18] But the situation is turned upside down as Jesus speaks of a knowledge she lacks about his identity and about the gift of God he can provide. If she had asked, Jesus continues, "you would have asked him, and he would have given you living water" (*hydōr zōon*) (v. 10).[19] Responding at an earthly level, the woman asks where Jesus obtains such living water, adding most ironically, "Are you greater than our ancestor Jacob . . . ?" (v. 12). Jesus' response contrasts all earthly water—which only temporarily quenches thirst—with the water he will provide, "a spring of water gushing up to eternal life" (v. 14). Remaining quite terrestrial, the woman asks politely that she have this water in order to avoid the daily trip to Jacob's well!

We are surprised by the shift in the conversation; this living water has been offered and the woman does request it, though on an "earthly level." Jesus now directs her: "Go, call your husband, and come back" (v. 16). Her response is to deny she has a husband, whereupon Jesus notes that she has had five husbands and the one she is living with now is not her husband. At this point, interpreters beg to differ. Some, including Raymond Brown, believe the interchange to "need have more than the obvious import."[20] Others see Johannine double-meaning at work in the exchange. Wes Howard-Brook speaks for this camp by first casting doubt on the clear literal meaning. The issue cannot be that of marital infidelity; "nowhere else in the fourth gospel is there expressed a concern for this kind of moralizing."[21]

What the latter interpreter holds is a more symbolic expression of the matter. The five previous "husbands," it is argued, pertain to the five foreign peoples that intermarried with the Samaritans, the latter also "marrying" their gods as well. And as for the one who "is not your husband" (v. 18a), it is suggested that the Roman occupation is being implied here. Once again, the most wholesome approach to John may be the most holistic. On one hand, the woman announces to her townspeople later that she has encountered "a man who told me everything I have ever done!" (4:29). On the other hand, the preachers who leave the matter at a personal, individual level of morality has probably not drunk deeply of this particular well. The response of the woman in either case is one of growing insight; she sees that Jesus is a prophet (*prophētēs*).

The issue now turns to theological geography. The woman speaks of the holy sites that stand in opposition between Samaritans and Jews—an issue that follows easily from both sides of the "husband" coin. Certainly the "five husbands" allusion to her people could evoke this comment. Moreover, it would be quite human to deflect the issue of her personal life by distancing Jesus with this question related to a very old family feud. Jesus' reply serves to render the ancient opposition obsolete. Neither location! Yet, there is more weight given to the Jerusalem option by Jesus. After all, "salvation is from the Jews" (v. 22).[22]

> Just as "living water" does not respect human boundaries but flows wherever it wills, so too are disciples of Jesus called to be free of ethnic and national boundaries.
> —Wes Howard-Brook[23]

Jesus now presents the woman and the readers of the Gospel with that distinctive present-future quality of his "hour." It both "now is here" and "is coming," in this case regarding true worship of the Father "in spirit and in truth" (v. 23). The mystery of Jesus' hour will finally be revealed as he is lifted up on the cross and in glory. Another perspective is needed, however, one that takes seriously John's role as spokesperson for his community. When Jesus comments that in comparison to the Samaritans, "we worship what we know" (v. 22), the alternative community of true worship may be that of John's own community. In such a case, worship "in spirit and in truth" is both present in the Word made flesh and in the community that eats his flesh and drinks his blood. John formulates the common faith of the community of the Beloved Disciple.[24] The dominical pronouncement continues with the reference to worship of God "in spirit and in truth." This doublet affirmation—closely linked in Johannine theology—renders null and void the old contest between Jerusalem and Gerizim and has replaced nationalist location with Spirit-filled true worship. Brown has suggested that the two terms are so closely related in the Fourth Gospel that they could be rendered as one phrase: "Spirit of truth."[25] Far from a vague "spiritualized" modern and liberal ideology of liturgical pluralism, the Evangelist rejects any geographical particularity to true worship while at the same time insisting upon a trinitarian location.

The children of God will worship the Father (*ho patēr*), and "must [*dei*] worship in spirit and truth" (v. 24). The woman's response is to affirm that she knows that the Messiah is coming, the One called Christ. Jesus' response to this partial faith is to bring it to full bloom; "*Egō eimi*," he proclaims—"I am he" (v. 26).

With these words of self-disclosure echoing near Jacob's well, the scene's cast of characters undergoes a dramatic shift. Abiding with "the rule of twos," the Evangelist notes the woman's departure to evangelize her kinsfolk in the town while also bringing the disciples back on stage from their trip into the city to secure provisions. The former leaves her now-obsolete water jar by the well while the latter, the disciples, are astonished that Jesus has been speaking to a woman. John traces the two narrative trajectories in sequence. First, he invites us to follow the woman on her mission. "Come and see," she invites, beckoning the townsfolk with a question she now knows has been answered. "He cannot be the Messiah, can he?" (v. 29). Her words have fallen on good soil; the townspeople leave the city and come toward Christ. Meanwhile, out at Jacob's well, the dialogue between Jesus and the disciples continues. They urge Jesus to eat, which evokes a response from the Lord concerning "food to eat that you do not know about" (v. 32). The disciples verify our suspicions that they follow Jesus only on an "earthly" level. They ponder whether some others have brought food for their rabbi. This evokes a response from Jesus that is entirely on the "heavenly" level: "My food is to do the will of him who sent me and to complete his work" (v. 34). What ensues is a pair of sayings, both related to sowing and harvesting. In the first, the prophetic vision is being fulfilled in this hour in Samaria. The seasons of the sowing and of reaping are being drawn together in a time of eschatological joy. Moreover, in the second image, another prophecy is being transformed. One sows while another reaps, not in exilic despair, but in fulfillment-time rejoicing.[27] "Look around you," Jesus says to his disciples, "and see how the fields are ripe for harvesting" (v. 35).

> In chaps. 4, 9, and 11 . . . , the Samaritan woman, Martha, and Mary are characters absolutely equal in importance to the blind man and Lazarus. In the portrayal of major male and female believers there is no difference of intelligence, vividness, or response.
> —Raymond E. Brown[26]

The harvest is begun by the woman—one of those who reaps having not sown. Many citizens of Zychar come to believe "because of the woman's testimony [*martyrountes*]" (v. 39a). Here is a startling and sudden reversal. Just prior to Jesus' Samaritan journey, the Baptist witnessed to some detractors that he is not the Messiah. The "one from above" has testified to what he has seen and has heard, "yet no one accepts his testimony [*martyrei*]" (3:32). Through the word of the woman's testimony, however, many Samaritans have come to believe. These are now certified days of eschatological harvest! Moreover, the Samaritans extend unexpected hospitality to the Christ. They ask Jesus to stay with them (literally, "abide"), and Jesus "abided" with them for two days. Now, they do not need the testimony of the woman, although her witness was crucial to this harvest. These new children of God "have heard for ourselves, and we know that this is truly the Savior of the world" (v. 42).

HOMILETICAL STRATEGIES

As I sketch an approach to a homily based on the story of the Woman at the Well for the Third Sunday of Lent, Year A, I will keep in mind the catechetical purposes of the season in general and the liturgical and pastoral context in particular. A number of homiletic voices have joined with the narrative tradition of African American preaching in the conviction that the best way to preach a biblical story is to let its plot—with its distinctive movement, sequence, and intention—shape the plot of the sermon. "Running the story," then, invites the assembly to journey through the biblical narrative with some real immediacy. This approach deals in what Henry Mitchell calls the "eyewitness" quality of preaching in the black church.[28] Rather than talking about the text, a narrative sermon invites the listeners to become part of the world of the text. The converse also obtains, however: as the story is run, inviting the listeners into its world, the preacher will also employ strategies for opening the biblical story out into the lived experience of the congregation. Among the various strategies available, I will focus on the identification of a number of locations within the narrative text where one may discern that an analogy exists with the contemporary congregation. I will identify these locations, putting the forward movement of the story on hold, and develop an excursus that invites the listeners to see how it is with them at this crucial place within the narrative. Most biblical narratives offer more possible locations than can be fully exploited. However, the congregational and worldly context will assist in deciding which locations will appropriately be developed into an excursus within this sermon (the choice of these narrative locations may vary as the preacher returns to the text). Clearly, the Woman at the Well story offers numerous potential locations for the development of such excursuses. With an imagined congregation in mind, I will identify the following places and explore means by which we may contemporize them. Following the excursus, of course, it is the preacher's task to reenter the biblical story and again invite the congregation to journey within its world. One caution: preachers will need to exert will exert a certain restrain with regard to the size of a story-illustration deployed within an excursus. If the contemporary illustration becomes too extensive and involved, listeners may have difficulty returning to the biblical story; they will remain stranded in the illustration!

Excursus 1: Journeying through Samaria. Although this location appears quite early in the text, there are powerful contemporary analogies to such a passage through alien territory. It is perhaps too early in this narrative sermon to employ a story-illustration. However, one or more examples (a more retrained reference out of the lived experience of the congregation) may well be offered for the listeners to grasp this experience of going through Samaria. For a suburban congregation, there may be a boundary to a part of the city that is rarely entered by choice. Sometimes the boundary even has a local name: "west of the river" or "east of I-5," and so forth. Sometimes, an entire community can be named that is a "Samaria" for the congregation. The example or examples should be selected with a clear analogy to the narrative's significance of "Samaria" for the first-century Jewish community in Galilee and Judea. We may also gesture toward some compelling motivation that makes it necessary (*dei*) for us to go through our Samaria.

Excursus 2: The oddity of the woman coming to the well at noon. Here, many preachers pause to provide the congregation with a brief scenario of the more "normal" times for women to gather at a well. They would come either very early in the morning or toward dusk, avoiding the heat of the day. They would gather to share in friendship and share any news. One contemporary analogy: in a farming community, for example, the early gathering at a favorite coffee shop before work begins in the fields. The preacher is cautioned not to develop this excursus too extensively. The congregation will need to move on as the plot thickens.

Excursus 3: Jesus violates the customs—he speaks to a Samaritan woman! At this point, it is most appropriate to pause and explore some contemporary analogies to Jesus' violation of these deeply held norms. One could shape a small rhetorical system as follows:

> So John tells us that "Jews do not share things in common with Samaritans." I expect, then, that John would understand that in New York City, strangers do not talk to each other in an elevator. Or that most people in a city don't look toward a homeless person sitting alongside an alley. Or that a bank executive doesn't often stop to chat with a teller. John might reply, "Well, it's something like those things, only it goes much deeper. Most Jews and Samaritans really believed that God ordained this enmity and distance between the two peoples."

Excursus 4: The offer of living water. One of the challenges in preaching is that negative examples come to us so easily, while images of grace are difficult to imagine. We are called to preach the gospel, however, and our images of grace will need to be as vivid as and even more powerful than those of darkness and sin.[29] One possible option is to depict for the congregation the baptism scene in the movie *O Brother, Where Art Thou*.

> The white-robed people move through the woods on the way to the river singing, "O brother, let's go down . . . O sister, let's go down, down to the river and pray." One of

184

THE SEASON
OF LENT
────────
RICHARD L.
ESLINGER

the three escaped cons watching the scene, Delmer, is suddenly moved to dash down the bank and he splashes out to the preacher. He is baptized, going down into the water and coming up gulping and laughing. Childlike, he's filled with joy. Delmer has heard this offer of living water, has responded, and thus has drunk deeply of its life-giving power.

This reference will function well for congregations somewhat familiar with the film. If that is not the case, perhaps the preacher will want to depict a baptism within the life of the congregation. Since we are anticipating the Easter Vigil here at the Third Sunday in Lent, the baptismal service from last year's Vigil could be deployed. In any case, Mary Catherine Hilkert's caution is that this scene of grace be named with concrete and imagistic speech.[30]

Excursus 5: "You have had five husbands." In this excursus, the personal morality dimension of Jesus' declaration will be briefly discussed and the issue rapidly expanded to deal with the social and theological issues of having "five husbands." After developing the latter aspect adequately, the preacher can gesture toward the kinds of "husbands" to whom we are wedded in North American culture. All of these can descend to the status of idolatry. Some examples may include:

a. The "husband" of our career
b. The "husband" of addiction
c. The "husband" of consumerism
d. The "husband" of nationalism
e. The "husband" of ideological certainties (liberal, evangelical, and so forth)

The list will not need to include a specific total of five examples. In order to provide a sense of multiple problem "husbands," however, one should perhaps offer three or more. Congregational, denominational, and regional context will shape the example system for the astute preacher.[31]

Excursus 6: Worship of God in spirit and in truth. Informed by the pericope, one understands this "worship in spirit and in truth" to include a community that transcends the most intractable human boundaries. Moreover, such worship will embody the truth of the Word made flesh and will be enlivened by the Spirit. The challenge for the preacher, though, is that one cannot speak of these qualities without concretely imaging them (otherwise, they fade from congregational consciousness). Related to the congregation's experience, for example, was there a recent ecumenical service of worship that did cross boundaries, and was filled with truth and Holy Spirit? Did representatives of the parish return from a mission trip celebrating the Spirit-filled worship of another people? Was a distinctive liturgy such as the "Celebration of the Rite of Election of Catechumens"[32] an examplar of such worship in spirit and in truth? One or more examples will serve to shape the assembly's understanding of Jesus' words about such worship.

Excursus 7: "Come and see," the woman announces. She bears witness to Jesus as the Christ. The woman left her town in the middle of the day as an outcast. After encountering Jesus and drinking deeply of the living water, she returns as a evangelist. And many believed because of her testimony. John's Gospel turns the tables on us once again. In the Synoptic Gospels and the Acts of the Apostles, the gospel radiates out from its epicenter at the empty tomb to all Judea, Galilee, and finally, to the Gentiles. But in the Fourth Gospel, two women evangelists bracket the narrative. Here, toward the beginning of the story of Jesus, the woman of Samaria takes the gospel to her neighbors, people who are considered by Jews to be outsiders and outcasts. Toward the end of the Gospel, Mary Magdalene takes the good news of the resurrection to the disciples, those closest to Jesus. The evangelization of the world, though, has begun in relation to those most distained and despised! But the Fourth Evangelist does not set this up as an either/or. So, the assembly might be asked whether their evangelization should now flow out to those most near (including, perhaps, neighbors and even members of the families in the parish) or most far away in social distance (who belongs to such groups for the parish?). Maybe, with John, the answer might be, "Both!" We tell the good news to both.

> As the woman of Samaria confessed her faith in Jesus Christ, the giver of the water of life, so the church confesses its need of Christ and its trust in God's mercy. We invite you whom God has chosen for baptism to join all the people of God in confessing the faith of the church.
> —"Blessing of Candidates for Baptism, Third Sunday in Lent."[33]

Notes

1. William H. C. Propp, *Exodus 1–18,* The Anchor Bible (New York: Doubleday, 1999), 603. Propp adds that it is "theoretically possible to divide vv 1b-3 into parallel accounts, supplying only an extra 'and Moses said.'"

2. George W. Coats, *Exodus 1–18,* The Forms of Old Testament Literature, vol. IIA (Grand Rapids, Mich.: Wm. B. Eerdmans, 1999), 137.

3. Coats states that the verb (from *nātan,* "give us") "is not necessarily negative in character. It can mean simply to process a (legal) demand"; ibid.

4. "Intercessions for the Elect, First Scrutiny," *Rite of Christian Initiation of Adults, Study Edition* (Chicago: Liturgy Training Publications, 1988), 83.

5. Coats, *Exodus 1–18,* 138.

6. Propp, *Exodus 1–18,* 606.

7. Ibid., 605.

8. Brevard S. Childs, *The Book of Exodus: A Critical Theological Commentary* (Philadelphia: The Westminster Press, 1974), 308.

9. See Ralph P. Martin, "Reconciliation: Romans 5:1-11," in *Romans and the*

People of God, ed. Sven K. Soderlund and N. T. Wright (Grand Rapids, Mich. and Cambridge, U.K.: Wm. B. Eerdmans, 1999), 36–48.

10. Thomas H. Tobin, *Paul's Rhetoric in Its Contents: The Argument of Romans* (Peabody, Mass.: Hendrickson, 2004), 159.

11. Ibid., 160.

12. Martin Luther, commentary on Rom. 5:4, from *Commentary on the Epistle to the Romans*, trans. J. Theodore Mueller (Grand Rapids, Mich.: Zondervan, 1954), 73.

13. The use of *agapē* here is one of Paul's infrequent mentions of the term. For an extensive and insightful exploration of Paul's witness to the love of God in this text, see Martin, "Reconciliation," 39–41.

14. Tobin, *Paul's Rhetoric in Its Contents,* 163–64.

15. Raymond Brown argues for an alternative location of the site near Jacob's well, the town of Shechem, adding that "Jacob's well is only 250 ft. from Shechem." Raymond E. Brown, *The Gospel According to John*, vol. 1, The Anchor Bible (New York: Doubleday, 1966), 169.

16. Gail R. O'Day, *Revelation in the Fourth Gospel: Narrative Mode and Theological Claim* (Philadelphia: Fortress Press, 1986), 52.

17. Wes Howard-Brook, *Becoming Children of God: John's Gospel and Radical Discipleship* (Maryknoll, N.Y.: Orbis Books, 1994), 113.

18. O'Day, *Revelation in the Fourth Gospel,* 59.

19. O'Day notes that the term is ambiguous and can be rendered "both as 'living' water and as spring, that is, 'running' water." Ibid., 60.

20. Brown, *The Gospel According to John*, vol. 1, 171.

21. Howard-Brook, *Becoming Children of God,* 106.

22. Wes Howard-Brook consistently translates the Johannine term *Ioudaioi* as "Judeans" rather than "Jews." The latter translation, as we know, has led to much anti-Semitism and persecution in the past, using the Fourth Gospel as a justification. Alternatively, most Johannine scholars would argue for a case-by-case approach to the various meanings of the term based upon context. Howard-Brook rejects this move, arguing that the negative depiction of the *Ioudaioi* relates to their representing the Judean ideology of dominance and economic exploitation. "The gospel is not anti-Semitic or anti-Jewish but anti-Judean, where "Judean" is a symbol for those whose allegiance is to the 'world'" (ibid., 43). In most instances, this writer agrees with such an assessment. However, there are a few times in the Gospel when the context does argue for the use of "Jews" rather than "Judeans." This occasion is one of those exceptions, I would argue. If the Evangelist only intends an anti-Judean usage of *Ioudaioi*, then this statement is most confusing. Besides, salvation would not come only from "Judeans," given the Fourth Gospel's use of the Hebrew Scriptures, it comes from "the Jews" in a most positive sense.

23. Wes Howard-Brook, *John's Gospel and the Renewal of the Church* (Maryknoll, N.Y.: Orbis Books, 1997), 42.

24. See Paul S. Minear, *John: The Martyr's Gospel* (New York: The Pilgrim Press, 1984), 10–13. Also see Raymond Brown, *The Community of the Beloved Disciple* (New York: Paulist Press, 1979).

25. Brown, *The Gospel According to John*, vol. 1, 187.

26. Raymond E. Brown, *The Churches the Apostles Left Behind* (New York: Paulist Press, 1984), 94.

27. See Howard-Brook, *Becoming Children of God,* 111–12, for a discussion of the interplay of prophetic allusions in the Hebrew Scriptures with these two dominical sayings related to harvest and the reign of God.

28. See Henry Mitchell, *Black Preaching: The Recovery of a Powerful Art* (Nashville: Abingdon Press, 1990).

29. See Mary Catherine Hilkert, *Naming Grace: Preaching and the Sacramental Imagination* (New York: Continuum, 1999).

30. Ibid.

31. The ability of congregations to retain these kinds of examples is undergoing a shift at present. If the example or example system is to provide concretion within some single meaning in the sermon—such as an excursus in a narrative sermon—it is increasingly the case that some brief perceptual element be added to the general statement of the example. Put simply, examples will not be heard if all we do is name them in some general way. In our present cultural context with its deepening imagistic and visual orientation, some imagery is now needed for examples to form in congregational hearing. So, for example, we will not only state the "husband" of consumer culture, but will invite the listeners to see the appeals for consumption in TV commercials.

32. *Rite of Christian Initiation of Adults, Study Edition*, 315–30.

33. "Blessing of Candidates for Baptism, Third Sunday in Lent" in *Welcome to Christ: Lutheran Rites for the Catechumenate* (Minneapolis: Augsburg Fortress, 1997), 23.

FOURTH SUNDAY OF LENT

MARCH 2, 2008

REVISED COMMON	EPISCOPAL (BCP)	ROMAN CATHOLIC
1 Sam. 16:1-13	1 Sam. 16:1-13	1 Sam. 16:1b, 6-7, 10-13a
Psalm 23	Psalm 23	Ps. 23:1-3a, 3b-4, 5, 6
Eph. 5:8-14	Eph. 5:(1-7) 8-14	Eph. 5:8-14
John 9:1-41	John 9:1-13 (14-27) 28-38	John 9:1-41 or 9:1, 6-9, 13-17, 34-38

KEY THEMES

- The elders at Bethlehem ask Samuel a critical question: "Do you come peaceably?" During the season of Lent, this question may well be posed to pastor and parish at every gathering during the Forty Days.
- John begins the Gospel story with a beggar who we come to discover represents blind humanity. With the gift of our sight by Jesus, will we, too, be cast out? Or, more directly, if we haven't been cast out, what's the problem?
- The parents of the man born blind are at the center of the Gospel narrative. John puts them on stage only long enough for the question to be answered: Will they bear witness to the Light? Will we?
- That "evangelical importance of exposing darkness to light" (Roy Jeal) includes exposing darkness within Christ's church.

FIRST READING
1 SAMUEL 16:1-13 (RCL, BCP)
1 SAMUEL 16:1b, 6-7, 10-13a (LFM)

The narrative of the anointing of David as king over Israel by Yahweh would at first glance be more fitting as a first lesson during the season of Advent. After all, the primary setting is Bethlehem ("David's royal city") and it is there that David is chosen as king and Jesus is heralded as Israel's "newborn king."

On the other hand, the Lenten journey is for Jesus one of movement toward the cross (where he will be announced by Pilate as "King of the Jews") and is for the catechumens one of movement toward their baptism in Christ and anointing with the gift of the same "spirit of the LORD" (1 Sam. 16:13). That the anointing of David is also accompanied by a sacrifice even more closely aligns this pericope and the spirituality of Lent. There is "divine intention,"[1] then, in the choosing of David as king and Jesus as God's anointed, both involving sacrifice.

The context for the anointing of David as Israel's king is provided in the last verse of the previous chapter. Samuel, the kingmaker, "grieved over Saul," while "the LORD was sorry that he made Saul king over Israel" (15:35). As the new chapter in Israel's story begins—for the beginning of chapter sixteen does mark a profoundly new chapter in God's dealings with God's people—the Lord has apparently moved beyond this deep regret over making Saul king. As the new scene opens, however, Samuel remains stuck in the past and continues to grieve over Saul. But it is time for a new thing to be accomplished, signaled in the Lord's words to Samuel: "How long will you grieve over Saul? I have rejected him from being king [mimlok] over Israel" (16:1a).[2] With the issue of Saul's status in God's eyes now resolved, Samuel is directed to fill his horn with oil and begin a most significant journey. "I will send you to Jesse the Bethlehemite, for I have provided for myself a king among his sons" (v. 1b). This word from Yahweh may resolve the "divine intention," but it seriously complicates matters for Samuel. For the kingmaker to anoint another as king while Saul retains the throne is seditious and dangerous. Quite rationally, Samuel responds to the Lord, "How can I go? If Saul hears of it, he will kill me" (v. 2a). Quite so. Our sympathies are with this beleaguered servant of the Lord!

The word to Samuel from Yahweh is a prescription for avoiding this deadly outcome and yet achieving the divine intention. Samuel is to take along a heifer and say to the Bethlehemites that he has come to offer a sacrifice to the Lord. "This may not be a blatant lie," Walter Brueggemann offers, "but this is clearly an authorized deception."[3] On this issue, scholars are divided. Others see the "heifer-ploy" as both an obvious cover for Samuel's Bethlehem visit (if Saul grows inquisitive) and as the provision of the heifer for a necessary ritual act at the ascension of a king. Moreover, there were any numbers of sacrifices upon the occasion of Saul's anointing (see 10:1-8)! At any rate, Jesse is invited to the sacrifice directed by the Lord. Moreover, and more importantly, the Lord tells Samuel that he is to anoint the one who will be named. Now at this point, the elders of Bethlehem come to Samuel trembling with fear. "Do you come peaceably [shalom]?" they ask (v. 4). This question is also quite realistic given the situation.

They know that Samuel is a kingmaker and a king breaker. Whenever the high officials of the court come to the village, there can be only trouble and risk. "Such officials never come to give but always take."[4]

Samuel's response relieves their trembling hearts, however. "Peaceably," he tells the elders, and he informs them of his intent to offer a sacrifice there. Now Jesse and his sons are sanctified and invited to the sacrifice. The narrator strongly aligns the readers with Samuel's perspective and inner thoughts as the sons of Jesse come before him; one will be the new king named by the Lord. The first, Eliab, seems to have all of the qualities for the office. With Samuel, we conclude, "Surely the LORD's anointed is now before the LORD" (v. 6). All of us will be wrong, however. God does not look on outward appearances (although the narrator has certainly made quite a point to emphasize Saul's outward appearance! [9:2]). Rather, "the LORD looks on the heart" (v. 7). So, consideration now shifts to a second son, Abinadab, but with the same absence of authorization by the Lord. So, too, with a third, Shammah, and with the others totaling seven sons. Samuel states the obvious: "The LORD has not chosen any of these" (v. 10). Given that the whole scene is dominated by visual terms—"seeing" (r'h), "eyes," "appearance"—we are now confused since none who are present before us appear to have been chosen by the Lord. We may even prematurely conclude that God has been wrong in sending Samuel on this mission since no one we have seen is the king-elect. We would be wrong.

Samuel's question to Jesse opens the door to this new chapter: "Are all your sons here?" (v. 11). Jesse replies that there is, indeed, another son, who is out tending sheep. He is the youngest (haqqaton), although the adjective can also mean the "smallest" as well.[5] With regard to the latter meaning, the contrasts are striking—Saul stands "head and shoulders above everyone else" (9:2b), while David could be the "smallest." On the other hand, Saul "came from the smallest clan of the smallest tribe (9:21)."[6] Samuel responds to this information from Jesse, directing that this shepherd-boy be sent for, adding, "we will not sit down until he comes here" (16:11). The Hebrew is ambiguous, but the NRSV has captured the core issue. Everything, including the movement of the plot itself, will be put on "pause" until young David is summoned from his flocks and arrives before Samuel. "The story waits, just as Israel has waited."[7] Upon the lad's arrival the narrator makes an ironic comment regarding David's appearance. (While the Lord only looks upon the heart, we were told earlier, the narrator invites us to see this ruddy, handsome, and lovely-eyed youngster!) Bypassing the irony, however, the Lord directs Samuel, "Rise and anoint him," adding, "this is the one" (v. 12).

He was beautiful beyond belief, and the wind came on him. David is clearly the one intended all along, to give YHWH's kabod staying power and visible form in the world.
—Walter Brueggemann[8]

Samuel does as the Lord ordered and "the spirit of the LORD came mightily upon David from that day forward" (v. 13). Israel has a new king, anointed by divine command and by the divine spirit. Of course, a problem remains for Israel and the Lord. The former already has a king who had also been anointed by Samuel and who, at times, displayed a strong share of the spirit of the Lord.

RESPONSIVE READING

PSALM 23 (RCL, BCP)
PSALM 23:1–3a, 3b–4, 5, 6 (LFM)

The Twenty-third Psalm is most appropriately chosen as the response of the congregation to the narrative of David's anointing. The imagery of story and psalm are shared and, in Jewish and Christian tradition, Psalm 23 is understood in multiple ways as "A Psalm of David."

SECOND READING

EPHESIANS 5:8–14 (RCL, LFM)
EPHESIANS 5:(1–7) 8–14 (BCP)

The epistle lesson for this Fourth Sunday in Lent is altogether appropriate to its liturgical context. Not only does it resonate with the motifs of light and darkness found in the Gospel lesson, this passage on its own has been associated with baptism in the history of interpretation. Even though explicit references to baptism are absent, it would be difficult, if not impossible, to conceive of the "children of light" apart from their calling—"one Lord, one faith, one baptism" (4:5). However, "[t]he thrust and function of the verses remain the same whether or not baptism is actually in view."[9]

The lection begins, "For once you were in darkness [skotos], but now in the Lord you are light [phōs]" (5:8a). The dominant opposition is now in place for the argument. One insight into this programmatic verse notes that those in darkness are described this baldly, with no qualifying identity, while those who are light are "in the Lord." "People in darkness are on their own or are there by their own doing, but not so with light."[10] Now, the deeper purpose of the argument begins to be disclosed. Those who are light should "live as children of light,"[11] bearing fruit "that is good and right and true" (vv. 8-9). Each of the three "fruits" brings an additional facet of Christian life into view. That which is "good" (agathōsynē) has the quality of generosity, of moral goodness, and, of course, that which is of God. The fruit that is "right" (dikaiosynē) implies "righteous actions or works."[12] Finally, the fruit that is "true" (*alētheia*) implies both the opposite of any falsehood as well as actions that model "covenant-like behavior toward God and [one's fellows] which reflects God's own loyalty."[13] The "children of light" are then encouraged to "Try to find out what is pleasing to the Lord" (v. 10). Given this exhortation, the writer of the epistle has at least two rhetorical strategies that present themselves: (1) proceed with specific examples of such good, right, and true behavior or, *via negativa*, (2) uncover ways that are not pleasing to the Lord. The writer chooses the second option.

This *via negativa* exhortation begins, "Take no part in the unfruitful [*akarpois*] works of darkness, but instead expose them" (v. 11). That which is to be "exposed" are any unfruitful works, but interpreters differ on whose works of darkness are to be exposed. One interpretation is that the children of light are to expose the works of the children of darkness (that is, those who do not have "one Lord, one faith, one baptism"). A more felicitous interpretation is that, with Paul in his epistles, the writer here is much more interested in exposing the actions of the faithful when they remain works of darkness. Harold Hoehner argues, for example, that "the context is speaking about believers" and Paul (with Matthew) "exposes, rebukes, and disciplines those in the church."[14] The Ephesians text goes on to add, "For it is shameful even to mention what such people do secretly . . ." (v. 12). Once again, the wording suggests some children of light who have fallen into works of the dark since "unbelievers sinned openly without shame (Eph. 4:19)."[15] The concluding statement of the pericope returns to a positive word regarding the baptized: "for everything that becomes visible is light." For some interpreters, the appropriate translation of *elegkomena* is "revealed," so that the phrase should read, "All that is revealed is light."[17] On the other hand, others maintain that the term does not carry the sense of something "revealed" but rather of that which is "manifest" or "*demonstrably evident*."[18] But what purpose is this exposing of any works of darkness by the children of light? The evangelical importance, Roy Jeal suggests, "of exposing darkness to light is justified by the resultant increase of light."[19]

> For we are not only in the dark, but we are also stark blind. The remedy therefore which the Son of God brings us by teaching us the doctrine of the gospel is that he gives us our sight again.
> —John Calvin[16]

The Gospel
JOHN 9:1-41 (RCL, LFM)
JOHN 9:1-13 (14-27) 28-38 (BCP)
JOHN 9:1, 6-9, 13-17, 34-38 (LFM alt.)

With the arrival of the Fourth Sunday in Lent, we encounter a Johannine sign for the first time in our forty-day journey. Therefore, it may be best to

first consider the nature and purpose of a "sign" (*sēmeion*) in the Fourth Gospel.
A sign is a miracle, of course, but much more is at stake than simply evidence that
a miracle worker is in our midst in Jesus of Nazareth. Each of the signs is at the
same time a disclosure of the true identity of Jesus and an opportunity for those
present to the sign either to see and believe or refuse to see and thereby disbelieve.
The miraculous event that discloses the glory of Jesus as Israel's Messiah and the
Son of God does not transpire in a way that compels faith. In fact, there is a narrative modesty to the signs that provides this open ground on which observers and
participants in the sign may make a decision for or against the light. (In the Cana
narrative, the steward tasted the water that now "had become wine" (2:9) while
in our present text, the man born blind washed at the Pool of Siloam "and came
back able to see" (9:7). Regarding responses to the signs, Raymond Brown has
identified four stages, two of which tend toward the positive while the other two
are decidedly negative. The stages include:

1. "The reaction of those who refuse to see the signs with any faith."
2. "The reaction of those who see the signs as wonders and believe in Jesus as
a miracle worker sent by God."
3. "The reaction of those who see the true significance of the signs, and thus
come to believe in Jesus and to know who he is and his relation to the Father."
4. "The reaction of those who believe in Jesus even without seeing signs."[20]

Given this span of possible reactions, it is fully consistent with the Fourth
Evangelist that the notion of "judgment" is frequently found in relation to the
narration of the sign.

The literary structure of a sign also distinguishes it from other miracle stories in
the Synoptics and even from other narratives within the Fourth Gospel. All of the
signs hold in common several structure elements. In each, the story opens with a
presented need or lack ("They have no wine" [2:3], "Where are we to buy bread
for these people to eat?" [6:5], and so forth). Following the establishment of this
need or lack, a pronouncement is typically made by Jesus that at first seems a *non
sequitur*; the comment seems not to follow. These dominical statements tend to
share several commonalities, however: (1) they locate the sign in relation to Jesus'
"hour" when he will be lifted up; (2) they locate the anticipated sign in relation
to the broader "works" of the Son, and (3) they resonate with the imagery of the
prologue ("light," glory," and so forth). Following the dominical statement (absent
entirely only in the miraculous feeding), the sign proceeds by way of narrative
drama toward an ending at which we will see who sees and who believes.

The story of the man born blind opens with a surprising calm following the
stormy confrontation between Jesus and his detractors at the Festival of Booths.

Remarkably, Jesus is walking along with his disciples in tow (they had been AWOL since the close of the Bread of Life discourse in chapter 6) while, just before this, he had been in hiding from those who were ready to stone him! They come upon a man blind from birth. The newly present disciples call attention to themselves in a nondisplay of pastoral sensitivity: "Rabbi," they ask, "who sinned, this man or his parents, that he was born blind?" (9:2). So here is both a need and a lack. The man lacks sight, has lacked it from birth, and the disciples need an answer to this old question about sin and suffering. Jesus' response is dominical *non sequitur* right on schedule. The man's blindness is "so that God's works might be revealed in him" (v. 3b). Recalling the prologue, Jesus proclaims, "I am the light of the world" (v. 5b). The reader remembers that this light shines in darkness and such an anamnesis prepares us for signs of darkness as the story unfolds. Now, the light of the world spits on the ground, creates mud with the saliva, and puts it on the man's eyes. "Go, wash in the pool of Siloam," Jesus commands (v. 7). The Fourth Evangelist helpfully informs us that the name of the pool means "Sent" (*apestalmenos*, from *apostellō*).[21] The man does as directed and comes back seeing.

Faithful to the rule of twos,[22] Jesus now disappears from center stage and the newly seeing man encounters both neighbors and people who knew him as a beggar. Although there is little opposition present in this new scene, the people who see the man born blind are of two minds on his identity. On one hand, some are convinced that this seeing individual is indeed the one born blind who used to sit and beg; others differ, saying, "No, but it is someone like him" (v. 9). They speak directly to the man—an issue regarding direct or indirect address will surface later—and ask him regarding his identity. His response is startling and unique: "*Egō eimi*," he announces. Only here in the Fourth Gospel does anyone other than Jesus use the emphatic expression that echoes God's self-disclosure to Moses at the burning bush. Wes Howard-Brook believes that this usage reveals "the acceptance by this now-seeing person of the very authority of Jesus to speak the truth."[23] In response to the crowd's questions concerning this feat, the truth-telling of the man is carefully stated. First, regarding the *how* of the healing, the man replies in a way that names Jesus as "the person" responsible for first making mud and then "anointing" his eyes. The shift here from the term *put* to *anoint* (or *spread*, NRSV) is telling. Thus anointed by Jesus, the man "becomes one chosen,"[24] although we will soon see how far he has to go to become aware of that election. The spiritual distance is revealed in his answer to the second question regarding his healer's whereabouts. "I do not know," responds the formerly blind beggar (v. 12).

The allegiances of the crowd are now more fully disclosed, for they lead the man to the Pharisees as the narrator provides a piece of dramatic new information. It was a Sabbath when Jesus did this "work of God" (cf. v. 4). The formerly blind man is again questioned regarding the "how" of his sight, and responds to the Pharisees,

"He put mud on my eyes. Then I washed, and now I see" (v. 15b). This version of his healing considerably lessens the scandal of the Sabbath healing. It also has the man reverting to the narrator's more neutral *put* rather than *anoint* in reference to Jesus' action. However, even this much more modest description of Jesus' work creates a more serious opposition within the narrative. Some of the Pharisees argue than Jesus has in fact violated Sabbath law and cannot be from God. Others of that party respond, "How can a man who is a sinner perform such signs [*sēmeia*]?" (v. 16). The Fourth Evangelist notes that there was a division (*schisma*) among them (v. 17b). The formerly blind man replied to their questioning: "He is a prophet" (v. 17).[25]

There is a consensus among Johannine scholars that the meeting of the Pharisees with the parents of the man born blind lies at the heart of the chiastic organization of the entire narrative. The questions that permeate this encounter are numerous, but the two that dominate the discussion are, first, that of the sin of the parents (recalling the disciples' question at the opening of the story: "who sinned?"). The second question is related and deals with this opportunity for the parents to join with their son—and the community of the Beloved Disciple—in bearing witness to the truth. "As the child is given a chance to recover from his blindness, so are the parents provided an opportunity to be redeemed by speaking the truth when questioned."[26] The Pharisees present the parents with a twofold question similar at first to those posed earlier by friends and neighbors: the issue of identity—"Is this your son?"—and of the particulars of the healing—"How then does he now see?" (v. 19). In response, the parents acknowledge that the man is their son and that he was born blind. Here, they speak the

> Unbelievers in John's Gospel never admit to needing anything.
> —Diana Culbertson[27]

truth openly. In response to the second question, however, they insist on a lack of knowledge and turn the issue back to their son, who is of age and should answer for himself. Our puzzlement as to this vague turn by the parents lasts only a moment. The Evangelist hastens to explain that they answered in this manner out of fear, for "anyone who confessed Jesus to be the Messiah would be put out of the synagogue" (v. 22).[28] Clearly, these two parents, just as did humanity's first parents, failed the test. The parents of the man born blind have opted for life in the darkness rather than risk a new community with the children of light. That core issue is now settled. The son is on his own in his journey toward full sight.

The next scene has the Pharisees returning to the formerly blind man and they bring with them the same accusatory rage displayed by Jesus' opponents during the Tabernacles Feast confrontation. Whatever calm was felt at the narratives' opening is now totally blown away. We are back to the anger and the threats and the irony. The Pharisees begin, "Give glory to God!" (suggesting a legal oath) and they state flatly, "We know this man is a sinner" (v. 24). The man born blind now shows more courage in his response. Replying that he is not sure whether Jesus is a sinner, however, he does know one thing: "that though I was blind, now I see" (v. 25). Again, in response, the "how" question is posed, a question whose truthful answer will convict Jesus of violating Sabbath law. Moreover, to fully answer this interrogation, the man will need to proclaim the identity of the One who has performed this sign. Rather than qualify his answer even further, the man takes the offensive in the argument. He has already told these people about this and they do not listen. In cutting satire, he then asks, "Why do you want to hear it again? Do you also want to become his disciples?" (v. 27). With such an answer, the formerly blind man is now risking a future with the One who healed him along with expulsion from the synagogue. In fact, the next words from the Pharisees do speak the truth, but the truth rapidly gets mixed up in falsehood. They begin, "You are his disciple," a reality becoming more and more the case, ironically propelled by such opposition. Now comes a piece of Johannine irony as they add, "but we are disciples of Moses" (v. 28). Jesus has already explained to the crowd in the Bread of Life discourse that the life-giving bread was not from Moses, "but it is my Father who gives you the true bread from heaven" (6:32). Therefore, true "disciples of Moses" would recognize the One who is the "true bread from heaven." But the Pharisees add another layer of irony; they state regarding Jesus, "we do not know where he comes from [*pothen*]" (v. 29). They thereby confirm Jesus' indictment during the Tabernacles controversy: "You do not know where I come from [*pothen*] or where I am going" (8:15). Now the man born blind finally bears witness to the truth:

Jesus spits, spits in the dust
Spits on a Saturday. Jesus!
—Tom Atwood[29]

> "Here is an astonishing thing! You do not know where he comes from, and yet he opened my eyes. We know that God does not listen to sinners, but he does listen to one who worships him and obeys his will. Never since the world began has it been heard that anyone opened the eyes of a person born blind. If this man were not from God, he could do nothing." (9:30-33)

What is striking in this testimony is not its fully accuracy—commentators hasten to list psalms in which sinners petition God—but its newly communal perspective. "We know," comments the formerly blind man. The contest is now between the Pharisees and the new community that witnesses to the One "from God."[30]

The response to this confessional outburst is predictable. No one is surprised that he is first slandered ("You were born entirely in sins") and then excommuni-cated ("And they drove him out"; v. 34). Now, the rule of twos is threatened. We cannot have the man simply alone in his new outcast status. Hearing of the man's ouster, however, Jesus finds the man and begins a conversation. "Do you believe in the Son of Man?" Jesus asks. The man replies, "And who is he, sir?"[31] The man

wishes Jesus to tell him about the Son of man that he may believe. Now is the
time for Jesus' self-disclosure, but it comes in an oddly indirect way. Readers would
naturally expect that of all occasions, this is one most ripe for *egō eimi* to fall upon
the man's ears. However, the reply is one of clarity, but also indirection. "You have
seen him, and the one speaking with you is he" (v. 37). Commentators note both
the hearing and seeing that are embedded in this dominical pronouncement. The
latter has been made possible by virtue of the healing itself; the former, the hearing, includes everything spoken by Jesus to the man born blind, including the initial word that his blindness was not due to his sin. And ironically, all of those words
of accusation and falsehood directed against Jesus by the Pharisees served to force
him toward the truth. His response was first one of confession: "Lord, I believe"
(*pisteuō, kyrie*). Then, "he worshiped him."[32] The man born blind now joins with
the Samaritan woman and the other outcasts in worshiping the Messiah. At the
same time, we wonder about Nicodemus and even the disciples (except for the
one Jesus loves). Will they also come outside to worship Christ?

The narrative does not come to its final moments with the worship of the Lord
by the man formerly blind. A postscript is added by the Fourth Evangelist, introduced by yet another dominical saying. (This sign is distinctive in having two such
pronouncements by Jesus, serving as bookends to the narrative.) We recall that the
opening statement spoke of the works of God that need to be done in the light
and that night is coming. Now, near the end of the story, Jesus provides the related
opposition of blindness and sight, one we have followed throughout the development of the sign: the significance of these alternatives is cosmic in scope. Jesus
announces that "I came into the world for judgment [*krima*] so that those who
do not see may see, and those who do see may become
blind" (v. 39). However, we are in for one further surprise. John reports that some of the Pharisees "near him"
responded in wonder, "Surely we are not blind, are we?"
(v. 40b). Jesus' response is direct: "If you were blind, you
would not have sin. But now that you say, 'We see,' your sin remains" (v. 41).
Immediately, we find ourselves in a reflective mode. "Just which Pharisees," we ask
ourselves and John, "have remained near Jesus?" Again, alternate solutions are proposed. On one hand, Brown believes that "their presence seems a bit contrived."[34]
On the other hand, Wes Howard-Brook is convinced that the Evangelist is quite
intentional in this concluding scene. Some Pharisees were really with Jesus, but
at the same time, were attempting to remain within that party and participate in
its practices and beliefs. Their sin? "The refusal to commit themselves openly and
allow themselves also to be thrown out!"[35] The hour of judgment is drawing near
and none will be able to hold both to the darkness and the light.

In John 9 Jesus' saliva incarnates "living water."
—Wes Howard-Brook[33]

The challenge for the preacher on the Fourth Sunday in Lent is the expanse of the Gospel narrative—all forty-one verses of it! While a number of distinctive thematics offer themselves to the preacher—including the blindness-sight testimony of verse 25—perhaps a more wholesome approach to this narrative text is by way of a narrative sermon. Happily, this particular pericope, though quite extensive, is nicely structured with regard to our interest in proclamation. As with one of the approaches to the Gospel lesson of the previous Sunday (the "Woman at the Well"), I will explore a strategy of "running the story," a method in which one recounts the biblical narrative while pausing at appropriate locations to explore "how it is for us at this time and place."

But observe the mind of the blind man, obedient in everything. He said not, "If it is really the clay or the spittle which gives me eyes, what need of Siloam? Or if there be need of Siloam, what need of the clay? Why did he anoint me? Why bid me wash?" But he entertained no such thoughts, he held himself prepared for one thing only, to obey in all things Him who gave the command, and nothing that was done offended him.
—St. John Chrysostom[37]

After the opening section of John 9 that deals with Jesus, the disciples, and the man born blind, there are several distinct scenes where one may put the story on hold and develop an excursus in which one searches for contemporary analogies. Once one has adequately explored the contemporary issues at stake in a particular location, the preacher is then free to close that excursus and resume the telling of the story. The pericope is structured and progresses by way of the motif of opposition and response, at least through 9:34 (when they throw the man out of the synagogue). From the moment of his healing to that excommunication, the man born blind comes to a new place of insight and empowerment in response to the growing hostility of his interrogators and detractors. As noted in the analysis of the lesson, a decisive shift in point of view occurs upon the man's banishment from the community. Jesus seeks out the man born blind and, by way of his self-disclosure as the Son of man, evokes both a confession of faith and extravagant worship. Having decided upon this strategy of running the story, it is now the preacher's task to identify the locations at which he or she will place the story on hold and in each respective place develop an excursus.

1. "Where is he now?" ask the neighbors of the man born blind. He replies, "I do not know." All the man does know is that a man named Jesus had something to do with his new life. As for the whereabouts of this Jesus, his response is familiar and frequent. The contemporizing possibilities here are abundant. We are still close enough to the old era of Christendom that we live among many persons—neighbors, workmates, or even family—who have been baptized but who, if asked where Jesus is in their lives today, would answer with the same poignant "I do not know." If the parish is blessed with a class of catechumens, the preacher could invite those who are becoming "illumined" to recall that time when with

the man born blind they would have given a similar response to such a question. And even for ourselves, there are times and seasons when the honest-to-God answer to that inquiry would be the same. With the man born blind, all we could muster as a response to the question is that our lives had something to do with Jesus. "Where is he now?" We blurt out the same reply during those times and seasons: "I do not know."

2. The accusers now attack the man born blind. "What do you say about him?" they hiss. The answer pops to the lips of the man: "He is a prophet." "A prophet, that's who he is!" But this seems an odd reply, doesn't it? Just how, we might ask, is Jesus any kind of prophet in this story? Just maybe, though, it is because Jesus did not even answer the disciples' boorish question, "Who sinned?" Jesus would not agree to its suffering-equals-sinning logic. Here is an opportunity for the preacher to explore how the ghost of such a logic still rattles around in our communal consciousness. Just let a newborn or little child become sick and the guilt can well up with that old thinking, "It's my fault." Or let a congregation come to a tough and challenging place in its life. The question automatically springs up within the parish: "Whose fault is this?" We may want to analyze other aspects of this old "stinking thinking."

3. The accusers of the man are now enraged by his honesty and his satire. They charge, "You do not know where he comes from!" The man previously known as the blind beggar suddenly blurts out, "He comes from God!" Finally, we can celebrate with the congregation all of the grace that has come "from God." The gift of life, of new life in Christ, of healing and forgiveness, of covenant love and life together, and the promise of eternal life—all of this and so much more coming "from God." (We may well find ourselves developing a celebration at this point in the sermon.)

4. The sudden shift in the narrative provides for this final excursus. Even the awareness of how much comes from God has not yet given us the status of mature disciples. There now arrives this concluding, essential stage where Jesus seeks us out, proclaims his Lordship, and invites both our confession of faith and our unrestrained worship. This is the place where we discover that being an outcast for the sake of the gospel is to find ourselves welcomed into a new community of witness and worship. How shall we image this new location within the assembly's imagination? If the liturgy concludes with the Eucharist, what better way to portray such a community of joy that is invited to share in new life in Christ?

Notes

1. Walter Brueggemann, *First and Second Samuel,* Interpretation: A Bible Commentary for Teaching and Preaching (Louisville: John Knox Press, 1990), 120.

2. David Jobling wonders whether God's rejection is entirely novel given that Saul's "reign" has been marked by such vacillation and inability to act as a king. Jobling concludes: "What this means in that kingship has not begun at all, nor judgeship ended." David Jobling, *1 Samuel,* Berit Olam: Studies in Hebrew Narrative & Poetry (Collegeville, Minn.: The Liturgical Press, 1998), 87.

3. Brueggemann, *First and Second Samuel,* 121.

4. Ibid.

5. Ralph W. Klein, *1 Samuel,* Word Biblical Commentary, vol. 10 (Waco, Tx.: Word Books, 1983), 161.

6. Ibid.

7. Brueggemann, *First and Second Samuel,* 122.

8. Walter Brueggemann, *Ichabod Toward Home: The Journey of God's Glory* (Grand Rapids, Mich.: Wm. B. Eerdmans, 2002), 66.

9. Roy R. Jeal, *Integrating Theology and Ethics in Ephesians: The Ethos of Communication* (Lewiston, N.Y.: The Edwin Mellen Press, 2000), 187.

10. Harold W. Hoehner, *Ephesians: An Exegetical Commentary* (Grand Rapids, Mich.: Baker Academic, 2002), 671.

11. The Greek verb is *peripateite* and the literal meaning is "walk." Found also in Eph. 4:1, 17; and 5:2, in every case the NRSV translates "walk" as "live."

12. Hoehner, *Ephesians,* 674.

13. Markus Barth, *Ephesians,* vol. 2, The Anchor Bible (Garden City, N.Y.: Doubleday, 1974), 568.

14. Hoehner, *Ephesians,* 679.

15. Ibid., 681.

16. John Calvin, "Sermon 36," in *Sermons on The Epistle to the Ephesians* (Edinburgh, Scotland: The Banner of Truth Trust, 1973), 532.

17. Barth, *Ephesians,* vol. 2, 573.

18. Hoehner, *Ephesians,* 683.

19. Jeal, *Integrating Theology and Ethics in Ephesians,* 188.

20. Raymond E. Brown, *The Gospel According to John,* vol. 1, The Anchor Bible (New York: Doubleday, 1966), 530–31. See ibid., 527–31, for an insightful analysis of the signs in the Fourth Gospel.

21. The post-New Testament church quickly took this narrative to be of great baptismal importance. Catechumens—those in final formation leading to their baptism at the Easter Vigil—were also named "Illuminates" (those becoming illumined). Brown adds that catacomb art frequently depicts this scene while the lesson gained prominence in the Lenten drama; ibid., 380–81.

22. In the Fourth Gospel, when more than one character is "on stage," there will typically be two but not three or more. Groups who act as one—the disciples, the crowds, the mourners, etc.—function as one character, preserving the rule of twos.

23. Wes Howard-Brook, *Becoming Children of God: John's Gospel and Radical Discipleship* (Maryknoll, N.Y.: Orbis Books, 1994), 219.

24. Ibid.

25. See Brown, *The Gospel According to John*, vol. 1, 373. Brown suggests that the miracle workers Elijah and Elisha are the referents here.

26. Howard-Brook, *Becoming Children of God,* 222.

27. Diana Culbertson, *The Poetics of Revelation: Recognition and the Narrative Tradition,* Studies in American Biblical Hermeneutics 4 (Macon, Ga.: Mercer University Press, 1989), 170.

28. See Brown, *The Gospel According to John*, vol. 1, 374, for an analysis of the various degrees of exclusion and banishment from the community in force in first-century Judaism.

29. From "The Man Born Blind (Jesus Spits, revised)" by Tom Atwood. Available online at http://www.macjams.com/song/14483 (accessed 1/15/07). Used by permission of the composer.

30. Paul Minear summarizes the situation: "Disciples were forced to choose between life within the synagogue and life in Christ." Paul S. Minear, *John: The Martyr's Gospel* (New York: The Pilgrim Press, 1984), 26.

31. "*Kyrie.*" Most translations decide for "Sir" at this point, reserving the alternate, "Lord," for the man's confessional statement in v. 38.

32. Wes Howard-Brook notes the significance of the term *prosekynēsen* in the Fourth Gospel. It does appear in the conversation between Jesus and the woman at the well concerning the place of true worship. Otherwise, "It does not occur elsewhere in connection with an act toward a person and was not used this way by contemporary Judaism, but rather referred to attitudes of respect and reverence toward the Temple and Torah. In light of the replacement themes in the gospel, the act seems to fulfill the idea that Jesus himself will take the place of both Temple and Torah as the site of respect and honor." Howard-Brook, *Becoming Children of God,* 229.

33. Wes Howard-Brook, *John's Gospel and the Renewal of the Church* (Maryknoll, N.Y.: Orbis Books, 1997), 60.

34. Brown, *The Gospel According to John*, vol. 1, 376.

35. Howard-Brook, *Becoming Children of God,* 230.

36. Some of the material in this homiletical strategy previously appeared in *Igniting Ministry Toolkit 2, Lent, 2002* (Nashville: United Methodist Communications, 2002).

37. St. John Chrysostom, "Homily LVII, John ix, 6, 7," from *Homilies on the Gospel of St. John and the Epistle to the Hebrews,* ed. Philip Schaff (Edinburgh: T & T Clark, n.d.). Available online at http://www.ccel.org/ccel/schaff/npnf114.iv.lix.html?highlight=john,9#%23highlight (accessed 1/17/07).

FIFTH SUNDAY OF LENT

REVISED COMMON	EPISCOPAL (BCP)	ROMAN CATHOLIC
Ezek. 37:1-14	Ezek. 37:1-3 (4-10) 11-14	Ezek. 37:12-14
Psalm 130	Psalm 130	Ps. 130:1-2, 3-4, 5-6, 7-8
Romans 8:6-11	Romans 6:16-23	Rom. 8:8-11
John 11:1-45	John 11:(1-16) 17-44	John 11:1-45 or 11:3-7, 17, 20-27, 33b-45

KEY THEMES

• The Fifth Sunday in Lent brings the catechumens to the third and last of their scrutinies. The time is drawing near for their dying and rising with Christ.

• The vision of the Dry Bones is read this Sunday and also as an Easter Vigil lesson. The point of view shifts somewhat, however. On this Fifth Sunday, the preacher will invite the congregation to focus on . . . well, itself. At the Vigil, the lesson is a type of Christ's glorious rising from the dead.

• We expect an "I am . . ." statement from Jesus as the story begins. But when it is completed, "resurrection and life," it almost leaves us speechless. Nevertheless, we will not simply talk about this revelation, but image it with vivid immediacy as we proclaim this great good news.

• One of the rhetorical "epics" in African American preaching elaborates on Jesus' command, "Lazarus, come out!" When moved by the Spirit, the preacher may add, "The reason Jesus called Lazarus by name is because if he didn't, all the graves would open and all the dead would arise!"

EZEKIEL 37:1-14 (RCL)
EZEKIEL 37:1-3 (4-10) 11-14 (BCP)
EZEKIEL 37:12-14 (LFM)

The "Valley of the Dry Bones" lesson from Ezekiel is paired with the "Raising of Lazarus" Gospel lesson for the Fifth Sunday in Lent. The pericope is also one of the lessons of the Easter Vigil in both the Revised Common Lectionary and the Roman Catholic Lectionary. Therefore, in parishes where the lections of Year A are the foundation of the Lenten catechumenate and where the candidates are baptized at the Easter Vigil, the congregation and the candidates will hear this text from Ezekiel on two occasions.

The vision of the "Valley of the Dry Bones" is among four striking visions contained within the Book of Ezekiel (3:22-27; chaps. 8–11; 37:1-14; and chaps. 40–48). The "Dry Bones" vision shares elements in common with the inaugural vision of 3:22-27, including the opening material that signals that a vision is at hand and the distinctive factors found at the onset of such an experience of the Holy. Each of these profound visions is introduced by a variation of the stock phrase, "The hand of the Lord [*yad-YHWH*] came upon me . . ." (see 3:22; 8:1c; 37:1; 40:1c). In the second and the fourth visions, the stock phrase is closely associated with a dating of the event, although the first vision is located within the temporal sequence first provided in 1:1. The absence of a temporal marker in this "Dry Bones" vision has led some commentators to offer that such dating was originally extant, but "later came to be omitted here for some necessary reason, perhaps editorial, which is no longer perceptible to us."[2] However, our pericope does have a significant correlation with the first in 3:22-27. In both, the prophet reports that he was taken (or directed) by the Lord and set down (or went out) in the middle of a valley. In the first vision, the valley is a domestic scene involving buildings and people; in the "Dry Bones" vision, the valley is now desolate—full of bones, "and they were very dry" (37:2b).

In spite of the profoundly unclean nature of the setting, Ezekiel is led by the hand of the Lord and set down in this valley filled with bones. Two terms qualify the bones—they were "many" and they were "very dry" (v. 2b). This is a place of ancient defeat, a place "where death holds triumph."[3] The Lord then asks Ezekiel a question whose answer mortals would already know: "Can these bones live?" (v. 3). However, the prophet does not immediately answer with other mortals, "No, there is no life here, Lord." On the other hand, the faith revealed here is not overwhelmingly positive either. "O Lord God, you know," Ezekiel answers (v. 3).

> Father, source of all life, in giving life to the living you seek out the image of your glory and in raising the dead you reveal your unbounded power.
> —"Prayer over the Elect"[1]

He is then directed by the Lord God to prophesy to the bones. The prophet's career seems disheartening. At his first vision, he was told to prophesy to an obtuse people, and now to a valley of "dessicated bones."[4] Above all, this command to proclaim God's Word to an antique battlefield with its defeated dead is a test of Ezekiel's fidelity to his call. It also comes gravid with promise. If the bones can live again, certainly God's obtuse people can find new life. As if to hearten Ezekiel's resolve, God indicates the sequence by which the bones will be brought to life. Most significantly, Ezekiel is to prophesy to the bones that the Lord will cause breath (*ruach,* also rendered "spirit") to enter them so they will live. Ezekiel does so prophesy and God's promise is fulfilled. Beginning with a rattling noise, the bones come together, sinews and flesh and skin cover them, "but there was no breath in them" (v. 8). In a powerful and poetic command, the Lord instructs Ezekiel to prophesy to the breath to come from the four winds "and breathe upon these slain, that they may live" (v. 9). The prophet does indeed prophesy to the breath and it comes into the lifeless multitude and they live.

As in other visions, an interpretation is now provided by God. The bones represent the whole house of Israel (*bet-yisra'el*), a people whose lament is "Our bones are dried up, and our hope is lost; we are cut off completely" (v. 11b). Walther Eichrodt comments, "Only now do we begin to realize that the vision has come as a mighty answer from God to the despairing laments of the exiles."[5] Not only will the exiles be revived and breathed upon, they will be brought back from exile. "I will put my spirit [*ruach*] within you, and you shall live, and I will place you on your own soil . . ." (v. 14b). And all Israel will know that the Lord has spoken these things and accomplished them.

RESPONSIVE READING

PSALM 130 (RCL, BCP)
PSALM 130:1-2, 3-4, 5-6, 7-8 (LFM)

Psalm 130, "De Profundis," has a tripartite focus on this Fifth Sunday in Lent. First, it is a most appropriate prayer response by the assembly upon hearing (and seeing) the vision of the dry bones. As the assembly comes to see the vision is about God's people now as well and then, we cry out of the depths to our saving God. Second, the psalm is especially appropriate as the catechumens come to their third and final scrutiny before baptism at the Easter Vigil. They wait for the Lord in a most distinctive and profound way. Finally, the psalm certainly could be that of Lazarus as he breathed his last breaths before dying and being entombed. Lazarus in that tomb does indeed wait for the Lord!

ROMANS 8:6-11 (RCL)
ROMANS 8:8-11 (LFM)

As the lesson opens, Paul has made a shift within his larger treatment of the work of the Spirit in relation to the mystery of salvation in Christ. At the beginning of the chapter, Paul has contrasted the Spirit with the law. The former is "the Spirit of life" (*pneumatos tēs zōēs*) while the latter is "the law of sin and of death" (*tou nomou tēs hamartias kai tou thanatou*) (8:2). Now, however, at the beginning of the lesson, the dialectic has shifted from Spirit/law to Spirit/flesh. Those who live according to the flesh have their minds set on "the flesh," while those who live according to the Spirit "set their minds on the Spirit" (v. 6). The former stance, Paul announces, "is death." But setting the mind on the things of the Spirit, he declares, "is life and peace" (v. 7). The latter terms—life and peace—recall the finale of the exhortation in 5:1-11: the purposes of justification are life through the resurrection and the gift of reconciliation that brings peace where there had been wrath. Notice, once again, that the Pauline dialectic between the flesh (*sarx*) and the Spirit is not a Hellenistic dualism of body and soul. Rather, the things of the flesh have to do with our whole being while we are trusting in our own works and hostile to God. Persons "who are in the flesh cannot please God" (v. 8). In fact, Paul can only speak of a mind-set of the flesh by virtue of this encompassing perspective. A critical issue emerges at this point when Paul adds that, being in the flesh, the person's mind "does not submit to God's law," and he adds, "indeed it cannot" (v. 7b). This "law of God" (*nomō tou theou*) does not refer to the Mosaic law. Yet, by such a choice of words, Paul "not only mutes any contrast between it and the Mosaic law; he also shows that the Spirit is not to be construed as freedom from 'law' in any general sense."[7] Freedom from the (Mosaic) law does not mean that the life in those who are in Christ is lawlessness! We also recall, however, that the flesh is incapable of following either the Mosaic law *or* the law of God. Hence, the life of the flesh is death.

> Lord Jesus, you are the resurrection and the life; call _____(*names of candidates*) out of the grave of old hurts so that they may enjoy eternal life with you and all your people.
> —Daniel T. Benedict[6]

On the other hand, life in the Spirit also encompasses the entirety of a person's being. Therefore, Paul can encourage the faithful in Rome, "But you are not in the flesh; you are in the Spirit, since the Spirit of God dwells in you" (v. 9). Paul now encounters one of the tensions within his flesh/Spirit dichotomy. To be sure, the life of the flesh is death. Whether in striving to obey God's righteous law—which leads only to condemnation—or in simple lawlessness apart from the law, death is the outcome of this life of the flesh. But the apostle now proclaims that through the righteousness of God, men and women may have life in the Spirit with its peace.

So how shall this life be celebrated when our earthly lives remain mortal? Two responses are now offered. First, while in our mortal existence, it remains the case that our body "is dead" (v. 10). That is, we remain mortal; our body will die. This condition derives from the old sin of a fallen race and it remains chronic. Still, while in this mortal life, having been given righteousness in Christ, the Spirit already enlivens us to virtues impossible to those of the flesh and graces us with reconciliation with God and others who are in Christ. Second, there is an eschatological dimension to life in the Spirit that will overcome the present tensions between death and life. Hence Paul affirms, "If the Spirit of him who raised Jesus from the dead dwells [*oikei*] in you, he who raised Christ from the dead will give life to your mortal bodies also through his Spirit that dwells in you" (v. 11). Paul refers back to the Spirit's work of raising Christ from the dead, but shifts to the future tense when speaking of the same Spirit's work in giving life to our mortal bodies. There is no body/soul dichotomy at work here; Paul's anthropology is thoroughly Hebraic. The Spirit will "give life to our mortal bodies." This promise of God is sure because through the power of the Spirit Christ has been raised from the dead. For those in the Spirit, nothing will be able to separate us from the love of God. But Paul will wait for the finale at the end of chapter eight to fully sing that song.

ROMANS 6:16-23 (BCP)

The context for this pericope is crucial. Paul has developed his theology of baptism and dying and rising in Christ (in 6:3-6). And the background of this baptismal affirmation is an allusion to a misunderstanding in the Roman church regarding freedom from the law.[8] So Paul begins his epistolary exodus toward the waters of baptism by asking, "Should we continue in sin in order that grace may abound?" and by answering his rhetorical question, "By no means!" (6:1b-2a). The issue is not fully explored, however, and in this pericope, Paul shifts to the social and legal metaphor of slavery. Any person subjecting themselves to slavery becomes obedient to the one over them. However, Paul pushes the metaphor to its most encompassing scope. All are either "slaves to sin" (*douloi tēs hamartias*), which leads to death (vv. 16b-17a), or slaves to God, leading to righteousness. By virtue of our baptism—and possibly resulting from our baptismal catechesis—we have been given a "form of teaching" (*typon didachēs*) that structures our Christian life. This *typos*, though, may be more expansive in meaning than the more literal meaning conveyed in "mark, copy, image."[9] The term also expands "to designate 'compendium' or 'terse presentation' of some topic."[10] The more extensive connotation of the term fits nicely with the overall baptismal theme of the argument.

Paul adds that he is "speaking in human terms" (v. 19a), perhaps explaining his use of the slavery metaphor. However, he presses on once more to interpret his "by no means!" response to the very notion of any Christian using Christian freedom as an excuse for further sin. Baptized into Christ, his death and rising, we are to "present our members as slaves to righteousness for sanctification" (v. 19). Once again, Paul reminds the Roman Christians that in slavery to sin, "The end [*telos*] of those things is death" (v. 21). On the other hand, for those enslaved to God and receiving sanctification, "The end is eternal life." Paul then returns to his earlier military metaphor: "For the wages of sin is death, but the free gift of God is eternal life in Christ Jesus our Lord" (v. 23). These "wages" (*opsōnion*) are rations or money "paid to a soldier" and "[u]nderlying the figure is the idea of regular recurrent payment."[11] For those whose allegiance is to Christ, and who receive the gift of righteousness and sanctification, there is a "free gift" rather than "wages" of eternal life.

THE GOSPEL
JOHN 11:1-45 (RCL, LFM)
JOHN 11:(1-16) 17-44 (BCP)
11:3-7, 17, 20-27, 33b-45 (LFM alt.)

Once again, John is faithful to the literary structure of a sign narrative. By now we expect some sort of need or lack to be stated at the outset and we are not disappointed. The need relates to information that a certain Lazarus was sick. A great deal of information is provided to locate this "certain man" in relation to Jesus and the readers. Lazarus is from Bethany, "the village of Mary and her sister Martha" (11:1). Moreover, Mary is surprisingly identified in a prolepsis as the one who would anoint Jesus with perfume (the phrase is told in the past tense, thereby locating the readers as the post-crucifixion and resurrection community). Lazarus is once again identified as ill with the additional knowledge being provided that he was Mary's brother. So the need has to do with Lazarus's illness and the implied concern and anxiety of the two sisters. A "lack" is also obvious—Jesus is not only *not* in Jerusalem (two miles from Bethany), but has sought refuge from those who were about to stone him, by descending from Zion and crossing the Jordan to an old familiar place. He is in the area of the Baptist's ministry recounted in 1:19-42. Through an amazing coincidence, that place of refuge and remembrance in the Trans-Jordan was also named "Bethany" (cf. 1:28)! So the irony is that while Lazarus needs the healing ministrations of Jesus, this Bethany is a long distance from the other Bethany. Across the distance comes the message, "Lord [*kyrie*], he whom you love is ill" (v. 3). (Here, the term for *love* is *phileis*. Much will turn on the interplay between such friendship and *agapē*.) However, for Jesus to respond to this call by showing true friendship—and being near him in his illness—also means that Jesus would need to place himself in grave danger from his Jerusalem opponents.

Also faithful to the anatomy of the Johannine sign, a dominical *non sequitur* immediately follows upon the statement of the lack or need. Jesus responds to the news: "This illness does not lead to death; rather it is for God's glory, so that the Son of God may be glorified through it" (v. 4). However, the readers (along with the disciples) are thrust deeper and deeper into a state of confused questioning. First, the Fourth Evangelist tells us that even though Jesus loved (*ēgapēsa*) Mary and Martha and Lazarus, after hearing of the illness, "he stayed two days longer in the place where he was" (v. 6). After the two days, Jesus then announced to the disciples, "Let us go to Judea again" (v. 7). The disciples remind Jesus (and the readers) that the Judeans had just attempted to stone him and now he is planning to return to that deadly location! This incredulous comment by the disciples provides an opportunity for a further dominical pronouncement, involving the oppositions of light and darkness, the twelve hours of day and of night, walking and stumbling,[12] wakefulness and sleep. Employing another double-meaning term, Jesus concludes this pronouncement by stating that "Our friend Lazarus has fallen asleep," adding, "but I am going there to awaken him" (v. 11).[13] For the first and only time, the disciples grasp an interpretation "from above." If he has fallen asleep, he will soon awaken. However, Jesus intends a very earthly meaning: "Lazarus is dead" (v. 14).[14] Jesus reveals that the delay in going to his now-dead friend is on behalf of his followers' belief. When Jesus states: "But let us go to him," Thomas tells the others, "Let us also go, that we may die with him" (v. 16). The reference is left ambiguous. Does Thomas mean Lazarus or Jesus? Of course, the statement will become deeply ironic when Jesus is arrested and killed and Thomas disappears until a week after the resurrection when he returns to doubt the Easter proclamation. But acting upon the earthly meaning of his words, Jesus turns again toward Bethany, and toward Jerusalem.

Paul Minear notes that "in telling the story the narrator turns the spotlight successively on three groups: the disciples, the sisters, and the Jews."[15] With the words of Thomas still echoing in our hearing—"that we may die with him"—the Fourth Evangelist now turns the spotlight on the sisters. Each of the three groups, Minear observes, "responds to Jesus in its own characteristic way."[16] As Jesus arrives in Bethany after his journey from the area of John's baptizing, the narrator tells us several significant pieces of information we need before this second scene (with "the sisters") unfolds. First, we are informed that Lazarus "had already been in the tomb four days" (v. 17). This settles matters for Jewish readers and for the sisters. Some rabbis opined that the soul hovered near the body for three days following death, Raymond Brown instructs, adding that the detail "is mentioned to make it clear that Lazarus was truly dead."[17] So the first piece of knowledge the Evangelist wishes to equip us with is this: Lazarus is really dead. Jesus is certainly needed for pastoral care of his friends, Mary and Martha, but the primary task of his dangerous mission is already out of the question. However, a related item of crucial information is immediately added. This location is "near Jerusalem, some two miles away" (literally, "fifteen stadia"; v. 18). Moreover, "many of the Jews had come to Martha and Mary to console them about their brother" (v. 19). This additional information, on one hand, confirms Jewish burial customs while, on the other, the presence of so many mourners makes the occasion a very public event. How can news of Jesus' arrival be kept from the irate and violent leaders in Jerusalem when the mourners return to the city? And what will be the outcome of this news getting out? We will soon learn of that outcome in the last scene of the story as the spotlight turns to those Judeans. But for now, a minute detail confirms our fears about this visit "going public" in Jerusalem. As "the sisters" scene opens, John tells us that Martha *heard* that Jesus was approaching Bethany. The Jerusalem grapevine was working and will work as expected!

The scene's action begins with the narrator's locating the two women and in so doing, confirming their stability as characters within the Gospels. After hearing of Jesus' approach, Martha "went and met him, while Mary stayed at home" (v. 20).[18] However, even as the stable characters of the two sisters are in the process of being confirmed by John—Martha is the active one, while Mary sits—there are, as we would expect, some shifts and turns from the Synoptic tradition here. Martha is the initially active one in coming out to meet Jesus, but John gives her activity a more positive interpretation:

> . . . whereas in Luke, Martha's activity is criticized as generating worry that distracts her from the important faith practice of contemplation, in John, her activity implies a measure of discipleship, as she leaves her culture to go to Jesus.[19]

What Wes Howard-Brook does not go on to say relates to the other side of the coin. Mary is sitting, to be sure. Yet she is not sitting at the feet of her Lord, but remains shut away in the house in her grief with the mourners. Both of the sisters are depicted as fulfilling the stable roles of their characters (as, for example, Peter does in all four Gospels), but in John, the action of each is given almost a reversed meaning. Is Martha showing real discipleship while Mary is "worried and distracted by many things" (Luke 10:41)? Martha initiates the conversation with a statement of a certain level of faith: "Lord [*kyrie*], if only you had been here, my brother would not have died." She adds, "But even now I know that God will give you whatever you ask of him" (vv. 21-22). Do the two statements add up to full faith from the perspective of the Fourth Gospel? Internally, we do not know.

To be sure, Martha acknowledges Jesus as "Lord," and holds to the conviction that his presence earlier would have changed the situation. Furthermore, she confesses belief in the intent of God to answer Jesus' every prayer. Put simply, these two statements sounds very much like expressions of the fullness of Johannine faith. However, that Martha still remains in some darkness is confirmed in her response to her Lord's pronouncement, "Your brother will rise again" (v. 23).[20] Martha's response discloses a much more conventional belief than full Johannine faith: "I know that he will rise again in the resurrection on the last day" (v. 24). In this, Martha shares the belief of the Pharisees and perhaps many in the community of the Beloved Disciple. What the Beloved Disciple's community knows, however, is that this *anastasis* has decisively happened with their Lord on the First Day. There is a contradiction between this "new knowledge" that Christ has risen from the dead and their "old knowledge" that, with Martha, all such risings will only occur on the last day. This opposition, Minear suggests, "produced pressures for them to modify their former notions, a procedure that is always difficult."[21] Jesus now sets about this difficult procedure with regard to the faith of his friend Martha. "*Egō eimi*," he proclaims, "I am the resurrection and the life" (v. 25).

The readers by now have come to expect that every "I am" pronouncement of Jesus will both more fully disclose his identity as the Lord and Son of God and propel the story in which it is embedded in new and deeper directions. "Living water," "bread of life," "gate for the sheep," "good shepherd"—the "*egō eimi*" imagery has tumbled out of the narratives, each taking on a life of its own. Yet they all are being woven *anōthen* ("from above") into a seamless garment by John. And now comes "resurrection and the life." In the present scene with Martha there outside Bethany, however, the statement needs to be interpreted more specifically so that this modification of former notions may proceed. Jesus adds, "Those who believe in me, even though they die, will live, and everyone who lives and believes in me will never die" (v. 26). Now, Martha has encountered the "earthquake shock" of the gospel; the conventional wisdom regarding life, death, and life beyond death is now turned upside down. Those who believe in Jesus "will never die"! The pronouncement comes in three successive utterances, each illuminating distinct aspects of Jesus' identity and vocation, his "works." The effect of all three is to leave behind irrevocably such inadequate attributions of Jesus such as "rabbi," "a good man," or the dim-sighted confessions of the man born blind before Jesus sought him out. Each statement of the pronouncement requires further elaboration:

• *"I am the resurrection and the life."* The "*egō eimi*" statement could be interpreted by the reader as one of John's prolepses: information provided ahead of time, before it is discovered in the course of the narrative. Thus, the narrator has given us Jesus' words about "the Son of Man being lifted up" (8:28) and about the "hour" that is to come but is not yet (2:4). Left by itself, this pronouncement could be heard by the Johannine community as yet another prediction of the events that so dramatically will erupt at Jesus' hour when the Son of man is lifted up—on a cross and in glory. Of course, a more radical assertion is being made here, but will need further uncovering.

• *"Those who believe in me, even though they die, will live. . . ."* Now, there is a more direct announcement that those who believe in Jesus will participate in the resurrection. Two issues are raised: First, the assertion, if left by itself, could be interpreted as ratifying the old knowledge of the Pharisees and the members of the Johannine community. Life—death—new life. Second, a closer scrutiny of the statement brings to the foreground its obverse as a real question. Those who do not believe in Jesus, even though they die, will they live? The question will be answered by way of a subsequent "I am . . ." statement: "I am the way, and the truth, and the life. No one comes to the Father except through me" (14:6).

• *"Everyone who lives and believes in me will never die."* It is this final pronouncement of the series that sets the "earthquake shock" into motion. The trajectory of this shock wave, though, will need to be traced, as Wes Howard-Brook notes, between a metaphorical and a literal interpretation.[22] On one hand, a literal interpretation would have it maintained that those who believe in Jesus simply do not die in the first place. On the other hand, a metaphorical interpretation could leave us detached from this world where bearing witness to the light encounters such fierce and constant opposition. Howard-Brook restates the question: "'[W]ill death separate the disciples from the community and from God?' And the corollary: 'Will the fear of death prevent discipleship from taking root in the first place?'"[23] Ultimately, answers will need to await the impending sign and the faithfulness of the response by Jesus' followers. For now, however, the spotlight on "the sisters" has narrowed to focus solely on Martha. Will death (either a fear of death or death itself) separate Martha from her friend who is the resurrection and the life?

Or more simply: what propels Jesus to his crucifixion in the Fourth Gospel is the calculated risk he takes in expressing his love for two women (11:7-10), and the calculated risk the women take by telling Jesus of their brother's illness.
—Jeffrey L. Staley[24]

Jesus brings all these questions to Martha by way of the most simple and most radical question: "Do you believe this?" (v. 26). It would appear that Martha's response will be clear cut, either remaining with the old knowledge of the Pharisees or coming to the new knowledge of this "*egō eimi.*" Her answer, however, is anything but clear cut. Martha exclaims, "Yes, Lord, I believe that you are the Messiah, the Son of God, the one coming into the world" (v. 27). But while this confession would align with some success with belief in Christ in the Gospel of Mark (see Mark 1:1), it may be wanting with regard to the Johannine understanding of faith. Paul Minear explains this dramatic point of decision for Martha:

If [Martha] believes, such belief should produce greater change in her attitude toward death than is thus far apparent. Of course, it is possible to accept her answer as being fully satisfactory: "Yes, Lord, I believe you are the Christ [11:27]." Rather, I think that the narrator intended to fault that answer. She is unable to say, "Lord, I believe that whoever lives and believes in you shall never die."[25]

As it stands, Martha leaves the spotlight with more questions for the viewers than answers. To be sure, she has confessed more true belief in Jesus than has any of the Twelve. Jesus is "Lord [kyrie]," "Messiah [Christos]," and "Son of God [hyios tou theou]." Certainly, in these confessions, she has ventured far beyond the belief of the Pharisees. Yet, does she know now that Jesus is the resurrection and the life? We will need to await any further words and actions. At this point, just outside Bethany, we are left with more questions than answers. And to be sure, for the community of the Beloved Disciple and for our communities of faith, perhaps at this point all have great solidarity with Martha.[26]

The spotlight now begins its shift to the other sister, to Mary. Martha goes back and secretly calls Mary, telling her, "The Teacher [didaskalos] is here and is calling for you" (v. 28). We laud Martha's wisdom in speaking "secretly" to Mary, remembering the threats to Jesus' life so recently encountered during Tabernacles. But what dismays or confuses us a bit is Martha's "downsizing" of her Christology. After all, many, even Jesus' most vociferous opponents, have called Jesus "rabbi" (teacher). On the other hand, perhaps this is the term of endearment for Jesus with this family in Bethany. Having heard this secret word, Mary "got up quickly and went to him" (v. 29). Oddly, Jesus has not moved from the place where Martha met him; he remains outside the town. But if this lack of movement is for safety's sake, it is soon rendered irrelevant. The mourners in the house see Mary quickly get up (anestē) and leave the house. Believing she was going to the tomb, they follow her, planning to weep there with her. However, Mary quickly walks out of Bethany to where Jesus is standing. This occasion has just become exactly the public event the disciples had feared. Even though this attempted secrecy has been thwarted, Mary propels the story ahead by bringing the mourners along. Her words, though, do not advance things all that much; they are identical to those of her sister. "Lord, if only . . . ," she begins. But upon seeing both Mary and "the Jews" weeping, Jesus was "greatly disturbed in spirit and deeply moved" (v. 33). These terms describe more than meets the eye. The Greek word translated "greatly disturbed," embrimasthai, most typically denotes a state of anger or indignation. Bodily turmoil is involved in this state—the verb is onomatopoetic, meant to imitate a horse snorting. The other Greek term, translating "deeply moved," etaraxen, also refers to deep bodily emotions and can be translated "shuddered" or "stirred." It can also mean "fearful." Raymond Brown translates the phrase, "shuddered, moved with the deepest emotions."[27] Some interesting theories have been proposed for this reaction of Jesus to the sight of Mary and the mourners all weeping. Two interpretations contend for preeminence. First, it is proposed that Jesus' disturbance is not in response to the grief that abounded, but to "the unbelief that accompanies it."[28] Second, along with John Chrysostom, it is suggested that, as in the Synoptics' Garden of Gethsemane incident, Jesus experiences "emotional distress prompted by the imminence of death and the struggle with Satan.[29] In either case, Jesus asks, "Where have you laid him?" (v. 34a).

The spotlight is now beginning to shift to "the Jews," as Paul Minear has noted. Their answer is "Lord, come and see." Once again, faith is revealed as faltering and inadequate. The response affirms Jesus as "Lord," but the "come and see" affirms death's last word. Jesus now weeps at this tragic situation. The mourners misunderstand that Jesus weeps in large part for them and they blurt out piously, "See how he loved him!" (v. 36). However, some cynics in the crowd were heard to comment, "Could not he who opened the eyes of the blind man have kept this man from dying?" (v. 37). Again, "greatly disturbed" (v. 38), Jesus comes to the tomb with its stone placed against the opening. He orders, "Take away the stone" (v. 39). Now Martha reappears with the obvious information about the stench that will come, it being four days. Her Lord's response is to remind her of the glory of God that he said would be revealed. The action now becomes tense and terse. The stone is rolled away. Jesus, looking upward, gives thanks (*eucharistō*) to the Father for always hearing him. But this prayer is said for the crowd's sake, "so that they may believe that you sent (*apesteilas*) me" (v. 43). Then, in a loud voice, Jesus calls, "Lazarus, come out!" Wes Howard-Brook comments, "The shepherd has called his sheep by name; will the one in the tomb hear his voice?"[30] Yes. Lazarus who was dead comes out of the tomb, "his hands and feet bound with strips of cloth, and his face covered with a cloth" (v. 44).[31] Jesus then orders the crowd, "Unbind him, and let him go" (v. 44b). One of the sheep has indeed heard the voice of his shepherd who is resurrection and life.

> Life for Lazarus means death for Jesus.
> —Paul S. Minear[32]

HOMILETICAL STRATEGIES

Once again, preachers are dealing with a Johannine pericope of considerable length. The preacher likely will be tempted to extract some "nugget" from the lengthy text and develop a sermon based on some distilled topic. Given the remarkable richness of the narrative, however, one may well decide upon a strategy for preaching "The Raising of Lazarus" that encompasses much more of its plot, characters, and intention. One approach that meets this criterion is that of David

Buttrick's "moves and structures."[33] For Buttrick, each move is designed to take form in the consciousness of the listeners while simultaneously becoming one element within the sermon's plot. The moves will follow upon each other in an easily traceable sequence and may—in this plotting derived from John 11—derive from the biblical text's actual sequence or may be assembled in a kind of reflection off the text. However, I will also heed Buttrick's admonition that each move will need not only some conceptual development, but will also require some imaging out of the lived experience of the people. (A move that depends solely on "talk-about" discourse, Buttrick maintains, will simply not form as thought in the congregational mind.[34]) One possible homiletical plot for John 11, then, may be shaped as follows:

Move 1. "Jesus, if only you had been here, my brother would not have died." "Jesus," we cry with Martha, "if only you had been here . . ." The opportunity now is to develop an opening move that speaks of our losses and our longings. We admit that Jesus has been our strength and shield once we are buffeted by such losses. But with Martha and Mary, our question is straightforward: "Jesus, if only you had been here . . ." And we dream of all those things that would *not* have happened if Jesus had been here.

Imagery: How shall one image this conceptual out of the lived experience of the hearers? Of all the moves in the sermon, perhaps only this one can be allowed to focus primarily on an individual sense of loss. So, the preacher may image a client pouring out his or her soul to the counselor in grief. (Note to preachers: Please decide upon the gender of the client rather than creating vagueness in the name of inclusivity.) According to the pastoral situations within the parish, some specific example of loss may be indicated. Also, in order to begin the movement toward the profoundly communal aspects of the pericope, the preacher could provide one example of individual loss spoken to a counselor and then have one example of loss from the congregation's story cited to a judicatory leader (bishop, synod president, and so forth). Each of the examples could end with the same lament: "Jesus, if only you had been here. . . ."

Move 2. The Lord's response is surprising. He announces, "I am the resurrection and the life." Imagine—this friend of ours is resurrection and life. Believe in him and we will live. Believe in him and we will never die!

Imagery: After further developing this center of our faith, preachers are challenged to provide some point of view by which listeners may hear and believe it as well. Since the perceptual modality is auditory—Jesus speaks this "I am" and we hear it—one may do best by remaining with oral/aural imagery. One possibility is to recall for the congregation how moved they were when the "Hallelujah Chorus" from Handel's *The Messiah* was sung at the Christmas Eve service. However, another musical and liturgical hearing of this witness to Christ would also function here. The song or anthem, however, would need to have as its focus this testimony to Jesus and resurrection and life. At issue is our perspective on whichever image is developed. *"And we hear the triumphant song somewhat muted, from behind our thick stone tomb door."*

Move 3. And now, our Lord looks straight at us and asks, "Do you believe this? Believe? "Well, yes," we stammer. But look. For John's Gospel, belief is not just an intellectual exercise. It involves a self-giving in response to our Lord's self-giving for us. So, if we answer in the affirmative, it means all of us (that old, "our souls and bodies" business). Nothing left behind. Anything less means, "No, Lord, I don't believe it."

Imagery: Perhaps an effective way to develop this Johannine sense of "belief" is to image the self-giving of a man and a woman in the Christian covenant of marriage. They are not asked just if they believe in one another. Rather, their vows spell out how this covenant will be lived out for them. Maybe a better way of putting the question is, "Are we wed to the Lamb?"

Move 4. So what if the world has it all wrong? What if new life is given right now in the midst of this world with its death and its darkness? And what if some of those the world lifts up as examples of "real living" are already among the dead? Maybe some of those who according to the world don't count for much are the ones who are really alive.

Imagery: There are revelations at times concerning this life and death business. A firefighter who continues to rescue survivors from a building until the tower collapses on him. The "odd" little woman who drives parishioners nuts but is there every time the church hosts their homeless guests. The retired man or woman (please choose which) who instead of now taking it easy is sweating through "Introduction to the Old Testament" and all the other first-year seminary courses because (he/she) finally said "yes" to Christ's call to become a pastor. (The example list can be expanded and modified.)

Move 5. Then comes the Lord's command: "Take away the stone!" Here is the necessary first step toward new life. This stone—the old sign of death and isolation—now being rolled away at Jesus' word. "Take away the stone," Jesus commands, wherever old death bottles up new life. The move is both deeply personal and yet communal. This stone has served as a sign of human captivity to the power of death. But by way of a command from the One who is resurrection and life, it is being rolled away. That which was so static and impervious is now mobile and responsive. It is becoming a symbol of liberation.[35]

Imagery: Other signs of the power of death can also become transformed into symbols of liberation. Precisely which signs of death will be imaged will depend upon the congregation's theological and social location. However, one that comes powerfully to mind is the old stone tomb door of apartheid in South Africa. Jesus

Christ's word of liberation went out and that stone was rolled away. Of course, much remained in the way of truth and reconciliation. But the rolled-away stone of apartheid had become liberation's symbol.

Conclusion: Now we hear our Lord's voice, calling our name. "_____, come out!" (The preacher might do a short roll call of some in the assembly at this point.) It is the Lord! The sheep of the fold do hear the voice of their Good Shepherd. Our name is called and Jesus commands us, "Come out!" Suddenly, there is a bright light as they roll away the stone from the tomb. We are carried, rushed out into the light. "Unbind her," "Unbind him," we hear. And now they are unwrapping those old grave clothes from around us like a nurse removes the bandage from a newly healed wound. What, we wonder, will we do now with our new life? Resurrection and life. Thanks be to God.

Notes

1. From "Prayer over the Elect," *Rite of Christian Initiation of Adults, Study Edition* (Chicago: Liturgy Training Publications, 1988), 107.

2. Walther Eichrodt, *Ezekiel: A Commentary* (Philadelphia: The Westminster Press, 1970), 506.

3. Ibid., 507.

4. Joseph Blenkinsopp, *Ezekiel,* Interpretation: A Bible Commentary for Teaching and Preaching (Louisville: John Knox Press, 1990), 171.

5. Eichrodt, *Ezekiel,* 509.

6. Daniel T. Benedict, prayer for candidates at an "Examination of Conscience," in *Come to the Waters: Baptism and Our Ministry of Welcoming Seekers and Making Disciples* (Nashville: Discipleship Resources, 1996), 119.

7. Ernst Käsemann, *Commentary on Romans*, trans. and ed. Geoffrey Bromily (Grand Rapids, Mich.: Wm. B. Eerdmans, 1980), 284.

8. See Ibid., 172–79, for an extensive analysis of the baptismal implications of Romans 6.

9. Joseph A. Fitzmyer, *Romans,* The Anchor Bible (New York: Doubleday, 1993), 449.

10. Ibid.

11. Ibid., 452.

12. Wes Howard-Brook notes that the Greek, *prosloptō,* is best translated as "bumping." *Becoming Children of God: John's Gospel and Radical Discipleship* (Maryknoll, N.Y.: Orbis Books, 1994), 253.

13. Paul Minear comments regarding the confusion all this evokes in the disciples, "When Jesus says *asleep* they assume he means *not dead*, but when he says *dead* they assume he means not *asleep*." *John: The Martyr's Gospel* (New York: The Pilgrim Press, 1984), 114.

14. Howard-Brook notes that here is the only place in the gospel "that the narrator directly explains the different interpretations of the conversation partners involved in misunderstanding." *Becoming Children of God,* 253–54.

15. Minear, *John,* 114.

16. Ibid.

17. Raymond E. Brown, *The Gospel According to John,* vol. 1, The Anchor Bible (New York: Doubleday, 1966), 424.

18. Howard-Brook notes that Mary "was sitting" (*ekathezeto*). He adds that "the only previous 'sitting' in the fourth gospel was when Jesus was sitting on the well in Samaria (4:6)." *John,* 256.

19. Ibid.

20. Brown notes that John employs the words *anastasis* and *anistanai* in this particular discourse, terms that will be used again in the resurrection narrative in 20:9. He adds that "*egeirein* in the passive is the more common term for the resurrection of Jesus in the Gospels." *The Gospel According to John,* vol. 1, 424.

21. Minear, *John,* 114.

22. See Howard-Brook, *Becoming Children of God,* 257–59.

23. Ibid., 259.

24. Jeffrey L. Staley, *Reading with a Passion: Rhetoric, Autobiography, and the American West in the Gospel of John* (New York: Continuum, 1995), 65.

25. Minear, *John,* 119.

26. Howard-Brook agrees on the ambiguities in Martha's confession at this point. Nevertheless, "even if Martha's answer may be seen as 'imperfect,' the fact that it is she who gives it rather than Peter is a strong affirmation of the right of women to participate in the community and of the importance of their opinions and commitment." Howard-Brook, *Becoming Children of God,* 259.

27. Brown, *The Gospel According to John,* vol. 1, 425. Also see Howard-Brook, *Becoming Children of God,* 261.

28. Howard-Brook, *Becoming Children of God,* 262.

29. Brown, *The Gospel According to John,* vol. 1, 435.

30. Howard-Brook, *Becoming Children of God,* 263.

31. This head cloth will come to mind when Simon Peter enters the tomb on the First Day and discovers Jesus' face cloth "rolled up in a place by itself" (20:7b).

32. Minear, *John,* 122.

33. See David Buttrick, *Homiletic: Moves and Structures* (Philadelphia: Fortress Press, 1987). Also see my *The Web of Preaching: New Options for Homiletic Method* (Nashville: Abingdon Press, 2002), chap. 4.

34. Buttrick, *Homiletic,* 193–98.

35. I am indebted for this insight to Dr. John W. Kinney, Dean of The Samuel DeWitt Proctor School of Theology, Richmond, Virginia.

HOLY WEEK

MELINDA A.
QUIVIK

Now, in this Holy Week, it is time for the church to own the primal stumbling block of Christian faith: the resurrection of Jesus. Now is the time to head right into all the hardest and most freeing symbols of the year. Now is the time for the church to let the ashes of Wednesday forty days ago come into full bloom as they fall upon the rabbi from Nazareth, bring his followers into true despair, and then vanish in the light of the empty tomb.

This is the most important time of the year. This is the heart of our faith. In the context of a society that always needs a miracle—and rarely searches for a real one—this is the week for every congregation to place itself deeply into the Word of God and the sacrament of the Holy Meal. Because our cultures are torn with wars over religious truth and tolerance and over political solutions to injustice and hardships, wherever our congregations can emphasize the events of Holy Week—as those events speak to our lives today—the communities those congregations serve will benefit.

Holy Week sets before us the image of God as One who does not enter into the quarrels resulting from human ignorance and sin, but instead falls down before the impossibility of solving them. The image is of God who becomes as nothing in order to bring us to a silence in which we might, then, finally hear the impossible word of hope.

Why the Liturgical Calendar Matters

Time is such an insidious aspect of our lives that we may forget to pay attention to the ways in which it dominates the structure of our days. We can become so accommodated to the pattern of weekday work schedules and weekend activities at home that we do not notice the many alternative foci that might serve to order our days.

The liturgical calendar is a blessing for its ability to disrupt our assumptions about time. The liturgical calendar overlays the secular calendar with its orderly months and weeks (that too often now begin, at least in print, on Monday rather than Sunday). But the liturgical calendar moves to a different rhythm: it does not respect weekdays. Instead, it interrupts weekdays with events of faith—if we take them to heart—like Monday, Tuesday, Wednesday in Holy Week—the last days in Lent—and then the great Three Days: Maundy Thursday, Good Friday, Easter Vigil. We could include in that inventory of days that interrupt the secular calendar all the special feast days during the year: the Annunciation, the Assumption, as well as commemorations of martyrs of the faith, renewers of the church, missionaries, pastors, bishops, theologians, musicians, and many more—remembering them on the date on which they are known or believed to have died. These days can become lost because we are too busy with work to come together for prayer.

O God, your Son chose the path that led to pain before joy and to the cross before glory. Plant his cross in our hearts, so that in its power and love we may come at last to joy and glory, through Jesus Christ, our Savior and Lord, who lives and reigns with you and the Holy Spirit, one God, now and forever. Amen.
—*Evangelical Lutheran Worship*[1]

But in Holy Week the church is compelled not to be too busy. We come together especially on Thursday to care for one another by taking each other's very feet in our hands (oh, what a powerful picture of self-giving on both sides of the washing), and then on Friday to pray for the world in the context of the crucifixion, and even on Saturday to sit in Vigil and hear the stories of our faith. In this way, we hold one liturgy situated in the presence of Scripture readings and sacraments that image God's deliverance in our world.

We need this disturbing calendar lest we come to believe that our own sense of time is the real time. God's time is, in fact, the real time. We need to be brought to that realization over and over again, to hear in the words of Holy Scripture the promises of eternity and the great scope of God's mercy. We cannot see that breadth in the clocks on our walls or in our appointment calendars. We require the patterns of a very serious and intentional tradition to even begin to approach what is meant by "he is risen, he is not here . . . go to Galilee . . . he has gone ahead of you. . . ." We require the treasures of a tradition much bigger than any of us or any of our congregations or even denominations to hold onto this unbelievable story. Although we revisit a plotted story line whenever we hear the Passion and resurrection, it isn't so much a narrative as it is an assertion of characters, events, fears, manipulations, and visions that become a part of our own present reality in the telling and hearing of them.

Without these signs of the ineffable Holy God, we are at a loss to explain our place in the universe—either in space or in time. So, we need Holy Week, the end of Lent leading to the Three Days. We need to live it fully and take it as the gift it is for every one of us.

Encouraging the Full Three Days

The new ELCA book for the Sunday assembly, *Evangelical Lutheran Worship* (ELW),[2] contains the Three Days for the first time in any Lutheran book of worship. Prior to this book, Lutheran congregations that treasured holding Maundy Thursday, Good Friday, and the Vigil of Easter had to find the worship orders in liturgical books published for the pastor's use and usually hidden from the congregation in the pastor's study. Now all the readings, symbols, movements, gestures, and logic of the Three Days can belong, quite visibly, to all who sit in the pew and look through the book of liturgies and songs, making sure that all the baptized "own" this liturgy.

Movement toward encouraging churches to observe the Three Days has been a commitment of liturgical renewal over the last several decades and has resulted in the inclusion of services for the Three Days in Methodist, Presbyterian, Episcopalian, and Lutheran as well as Roman Catholic worship books. As liturgical scholars increasingly emphasized the liturgical link between sacraments and Jesus' resurrection, baptism came to be understood by many churches as appropriately central to the Easter Vigil. Scholars also made the case that without the full thrust of the Three Days—the command to serve, meditation on the cross, and hearing the full story of God's power in our midst—the movement from Palm/Passion Sunday to Easter could not convey enough about the Christian faith.

> God, of your goodness give me yourself for you are sufficient for me. I cannot properly ask anything less, to be worthy of you. If I were to ask less, I should always be in want. In you alone do I have all.
> —Julian of Norwich[3]

It has long been a source of wonderment that congregations could be expected to receive the import of the resurrection without having it set in the context of the full Passion story: the foot washing at the Last Supper, the crucifixion, and most importantly, the waiting—holding vigil—at the tomb, not sure what it would come to. For this plot mirrors our own lives. When we visit the symbols of its actions every year, year after year, we are in fact reengaging the story of our daily lives. We have always before us the possibility of truly caring for one another, turning to each other in loving and steadfast kindness, yet death by cruelty, poverty, and injustice tramples on our hopes. These are facts of life. They are no less real for us than was the dinner in the upper room for Jesus and the disciples and the betrayal. Certainly, we know destruction on our city streets, our desolated landscapes, our brothers and sisters who die from lack of proper nutrition and so many other unnecessary lacks. We also know the surprise of returning hope, the unbelievable resurgence of possibility made real for us through Christ's daily presence and the inexplicable goodness that can and does come, both to those who suffer the most and to those who ease suffering. So it is that the empty tomb is manifest in our midst.

When we do not give ourselves time to reside fully in these signs of God's recognition of our reality, we are shortchanged. Our comprehension, our realization (to get away from suggesting that this is a cognitive matter), is blunted. There is no Easter Sunday without Good Friday, as the slogan says.

If we believe that the meal is enough on Maundy Thursday or that the so-called Seven Last Words are enough on Good Friday and we can skip over the Vigil and head right on into Easter Sunday, we have missed the point. The meal and the foot washing belong together on Thursday. The meal is about Jesus' sacrifice. The foot washing is about Jesus' example to us of service. We are fed by him so that we can serve like him. We are not able to wash the feet of others without first having received Jesus' gift of his body and blood, without, in effect, taking into ourselves the reality of Jesus. A meal without foot washing does not make this connection clearly enough. And once we have eaten the meal, who are we meant to be if not persons devoted to the care of our sisters and brothers?

And then, if on Good Friday—instead of silence, adoration of the cross, and prayer—we hear the Last Words, we are given an amalgamated experience of the crucifixion. Those words do not appear *together* in any one of the Gospel accounts. To string them together is to do as Mel Gibson's movie *The Passion of Christ* did with the Gospel accounts of the crucifixion; in the end, there is no dependable substance because the ingredients have been pureed into a flavorless soup. It is the differences between the Gospel accounts that tell us the most about Jesus.

In many cultures there is an ancient custom of giving a tenth of each year's income to some holy use. For Christians, to observe the forty days of Lent is to do the same thing with roughly a tenth of each year's days.
—Frederick Buechner[4]

Comb the Three Days texts in worship books of many of our Christian denominations for the brilliance of these liturgies as they appear. They are meant to lay out what the end of Holy Week brings us to grasp: a risen Christ who, in the beginning of his Passion, taught washing and eating, whose death we need to see as a cross rather than as tea lights to be extinguished (they are easy to purchase and replace, but a cross . . . !), and for whom we wait beside the tomb.

Which brings us to the reason for the Vigil of Easter: the darkness of doubting, the ignorance about it all, the sad inevitability of Jesus' death, and the suffering of all who spend their lives as prophets pointing the way to something better than what we have now. Those voices are among us today. As with the poor, they, too, are always with us. We simply don't listen. But none has the power and eternal weight of Jesus of Nazareth. So, at the Vigil we contemplate his dying while we hear the stories that have brought us to this night.

The readings from the Old Testament pile up the images of our heritage: the creation, flood, Abraham and Isaac, the exodus, Isaiah announcing salvation free for all, God's wisdom, Ezekiel's announcement of a new heart and spirit, his vision of the dry bones, the in-gathering of the people, clothed in salvation, and delivered from a fiery furnace. Without these images the impact of the resurrection is bereft of its full context, and we are the poorer. When we gather for the Vigil, we physically rest inside these witnesses who proclaim to us what gives meaning to our lives.

The Vigil of Easter is essential to the trombone-blasting celebration of the resurrection meal of Jesus' body and blood. There is a rhythm to the Three Days that even has a sensate emotional beat, moving from a table feast with friends on Thursday and then a disrupting command to serve to the Friday silence out of which prayer for the world cries out. Saturday continues the silence and solemnity with candles and song and stories until the Gospel is proclaimed and we see with joy—and confusion!—the gardener who says, "Don't cling to me. . . ." The liturgy of the Passion moves from regular meal to oddness to silence to more silence and finally to trumpets. This is the heart of things. Do not believe me. Believe in the Risen One. Fully embrace the signs and words by which Christ Jesus is known in this world.

About Preaching the Heart of the Gospel

In Martin Luther's terms, the preacher's task is to find the *Herzpunkt* of the text(s) and preach the gospel out of that core. The "heart-point" is a provocative image of the lifeblood, the beating pulp of God's Word. To find it, again in Luther's common terms, the preacher looks for the law and the gospel in the text(s).

On a Sunday, for the sake of the gathered people, the preacher considers all three texts read from those appointed by the lectionary: from the Hebrew Scriptures, from the Epistles, and from the Synoptic Gospels or Gospel of John.

The Revised Common Lectionary includes both sequential and complementary options for most Sunday's readings. Both patterns have strengths and drawbacks. The sequential list offers larger pieces of Scripture read "in sequence" week by week, which is helpful especially for teaching. They can include texts the assembly might not otherwise encounter, given the difficulty people have engaging in Bible study either in groups or individually due to time constraints in our overly busy worlds. The complementary lectionary is based on typological, imaginal, and liturgical relationships between the texts. The complementary lectionary connects the two testaments by inviting the assembly to encounter faith through the lens of sometimes obviously—sometimes disparately—associated symbols and signs. Using either lectionary rationale, it is possible to go deeply enough into the texts to find the common thread of law and gospel.

Sometimes the best thing to do with the Epistle reading is to delink its specific law and gospel dichotomy from the other two texts and instead see it as a proclamation about the church's task. But even this is not necessary. The Holy Spirit runs through every word binding them all to the contemporary moment. Look and you will find the heart of it.

By the end of the sermon listeners should rely not upon their own inadequate resources and strength to make the needed reparations in their lives, but on the strength of God in Christ who empowers all people both to discern and carry out what is required. —Paul Scott Wilson[5]

In all three texts, the Word of God tells the truth of our lives. This is the law. It might come in the form of a command from the narrator or prophet or apostle or from the Lord. It might not be a "command," as such, but an assertion of how we creatures live with one another or an implication that gets at something about our troubled lives. The preacher will also find the gospel, the promises of God, in each of the three texts. The gospel might be the words of an angel saying, "do not be afraid," the image of a pillar of cloud by day and a pillar of fire by night, the steadfast faith of someone persecuted, the still small voice Elijah "heard," or, indeed, the empty tomb. Both law and gospel shine through every text of the Scriptures either overtly stated or covertly inferred as the background context out of which its opposite comes forth.

Preachers are notorious for saying that lectionary texts do not connect with each other. The preacher's challenge for every sermon is to defy that possibility and find the *herzpunkt*. The preacher first locates and articulates in simple, short phrases what seems to be the law and gospel crux of each text. By doing this, the preacher can then boil these down to get at the very "heart-point" of the texts. This exercise is to ask oneself while praying with the Scriptures in preparation for preaching: What is the law in this text? What is the gospel? And then, having answered those two questions, ask: What is the commonality between them in terms of law? In terms of gospel?

While it is true that some texts and phrases can be understood as expressing law and gospel simultaneously—and this is a great gift of the Holy Scriptures and of the paradoxes of God's Word—the complexity of this overlap is most apparent and useful when first seen separately.

Once the preacher has named the *Herzpunkt* of the readings, the task of sermon preparation turns to sermon structure. Homiletics professor Paul Scott Wilson conceives the sermon as a document in four pages. (These pages are simply a handy conceptual tool and do not mean to dictate the length of a sermon.) The basic proposal breaks down the focus of each page in this way:

Page One: Trouble in the Text
Page Two: Trouble in the World
Page Three: Grace in the Text
Page Four: Grace in the World

Wilson uses the words *Trouble* and *Grace* for what others would call *law* and *gospel*.[6] Trouble and Law are not exactly equal in what the terms suggest, but we can let them stand as synonyms for the truth about human and creation's reality. Grace and gospel stand for what God is doing in our midst to transform what is troubled into something whole and life-giving. A quick glance at the content of the pages above reveals that Wilson advocates a 50-50 balance in the sermon between (1) Trouble/Grace and (2) Text/World.

Using, for example, the Holy Week text from Monday—John 12:1-11, in which Mary anoints Jesus' feet—the preacher might begin the sermon on Page One (Trouble in the Text), describing what the text reveals about the difficulties for Mary in that event, the conflict between Mary's extravagance and Judas's concern not to "waste" the costly ointment. Page Two (Trouble in the World) might deal with the society's conflicts over use of tax monies or the inability of some of us to understand others' choices with regard to resources or the ways in which Jesus' statement about the poor always being with us has been abused to excuse disregard for the poor. Page Three (Grace in the Text) would return to the text and talk about Jesus' defense of Mary (how good it must have been for her to feel defended and protected by his commanding wisdom!) and Jesus' turning her action into permission to do things that don't seem immediately practical or valuable in any way. Then Page Four (Grace in the World) would show how this very defense and permission operates even in our lives as we struggle with the value of things and how to use our time, where to place our energies, and how to accept thankfully the incredible extravagance of God's bounty being poured out today for us and for our neighbors.

Preachers confuse nonaction verbs with grace. Statements such as, "God is present; God hears; God cares," etc. are good as far as they go but they are not much better than Bette Midler's song verse, "From a distance God is watching." On their own, such words are not much help if listeners are in trouble and need God to do something. God is no mere spectator, onlooker, sightseer, or voyeur. God cares enough to do something, to become involved, to get messed up in human affairs, to work for good, to bring forth transformation, to be vulnerable, to suffer, even to die on a cross.
—Paul Scott Wilson[7]

This structure leaves plenty of room for rearranging the pages and, thus, rearranging the content as it is presented. These pages can be reshuffled or woven together. It may be that a sermon does not explicitly spell out the subject matter of one of the pages, but instead suggests it so well the assembly hears it anyway.

The point is that the sermon—especially in this structure of Trouble and then Grace in a 50-50 apportionment—moves from reality to promise, from what *is* to what *will be*, from what *we* see to what *God* sees, from how we struggle to how God's power is alive in our communities, and on and on. When the preacher begins from the *Herzpunkt*, the assembly is drawn into an experience of clarified paradox through which the whole truth in all its depth is offered.

IMAGES IN THE TEXTS

The primary trajectory of images in this week begins with the paradox of Palm/Passion Sunday. Why do we read both of these stories on the same day? To those who think we are "enacting" the story of Jesus' crucifixion this Holy Week, it will seem ludicrous to read about his triumphant procession and his death on the same day. How can we leap into the death before we have arrived at Good Friday? Others may believe that we read both of these texts on this Sunday because "nobody comes on Thursday or Friday, so they better hear it now." Ah, a practical but liturgically faulty reasoning. Christians are formed through paradox, letting conflicting images stand together so that through their incongruity, through their impossibility, we might get a glimpse of something true.

• *Palm/Passion Sunday*, by creating a paradoxical occasion, sets us out on *that* journey. And it is Jesus' journey, too: from death into life.

• *Monday*'s imagery is dominated by Mary's exquisite witness to Jesus' impending death. She anoints the feet of the bruised reed who gives light to the nations. Here is parallel or foreshadowing of the Thursday foot washing. These images feed each other.

• The text on *Tuesday* common to all these lectionaries is from Isaiah—the servant who is sword and arrow *and* light to the nations. Light is in John, as well.

• Light is obscured on *Wednesday* with the revelation of Judas's role in Jesus' death. Without the appalling nature of this betrayal by a friend, there can be no light shining in the darkness.

• *Thursday* is about the Passover and the servanthood exemplified in foot washing. Can we imagine this coupling of texts linking freedom with obedience, and release from slavery with being tethered to those around us?

• The adoration of the cross on *Good Friday* and the bidding prayers offer the assembly a means by which to endure and ponder the healing we receive by Jesus' bruises.

• On *Saturday* before the Vigil, the image is the tomb, the very real description of retrieving the body and taking it to Joseph's hewn-out place. Somber, sober death is Job's poetic song as well, driving home the finality of loss. The dichotomy here is in the clash of two beauties: the gift given through this death (the most beautiful image we have) and the gift of the assembly together because of it, mourning and praying and in that action being the body of Christ not dead.

• The *Vigil* takes all the dear and difficult images and lays them out together for us to stand with, risen to our feet in God's forgiveness, hearing our names along with Mary's.

There are other images. There are innumerable images for preaching. But there is also a trajectory of images that lead from the law of our daily lives to the emptiness of the tomb where good news pours itself out for us. The images are the pathway strewn before the assembly on this week. They are the Word of God, a lamp and a cross and an appearance.

Notes

1. *Evangelical Lutheran Worship* (Minneapolis: Augsburg Fortress, 2006).

2. Prayer for Monday in Holy Week, Years A, B, C, in *Evangelical Lutheran Worship*.

3. Julian of Norwich, quoted in *A Lent Sourcebook: The Forty Days, Book Two* (Chicago: Liturgy Training Publications, 1990), 193.

4. Frederick Buechner, *Wishful Thinking: A Seeker's ABC* (San Francisco: HarperSanFrancisco, 1993), 74.

5. Paul Scott Wilson, *The Four Pages of the Sermon: A Guide to Biblical Preaching* (Nashville: Abingdon Press, 1999), 104.

6. Ibid.

7. Ibid., 162.

PALM SUNDAY /
PASSION SUNDAY

MARCH 16, 2008

REVISED COMMON	EPISCOPAL (BCP)	ROMAN CATHOLIC
Liturgy of Palms	*Liturgy of Palms*	*Processional Gospel*
Ps. 118:1-2, 19-29	Ps. 118:19-29	
Matt. 21:1-11	Matt. 21:1-11	Matt. 21:1-11
Liturgy of the Passion	*Liturgy of the Word*	*Palm Sunday: At the*
Isa. 50:4-9a	Isa. 45:21-25 or	*Mass*
	Isa. 52:13—53:12	Isa. 50:4-7
Ps. 31:9-16	Ps. 22:1-21 or	Ps. 22:8-9, 17-18,
	22:1-11	19-20, 23-24
Phil. 2:5-11	Phil. 2:5-11	Phil. 2:6-11
Matt. 26:14—27:66	Matt. (26:36-75)	Matt. 26:14—27:66
or 27:11-54	27:1-54 (55-66)	or 27:11-54

KEY THEMES

• Christians are formed through paradox: palms and Passion

• A celebratory parade contains the irony of impending defeat.

• Christ emptied himself. "Let the same mind be in you . . ."

FIRST RESPONSIVE READING
PSALM 118:1-2, 19-29 (RCL)
PSALM 118:19-29 (BCP)

The liturgy for Sunday of the Passion (Palm Sunday) in *Evangelical Lutheran Worship* does not include Psalm 118 except for the responsive use of verse 26 as the opening of the liturgy when the people gather with their palms outside the worship space. The presider cries out, "Blessed is the one who comes in the name of the LORD," and the assembly replies, "Hosanna in the highest." The rubric suggests that this acclamation could be repeated several times.

These words are heard again immediately in the Gospel reading that follows from either Matthew 21 (RCL, BCP) or Luke 19 (LFM). Use of these texts and the Gospel story of Jesus of Nazareth links the songbook of the Hebrew people, the ancestors of Jesus, with the Gospel accounts of Jesus' last triumphal entry into the city that will be his place of death. This is not a link that can be understood except typologically, and to see it in those terms is to see into a common experience of people's rejoicing across many centuries with differing languages and yet with the same power and steadfast love at its center.

This acclamation of blessing is the heart of Psalm 118, giving thanks to the Lord who is faithful, who answers need, and who is the chief cornerstone. In verse 27, the procession of branches is praised and the closing in verse 29 rejoices: "Give thanks to the LORD, for the LORD is good; God's mercy endures forever." The parallels are enormously rich, and the people will benefit both from singing the entire psalm selection and from the acclamation. Attention might be given to using the psalm as a song with the acclamation as a repeated antiphon.

PALM SUNDAY / PROCESSIONAL GOSPEL
MATTHEW 21:1-11 (RCL, BCP, LFM)

The narratives from Matthew deals with the acquisition of the donkey Jesus needed for his ride into the place of power and danger, Jerusalem. Matthew includes in verse 4 an aside to the reader explaining that the use of a donkey fulfills the ancient prophecies. Then in verse 5, Matthew echoes the prophets: "Tell the daughter of Zion, Look, your king is coming to you, humble, and mounted on a donkey, and on a colt, the foal of a donkey."

Matthew's use of the text from Zechariah 9:9, however, omits the prophet's declaration of triumph. Zechariah reads: "Rejoice greatly, O daughter Zion! Shout aloud, O daughter Jerusalem! Lo, your king comes to you; triumphant and victorious is he, humble and riding on a donkey, on a colt, the foal of a donkey." Instead of the full thrust of the passage, Matthew only refers to the humility of the rider.

> Our Lord comes from the Mount of Olives to plant young olive trees by his power from on high. Their mother is that Jerusalem which is above. And on this mountain is the heavenly Farmer.
> —Ambrose of Milan[1]

Matthew's version of this event shapes the assembly's vision of the Lord by pressing upon the ambiguity of this occasion. That ambiguity is held even in the title of this Sunday that is named by paradox: palm and passion (joy and pain). The palms are, of course, the branches spread on the road for the donkey to walk upon. All is joyous and welcome.

But as soon as Jesus enters into the city gates, Matthew tells us, murmurs are heard asking what is going on. "The whole city was in turmoil, asking, 'Who is this?'"—a fitting question that we are still asking today.

We do not need to conflate the stories artificially to recognize that this is turmoil indeed. What appears to be a celebratory parade contains the irony of impending defeat. The One who is hailed in this scene will, in the next, be nailed. The ones who are shouting with glee will turn their backs and pretend they do not know him. Those who are the keepers of religious order and holiness will become complicit in the death of the One at the center of the celebration. The greatest will be least, or this will, at any rate, appear to be the case very soon. The reading sets up the dis-ease that will put hearing the story of the Passion into an appropriate context: the paradox of triumph through crucifixion.

FIRST READING
ISAIAH 50:4-9A (RCL)
ISAIAH 50:4-7 (LFM)

For discussion of this text, please see the first reading for Wednesday in Holy Week, below.

ISAIAH 45:21-25 (BCP)

The voice of the Lord in this end of Isaiah 45 is a juridical argument put forth to assert God's superiority over all other gods: "Turn to me and be saved, all the ends of the earth! For I am God, and there is no other" (v. 22). God calls all the nations to assemble and make argument. God's case is that in God alone is all righteousness to be found, and whoever does not recognize that will "be ashamed." It is as if the nations who do not turn to the Lord will eventually come around because, after all, there isn't any option! No one and no nation can live without this only-righteous God. What rings in modern ears as a command—"To me every knee shall bow, every tongue shall swear" (v. 23b)—may, in fact, be more a promise than a scolding! There is simply no way to avoid being entranced by this God and turning toward this power.

Romans 14:11 and Philippians 2:10-11, of course, include this command/promise but couch it for their own purposes. Paul's use of the image concludes with what could be taken as a threat: "So then, each of us will be accountable to God" (Rom. 14:12). In Philippians, the same twist occurs in the command to "work out your own salvation with fear and trembling" (2:12).

It may seem stunning to think of Old Testament texts containing a clearer gospel message than their use in the New Testament would suggest, and yet that is often the case. It may mean that the way we read and preach this Isaiah text can offer to the imagination the God whose steadfast love and righteousness was what Jesus saw.

ISAIAH 52:13—53:12 (BCP alt.)

For discussion of this text, please see the first reading for Good Friday in Holy Week, below.

SECOND RESPONSIVE READING
PSALM 31:9-16 (RCL)
PSALM 22:1-21 or 22:1-11 (BCP)
PSALM 22:8-9, 17-18, 19-20, 23-24 (LFM)

These songs shape a common human cry. In the midst of adversity—even terror! (oh prescient words for our time!)—the psalmists sing of trust in the Lord. The toughest neighborhoods of our cities and the loneliest villages of our sparse places comprehend this fear, this dread. Wherever people are frightened, lost, looking for housing, fleeing from traitors and warlords, this agony is a daily reality. And even in homes that look the most comfortable, broken vessels are surely to be found whose bones are out of joint. These songs are for both the One who goes to his crucifixion and the one who watches helplessly. These songs are for the church on this day as a response to the suffering servant everywhere: "My God, my God, why have you forsaken me?"

SECOND READING
PHILIPPIANS 2:5-11 (RCL, BCP)
PHILIPPIANS 2:6-11 (LFM)

Fred Craddock's analysis[2] of this passage extols the wisdom of the church in appointing this text to be heard every year on Palm Sunday. There are several reasons to agree with Craddock, as those who have read him and heard him preach already know. First, this text has been long thought to be a hymn, and whether or not that is true, it is language so compact and beautiful that one can readily imagine singing it! Second, this is a christological portrait of the One who is proclaimed as human and divine, who *was and is and is to come.* These verbs of existence echo in the hymn in several phrases: Christ "emptied himself, taking the form of a slave . . . being found in human form, he humbled himself. . . . Therefore God also highly exalted him and gave him the name that is above every name . . ." Third, this hymn reminds the assembly that as we hear the astounding story of One who did not aim to be equal with God, did not hold himself up as being above other people, did not seek power and wealth and prestige but gave himself instead to the building up of community and common wealth, so, too, does that witness call to us.

The RCL and BCP lectionaries include verse 5 as the opening phrase ("Let the same mind be in you . . ."), pointing out from the very start that this image of the emptying Christ is meant for us to see in it an image of our own lives. The LFM omission of this phrase means that the text begins with Christ rather than with us. The difference created by that omission is huge in theological terms. Including verse 5 means the text is, from the beginning, about our response to Jesus' sacrifice; without verse 5, it is focused from the start on what God accomplished in Christ.

Most provocative, perhaps, is the realization we are given here—and elsewhere in the Passion accounts—that Christ had no assurance of a reward for his self-emptying. According to Craddock, "Christ acted in our behalf without view of gain. That is precisely what God has exalted and vindicated: self-denying service for others to the point of death with no claim of return, no eye upon a reward."[3] This is a giving beyond all human imagination. Perhaps it is for that reason the LFM does not unduly burden the hearer on this paradoxical day of both celebration and mourning with the command to *be* the same as Christ.

On the other hand, to *let* something *be* in one's self is a restful, gracious reception. It is not a grasping but a welcome. It is visible in infant baptism where the one who is baptized cannot possibly give assent to the event but can only be given what the church offers through Christ Jesus. It is visible and palpable in the reception of bread and wine when the presider or assisting minister hands to each person in the assembly the elements in which Jesus has located his presence. The members of the assembly are not expected to *take* the elements; they *receive* them. The invocation of the Holy Spirit upon the baptized and the invocation of the Holy Spirit upon people and meal are regular glimpses we all receive of the words *let the same mind be in you* that Paul prays even for us in this letter.

> While Christ's obedience is, in the final analysis, unto God, very likely the statement refers more immediately to all the forces and powers that determine human life . . . *principalities, powers, angels, thrones, dominions, elemental spirits. . . .* Those who teach and preach that the saving work of Christ is solely a private and subjective experience in the heart are guilty of unacceptable reductionism.
> —Fred Craddock[4]

THE GOSPEL

MATTHEW 26:14—27:66 (RCL, LFM)
MATTHEW 27:11-54 (RCL alt., LFM alt.)
MATTHEW (26:36-75) 27:1-54 (55-66) (BCP)

The plot to kill Jesus is set in the Gospels at the time of Passover. In this central fact of the setting, a major irony is put in place: the popular and dangerous rabbi who preaches freedom will be killed when the people come together in Jerusalem to celebrate their freedom from slavery in Egypt.

That Jesus knows he is closely watched for the turmoil he might create—in a city that doubles in size during the Passover days—is clear from the word Matthew has Jesus use to describe himself. In the Garden of Gethsemane Jesus asks his accusers if they have come to arrest a "terrorist" (*lēstēn*). The NRSV uses the word *robber*, but *lēstēn* has more political overtones than burglary suggests. Jesus' mocking description of himself is used in extrabiblical literature to refer to "assassins." His opponents may have ample evidence for considering him a potent enemy given his comments critical of the Temple priests (Matt. 21:12-13) and about tearing down the Temple (Matt. 24:2). Yet, in keeping with the pervasive paradoxes in this story, right after the crowd confronts Jesus in the Garden, Jesus repudiates the one who violently attacked one of the soldiers. This is not the terrorist behavior we have come to expect in a world where bystanders are kidnapped and innocent people are tortured every day.

Was he more offensive to the religious leaders or to the political leaders? In truth, everyone in this account is responsible. Although the so-called council held at Caiaphas's house is hard to decipher (it is oddly held on the first day of Passover and is described as a trial by the whole Sanhedrin), the council finds someone who testifies to Jesus' statement as recorded in Matthew 24:2 that he will tear down the Temple. The religious leaders' judgment is death.

This same judgment, in effect, is rendered by Pilate with Jesus' refusal to answer the charges against him. It is remarkable that someone would stand before political power and say nothing. Imagine being lied about and letting the words stand without opposition. Even Pilate's questioning the crowd for the second time and hearing his wife's admonition based on a dream do not move him enough to oppose the cry for blood. Like the religious leaders, Pilate lacks vision—not only about the power that he holds and how it might be used but also about his own place in time. The myopia of expedience, and impatience with complexity, blinds all of them to the larger scope of things. In our own time, we can certainly name leaders who use slogans to describe the bases of their policies, thus pandering to lazy minds rather than teaching the people how to reason with real compassion. This practice is in full evidence at Jesus' appearance before both the religious and the Roman leaders. It serves as a poignant commentary on all of human relationships.

> The Son of Man, who is King of the Jews, will be crucified at the Jewish festival of freedom. . . . Those who should be celebrating freedom make plans to preserve their servitude by killing the one who can give them true freedom.
> —Daniel J. Harrington[5]

Matthew's Gospel has all the characteristics of a good novel: an impeccable main character whose goodness is betrayed; a complicated conflict that involves everyone; a shamed betrayer; nearly comic followers of the good main character who swear their allegiance and then fail; the Powers That Be—religious and political—swaggering with trick questions and their own impunity; a hapless scoundrel whose freedom becomes barter for the good man's capture; a couple of bandits; a very frightening natural disaster at the moment when the good man dies; an important soldier whose epiphanic words ring through the next two thousand years; some women who silently watch it all; a rich man who has a new tomb; and a stone.

What is the preacher to make of all this? Any of the myriad details could serve up plenty of means by which to explicate the text's expression of both law and gospel. The preacher could explore plot movement, recurring images, particular characters and how they change, language used for critical specific incidents, or any of the dominant theological issues raised.

Each of the characters is rich with complexity. Judas betrays Jesus, but Judas also realizes what he has done and the enormity of it drives him out of his mind, or perhaps in his right mind he so despises what his deed has made him become that he can no longer bear to live. Peter believes he will never reject Jesus, but of course he does, and then he, too, realizes it. The women say nothing, stand at a distance, but they witness and they "had provided for him." Even Jesus is without words in the face of distortions and lies. He who has had so many words through so many stories suddenly seems to act according to the notion that one picture really is worth a thousand words. As we know from this side of the resurrection, the empty tomb is eloquent and articulate above and beyond any clarity that might come from a debate over the definition and meaning of God's reign.

Yet, with so many details, how does one choose what the primary focus might be for a sermon on this day? And furthermore, the reading ends with Pilate's hacks having sealed the tomb. It is not an image replete with hopefulness. Where is the gospel in this text? Where is the reign of God here? Could an exploration of that question through each of the characters yield the necessary transforming vision? Could the parallels in our world today help the assembly see the work of the Lord in our midst?

In each of these people and scenes, we readily see the *circumstances* of human life (the trouble we are in, the need we have for God's mercy, the "law" that burdens us because we cannot fulfill it) and we also see inexplicable *beauty* (the release we have been given through Jesus' silence and death, the desire of his friends to maintain fellowship with him, the desire of human beings to follow and to comfort, the "gospel" that gives freedom). The beauty is in the unfathomable and yet undeniable power of this entire story. In order for the sermon to make sense of something horrible being a triumph, and turning the vision of the assembly toward the presence of that victim even today, the preacher might best hone in on one facet of the event and make it very palpable.

Images of treason and irony, of arguments versus lies, of cowardice and silent ultimate power abound in this text. Especially if the preacher can lift up the strongest image, certain details that help give coherence to the entire event, this would give the assembly an opportunity to comprehend a tone for the entire week. I think of the stones Jesus was accused of taking down and the stone at the very end of the reading, sealed against him. We know he becomes the "cornerstone," the "stumbling block," and then the "gate" (a kind of door, possible a stone?) for the sheep. The lamb becomes the gate. The stumbling turns us into creatures who see our own inabilities and then fall into the hands of a powerful God. This is so rich, these words. Perhaps the preacher's greatest difficulty is to find the one image that is really apt for the assembly, really pivotal for the entire text and liturgical moment, and can be dealt with in a complete enough and strong enough way that it will carry throughout the week.

Or could the preacher remind the assembly of the triumph of the palms and let the people's joy serve as a kind of backdrop to the horrible killing of their leader? Could the palms and the passion themselves become the image of resurrection? They are exemplary of the reality of triumph and defeat, gospel and law in all times and places lifted up together as the image of the crucified Lord.

Notes

1. Ambrose of Milan, in *A Lent Sourcebook: The Forty Days, Book Two* (Chicago: Liturgy Training Publications, 1990), 178.

2. Fred B. Craddock, *Philippians, Interpretation: A Bible Commentary for Teaching and Preaching* (Atlanta: John Knox Press, 1985).

3. Ibid., 42.

4. Ibid., 39.

5. Daniel J. Harrington, S.J., *The Gospel of Matthew, Sacra Pagina* (Collegeville, Minn.: The Liturgical Press, 1991), 364.

MONDAY OF HOLY WEEK

REVISED COMMON	EPISCOPAL (BCP)	ROMAN CATHOLIC
Isa. 42:1-9	Isa. 42:1-9	Isa. 42:1-7
Ps. 36:5-11	Ps. 36:5-10	Ps. 27:1-3, 13-14
Heb. 9:11-15	Heb. 11:39—12:3	
John 12:1-11	John 12:1-11	John 12:1-11
	or Mark 14:3-9	

KEY THEMES

• Anointing the feet of the bruised reed prepares the disciples for foot washing.
• Through the servant, the Lord gives compassion and insight to see ourselves, too, as gift.
• Who is this self-giving Christ?
• The woman's extravagant desire is poured out as gratitude.

FIRST READING

ISAIAH 42:1-9 (RCL, BCP)
ISAIAH 42:1-7 (LFM)

It is a blessing that the first reading for the first day in Holy Week so clearly expresses human need for the servant given by the Lord, for that is the existential place in which we human beings find ourselves. We are bruised and dimly burning. And not only are *we* so, but even the lands along the sea need insight: "the coastlands wait for his teaching." The whole of creation, in effect, resides in the darkness of ignorance, yearning for something remarkable to bring relief.

This song (the first, as it is called, of the three Servant Songs in Isaiah) offers a glimpse of what is coming: a servant. This figure has been variously interpreted as either the nation of Israel or an individual supremely admired for having suffered for others. Recent scholarship has cautioned Christians against a readiness to see this servant as Jesus the crucified. The parallels are there, to be sure (bruises, harassment, blood), but postmodern minds have learned that one of the sins of human

236

arrogance and injustice is usurping others' perspectives by defining them away on our own terms. To redefine the suffering servant in terms not operative when Isaiah was written is to read into the text what is not there.

Of further danger is losing—through co-optation—the profundity of the suffering servant as a figure from another faith or time (or even from a different faith paradigm than our own) who, by offering yet another typology, adds weight to our understanding of the Christ. Walter Brueggemann holds that "it is more important to recognize the commonality and parallel structure of Jewish claims and Christian claims at the core of faith than it is to dispute about which presentation of the claim is primary."[1] This isn't a contest. It is not necessarily true that only one interpretation can be right, or that only one faith perspective is appropriate to the mysterious promises God holds out toward humanity. For that reason, the caution stands: beware of too easily assuming this servant is Jesus, a prophecy foretold and later brought to reality. Beware of listening uncritically to the voices that rehearse the trials of this servant as if they were the tribulations of the figure we Christians honor on Good Friday.

What matters is that through the servant, the Lord gives compassion, justice, creation itself, and the breath or spirit (*ruah*—"breath of humans") that makes possible our consciousness of what gifts we are in ourselves and what gifts we receive. To the servant, the Lord gives a call, support, shelter, the power to free, and the power to bring light. These are huge images that set the promise for the rest of the week.

Because the LFM lectionary omits verses 8-9, the assembly is left at the end of the reading with the word *darkness* rather than with the "I am" of God's name. The assembly is left, in effect, with the law that describes the devastating difficulty of life. We do, in fact, "sit in darkness"—as both saint and sinner—so to end the reading with that image reinforces in the listeners our common identity as "bruised" and "dimly burning." When the reading includes verses 8-9, it ends with God's promise that "new things" will "spring forth." This leaves the assembly with the gospel, which tells of God's actions on our behalf.

The effect of either ending, while certainly placing a different emphasis on what the assembly is given to contemplate, does not alter the impact of God's Word because all through verses 1-7 (which are heard in all lectionaries), this text moves from law to gospel and back again, setting each in the listeners' ears with hardly a breath between them. Speaking to the servant directly, for example, the Lord says: "I have called you . . . taken you by the hand . . . to open the eyes that are blind . . ." The Lord promises to heal what is broken. But what is broken is, indeed, real and in need of healing. Both law and gospel are present, and both are required if the vision of this servant's gifts is to be grasped, for it is in the gap between them that the light comes in.

PSALM 36:5-11 (RCL)
PSALM 36:5-10 (BCP)

The psalm as a response to the Isaiah 42 reading continues praise for God's gifts with images of God drawn from nature: clouds, mountains, wings (things on high) and river, fountain, and light (things that come to us at eye level). All around, close at hand and in the distance, reside the images of God's goodness.

This is particularly true for verses 5-10, the appointed reading for the BCP. The RCL, adding verse 11, introduces a balancing image: a petition for salvation from that which seeks to destroy. The arrogant and wicked continuously threaten. Despite the heights to which verses 5-10 soar, verse 11 alone brings the hearers down from the heights to the pain and danger of earthly life that is surely the singer's location. That place is akin to where the suffering servant can be found. Both are in trouble and both are holding fast to rescue in the Lord.

PSALM 27:1-3, 13-14 (LFM)

This psalm continues the song of praise from Isaiah 42 by lifting up the images of the Lord's rescue as light and stronghold. The visages of evildoers and an enemy army stand for what seeks to overwhelm the psalmist. But the power of the Lord will prevail, and the psalmist is bolstered even by the song's words of hope affirming that the faithful must "wait for the LORD; be strong . . . take courage . . ." The assembly singing these words may find its own affinity with them if the Taizé chant to this text is part of the congregation's familiar songs.

HEBREWS 9:11-15 (RCL)

This letter, written to an uneasy Christian people to encourage them, reminds them that Christ, the great high priest, stands in contrast with the worldly priests who must day after day and season after season perform the rituals that occur inside the sanctuary. In verses 1-10 the writer describes the priests' work, bringing blood offerings into the first tent on a regular basis but only into the Holy of Holies by the high priest once a year. Thus do the human priests carry out the necessary oblations to the Lord on behalf of the people.

Verse 11 announces a radical shift: "But when Christ came as a high priest . . . he entered once for all into the Holy Place . . ." Jesus' example—through his life, death, and resurrection—is one of self-giving rather than offering something out-

side of himself: "he entered . . . into the Holy Place . . . with his own blood . . ."
What is most provocative here is the assertion that Christ's self-giving informs our
own. We are not called to *be* Christ, but we are reminded that his gift as mediator
has become the means by which we also give to others. We do not give something
outside of ourselves but give our own selves. Christ must not remain outside of us
lest we use him as our "sacrifice," as if we would make Christ into an offering we
can, in fact, give up to God. Instead, because we are now the body of Christ, we
have become the gifts to be given away.

We, the body of Christ now, are the ones who have been released from "dead
works" to become creatures who worship "the living God." Instead of killing, we are
to feast. Instead of offering up other human beings in acts of righteousness, we are
invited to a banquet that brings hope to all people. Christ's blood purifies the con-
sciences of the faithful, but it remains for the preacher—if this text's focus is central
for a Monday preaching service—to speak to the meaning of Christ as "mediator of a
new covenant." This mediator does not stand outside of human reality here and now.
Rather, Christ makes us his own through the body and blood we ingest. This meal is
not eaten alone. We become the body of Christ corporately by eating together.

Spending some time in the early hours of Holy Week on the meaning of the
self-giving of Christ Jesus will help to prepare the assembly for the coming images,
especially on Maundy Thursday in the foot-washing image of servanthood and
the words of institution at the Last Supper. Each day this week can be understood
to build and deepen the imagery offered by the readings. Monday of Holy Week
lays groundwork that is, in fact, eschatological, beginning here with an emphasis
on where we are going.

HEBREWS 11:39—12:3 (BCP)

For those who use the BCP, the epistle focuses not on Christ as high
priest and mediator but on those who have followed him through the centuries,
becoming in all times the "great cloud of witnesses." Yet, this is not so different an
emphasis, since it works together with the same Isaiah 42 and John 12 readings to
speak of the limitations of human capability and the need we have for each other.

Were this text alone to be the focus for the preacher, it could well be time for
remembrance of the witness of this particular congregation in this specific community. Who are the witnesses who have built and nourished this church? Who
are the ones who have taught the young, raised the money, remembered the work
of missionaries, and tended to the sick? Who reads the Scriptures week after week
and tends the church's furnace? It is a good thing for a congregation to be able
to see itself in the mirror of the preacher's words. These readings all (including
especially this Hebrews celebration of the real substantial work of the church that

day after day sustains the faithful) point us to the body of Christ in whose presence we find ourselves enlivened.

THE GOSPEL

JOHN 12:1-11 (RCL, BCP, LFM)

For Monday in Holy Week, the Gospel reading invites the assembly to stand back and survey the spectrum of perspectives people hold toward Jesus. At an ordinary situation, a dinner, attended by differing classes of people, the various issues aroused by commitments to social, political, and religious matters come to light. This text, offered in all the lectionaries concerned with Holy Week, is about how people respond to Jesus, and it encompasses a range of views of him from deep honor to disdain for the symbol of honor. In one perspective, it is as if, in weighing Jesus and the poor, Jesus loses.

The disciples hold the dinner to honor Jesus. Opposed to their respectful relationship with Jesus—or oblivious of it—stands the crowd outside the house, come to gawk at Lazarus (a dead man raised!) rather than to stand in awe of the rabbi from Nazareth. Mention is made of the chief priests who are planning to have Lazarus killed along with Jesus. And over against their nefarious plotting, we hear of the many people who "were deserting" the chief priests to follow Jesus. Even the gape-jawed crowd comes to be a source of believers.

Opposite Mary's extravagant expression of devotion stands Judas's rendition of how money should be spent with regard to social justice and acts of charity. This question, of course, constantly and incessantly plaguing human beings, is as strong as ever in our own time. What is the value of desire? How do we discern the worth of one desire (to feed the hungry) over another (to honor the Lord)? Is it really an either/or issue? What is enough regarding possessions and giving possessions away? Whole religious wars, political parties, and revolutions have been created and waged in order to battle for the right to answer these questions.

The oppositions established in this text invite the assembly to locate its own allegiances in the persons found in the scene and in the spaces between their ideologies. The hearer is compelled to locate herself or himself in some quadrant of the room in the text. By way of assessing one's prejudices, the hearer confronts the striking fact that Jesus defends Mary's gesture with great force. Jesus cuts through the contradictions that set people in opposition to each other and asks that Judas—in other words, we—stop condemning others based on competing needs. Instead, we should embrace gestures of honor for what is most deeply true.

We are, thereby, in the hearing of this text on this day, set up to spend the rest of Holy Week contemplating what, in fact, is most deep, abiding, and true in Christ

Jesus, for he defends all of us in our feeble but well-meant "waste" of ourselves, our time, and our possessions. The question that haunts us is whether the waste is lame or blessed.

We are also invited to come to terms with the assertion that we will "always have the poor with [us]." In Jesus' mouth—in the context of his imperative to stop hounding Mary about her care for him—mention of the poor is in no stretch of the imagination a cynical or resigned pronouncement. It is only a fact of weighing honor. It remains with us to ponder.

MARK 14:3-9 (BCP alt.)

Here is a different meal than the one described in John 12. Here is a meal at the home of Simon the leper. A woman comes with expensive ointment in an alabaster jar and pours it on Jesus' head. Someone unnamed complains about the "waste," but Jesus defends her in the same root words as in John, "Leave her alone" (*aphete autēn*).

A crucial phrase is inserted here regarding the poor. Just as with the John text, Jesus acknowledges that the poor will always be present and he will not. But here in Mark, Jesus reminds the complainer that "whenever you wish," kindness can be extended to the poor. He, on the other hand, will not always be available.

Especially in company with Isaiah's pronouncement about the servant and the Hebrews' focus on the manifestation of Christ in the present time in the body of Christ made from his own body and blood, the commonalities between the John and Mark readings of a nearly identical event amount to a meditation on the scope of Jesus' relationship with his followers. In short, at a meal among disciples, one woman, recognizing Jesus' vast import, lavishes on him an extravagance that is not understood by those who cannot see beyond temporal reality. Jesus' defense of her—strong and clear—should serve to embolden all of us to pour out our own hearts in the direction of what we perceive to be most worthy and most abiding. Sometimes that means we will not—at least for a little while (perhaps for the space of a dinner)—fix our attention on the pain of our fellow creatures, or even on our own pain! Instead, we will honor what is most deeply nourishing: the One who feeds us with the bread of life.

> Thanks to the cross we are no longer wandering in the wilderness, because we know the right road; we are no longer outside the royal palace because we have found the way in; we are not afraid of the devil's fiery darts because we have discovered the fountain. Thanks to the cross we are no longer in a state of widowhood for we are reunited to the Bridegroom; we are not afraid of the wolf because we have the Good Shepherd. Thanks to the cross we dread no usurper, since we are sitting beside the King.
> —John Chrysostom[2]

A drawback in using the Mark text for Monday in Holy Week is that the anointing is of Jesus' head rather than his feet, thus losing the connection between anointing feet (as in John) and the washing of feet on Maundy Thursday. When possible, fomenting rich images day after day throughout this time can help compile a sense of the layering, the depth, of the signs of Jesus' meaning. Anointing feet on Monday, as in the John story, leads to foot washing on Thursday in the context of our own communities. It is a different matter to try to connect Mark's story of the anointing of Jesus' head with a later aspect of the Passion, although singing "O Sacred Head Now Wounded" might be allowed to supply continuity of images.

PREACHING THE HEART OF THE GOSPEL

As we gather for the readings on this day, we might imagine a simple Evening Prayer service in which the assembly sings the light of Christ into the assembly, sings Psalm 141 ("Let my prayer rise before you as incense . . ."), hears these readings, sings the Magnificat in one of the many forms available now, and prays for the world through the chanting of the Great Litany and singing the Lord's Prayer.

Here at the beginning of Holy Week, the Gospel story invites us to place ourselves (today!) in the position of the one who anoints Jesus for burial. She was the one in the scene who seems to have understood that he would be dying soon. The others remain ignorant of that fact even though he has told them his journey toward Jerusalem will result in his execution.

The woman—whether Mary of Bethany (in John) or the unnamed woman (in Mark)—invites us to imagine ourselves as someone without any standing in a culture antagonistic to women who, even in the company of like-minded followers of Jesus, is alone in her perception of the events unfolding around him. She honors Jesus in a way only possible for someone who sees deeply into the situation and what his presence means for the people, and she is chided for her vision and her gesture.

> A very beautiful woman who looks at her reflection in the mirror can very well believe that she is that. An ugly woman knows that she is not that.
> —Simone Weil[3]

Perhaps we can use this Monday reading and preaching to explore the possibility that the ones who can most point us toward Jesus may be the very people in our midst who are without stature or respect. If we imagine ourselves in this woman's place, we are given insight into either our own circumstances (perhaps we are similarly faithful and derided and outside of the power structures) or the situation of others in our society. These texts set us up to spend Holy Week in the company of those who are abused by the expectations of the religiously powerful. In these texts, we see Jesus through the eyes of others like ourselves who do, indeed, feel the poverty of our gifts in comparison with the gifts given to us in the cross and the empty tomb.

Notes

1. Walter Brueggemann, *Isaiah 40–66*, Westminster Bible Companion (Louisville: Westminster John Knox, 1998), 143–44.

2. John Chrysostom, *Homily 1, "On the Cross and the Thief,"* in *Patrologiae cursus completus: Series Graeca*, vol. 49, cols. 399–400; English translation by ICEL—from Robert Atwell, *Celebrating the Seasons* (Harrisburg, Pa.: Morehouse Publishing, 2001), 206.

3. Simone Weil, *Gravity and Grace* (London: Routledge and Kegan Paul, 1972), 29.

TUESDAY OF HOLY WEEK

MARCH 18, 2008

REVISED COMMON	EPISCOPAL (BCP)	ROMAN CATHOLIC
Isa. 49:1-7	Isa. 49:1-6	Isa. 49:1-6
Ps. 71:1-14	Ps. 71:1-12	Ps. 71:1-4a, 5-6b,
		15-17
1 Cor. 1:18-31	1 Cor. 1:18-31	
John 12:20-36	John 12:37-38, 42-50	John 13:21-33, 36-38
	or Mark 11:15-19	

KEY THEMES

• God holds the suffering servant in absolute security.
• The cross holds foolishness and wisdom in tension with each other.
• The cross speaks beyond logic where true wisdom resides.

FIRST READING
ISAIAH 49:1-7 (RCL)
ISAIAH 49:1-6 (BCP, LFM)

This text is in two voices: the suffering servant and the Lord. The first narrator is the servant. When the servant calls out to be heard, the first entity addressed is the very perimeter of the place where people live. "Listen to me, O coastlands!" is the voice of a servant whose identity has eluded people of faith both Jewish and Christian. It may be Israel itself. It may be the Christ described by Dietrich Bonhoeffer whose death and resurrection means to effect transformation not just for human creatures but for the entire earth. "Christ is *the* new creature. Thereby he shows all other creatures to be old creatures. Nature stands under the curse which God laid upon Adam's ground. . . . As the fallen creation it is now dumb, enslaved under the guilt of man. Like history, it suffers from the loss of its meaning and its freedom. . . . Nature, unlike man and history, will not be reconciled, but it will be set free for a new freedom."[1] Because all proposals about the servant's identity lead to further questions, this difficulty may best point the exegete to think of an open-

ended image, one who is capable of entertaining many identities but at least someone (certainly a person of faith) called and sent by God for the fulfillment of God's
good purposes. And that purpose is large enough to embrace all of creation.

The narrator, then, as servant, describes how the servant has experienced God's
call and what God caused in the narrator in order to make answering the call possible. God made the narrator a "mouth like a sharp sword" and shaped the narrator
into a "polished arrow." Such a weapon can fly smooth and straight into its target,
drawn out of the Lord's own quiver where the arrow is kept hidden, safe, until
the right moment. God as a bow hunter! This was once a sophisticated means for
getting meat, enabling the hunter to tackle animals at a distance.

Today, special times at the beginning of the autumn hunting season are set aside
for bow hunters because some people still recognize the value of such skill. With
the bow and arrow, they move soundlessly through the woods and fields, striking
their prey with only the force of human muscle, braced wood, strung sinew, and
focus of the eye. God has made the servant into a thing of sharp and ingenious
technological beauty who can hit a target with just a whoosh of air.

God hides the servant in "the shadow of [God's] hand," a place of retreat, of
absolute security. To hide in the palm of a hand depicts an image of a size imbalance and therefore a power imbalance. The smaller one who hides is weaker, we
assume, than the one who holds the palm. A quick glance at the mention of "hand"
in the Scriptures reveals a long list with many familiar
recurring phrases referring to the hand of the Lord used
either to rescue or to punish. In Job, for example, "the
hand of the LORD has done this" (Job 12:9) and "the Son
of Man [is] seated at the right hand of Power" (Matt.
26:64). The hand of God holds all manner of influence
over human life.

The characteristics and qualities given by God to the
servant are certainly paradoxical: both cutting and cra-
dling. If the servant is so swift to kill, so sharp of wit, why
does the servant need to hide in a shadow? Could it be
that God understands human incapacity for standing up

The form of the eschatological presence
of God is in "law" and "gospel," in the
articulation of local need and the proclamation of the presence of holy mercy, in
telling the truth about death and life. A
preacher does not need to pretend. What
she or he must do is honestly speak of
our common need and faithfully speak
of the present mercy of the triune God.
—Gordon W. Lathrop[2]

and charging forward into the tasks set before us? Does God know that instead of
taking the old proverbial "bull by the horns," we need a cupped palm in which to
take our rest before and between and during the battles? In fact, God's armaments,
as weaponry, are undercut by the image of the servant hiding. It is an accurate
portrait of human need. It is a statement of law. Were it not for hiding in the palm
of God's hand, in the shadows of security, we could do nothing.

The second narrator is the Lord who speaks for the first time in this text in
juxtaposition with this hiding in the privacy of God's own person. God says to

this little creature, "You are my servant . . ." God, who is much bigger and much more powerful, exclaims that this little servant will glorify God's own self. Imagine this. Imagine that you and all the earth's people are those little ones called out to servanthood while also being held by God.

How will God be glorified? Well, the narrator thought it had to do with gathering the exiles back into the land that the Lord had given them. But this (v. 6) comes to seem "too light a thing" and instead the Lord pronounces to the servant: "I will give you as a light to the nations, that my salvation may reach to the end of the earth." God's glory is in saving the farthest reaches of this world. The image is of an entirely redeemed earth: coastlands and peoples, all nations. This is a statement of gospel.

The omission of verse 7 in both the BCP and LFM ends the reading with the image of the servant as light itself. Inclusion of verse 7 adds a political dimension to the image: invoking the promise that even the most powerful among humans— kings and princes—who hold power over vast numbers of societies will not be able to remain standing upright in the presence of this light. They will fall on the ground in obeisance. The light becomes a source of strength emitted far beyond the needs of only one people (say, those most immediately in the hearing of Isaiah's prophetic utterances), stretched and beamed to encompass all power structures. Rather than being imaged by the proverbial "candle in the darkness," this light is nuclear.

RESPONSIVE READING

PSALM 71:1-14 (RCL)
PSALM 71:1-12 (BCP)
PSALM 71:1-4a, 5-6b, 15-17 (LFM)

This could be the song of the suffering servant as he or she cries out for refuge and help in a time of great persecution. In response to the Isaiah text, the assembly might be singing this song on several levels at once: on behalf of the servant and of the One who will be betrayed and on its own behalf as the members of the assembly face each our own daily betrayal of the Lord despite our desire to live in praise of the One who rescues us. The song may be of an elder, pulling together fragments of quotations from other prayers into a kind of prayer song found in postexilic Israel. The movement back and forth between trust and fear surely mirrors the experience of faith life in every age.

The BCP pericope omits the last two verses (included in the RCL), leaving off the cry that the psalmist's tormenters be themselves tormented. The verses included in the LFM rendition of this psalm speak only words of petition to the Lord for rescue and trust that the Lord will, indeed, come through. It contains nothing of what is tormenting the singer: only a pronouncement of trust in God.

1 CORINTHIANS 1:18-31 (RCL, BCP)

Paul's argumentative skills are in full force here, in phrases so resonant for us that this passage can sometimes seem like a song: "the cross is foolishness to those who are perishing, but to us who are being saved it is the power of God" (v. 18). The verb tenses caution us to refrain from letting this announcement cause us to believe we know who is foolish and who is wise. Those for whom the cross is the power of God are, it should be noted, "being saved" (*sōzomenois*). Eugene Peterson renders this phrase as "those on the way of salvation."[3]

Set this foolish cross next to a light that renews all of creation and the epistle reading becomes an endorsement of Jesus' own hermeneutic. In his ordinary birth, his not eluding capture by the aggrieved authorities (that is, he did not display or use power), and his humiliating death, no knowledgeable or skilled person could find much hope.

> The gospel is not an esoteric body of religious knowledge, not a slickly packaged philosophy, not a scheme for living a better life; instead, it is an announcement about God's apocalyptic intervention in the world, for the sake of the world.
> —Richard B. Hays[4]

But here the cross is precisely the image of God's power: pulling together wisdom and foolishness—things "wise" people would otherwise insist on distinguishing between. The cross, in other words, embodies contradictions. The cross has no rhetorical skill. It speaks beyond speech where the true wisdom resides.

The play between definitions of wisdom and foolishness reveals that they hide inside each other as if to embody what it is to throw aside all human conceptions of rational thought and instead leap into something called "believing." This text, in fact, invites the hearer to move away from the clever intellectual games we play with conundrums when we pin their parts to a wall as if they were insects we could splay out and explain. This text calls us to stop dissecting and pining and instead become like little children who do not yet know to make false dichotomies. God has "made foolish the wisdom of the world" (v. 20), which says that God has hung the wisdom we cherish on a cross for all to see its ultimate failure—"to reduce to nothing things that are . . ."—so that the outrageous resurrection could reveal the poverty of our perceptions and expectations.

In verse 19 Paul builds on Isaiah 29:14; in verses 27-28 on both 1 Samuel 2:1-10 (Hannah's song) and Luke 1:46-55 (Mary's Magnificat); in verse 31 on Jeremiah 9:23 and others, drawing on the ancient sources to evoke God's astounding reversals. The culmination of this conjunction of foolishness and wisdom—as with the other readings, especially John 12—names a specific human propensity: boasting. All of the grand language is summed up in a reminder that the only pride available is not our own, it is "*in* the Lord."

MELINDA A.
QUIVIK

The Gospel
JOHN 12:20-36 (RCL)

The image of light again emerges in this reading, echoing the light of Isaiah 49. After a long string of events from the formation of the church (one follower bringing other outsiders to Jesus) through enigmatic statements about dying to rise again, the passage reaches a summit in Jesus' identification of the Messiah or Son of man as light. As with the series of paradoxes of dying and rising, loving and losing, hating and keeping, the final speech admonishes the crowd to walk in light not darkness, to have freedom ("so that darkness may not overtake you") rather than being lost ("you do not know where you are going").

Finally, Jesus adds one more twist: not simply to *use* the light in order to see the path, but "believe in the light, so that you may become children of light." Up until this point, Jesus has been dealing with tangible realities—what happens to grain, the fact that people love or hate life, having light in order to see the path, getting lost in the dark—all of which dissolve in a concluding suggestion of a more encompassing relationship with the light, offering a deeper structure to all of his remonstrances. The meaning of the need for death in order to bear fruit becomes, in the end, about the fruit bearing which results from a faith that offers a new identity.

If we couple what Jesus has to say with the promises of the servant in the Isaiah text for this day, a new identity is open to everyone, even the coastlands themselves. The servant does not need to *be* Jesus in order to be drawing the hearer to the same place: into a realm of light where we are invited to see all people on the lighted road as "children," all alike in our relationship to the light. The light itself is what binds the children together. The exact parameters of the walking are not spelled out. It is an open road, in many respects, with only Jesus' command to "believe in the light" (*pisteuete eis to phōs*) left sounding like a conditional route to becoming "children of light."

The church, of course, continues to ruminate and propose systematic measures for how best to define "believing." Jesus doesn't define believing. He uses images to lay out options: it's either light or dark. Take your pick. It's either loving life and clinging to it in a way that will inevitably devalue it or letting go of the desperate clinging so that one's hands, we might say, can be opened to what comes, so that the path can bear fruit, rather than making a fist in fear of the future. We might all well ask ourselves whether the theological constructs of our own denominations or our own congregations or our own hearts result from clinging or from letting go. Do we feed the fires of division or by being peace, make peace?

Jesus' imagery—albeit in the language of the writer of John's Gospel—is commensurate with the wealth of images in the parables Jesus tells. By opposing two of those images, followers can see the options and come to appropriate more deeply where they stand. This appropriation might best be understood as a *re*-cognition, a *re*-learning, a *real*-ization of who Jesus is through the images he uses.

JOHN 12:37-38, 42-50 (BCP)

As with John 12:20-36, Jesus here pits human against divine glory, light against dark, rejection against belief, and judgment against salvation. In contrast, however, with the earlier reading that contained the image of the Messiah and Son of man as light without specifically naming Jesus as either of those figures, here Jesus explicitly refers to himself as light: "I have come as light into the world, so that everyone who believes in me should not remain in the darkness" (v. 46).

It may be more elusive for the preacher to get at the meaning of belief here because the focus is on the promise that comes from believing without describing the relationship of the hearers to the light or to belief. The provocative distinction Jesus makes between coming not to judge but to save could serve to help the preacher lead the assembly from the Tuesday texts toward the meaning of the cross and resurrection as gift rather than fault.

MARK 11:15-19 (BCP alt.)

If an assembly on Tuesday in Holy Week is fed this text paired with Isaiah 49, the suffering servant gains a concrete edge. The figure becomes a prophetic and revolutionary critic of the economic structures (read: power structures) that shape even religious life. Jesus here takes on the Temple guardians, the taxing structures, a system of redemption payments to the priests.

Jesus calls the Temple a "den of robbers" (Mark 11:17). He drives them out and overturns the tables. Ched Myers calls this a "direct action campaign: Jesus' showdown with the powers in Jerusalem."[5] Might we say this is Jesus as Rosa Parks, Che Guevara, Nelson Mandela, The Mothers of the Disappeared, Desmond Tutu, Hugo Chavez, Cindy Sheehan, Martin Luther King Jr.? This may be uncomfortable to think about, but it is apt, for although human being can be equated with the offering made by Jesus, typologically we can trace a thread through the servant of Isaiah as a "polished arrow" who cuts through hopelessness and self-deception to show a harbor in the hand of the Lord. Visions of what is righteous in God's eyes reveal the ways in which we human beings shield ourselves from our own iniquity. Turning over the tables makes possible a whole new way of functioning in the Temple, and it threatens the powerful so that they seek a way to stop the direct action campaign.

Spend Tuesday in Holy Week pondering the need to drive out systems and structures that stand in the way of prayer for all nations.

This text along with Isaiah's servant song has its own peculiar brilliance in that in John it follows the foot washing (John 13:1-17) and Jesus' announcement to the disciples that to receive him is to receive the One from whom he was sent (vv. 18-20). The other textual matter of note is the omission of verses 34-35, which contain the commandment to "love one another." The focus in this text, in other words, is not on Jesus' followers and what we are to do but on Jesus.

If we look at Isaiah and John together we see parallels between the servant and Jesus. This comparison is not meant to say that the suffering servant *is* Jesus, but rather that, as a common type, the two have an astonishing paradox in common: both are described in their respective texts as containing (offering) the capacities both to cradle and to cut. The servant is made like "a polished arrow" and also "a light to the nations." Jesus feeds his betrayer, and only then is the betrayer infused with Satan. Once the betrayer has left the dinner, Jesus says the "Son of Man has been glorified." He does not here identify himself as that Son of man, but the pronouncement, falling close on Judas's heels, indicates a connection between the revelation of the one who will be betrayed and Jesus.

Many scholars have chewed on the possibility that the morsel is the bread of the Eucharist. While no agreement exists on this matter, it is nevertheless clear that just as Jesus feeds us now in the Eucharist with his body and blood, so too does this scene show him feeding Judas. We need not debate the substance and essence of the bread in order to draw a parallel between feeding in one situation and feeding in another. That the morsel given to Judas is a sign of betrayal as well as nourishment might serve to nudge the people of God in our time to approach the meal every week with a reminder that this bread is a sign of both death and life. What we celebrate also pierces us, like "a polished arrow."

Judas walks away from the light of the world . . . into the night and the darkness of those who reject Jesus and plan to kill him.
—Francis J. Moloney, S.D.B.[6]

When we ask about the law and the gospel in this text, we come upon the problem of needing to look beneath the text for its shadow . . . or its light! The fact that Judas will betray Jesus and that the disciples cannot go where Jesus is going, point to the radical paucity of human goodness and ability. That is a law of our world, a founding reality from our Creator.

The flip side of that law is the promise from Jesus in this text that "you will follow afterward" (v. 36). This will occur because the Son of man, by the betrayal and ensuing events, will be glorified. We might even say that the glorification is based on the betrayal. Not knowing how to follow is part and parcel of the ignorance expressed in Peter's question. The eventual ability to follow where Jesus goes is promised even though Jesus flatly asserts that more betrayal is inevitable "before the cock crows" (v. 38). We know it was and is every day still the case.

The key in John 13 is that Jesus finally will lay down his life for his beloved disciples. Despite being "troubled in spirit" (v. 21) and knowing his betrayer, Jesus nourishes his betrayer and, in fact, feeds all of his unworthy disciples.

We will betray him. We do betray him. We do not adequately own his family, his body, our sisters and brothers, his "little children" (v. 33)—of whom each of us is also a part—and yet we are told that we will and are able to follow him. These words are enigmatic and lush, and we spend this week bathed in them, listening for a clue yet again this Holy Week, as in every year, for how the Word of God feeds us with light.

PREACHING THE HEART OF THE GOSPEL

In each text for this day, we hear of reward and betrayal, reward and ignorance, and light and darkness. The paradoxes abound. They form the tensions through which we are able to gaze at a deeper truth than either end of the polarization can convey on its own. The images are of contrast and contradiction between God's gifts of light and hope and the human sense of futility. This is the classic conflict between law and gospel that leads so many preachers to misinterpret the differences and connections between them.

The law tells us the truth about our lives and tells us we need the gifts that God holds out to us. It isn't enough to say that the law shows us our need for God; the law also always shows us that God *is* and that we have been created to hearken when God's voice breaks through the mute universe of fear. We are called in the same way as the servant speaks of being called, and we are held and equipped by God for the tasks needing attention in our several spheres of influence.

This voice of God calling to us is obviously capable of bearing in itself both law and gospel. It is a trumpet announcing our responsibilities while also in its very existence revealing to us the fact that what God calls us to undertake and *be* in this world is possible. This is good news, indeed. The gospel reveals God's promises of eternal reward *and* God's presence in our midst as joyous celebration and even—especially—when we suffer from doubts and despair in this life. The gospel does not abbreviate the "good news" to a sort of "You Are the Lottery Winner" telegram, but says to us that underneath those things we readily understand to be "good" in our world lies a foundation of power sometimes less easily discernible as positive.

The preacher could fruitfully work with the images from the second reading of pathway, lighted route, journey, and an ongoing event, which, at the very least, are mysterious enough and diffuse enough for no one to boast of having figured them out!

While preachers have never had, and do not now have, the luxury (or burden) of an A-B-C approach to preaching—and while no single form is the best for all situations—I affirm that a sermon which begins by acknowledging the crisis and then moves to God's hopeful word for us has a better chance of being heard and being helpful.
—Joseph R. Jeter, Jr.[7]

Notes

1. Dietrich Bonhoeffer, *Christ the Center* (New York: Harper & Row, 1960), 64–65.

2. Gordon W. Lathrop, *The Pastor: A Spirituality* (Minneapolis: Fortress Press, 2006), 50.

3. Eugene Peterson, *The Message* (Colorado Springs: NAVPress, 1993), 339.

4. Richard B. Hays, *First Corinthians,* Interpretation: A Bible Commentary for Teaching and Preaching (Louisville: John Knox Press, 1997), 27–28.

5. Ched Myers, *Binding the Strong Man: A Political Reading of Mark's Story of Jesus* (Maryknoll, N.Y.: Orbis Books, 1997), 290.

6. Francis J. Moloney, S.D.B. *The Gospel of John,* Sacra Pagina (Collegeville, Minn.: Liturgical Press, 1998), 385.

7. Joseph R. Jeter, Jr., *Crisis Preaching: Personal and Public* (Nashville: Abingdon Press, 1998), 105.

WEDNESDAY OF HOLY WEEK

REVISED COMMON	EPISCOPAL (BCP)	ROMAN CATHOLIC
Isa. 50:4-9a	Isa. 50:4-9a	Isa. 50:4-9a
Psalm 70	Ps. 69:7-15, 22-23	Ps. 69:8-10, 21-22, 31, 33-34
Heb. 12:1-3	Heb. 9:11-15, 24-28	
John 13:21-32	John 13:21-35 or Matt. 26:1-5, 14-25	Matt. 26:14-25

KEY THEMES

• How would Judas know whose voice he was obeying? How would the suffering servant know? How do we know who voice we are obeying?

• Judas is an image of the need for all of us to remain at the table.

• The great high priest feeds even the betrayer.

FIRST READING

ISAIAH 50:4-9a (RCL, BCP, LFM)

Note the significance of Isaiah 50 for this day in Holy Week: All three lectionaries agree on its use. The text is suffused with gifts given by the Lord to the one who is a teacher, a pastor, a sufferer, and a strong but harassed servant of the Lord.

The servant we heard on Tuesday speaking with some confidence of the Lord's call to be "a light to the nations" here sets out the treacherous nature of that mission. The servant is abused, insulted, and spat upon, in vivid language showing the tormenters' very particular provocations meant to inflict shame. They strike the servant; pull out his beard. The servant tries to hide, to protect his face.

The servant, however, is not alone, for the Lord God has showered gifts abundant: (1) a tongue to speak comfort to any who are similarly afflicted ("to sustain the weary with a word"—v. 4) and (2) an ear opened to listen to the teachings available every day. In other words, the servant is given the tools needed for a life of combat. The servant is daily awakened to the posture of a student, a listener, a learner, in order that the tongue with which the servant speaks may be a blessing to those made tired by the pain and struggle of this world.

Isaiah's "poetry conjures a judicial context,"[1] writes Walter Brueggemann, noting that in verses 8-9 we find words used in a law court: vindication, guilty, and adversaries. The brutality of the servant's contentious life is full of oppositions, but they are not just the tug of war between comfort and suffering.

There is also a tension within the servant's own role: that of listener and speaker. Ear and tongue are the images that rise to point the way for the servant in this difficult task. The servant does not just have at the ready all the words that need to be said but is, rather, given them steadily, daily, with ears the servant doesn't open himself but that the Lord God makes open for the hearing. This is a depiction of mercies given so that, in turn, mercy may be offered to others. The direction of the action is clearly from the Lord to the servant and through the servant to those who need the word. This is all grace, all gospel.

> The heart of the Christian ascesis—and the work of Lent—is to face the unconscious values that underlie the emotional programs for happiness and *to change them.* Hence the need of a discipline of contemplative prayer and action. . . . The external word of God and the liturgy dispose us for the experience of Christ's risen life within us.
> —Thomas Keating[2]

RESPONSIVE READING

PSALM 70 (RCL)

Only five verses long, this psalm cries out, even in its brevity, the intense need of the singer. Death is immanent; the Lord must hurry to the rescue. "You are my help and my deliverer; O LORD, do not delay!" Of special note is that in the midst of the plea for quick intervention, the psalmist (v. 4) moves out of the immediate threat to sing praise of God in whom the faithful can rejoice. This is a remarkable moment in the impact it provides, set within such a heartfelt urging: even in the middle of a crisis, the faithful can sing of joy. This is very provocative language for the middle of Holy Week.

PSALM 69:7-15, 22-23 (BCP)
PSALM 69:8-10, 21-22, 31, 33-34 (LFM)

In each of these assemblages of verses from Psalm 69, the psalmist is in deep trouble and knows why it has come. Having held zeal for the house of the Lord, those who hate the Lord have come to turn their contempt onto the psalmist. Alienated from family, insulted, mocked, "sinking in the mire," the psalmist pleads for rescue and for the enemies to be snared, blinded, and frightened to the core.

Such psalms as these, expressing stark clarity about the pains of being threatened for remaining faithful in the midst of an unfaithful community, can bring to the assembly's mind the suffering servant of Isaiah and the suffering of Jesus as he faces his enemies daily. The psalm may well be a voice for members of the assembly today who struggle to maintain courage in their places of work (against unethical practices) or in their families (who misunderstand or abuse them) or in their sheer need (with all the insults that poverty, homelessness, unemployment, and hunger bring on a person). Often people do not have enough experience praying or singing the psalms to realize the extent to which these ancient hymns and prayers contain very negative truths about life. Holy Week is a prime time in the life of a congregation for the worship services to offer the real depth of the psalms. Neither the psalmist nor we are alien from each other. The same struggles apply in every era.

Second Reading
HEBREWS 12:1-3 (RCL)

Christian faith is not formed by an esoteric idea but by the one who endured all pains for the sake of the world: "Jesus the pioneer and perfecter of our faith." Because of him, we need not "grow weary or lose heart." We are uplifted continually by the nearness of the "great cloud of witnesses" upon whose shoulders—words and deeds, teachings and sufferings, embodiments and imaginings—we stand.

This second reading for this day brings home to the assembly its own importance in this venture we call faith. Together with the Isaiah servant and the Judas betrayer, the assembly sees the body of Christ, the church itself, as its present strength in times of trouble. The witnesses ring us round, having raised us up to belong. Some were parents and grandparents, aunts and uncles; others, strangers or friends, neighbors, even people we read about or whose stories we heard thirdhand. The pronouncements and the examples of faith keep us mindful, help us run, help us persevere.

HEBREWS 9:11-15, 24-28 (BCP)

The reading here of a text that speaks a high Christology differs markedly from the RCL Hebrews 12 text with its emphasis on the cloud of witnesses. In Hebrews 9, only Christ is in sight. The witnesses are mute, perhaps gape-mouthed before the great high priest. (For discussion of Hebrews 9:11-15, please see the second reading, RCL, for Monday in Holy Week, above.)

Verses 24-28 reinforce the point in verses 11-15 but with an eschatological coda. In other words, we humans create for ourselves ways of worship that meet certain of our human needs—the needs for continuity, regularity, stability, for "something" to be performed that will make a difference in the larger scheme of things which we do not understand and yet for which we yearn.

Despite our deepest and dearest intents, the sanctuary we create cannot endure. The priests we call to serve in our sanctuaries can never do the work that the great high priest has already done. We look to Christ the high priest as the One who has once and for all time, for all ages, performed the sacrifice that renders moot our inabilities. Christ, the "mediator of a new covenant," has shed his own blood, not the blood of others, and in so doing now appears "in the presence of God on our behalf." The old covenant has been fulfilled in a new covenant: the Christ, the only perfection.

Imagine a great chasm between God on the one side and suffering and broken humanity on the other that must be bridged if human beings are to be rescued and creation brought to its consummation. In order to span the gap, God engages in a series of saving acts, redemptive "words," that are forged together like links on a great chain stretched across the divide. God calls Abraham to leave his ancestral lands, stirs up the midwives Shiphrah and Puah . . . summons Moses . . . enrolls Isaiah . . . [and] Jesus is the final link.
—Thomas G. Long[3]

THE GOSPEL
JOHN 13:21-32 (RCL)
JOHN 13:21-35 (BCP)

These texts are discussed in Tuesday's lectionary readings (LFM) with this difference: how the Isaiah text is understood will alter the interpretation of the Gospel text. The reading from Isaiah on this day draws the servant's picture as one who has specific gifts and particular troubles rather than showing us the servant in a broader frame, as one who has received a call to the nations. To be hearing the John 13 text (either one, actually) in company with Isaiah 50 means that the accent may well be on the particular agony of the One who is betrayed—in much the way the servant's particular pain is delineated.

Note also that the RCL text for this day does not include the last five verses of the Tuesday text and so does not offer the comparison between Judas as betrayer and Peter as denier. If the hearer has only Judas to consider—as one to whom Jesus gives bread—the hearer may be allowed to disengage from the scene, for without Peter in the story, we are more inclined to point a finger only in Judas's direction.

Additionally, the BCP text includes verses 34-35, omitted on Tuesday. They speak Jesus' command to "love one another." Said here in the context of Judas's coming betrayal and Jesus' glorification, they narrow these large themes down into our daily lives where each of us confronts the meaning of loving the neighbor. This sets up rather nicely the move from Wednesday to Maundy Thursday's instruction and example of foot washing.

With either of these texts, the preacher will want to ponder what difference it makes that certain verses are either included (extending the Tuesday reading in a new direction or with a slightly altered emphasis) or omitted (yielding a slightly amended movement into the next themes of Holy Week).

MATTHEW 26:1-5,14-25 (BCP alt.)

Anticipating the story from Tuesday when the Gospel text honed in on the moment before Judas leaves the table, this text follows Judas going to the high priest to offer his services as a betrayer of Jesus. Set here in the context of the Isaiah 50 images of the persecuted servant (who nevertheless owns a tongue and ears with which to teach and learn), we see Judas living, in comparison, a far more impoverished life. Unlike the servant who is faithful though abused, Judas has no ear to hear what the Lord God wants to teach and no tongue to speak something other than "What will you give me?" (v. 15). Or does he? Judas asks, "Surely not I, Rabbi?" (v. 25). One who has no such inkling will not be inclined to inquire.

We are set up by this reading to know already the end of the story, as it were. We know Judas has made the deal with the religious leaders and elders who mean to kill Jesus. We know that Judas will help them. And we also see Judas coming one last time to sit at the table with Jesus and the other disciples.

In contrast to the John account of this supper (but in keeping with the events described by Mark and Luke), here Jesus does not point to Judas specifically as the betrayer by handing him bread. In all the Synoptic Gospels, Jesus simply says that one of the Twelve is the betrayer. In each case, the disciples all ask the identity of the betrayer with an open question ("Is it I?"). Along with the others, Judas asks the same question but only in Matthew is he singled out for asking. Jesus' reply could seem unclear unless we apply hindsight and the fact that Judas is the only one to whom (in this text, at any rate) Jesus gives an answer. Additionally, it may be important that Jesus uses the same answer in his responses to the high priest (Matt. 26:64) and to Pilate (Matt. 27:11). The text is not clear.

Following the eating of the morsel, Judas is said (vs. 30) to have gone out. It is usually supposed that he went to the authorities to betray Jesus for the next time he appears (xviii 2-5) he comes with police from the priests and the Pharisees to arrest Jesus. . . . By having Judas depart from the Supper only after Jesus has told him to leave, John stresses Jesus' control over his destiny; no one can take Jesus' life from him unless he consents (x 18).
—Raymond E. Brown[4]

One more remarkable thing about this pericope is that the story at the heart of these verses is torn out: the story of the woman with the alabaster jar of ointment. She anointed Jesus' head with it. Without this story, the questions of extravagant honor toward Jesus, the relationship between worship and poverty, the relationship between Jesus and those who are devalued (a woman, in this case), the relationships between those who give scorn and those who have to endure it, and Jesus' unequivocal defense of her and her gesture are mute. Yet, the echo of all of these matters is still present in the story as it stands.

In addition to the discussion above, the omission of verses 1-5 in the LFM text focuses attention on the event of Judas's contracting for the betrayal and of the supper events. Thus is omitted the context in which we learn about the plotting behind the scenes. This may simply leave out an enhancing of the plotting climate, or it may leave the impression for the assembly that Judas's decision stood outside an environment that conspired against Jesus in a broader community and context than Judas's own frustration with Jesus (if that was what drove him; we don't know).

Preaching the Heart of the Gospel

It is particularly critical in Holy Week every year to maintain vigilance against language that denigrates Jews. This becomes most acute on Good Friday, given the hostility Jewish people have experienced (even to death!) following Good Friday services in many countries and times. But here, too, in the language that surrounds the movement from old to new covenant, preachers do well to consider the meaning of Jesus' saying that he did not come to remove the law but to fulfill it.

The First Testament, as some scholars have come to call the Hebrew Bible, is also a witness to the faith Christians proclaim. We cannot have a "new" covenant without the "old" one. We cannot know Jesus as the Son if we do not already know the Father, the Creator God, YHWH, revealed in the Scriptures Jesus himself read in the Temple. We do nothing to proclaim the witness of that Holy One if we speak chasms into being between Jews and Christians.

If preachers only denigrate the work of the human priests in favor of the work of the great high priest, we also do not do justice to the witness and work of the body of Christ. We are Christ's members, children of God, brothers and sisters, and among us are those called to be pastors, priests, rectors, ministers, who preach the gospel and administer the sacraments, teach the faith, call the people to prayer, and serve in their best capacities to faithfully respond to Jesus' gospel invitation. If the priests of the Old Testament are demeaned, so are our own, for in no age can the human being and the structures we set up—even in the best of times and the best of faithfulness—begin to approach the grace of the great high priest. This isn't a contest between faiths or priests. This is good to remember.

The great themes for this day of Holy Week—the final day before the Three Days begins, the beginning of the final day of Lent, actually!—revolve around betrayal. Set next to the servant in Isaiah, we can see a parallel with persons in whom the Lord plants capacities for the exercising of God's purposes. Judas is not stopped. The suffering servant is not left without the abilities (the tongue and ear) to teach in a way that is perhaps the reason his persecutors so tormented him. By spending time on the meaning of betrayal here, we end up meditating on the questions of evil: theodicy. Did God put into the suffering servant the very means for performing what, then, gets him in trouble? Did God put it into Judas's head that this handing-over was just what he needed to do? How would Judas know whose voice he was obeying? How would the suffering servant in Isaiah know? How do we know whose voice we are obeying? Assemblies that have had some experience dealing with spiritual discernment will benefit from being given time to enter into these questions, for we are all called upon to discern what courses of action are most in keeping with our intentions to be faithful followers of the Lord.

One remarkable example of this discernment is the Quaker practice of holding a "clearness committee." A person with a life question asks several members of the assembly to meet together to hear the question. Then, over a period of time—usually a few hours, and perhaps meeting more than once—the group, agreeing to absolute confidentiality, will only ask questions of the one who is in discernment. The questions must be probing in the way that really good friends will sometimes ask a question. It may come in the form of: "I hear you saying that you would really like to do x and y. Can you say more about the difference between x and y?" It is a nonjudgmental question. It is only asking for further clarification. The clarifying comes from the one being asked to articulate. (To learn more about this practice, see several works by Parker Palmer, especially *Let Your Life Speak: Listening for the Voice of Vocation.*[5])

We usually have many different avenues, and if not many, there is hardly a person who does not have at least two choices every day. Some of our choices will prove fruitful beyond our dreams while others will wither. We use our best faculties to peer into our own hearts and see into the future, but the pathways are often strewn with unknown obstacles. For the task of discernment, we have been given the body of Christ. We do not discern best alone but extend to others a request for help with hearing the voice that calls.

Something in the scene at the table with Jesus and the disciples tells me that even for the terrible task Judas was about, he met with the others—found himself *in company*—at the moment of the final choice. What that meant for him, and finally for us, is extremely complex. The preacher will not want to pretend it is possible to crawl inside the mind and heart of Judas and imagine his thinking. But Judas may be a window for us into the helplessness we encounter in ourselves when we ultimately make a move that is destructive. Judas might also be an image for us of the need to stay at the table and not run out to find the enemies of the One who most feeds us. What would that look like in your congregation on this day?

Notes

1. Walter Brueggemann, *Isaiah 40–66,* Westminster Bible Companion (Louisville: Westminster John Knox, 1998), 122.

2. Thomas Keating, *The Mystery of Christ: The Liturgy as Spiritual Experience* (New York: Continuum, 2000), 39, 45.

3. Thomas G. Long, *Hebrews,* Interpretation: A Bible Commentary for Teaching and Preaching (Louisville: John Knox Press, 1997), 13.

4. Raymond E. Brown, *The Gospel According to John XIII–XXI,* The Anchor Bible (New York: Doubleday, 1970), 578.

5. Parker Palmer, *Let Your Life Speak: Listening for the Voice of Vocation* (San Francisco: Jossey-Bass, 2000).

MAUNDY THURSDAY / HOLY THURSDAY

MARCH 20, 2008

REVISED COMMON	EPISCOPAL (BCP)	ROMAN CATHOLIC
Exod. 12:1-4 (5-10) 11-14	Exod. 12:1-14a	Exod. 12:1-8, 11-14
Ps. 116:1-2, 12-19	Ps. 78:14-20, 23-25	Ps. 116:12-13, 15-16bc, 17-18
1 Cor. 11:23-26	1 Cor. 11:23-26 (27-32)	1 Cor. 11:23-26
John 13:1-17, 31b-35	John 13:1-15 or Luke 22:14-30	John 13:1-15

KEY THEMES

- Foot washing tethers us to those around us.
- We hear of the Passover and remember our ancestors.
- Jesus institutes a meal at which there is enough for everyone and everyone is welcome.
- At Passover and at the beginning of the Three Days, the people of God hear the command and promise: Remember that I have brought you freedom.
- The preaching on this day is about the sacraments: Baptism and Eucharist.

FIRST READING

EXODUS 12:1-4 (5-10) 11-14 (RCL)
EXODUS 12:1-14a (BCP)
EXODUS 12:1-8, 11-14 (LFM)

The Lord's instructions to Israel on the eve of the Passover constitute a deeply liturgical text. The people are to do certain actions (get a lamb, cook it, eat it, put blood on the doorposts) and do them in a certain way (loins girded, sandals on feet, staff in hand, eat hurriedly). Most significantly, they are to remember the day.

This is a description of a "liturgical" event because the people themselves enact a public ritual that is intended to be repeated. ("Liturgy" derives from *leit-ourgia*:

261

services performed for the well-being of the public. The Greek parallels with the public Word and Sacrament services are legion.) The people of the exodus are to consider this day and these instructions so important that they will celebrate in the future, again and again, "as a perpetual ordinance" (v. 14). These instructions mean that this day changes everything, every day, every year, for all time. In other words, time itself is altered by this day's liberation.[1]

In the very beginning of the text, the Lord speaks of time: "This month shall mark for you the beginning of months; it shall be the first month of the year for you" (v. 2). This speaking is enveloped by two strong statements about this new understanding of time:

1. At the start, it is a time that makes all time new. All months before have been laid waste compared to the new thing that is about to happen. It is as significant as saying that our weeks begin with Sunday not Monday; that our liturgical year, the Christian calendar, begins in Advent with the eschatological breadth of the incarnation about to happen.

2. The final verse (14) turns this new beginning into a liturgy in that it will be in some way (unspecified as yet) ritually made present again and again. In the liturgical enactment of its remembrance, the Passover will become a gift not only to the first people to whom it came but to all people who live in its mind-set, its perspective, its promise. Liturgical remembrance is an appropriation of others' realities. Here it is ordained by the Lord for the people of Israel.

We Christians, too, remember the Passover when, even in our time, our Jewish sisters and brothers help us to hold this pivotal event of God's salvation by keeping certain behaviors, rituals, and meal gatherings every year. Additionally, in the Christian witness, there is also this Holy Week—the time of the Triduum, celebrating the Three Days of Jesus' Passion—in which we begin, actually, by reading the story of the Passover! We remember every year the very precise—and for that reason, very personal—requirements to the enslaved Israelites laid out by the Lord so that they would be spared the bloodshed of justice about to be visited upon their masters, the Egyptians.

The text is full of details that speak justice:

1. As described above, the Lord gives the people a new beginning. Everyone is to eat. If a family is too small to afford a whole lamb, the families should come together and share.

2. That way, a second justice is created: plenty for all and no one left out for want of means. No one is made hungry by being in too small a community. Room is made for everyone at some table.

3. The hurried eating is a way to focus on the Lord's work rather than the sheer goodness of the meal, the taste of the lamb with all those bitter herbs, roasted, and served with bread. A family might get involved with the joys of the feast itself if it weren't for the remonstrance to eat quickly and not settle in to the present moment. This is a justice word because keeping an eye open—and the body ready—for the coming of horrendous righteous reckoning is a stance that breeds expectation rather than complacency. We might all be better off training our attention to be set for the Lord to do something utterly freeing, something that will unbolt us from our comforts and set us off in new directions. Thus does justice roll down from heaven onto people who actually expect it!

4. The very "gods of Egypt" will receive their reward: the attachments and the powers, the greed and desire, the people who set up the structures of oppression, everything that mitigates against what is good. All will receive God's wrath. There will be blood.

5. But the blood on the doorposts of the Israelite slaves will be a sign that the vengeance will pass them by. This is the fifth sign of justice in this Passover instruction from the Lord. Justice not only entails visiting suffering upon those who have done ill to others, but also that the ill-treated will be spared.

Strikingly, although the BCP has the longest and most complete pericope, it omits the final parts of verse 14 that reiterate the importance of the day as a celebration. One could argue that the full text ought to be included, chiefly to emphasize the facet of time as a bookend to this scene. Verse 14 as a whole offers a sharp insistence on the remembrance of the day in festival for all time. To omit it is to lose that perspective.

The RCL omits the discussion of the lamb's actual roasting, the direction about putting blood on the doorposts, and the stance of the family gathered to eat it. The omission of these details, for one thing, lessens the power of the Lord's involvement with the mundane. For another, failure to read the Lord's instructions that the blood should be put on the doorposts renders unintelligible the final (v. 13) mention that the Lord will see on the doorposts and pass by. The loss, especially, of the unblemished lamb and the blood on the doorposts is also the loss of typological connection between the lamb eaten for the Passover meal

> Our rabbis taught: When the Egyptian armies were drowning in the sea, the Heavenly Hosts broke out in songs of jubilation. God silenced them and said, "My creatures are perishing, and you sing praises?" Though we descend from those redeemed from brutal Egypt, / and have ourselves rejoiced to see oppressors overcome, / yet our triumph is diminished / by the slaughter of the foe ...
> —*A Passover Haggadah*[2]

and the Son of Man dying unblemished on the cross. Why disconnect those types? Why lose that powerful imagery?

The LFM retains the lamb as unblemished but omits the way it should be roasted and eaten. Again, this omission turns the text's emphasis to finding the lamb and roasting it but does not tell the people how to eat the lamb. In this way, the imagery admonishing the people to ready themselves for eschatological time to break forth into this world vanishes.

The theodicy problem in verse 12 is transparent and difficult. Why should the firstborn of human beings and animals be killed for the evil done by the human parents? One response of contemporary Jews is the prayer of sorrow for the innocent who died.

RESPONSIVE READING
PSALM 116:1-2, 12-19 (RCL)
PSALM 116:12-13, 15-16C, 17-18 (LFM)

What can be offered up to the Lord in response to the deliverance from slavery into the freedom of the wilderness where the Lord still provides water and manna? The people's response to this story of steadfast love and rescue is perfectly summed up in this psalm of joy. The response begins, "I love the LORD," and ends with "Hallelujah!" The liturgical refrain is in verse 14, included in both the RCL and LFM: "I will fulfill my vows to the LORD in the presence of all God's people."

In other words, the assembly's response to the recounting of the Passover is to give thanks and, in so doing, link that thanksgiving with the liturgical event of gathering, Word, meal, and sending. We may not always make this connection consciously but the doing can help us to re-cognize the bonds we have with our ancestors.

PSALM 78:14-20, 23-25 (BCP)

This psalm directly responds to the events following the Passover, first describing what God provided for the people in the wilderness, then remembering the people's fear and their anger against God, and finally recounting God's gifts of water and food in the desert ("mortals ate the bread of angels . . ."). To tell and retell a story of great danger and release, the truthful reluctance of the people to go where God was leading them, and then to end with the proclamation of God's liberating way, is to tell also the story of our own existences.

1 CORINTHIANS 11:23-26 (RCL, LFM)
1 CORINTHIANS 11:23-26 (27-32) (BCP)

The words Jesus said over the bread and wine at the Lord's Supper carry the central promise of the meal institution celebrated this night along with the foot washing. They are the *verba* (words of institution) without which the holy meal is not usually held. These are the words said by the presider over the bread and wine either (1) in a prayer of thanksgiving that includes the whole of God's actions in creation or (2) alone as proclamation of that for which Jesus is to be remembered, namely, salvation through the cross and resurrection.

The full "eucharistic prayer"—thanksgiving prayer—has a trinitarian structure. It begins by giving thanks for the Creator's act of making all things. Then the prayer gives thanks for the Son who was betrayed and at his last meal gave thanks himself for bread and wine, commanding his friends and followers to eat and drink to remember him. Finally, the prayer ends with thanks for the breath and fire of the Holy Spirit. This prayer offers the thanksgiving itself as proclamation and sets the Last Supper—the event remembered on this Maundy Thursday night—in the context of the widest scope of God's work in the cosmos.

Where only the *verba* are used, the context becomes the proclamation in and of itself. Some churches insist that the meal words must proclaim what Christ has done and can do so only in his words. Christians who take seriously our heritage even prior to the Reformation, note that one of the very oldest liturgical documents of the church, the *Didache*, in fact, does not contain the *verba* at all in its recounting of the presider's words over the bread and wine. And yet, the point of the meal—the gathering as Jesus commanded, the eating and the remembering—still hold.

Here is the parallel with the Passover commands from the Lord. Do this. Remember my rescue of you. Remember I have brought you freedom. Do not fail to hold this feast lest you forget what I have done. Do not fail to gather in my name and eat the food I offer lest you forget that you, too, once lived a wandering existence totally dependent on my bounty, and that now you are the food for others who still wander. Do not neglect the poor. Do not neglect to feed on what I most long to give you.

> Confession contains such a noble thing. I would not give up confession for all the riches in the world, even if all leaves and grains of sand were gold. And save for the sacrament, I know of no greater treasure and comfort than confession. Whoever does not know this comfort is not worthy to confess.
> —Martin Luther[3]

THE GOSPEL
JOHN 13:1-17, 31B-35 (RCL)
JOHN 13:1-15 (BCP, LFM)

The crux of the John text is the foot-washing scene at the Last Supper. All three lectionaries include verses 1-15 that form the story and, thus, the basic insights into Jesus' teachings on that occasion. As verse 15 has it, Jesus sums up his ministry: "I have set you an example, that you also should do as I have done to you." In this specific instance, the thing the disciples should do is wash one another's feet.

What is it to wash feet? In a time and place where transportation is primarily by foot in a dusty land, washing feet is a welcome relief for the truly foot-weary. Even in our day—where we in the developed world, especially, are accustomed to wearing sturdy shoes that keep our feet from feeling the stones and sticks in our paths—we know the comfort of having clean feet. In fact, newly clean feet actually can tingle. Washed and dried feet have a life of their own. They are the very definition of a simple way for a person to feel pampered.

Feet are important because of the enormous amount of work feet are asked to do. The weight of the entire body rests on them. They have to maintain balance, stand still, move, and even run. They manage to sense a thousand bits of information about the body pressing down on them and turn that data into a power without which we would have a much harder time keeping ourselves alive. Feet work hard. And those who have lost limbs know the miracle of prosthetics that give them back their freedom and strength.

It is, alas, also true that feet are not considered a delightful part of the body. Congregations faced with Maundy Thursday's command to wash each other's feet often find themselves cringing at the prospect. Feet are often smelly and unattractive. They are private, intimate, and sometimes contorted because of birth or shoes or injuries. They are an abused part of the body.

In a culture like our own North American culture in which, for many of our sisters and brothers, touching the feet of a stranger is an awkward if not disgusting idea, this day's liturgy can challenge the body of Christ to engage in deep growth. We are all members of one another, and yet we often reluctantly involve ourselves in the messy and distorted aspects of each other's lives. To wash someone's feet—those of a stranger or of someone with whom one has had a quarrel or stood in awe or been uninterested—can be the beginning of an entirely new way to see one's own faith in relationship to others.

Jesus never failed to call his followers to radical changes. This is one of the big ones. Washing feet. No wonder it is a sacramental act for some of our denominations, namely the Mennonites. They understand that Jesus instituted this action in the same way he instituted the meal of bread and wine and the command to "go and baptize." Those of our denominations who do not see the foot washing as sacramental might nevertheless see its increasing importance as a radical disavowal of the isolation of the technological age.

To a culture with telephones hanging from ears, text-messaging devices slipped into shirt pockets, and people on airplanes working their spreadsheets on computers instead of reading a book, the experience of kneeling before someone who is not in one's immediate family and washing her or his feet is a fantastic departure. It has life-changing promise. Unhooked momentarily from the electronic breadth of the computer world, the foot washer is immersed in a sensual, unprotected, personal, and life-giving encounter with another human being. It is a moment when the virtual world is disavowed. Just for a small snippet of time, something real happens in the name of Jesus Christ who taught us to do this. "If I, your Lord and Teacher, have washed your feet, you also ought to wash one another's feet."

It is acceptable sophistication to many Christians in our day that Jesus "didn't really mean we have to wash each other's feet; it's just a figure of speech; it's just a way of describing service." Yet, what if his "example" is precisely what is needed for us to physically, emotionally, personally understand what he was all about? It is unlikely that many of us are going to follow his example by inviting our own executions or failing to speak up for ourselves when put on trial or look upon our tormentors with pity as he did. Short of all that, we might see that Jesus still invites us in this foot washing to come to a greater grasp of his meaning by doing something both very simple and very hard. Can we not, in our small and large congregations, find a way to invite each other into vulnerability—to be washed—and into servanthood—to do the washing of someone else—in order to glimpse a truth that Jesus could only show us in this way? Can we imagine ourselves into that?

The BCP and LFM readings of this John text stop at the point where the text begins an additional, and didactic, section. They ask us to hear the story of the foot washing itself, letting the scene speak its own language so that it rests in us as an event.

To know Christ sacramentally only in terms of bread and wine is to know him only partially, in the dining room as host and guest. It is a valid enough knowledge, but its ultimate weakness when isolated is that it is perhaps too civil. . . . [H]owever elegant the knowledge of the dining room may be, it begins in the soil, in the barnyard, in the slaughterhouse; amid the quiet violence of the garden, strangled cries, and fat spitting in the pan. Table manners depend on something's having been grabbed by the throat. A knowledge that ignores these dark and murderous human *gestes* is losing its grip on the human condition.
—Aidan Kavanagh[4]

The RCL includes the didactic last section from verses 16-35 in which Jesus explains the glorification of the Son of man and the distance between the glorified Son and the followers who cannot follow where Jesus will go. The lesson is summarized: "I give you a new commandment, that you love one another."

A curious result of the teaching summary is that by seeming to clarify the foot washing that just occurred, the "new commandment" obfuscates the splendid specificity of the action it addresses. There is, in other words, less clarity in verses 16-35 than in verses 1-15 because the foot washing itself is so specific it carries the capacity to serve as a metaphor larger than itself. It is vivid and concrete. "Love one another" calls up a broad and less inductive comprehension of Jesus' meaning because "love" is more vague than "wash." It is easier to pay less attention to—or give less credence to—the command to "love" because we are prone to assume we are either doing it or cannot do it. Washing feet is, frankly and obviously, not beyond the capability of anyone who has one or two hands. Under most normal conditions, we have no excuses.

LUKE 22:14-20 (BCP alt.)

In addition to the slightly altered *verba* in this text, its use offers the reference Jesus makes to the coming events: "I have eagerly desired to eat this Passover with you before I suffer; for I tell you, I will not eat it until it is fulfilled in the kingdom of God" (v. 15). It could be interesting to wonder at the double mention in this text of the cup (did he not pass it when he first picked it up?) and the discrepancy between this account of the Supper and the other Synoptic accounts, but liturgical scholars have emphasized, instead, the commonality between all versions of the *verba* in terms of Jesus' taking the elements into his hands, giving thanks over them, and distributing them to his followers. This is the crux of the meal remembrance.

Preaching the Heart of the Gospel

Jesus uses the servant action of washing feet as a metaphor for the comprehension of self that allows the giving of the self for sake of the other. He knew ". . . that he had come from God and was going to God" (John 13:3). His knowing is that he lives in concert with a grand and eternal source and summit. He is, in effect, not a "self" in the sense we often use that word in our time to speak of a disconnected, competitive, and this-world-oriented entity. He is entwined with a purpose beyond himself. He is gift for others. And his action intends for the disciples to see and feel the reality of that giftedness which is also being given to them. The leader is on his knees. The rabbi is bending over my feet. Who am I, then? What does this gift make me? What would it be to refuse this gift? What image of myself would that come to form in me? What would it mean for my sense of self if I was to refuse to give it to others?

Likewise, Jesus uses the foot washing also as a type of baptism: "Unless I wash you," he says to Peter, "you have no share with me" (John 13:8). Christians understand baptism as initiation into the body of Christ. We have "no share" in who that body is, who Jesus is, unless we are washed in the name of the triune God. So it is with this foot washing. The two kinds of washing—for they are distinct despite their congress—are set close together through the words used to describe them, and in that way, each washing articulates something important about the other.

Both washings mean to bring us into a comprehension of our separate selves as larger than we are on our own. As members, finally, of all of humanity—and creation, too!—we see our "selves" in a new light: expansive, responsible, and cared for by the other persons of our "selves."

The preaching on this day could never over-spend itself on the meaning of the Passover as it is reimaged in the foot washing and the meal of Jesus' body and blood. This is a sacramental preaching moment. The Word of God on this day is fixed on the meaning of the sacraments of Baptism and Eucharist. The preacher's task is to bring into the present congregation's fundamental life the importance of these liturgical moments. Why do we baptize? Why do we eat the meal? How does this day mark us as a people called by God to live in freedom?

Notes

1. Thomas W. Mann, "Passover: The Time of Our Lives," in *Interpretation* 50, no. 3 (July 1996): 240–50.

2. *A Passover Haggadah*, ed. Herbert Bronstein, Central Conference of American Rabbis (New York: Penguin, 1982), 48–49.

3. Martin Luther, Sermon March 21, 1529 in *The 1529 Holy Week and Easter Sermons of Dr. Martin Luther* (St. Louis: Concordia Publishing House, 1998), 34.

4. Aidan Kavanagh, *The Shape of Baptism: The Rite of Christian Initiation* (New York: Pueblo Publishing, 1987), 160.

GOOD FRIDAY

MARCH 21, 2008

REVISED COMMON	EPISCOPAL (BCP)	ROMAN CATHOLIC
Isa. 52:13—53:12	Isa. 52:13—53:12 or Gen. 22:1-18 or Wisd. of Sol. 2:1, 12-24	Isa. 52:13—53:12
Psalm 22	Ps. 22:1-21 or 22:1-11 or 40:1-14 or 69:1-23	Ps. 31:2, 6, 12-13, 15-16, 17, 25
Heb. 10:16-25 or Heb. 4:14-16; 5:7-9	Heb. 10:1-25	Heb. 4:14-16; 5:7-9
John 18:1—19:42	John (18:1-40) 19:1-37	John 18:1—19:42

KEY THEMES

- Good Friday is the day to spend enough time with what we do not know and yet yearn to grasp.
- The reading of the Passion story stands alone in this liturgy as the pivotal proclamation, the reason for the assembly itself.
- Good Friday lifts high the cross in adoration and prays for the whole world in careful words and plenty of silence.

FIRST READING
ISAIAH 52:13—53:12 (RCL, BCP, LFM)

It is no small thing that on each of the days of Holy Week, the lectionaries agree about these readings from Isaiah. (For introductory commentary on the identity of the suffering servant, please see the first reading for Monday in Holy Week, above.) Variations in verse are minor, testifying to the fact that the prophet's imagery of this sufferer has figured prominently in the way the church understands the suffering of Jesus, otherwise these texts would not have been appointed for so long to be read on the day when the church hears the Passion, prays long and hard for the world, and venerates the cross.

The mostly Isaiah Old Testament readings for Holy Week have thus far taken the assembly from chapter 42 on Monday (servant as bruised reed) to chapter 49 on Tuesday (servant as polished arrow) to chapter 50 on Wednesday (servant with tongue and ear who vindicates) to this culminating Friday text from Isaiah 52. Here the bruises by which the suffering servant is tormented become the wounds by which the people are made whole: "by his bruises we are healed."

This text is complex in its use of language, its form, the ambiguity of the pronouns (I, he, we, they) and the fact that it hangs together despite inexplicable leaps in perspective. Many scholars have pored over this passage. Their attention is itself testimony to the power of the image described: one—or a number of persons, such as a nation—carries the burdens of others and thus brings about healing. But what does it mean? Despite all the centuries of the faithful reading and rereading this text, we are still in doubt about it.

It is better to lift up the image as one that depicts a radical giving for the sake of the other. The image of the suffering servant shows the sort of torture Jesus experienced but not specifically as a foretelling of his coming and his end. The appreciation that Christians have shown for this Isaiah image tells us mostly that the church has consistently found this description to be revelatory of the death that Jesus underwent primarily for its salvific effect ("by his bruises we are healed"). The torment of the suffering servant is laid out in such a way that by its vividness, the hearer is brought to a deep sense of awe for the one who would silently endure the cruelty and thereby achieve a far greater aim than his opposition would have given him.

The image of the servant expresses, in fact, what Christians have long said when we gather in Holy Week and on each Sunday to celebrate the resurrection in bread and wine: "Lord, have mercy." The cry for mercy—based on the guilt we must assume—is, however, an open plea. We do not know how Isaiah understood the suffering of the "one" who was unfairly singled out. We only know that in these chapters stands an image of the brutality of our world—an image we certainly share with the prophet—and the amazing brilliance of those who unmask the torturers.

> A god is known by the system it sanctions. Theodicy becomes in fact an irrelevant speculative issue if the God question is not linked to systems of social access and goods.
> —Walter Brueggemann[1]

Depending on how we understand the suffering servant, we come to face similar questions about Jesus' Passion: Is the Abba of Jesus a God who intentionally commits child abuse? What does it mean that Jesus took on our sins if we still commit them?

This Holy Week—and particularly this Good Friday of both death and our adoration for the one who died—is too full of serious theological questions to let its substance be lost in facile answers.

GENESIS 22:1-18 (BCP alt.)

For those churches that hear on this day the story of Abraham's near-sacrifice of Isaac instead of the Isaiah depiction of the suffering servant, the parallels with the Passion of Jesus are just as stark but may carry, at least for some worshipers, an even more poignant note. The figure of Abraham and the trusting, unsophisticated figure of Isaac are drawn in more personal detail than that of the suffering servant. In its detail (early in the morning, with a donkey, carrying fire and a knife, arranging wood, seeing the ram), the scene is intense with smells and textures. Abraham's obedience is beyond the reach of most of us. Isaac's ignorance is more in keeping with human comprehension.

We know, of course, how dearly Abraham longed for a son and how amazing the birth was for him and Sarah. The thought of such a sacrifice is too much for most of us to bear, and there may well be some people in the congregation on this night for whom this story is too close for many reasons.

And then the miracle of rescue comes. The great divide between what is human and what is divine capacity grows more apparent than ever: God the Father can, on Good Friday, be depicted as one who lets the Son be killed, but the Lord does not require that human beings sacrifice their own children. The assembly, on this day, hears of both results: Jesus' death and Isaac's life.

Whether the focus here is on the trust that Abraham acted on or the reprieve shown to both Abraham and Isaac by the angel of the Lord, there is, for the preacher, a very gracious truth to proclaim: God does not desire that we torment ourselves or our children in order to prove our faithfulness.

WISDOM OF SOLOMON 2:1, 12-24 (BCP alt.)

This Wisdom text—with its description of what the narrators will do to "test" the righteous one "with insult and torture"—adds to the Passion story the voice of those who live with such enormous envy and anger, resentment and unhappiness, that they find pleasure (or so it seems) in planning cruelty. We do not know the identity of those who are said to reason "unsoundly" in this text or of the one against whom they are plotting. Just as with the suffering servant of Isaiah, the figures are types that call to mind those who meant to harm Jesus and his followers.

In the RCL for Proper 20 (or 25) in Year B (the Sunday between September 18–24), this pericope is paired with Mark 9:30-37 in which Jesus teaches the disciples about the greatest being the least by setting a child in the midst of them. What wisdom there is in that conjunction of one who taught an other-oriented compassion and the voices in this text that clearly resent the one they plot to kill.

RESPONSIVE READING

PSALM 22 (RCL)
PSALM 22:1-21 or 22:1-11 (BCP)
PSALM 31:2, 6, 12-13, 15-17, 25 (LFM)

These songs, also heard in slightly nuanced form in the Passion/Palm Sunday liturgy, sing of abandonment and need. Familiar language from Jesus' suffering—so immediately present on Good Friday—brings us phrases that have come to embody the crucifixion: "My God, my God, why have you forsaken me?" (Ps. 22:1) and "Into your hands I commend my spirit . . ." (Ps. 31:6). These are songs of trust in a moment of great ordeal. They are for everyone to sing as we remember the One who knows all suffering. (*For further discussion of these psalms, please see the responsive readings for Passion/Palm Sunday in Holy Week, above.*)

PSALM 40:1-14 (BCP alt.)
PSALM 69:1-23 (BCP alt.)

These are the cries of someone who knows salvation firsthand ("the LORD lifted me out of the desolate pit"—Ps. 40:2), trusts that again and again deliverance will come, and asks that the tormenters be rightly dealt their own pains ("Let their eyes be darkened . . . and give them continual trembling in their loins"—Ps. 69:23). For Good Friday, these could be the songs of all people who honestly voice the suffering of unjust treatment and the desire for the enemy to be humiliated. What other day in the liturgical year could more appropriately hold these truths? It is especially on this day that, even in the midst of Jesus' suffering, the people of God hear—in the story of the Passion—no reproaches from his lips. In the difference between our own human desire for revenge and Jesus' distance from such desires, we see the measure of his gift to us.

SECOND READING

HEBREWS 10:16-25 (RCL)
HEBREWS 10:1-25 (BCP)

This difficult and rich epistle was written to a people believed to be in great danger of turning away from the Christian witness because of enormous pressures being brought to bear on them. A thread through the whole epistle is that Christ is the great high priest to whom we may hold fast. He is likened to King Melchizedek about whom we know little except that he did not descend from a line of kings but was appointed king, coming to power in a new order.

So, too, Christ entered into the Holy Place of priests. But he entered with his own blood rather than the blood of others, and he entered only once, not through repeated sacrifices. The litany of prior giants in faith following this pericope in chapter 11 (Abel and Cain, Abraham and Sarah, Moses, the Israelites, as well as martyrs and prophets—the great cloud of witnesses) is evidence of a pastoral approach for the recipients of the letter. The writer sends them strong images of those on whose shoulders they now find themselves struggling to maintain balance. The writer lays out many arguments throughout the letter to offer means by which those who are teetering in faith might receive a solid hold.

Let us pray for all who have not received the
  gospel of Christ:
for all who have not heard the words
  of salvation,
for all who have lost their faith,
for all whose sin has made them indifferent to
Christ, for all who actively oppose Christ
  by word or deed,
for all who are enemies of the cross of Christ,
and persecutors of his disciples,
for all who in the name of Christ have
  persecuted others,
that God will open their hearts to the truth
and lead them to faith and obedience.[2]

The BCP text (vv. 1-25) carries a larger frame than the RCL (vv. 16-25) because it includes the beginning verses of Hebrews 10 in which the author engages in a doctrinal interpretation of the crucifixion and resurrection of Jesus of Nazareth. This description compares the sacrifice of the Temple priests' repeated offerings with that of Jesus who offered himself and only once. In verses 1-15 (those omitted in the RCL) the author describes the ineffectiveness of the continual sacrifices of the priests for achieving the goal of cleansing the people. Repeated sacrifice at the Temple reminds the worshipers of their need for cleansing. Without sacrifice, "the worshipers, cleansed once for all, would no longer have any consciousness of sin" (v. 2). Before Christ's self-offering, the way to return to the Lord was through the yearly Temple offering.

In short, the text tells us: "the law . . . can never . . . make perfect those who approach" (v. 1). The writer argues that the Temple priests' need for continual sacrifices means they are not the ones through whom salvation is found but rather, in contrast, salvation is in the sacrifice of the crucified and risen Christ who died once for all, the great high priest. By omitting verses 1-15, the RCL text goes directly to the gospel: God's covenant with the people, opening the Temple to all people through forgiveness, and the assertion of hope that enables a community of faith to live in such a way that the members hold each other accountable.

According to homiletician Thomas Long, the narrator of Hebrews—maybe the writer or the voice of the letter—is nevertheless a preacher who, having previously established the confidence and hope the people may rightly place in Jesus, now asserts that the people may find in the Risen One the courage to pray with absolute trust. Long writes, "how we speak our prayers of petition and intercession derives from how firmly we hold the creed. That is why the Preacher begins this section by urging that the congregation 'hold fast to our confession . . .' that is, to the conviction that Jesus is God's Son . . ."[3]

As the "great high priest," Jesus is the one who hears our deep pleas because he completely understands human suffering. "In the days of his flesh, Jesus offered up prayers and supplications, with loud cries and tears" (5:7) and so he can be trusted. The cries of the faithful must not wither as if the confession of Jesus' place is not sure, but must be said with boldness.

The Gospel
JOHN 18:1—19:42 (RCL, LFM)
JOHN (18:1-40) 19:1-37 (BCP)

Many church traditions have long held that on Good Friday the church hears the Passion story from the betrayal in the Garden of Gethsemane to the burial of Jesus' body in the tomb provided by Joseph of Arimathea. This long sweep is still the text used in the RCL and LFM.

The BCP reading omits portions at the beginning and at the end, taking up only the heart of Jesus' Passion: the flogging, sentencing, and actual crucifixion. Omitting the betrayal in the Garden and the burial, however, does not necessarily jeopardize the enormity of what is heard because, in fact, the betrayal of the human community through Judas's action is all there in the scenes with the crowd and Pilate.

There are, nevertheless, several major differences between the Passion story heard on Good Friday from John and that heard on Palm/Passion Sunday. The major shape of the events are, of course, the same in each, but certain aspects of the story—emphasized or omitted in John—suggest ways in which the lectionary choices inform the liturgical day.

The Johannine Passion does not include the account of Judas's attempt to return the payment he received for betraying Jesus. It is as if Judas ceases to be important as soon as the story moves away from Gethsemane. Who Judas becomes or what he thinks of himself has little relevance any longer.

In contrast, Pilate's role is much larger here than in the Matthew account heard last Sunday. Pilate's deliberations are intensely indecisive even while he can be imagined conducting himself with the utmost authority: he wants to acquit Jesus, he finds no fault in him. This judgment is repeated until the final hand washing only provides a visual and tangible expression of what his words have been saying all along. Despite the unusual appearance of Pilate's wife and her evocative mention of a dream, he is unable to extricate himself from the situation.

For many Christians the sense of the presence of the suffering Christ, who in their thought is also the suffering God, makes it possible through His fellowship to abide their own suffering of whatever kind or character. To know Him in the fellowship of His suffering is to be transformed by the glory of His life, and for these individuals this is enough—in His name they can stand anything that life can do to them. This is the resource and the discipline that comes to their rescue under the siege of pain.
—Howard Thurman[4]

And something, certainly, needs to be noticed about the fact that John's story has no earthquake. If the earthquake in Matthew had something to do with a sign of a remaking of God's relationship with creation or with resurrection in the end times, its omission does not necessarily signal a lack of importance at the moment of Jesus' death. On the other hand, it could be read as silence on the part of creation at the crucifixion of God. For a sign to have meaning when present, its failure to materialize makes just as fruitful a basis for pondering this different expression of Jesus' death.

One more intriguing note of difference is the appearance of Nicodemus at the burial. He brings an inordinate amount of spices.

The crux of the issue largely swirls around human complicity in the murder of the One the church proclaims to be the second person of the Trinity. This story, whether read in its entirety by one voice or by several voices, stands alone in this liturgy as the pivotal proclamation, the reason for the assembly itself. It is not yet about the resurrection; it is a time to focus on the narrative of events that resulted in the death of an innocent human being.

PREACHING THE HEART OF THE GOSPEL

Hearing the story of the Passion again and again, the church proclaims the questions raised by this event: How did it happen? Why did it happen? Is it still happening? What is our relationship to such a thing as a community and as individuals? Who is the one who was killed?

Jesus, we know, is the supreme light shining in the blackness of our painful lives. Still, there may have been another (or others) who, in the exile and oppression of Isaiah's time, also showed the people another way to live, one not dependent on power and killing. The pairing of Isaiah with John invites the hearers to multilayered meditations. Good Friday is just the day for silence enough to spend time with what we do not know and yet yearn to grasp. But where speech breaks through the silent wonder at the events adored in this assembly, the preacher may address some of the questions these texts invite us to consider:

- How are we to understand the meaning of "God's will" in the torture of God's servant?
- What is really meant by "original sin?" Is it a fixed identity we must own? Or is it a self-perception in which we see the beauty of Jesus' silence before Pilate as metaphor for the impossibility of human unity?
- How does the atonement work?
- Who is tormenting the suffering servant?
- How is it that the suffering servant's bruises cause healing for the plurality of voices speaking?

This day is not necessarily appropriate for a sermon that attempts to work through a teaching on a difficult doctrine like the atonement, but perhaps in preparation for this day's brief sermon, the preacher might consider a focus on that doctrinal puzzle during Lent, either in a lecture format (adult forum, Bible study, and so forth) or as a part of a sermon leading up to Holy Week. The substitutionary language around the Isaiah figure—and in the way Christians have long referred to the crucifixion in hymns—makes it almost a foregone conclusion that many faithful people think of Jesus' gift as ransom rather than as the result of brokenness or as a witness to a nonviolent way of life. An emphasis on the atonement—helping people to think about it in more expansive ways—would be a worthy attempt to get away from what can sound like an almost magical quality to the crucifixion while, simultaneously, deepening the significance of Jesus' gift in its eschatological dimensions.

At the heart of this service is the passion reading according to John, which celebrates Christ's victory on the cross. As Jesus draws all people to himself, we pray for the whole world for which Christ died. Finally, we honor the cross as the sign of forgiveness, healing, and salvation.
—*Evangelical Lutheran Worship*[5]

Notes

1. Walter Brueggemann, "Theodicy in a Social Dimension," in *Journal for the Study of the Old Testament* 33, no. 1 (Oct 1985): 3–25; quote is on p. 5.

2. Good Friday Prayers, in *Book of Common Worship* (Louisville: Westminster John Knox Press, 1993), 285.

3. Thomas G. Long, *Hebrews,* Interpretation: A Bible Commentary for Teaching and Preaching (Louisville: John Knox Press, 1997), 64.

4. Howard Thurman, *Disciplines of the Spirit* (Richmond, Ind.: Friends United Press, 1987), 78.

5. *Evangelical Lutheran Worship* (Minneapolis: Augsburg Fortress, 2006), 249.

HOLY SATURDAY

REVISED COMMON	EPISCOPAL (BCP)
Job 14:1-14	Job 14:1-14
or Lam. 3:1-9, 19-24	
Ps. 31:1-4,15-16	Psalm 130
	or 31:1-15
1 Peter 4:1-8	1 Peter 4:1-8
Matt. 27:57-66	Matt. 27:57-66
or John 19:38-42	or John 19:38-42

KEY THEMES

• This is the day when we as Jesus' followers set ourselves in the mode of funeral preparation. This is the day for reality to sink in.

• Holy Saturday is about seemingly endless waiting. We wait with Job and at the tomb of Jesus.

• Christians comprise a new household that resides in the world as alien to it by reason of the hope we hold in the impossible.

• "The end of all things is near . . ."

FIRST READING
JOB 14:1-14 (RCL, BCP)

The book of Job includes three dialogues enveloped by an opening set-up of Job's predicament and concluding with Job's soliloquy and God's restoration. The issue is whether God can be just if God allows the innocent to suffer. Dealing with the question of theodicy (*theos* + *dike* = God + justice) utilizes the language of the court in that accusation and defense constitute the currency. But Job also employs metaphor, rhetorical strategies, oppositions, and the language of power.

This Holy Saturday reading carries stark metaphors to compare mortals—humans and plants—to state the finality of human death. This text comes at the end of the first dialogue between Job and his friends. The friends insist that Job must repent for surely he has been complicit in his own troubles.

Job's response begins in chapters 12 to 13. He argues that only God could have brought this misfortune upon him and that his so-called friends, full of deceit regarding God's powers, have demeaned Job.

Then, in the verses appointed for today, Job compares a human being to a tree and declares the difference between them: a tree may rise from the dead; a human being cannot. A tree left even as a mere stump can, with a bit of water, send up a shoot. Once dead, a human has no prospect of coming to life again. Job sees in this truth a hard burden for human life. In his sorrow, all that he might have hoped for has vanished. Job's desire is to be hidden until God's wrath has gone away. He seems to believe that since everything is being taken from him, his life will soon be taken, too.

> I am convinced that neither death, nor life, nor angels, nor rulers, nor things present, nor things to come, nor powers, nor height, nor depth, nor anything else in all creation, will be able to separate us from the love of God in Christ Jesus our Lord.
> —Romans 8:38-39

In a service of Morning Prayer, Noon Prayer, Evening Prayer—or something else on this Holy Saturday before the Vigil begins—this reading offers a meditation on the crass reality of death. Holy Saturday is about seemingly endless waiting. To wait with Job in the presence of his foolish-though-well-intentioned friends (perhaps it would be more charitable to call them theologically unhelpful) is to wait at the tomb of Jesus, hearing Job's ironic question. "If mortals die, will they live again?" (v. 14). But we know that to wait at Jesus' tomb is to await the answer given in the resurrection.

LAMENTATIONS 3:1-9, 19-24 (RCL alt.)

Lament is a cry of grief. This is the day for such a cry, while Jesus' tomb remains sealed, while the religious leaders are not yet faced with their ignorance of him, while the disciples shudder in fear, while we ponder the crucifixion and wait. Most of this reading describes concrete conditions for justifiable lament. We might, in our time, use this text for a meditation on the use of torture and the pain of those in our own world who have to endure unimaginable suffering.

We must also notice that the images of great wretchedness are abruptly ended in a statement that contradicts depression: "I have hope . . ." for "the steadfast love of the LORD never ceases . . ." There is no easy transition between the catalog of horrors and this wild, bright assertion of mercy. Hope and pain are entwined in this text in the same amazing way they live beside each other each day of our lives. The move from darkness to light has no slick pathway. It is a stone rolled away. It is a blinding vision. It is an assertion without context. "The LORD is my portion . . . therefore I will hope . . ."

RESPONSIVE READING
PSALM 31:1-4, 15-16 (RCL)
PSALM 130 (BCP)
PSALM 31:1-15 (BCP alt.)

Both of these psalms (and in both versions appointed for Psalm 31) are cries of hope and trust in the Lord in the midst of suffering. They can be heard as the cries of the One who was crucified. They can also be heard as the cries of all those who pray for any kind of deliverance. It should be remembered that the psalms are songs, so that if they are used in worship on this Holy Saturday, in the midst of the solemnity of the day and in keeping with the move toward holding vigil, it would be appropriate for the assembly to sing or chant these strong words.

SECOND READING

1 PETER 4:1-8 (RCL, BCP)

In sync with the suffering of Jesus that brings the assembly to a Holy Saturday service, this reading from a time of Christian persecution in possibly the late first century links Jesus' suffering with that of his followers. This letter sets before the church of exiles in five remote Asia Minor regions (the eastern edge of the Roman Empire) the deadly torment of Jesus so that in it the people to whom the letter is addressed may find comfort for their own situation.

It is enough that we know that Christ descended into hell and destroyed hell for all believers and that he redeemed them from the power of death, the devil, and the eternal damnation of hellish retribution. How that happened we should save for the next world, where not only this matter but many others, which here we have simply believed and cannot comprehend with our blind reason, will be revealed. —*Epitome of the Formula of Concord*[1]

They have been reminded in the first three chapters of 1 Peter that Christians comprise a new household that resides in the world as alien to it by reason of the suffering that must be endured. The suffering is not the usual human trials and tribulations that come with daily problems and aging, but the sort that comes from rejection by one's neighbors. It is not clear that the persecution is of the officially sanctioned governmental sort. Rather, it may be ostracism and hatred. The point is that the Christians in these churches—especially because it seems they are new to being called "Christian"—are reminded that Jesus Christ also knew suffering.

The fourth chapter begins with a turn toward concluding admonitions, "Since therefore Christ suffered in the flesh, arm yourselves also . . ." The suffering of Christ is at the heart of what has created the church and it is in that suffering— mirrored in the persecution of Christ's followers—that the church will know the meaning of the will of God. Verses 1-2 might well be rendered: accept death so that you die to sin and live by God's will. Fred Craddock suggests that these verses are best understood through Romans 6:7-11: "For whoever has died is freed from sin . . ."[2] It is probably not wise or necessary to interpret these verses to mean that the author of this letter wants the recipients to welcome death. Instead, they are to understand that they have become "dead" to their former way of life, and by *that* death—which has given them a new measure for the value of things—they are encouraged to persevere.

Toward what—and how—is the church called to live in the time of suffering? Toward what—and how—is the church called to live in the time of waiting? This Holy Saturday, after all, is the day of waiting even for the vigil that is its own time of waiting. This day is an immense ocean of being on hold! In that holding pattern, when "the end of all things is near" (what a provocative statement of apocalyptic promise we find in v. 7), the church is called to "be serious," "discipline yourselves for the sake of your prayers," and "love one another." In other words, in the pattern of waiting, the church's task is prayer and love.

THE GOSPEL

MATTHEW 27:57-66 (RCL, BCP)

Each of the accounts of Jesus' Passion tells about the burial of Jesus. On Holy Saturday, we are offered some time to meditate on the honor shown to Jesus by Joseph of Arimathea, a disciple who had the courage to step forward from the crowd and go directly to Pilate to request Jesus' body. The conventional portrait of Jesus' disciples at this point in the narrative has them cowering for fear—except for the women who stand close by Jesus and witness all the events.

Why does Joseph stand out like this? What is it about him that would make it possible for him to expose himself to the potential dangers of being identified with the One who was just crucified? What was so important about burial that he would risk himself?

Throughout the Old Testament, stories of burials either serve as testaments to the importance of the one who is dead or as testaments to the shame under which they died. A few examples will demonstrate the point.

In Genesis 23, Abraham negotiates for purchase of the tomb in which he will bury Sarah. It is the first tomb so described in the Bible. It is for a woman. This is remarkable in that burial itself is not always mentioned and never in such great detail. Sarah's tomb becomes the burial place for many, a sort of shrine for a long line of illustrious descendants. But she is the first, so honored is she by Abraham.

The death of Jezebel in 2 Kings 9, in contrast, arouses no such honor. Her body is left to the dogs to eat, lying in a field where animal excrement can be found.

This is the height of disrespect for a woman who had no respect for others when she was alive and held power over them.

There are other deaths as well, such as of Saul and his sons in battle with the Philistines in 1 Samuel 31, which describes them hugely dishonored, dismembered, and left in the field. Adding to the dishonor is that the mortally wounded Saul tried to convince one of his own soldiers (1 Sam. 31:4) to kill him in order to deprive the enemy of being able "to make sport" of him. The soldier couldn't do it, and so Saul committed suicide. (This account is contradicted in 2 Samuel 1:10, but the point, as we shall see, is the non-burial rather than the suicide.)

Grateful warriors, who appreciated Saul's attempt to side with them against their enemies, took great pains to retrieve the bodies and then cremate them. Some scholars suggest that prejudice against cremation in some societies and cultures—especially in the West—comes in part from the link between Saul's suicide and the dishonor toward his body when the Philistines left him and his fellow soldiers on the hillside. There is shame in not being buried and particularly in the body not being left intact. Whether or not his manner of death is the reason for centuries of avoiding cremation (other scholars note the belief that the resurrection on the last day requires whole bones rather than ashes—so powerfully and literally do many of our sisters and brothers take the promises of life eternal), we can see in this story the final respect shown to Saul, his sons, Jonathan, and other warriors when their bodies were retrieved and dispatched with care by being burned. Not caring for the dead creates a common outrage that the United States saw when the bodies of flood victims were left to wash in waters following Hurricane Katrina's destruction in New Orleans in 2005.

Joseph risked his own safety to properly care for Jesus' body. We can reasonably assume that he did not know more about the resurrection than the other disciples (see John 20:9). This means that even before Jesus' identity was fully revealed, Joseph understood something about caring even for One who was thoroughly disgraced in the eyes of the world. Jesus' disgraceful execution did not stop Joseph from honoring the One who had so transformed his life. Even before the resurrection, Joseph the disciple was so filled with gratitude that Roman threats on him as a follower of Jesus (John 20:19; 19:38) could not keep him from paying homage to Jesus. Despite his fear (v. 38), he went to speak with the powerful Roman governor and, by asking for Jesus' body, made public his allegiance to Jesus. He risked his own life to honor the life of someone who was no longer able to notice the gift.

There is no need to choose between prayer and silence, privacy or conversation, reading or writing, reflection or the abandonment of thought, the frequentation or avoidance of spiritual people, abundance or famine, illness or health, life or death; the "one thing necessary" is what each moment produces by God's design.
—Mary Margaret Funk[3]

To what is said above regarding Joseph of Arimathea (in Matthew 27:57-66), who also appears in this reading from John 19, we must add the courage of Nicodemus who joins Joseph to prepare the body of the outcast Jesus for burial. Nicodemus is the one who had earlier gone to see Jesus in the dark, under cover, hidden from all eyes (John 3:2), and here he is again. This time, however, he is defying his own fears, if they are like the fears Joseph is said to have (v. 38). Here is Nicodemus with an unimaginable amount of spices, nearly one hundred pounds. It is far more than enough for burial. Scholars have argued whether he is assuaging guilt or perhaps expressing his desire to ward off decay because the resurrection is still too preposterous.

There is no agreement on Nicodemus's underlying motivation, but on the surface we can see an image of the disciple still operating "in the dark"—without full knowledge—just as we function even today on this side of the resurrection. Like Nicodemus, we do not understand who Jesus is and we turn to him too often with our arms full of too many bribes and excuses.

Preaching the Heart of the Gospel

This is really the day when we as Jesus' followers can set ourselves in the mode of funeral preparers. And so it is fitting that this is the day the Gospel texts speak of Joseph and Nicodemus, of asking for Jesus' body and preparing it, of offering up a new grave and rolling the stone over the entrance. This is the day for reality to sink in. This is what a funeral will do, and in fact, there is, as we can see, no account of a ritual moment of remembrance and celebration for Jesus' life as we have come to know funerals. Instead, the ritual is boiled down to honoring the body by caring for it in a respectful way.

During the Black Plague, this is something for which Christians came to be known: we buried the dead. I wasn't there, of course, and neither were you. But *we* buried the dead, taking a risk that we might become infected, and we did it—through our brothers and sisters then—because we know that death is not the final act in God's purposes. Those with whom we share fellowship in the communion of saints, living and dead, make it possible for our identity to transcend both time and space. This is one meaning for the resurrection. We do not fear death. We do not necessarily know the shape of the next act, but we know it has ultimate implications and makes life here in our sphere one with commensurate ultimate implications. We are given a perspective through which to barely nose our way toward grasping Job's hope (he is the one we quote at funerals: "I know that my redeemer lives") and grasping Joseph's courage in confronting Pilate to get the body.

> Good though it may be to think of God's acts of kindness, and to love and praise him for them, it is far better to think of his bare existence, and to love and praise him for himself.
> —*The Cloud of Unknowing*[4]

Can you preach this? Can you and I hear that in the midst of sorrow over the reality of death—the unthinkable truth that we will all die eventually—the truth is a different word about life? What is the word?

Notes

1. "Formula of Concord, Epitome," from *The Book of Concord,* ed. Robert Kolb and Timothy J. Wengert (Minneapolis: Fortress Press, 2000), 514.4.

2. Fred B. Craddock, *First and Second Peter and Jude,* Westminster Bible Companion (Louisville: Westminster John Knox Press, 1995), 66.

3. Mary Margaret Funk, *Tools Matter for Practicing the Spiritual Life* (New York: Continuum, 2004), 108.

4. *The Cloud of Unknowing and Other Works,* chap. 5, trans. A. C. Spearing (New York: Penguin Books, 2001), 27.

EASTER VIGIL

MARCH 22, 2008

REVISED COMMON	EPISCOPAL (BCP)	ROMAN CATHOLIC
Gen. 1:1—2.4a	Gen. 1:1—2:2	Gen. 1:1—2:2 or 1:1, 26-31a
Gen. 7:1-5,11-18; 8:6-18; 9:8-13	Gen. 7:1-5, 11-18; 8:6-18; 9:8-13	
Gen. 22:1-18	Gen. 22:1-18	Gen. 22:1-18 or 22:1-2, 9a-13, 15-18
Exod. 14:10-31; 15:20-21	Exod. 14:10—15:1	Exod. 14:15—15:1
	Isa. 4:2-6	Isa. 54:5-14
Isa. 55:1-11	Isa. 55:1-11	Isa. 55:1-11
Prov. 8:1-8, 19-21; 9:4b-6 or Bar. 3:9-15, 32—4:4		Bar. 3:9-15, 32—4:4
Ezek. 36:24-28	Ezek. 36:24-28	Ezek. 36:16-17a, 18-28
Ezek. 37:1-14	Ezek. 37:1-14	
Zeph. 3:14-20	Zeph. 3:12-20	
ELW adds: Jon. 1:1—2:1 Isa. 61:1-4, 9-11 Dan. 3:1-29		
Rom. 6:3-11	Rom. 6:3-11	Rom. 6:3-11
Psalm 114	Psalm 114	Ps. 118:1-2, 16-17, 22-23
Matt. 28:1-10 or John 20:1-18 (ELW)	Matt. 28:1-10	Matt. 28:1-10

KEY THEMES

- The image of our lives is a very long and beautiful story. It is the story of all who have followed the Lord.
- Out of the empty tomb, good news is poured upon us.
- Along with Mary's, Jesus speaks our names.
- We need to go where Jesus said we would find him: in the bread and wine, wherever there is need, and wherever two or three are gathered in his name.
- "Do not be afraid."

OLD TESTAMENT READINGS AND RESPONSES

GENESIS 1:1—2:4a (RCL)
GENESIS 1:1—2:2 (BCP, LFM)
GENESIS 1:1, 26-31a (LFM alt.)

Creation. Some congregations begin the Easter Vigil outdoors around a fire—a big bonfire or a rousing brazier fire—whose flame is used then to light the Paschal candle and from that to light the individual candles carried into the sanctuary. Around this large, communal fire, the story of creation is read. Depending on the time of year—earlier or later in the spring—the sky may be light or already darkening, adding to the mystery of God bringing something out of nothing and making our world possible.

The place to start in telling the story of time is, of course, at the beginning. This is, in some respects, a startling point to set out on the journey because, in the postmodern world of awareness about social location and self-consciousness about beginnings, the place to begin might be thought to be with who we are at present, moving then backwards into the beginnings. But with God's Word, the origin is the first words, "In the beginning . . ."—which not only tells the gathering where we are located (we are not *in* the beginning any longer, we are after *it* began), but also tells us that the beginning words, as the church has heard them from the beginning of the book, are also *our* beginning now.

With the candles lit, the Easter Proclamation sung, and the Prayer of the Day asking for the renewal of the church, the Word continues with the readings that lead the assembly to hear and remember how God has acted throughout the life of all Christians.

Flood. The RCL and BCP appoint the story of the Flood, with its implications for a creation gone wrong and yet a God who holds out a promise for the rest of time. God will remember whenever God sees the bow in the sky! This story acknowledges that creation is not Eden-like, everyone does not escape the natural disasters ravaging our settlements, some people find haven and others do not, but through it all even the animals and birds are beloved by God. Such is the way faithful humans understood our relationship with the Creator. It is not a simple journey, this life. It is fraught with dangers. But the rainbow remains, and we wonder—together—at its meaning.

GENESIS 22:1-18 (RCL, BCP, LFM)
GENESIS 22:1-2, 9a, 10-13, 15-18 (LFM alt.)

Testing of Abraham. The story of Abraham's journey up the mountain with Isaac and rescue by God's sending a ram to sacrifice confronts us with the meaning of a faith that has deepened beyond the physical rescue from floodwaters. God has already cut off Abraham and Sarah from their past by calling them to wander into a land not their own. Abraham now acts on his belief that God has asked him to sacrifice his own future in the person of Isaac. Abraham's testing is beyond the ken of most of us who cannot begin to approach preparing to let go of both our past and our future. To do so sets a person in an excruciating and existential place. This is where God has brought Abraham, and he faces it with a clarity and certainty that, despite its terror—or perhaps because of it—is sorely needed by people of faith. In Abraham's story we find ourselves imagining a reality that stands apart from all that surrounds us daily, suspending us in a realm only God can fashion and mend.

EXODUS 14:10-31; 15:20-21 (RCL)
EXODUS 14:10—15:1 (BCP)
EXODUS 14:15—15:1 (LFM)

Deliverance at the Red Sea. Yet, the rescue only God can send is repeatedly difficult to grasp. (Certainly this is one reason people of faith need to hear the stories again and again.) The difficulty is evident in the glimpse the exodus story gives us of the Hebrew slaves being liberated. Salvation does not usher in a response to life that is emotionally one-dimensional. The freed people are not merely joyous; they are fearful and angry with Moses, who has brought them to a place where they can only imagine dying. Moses' assurances are met with incredulity until the waters part and the people cross over to the other side, watching from there as their enemies are brought down.

Verses 20-21 are Miriam's song of triumph. In a lecture in Montana several years ago, Hebrew Bible scholar Phyllis Trible made the case that because so few women are named in the Scriptures and because so few are shown as religious leaders, we should put great stock in the portrayal of Miriam here as just such a leader. She is, in effect, a liturgical leader in this scene. With tambourine in hand, she is the musician of the people, the cantor, the liturgical dancer. She leads the song of rejoicing. These verses and, in fact, the previous song attributed to Moses and the Israelites are considered some of the oldest pieces of Scripture.

We do not have historical data on this liberation event, this exodus of the Israelites from Egypt. But we can recognize in this story the elements of many liberation histories: the oppressive government, the economic enslavement, the destruction of families and spirits, and the leader who arises from the people with a vision that seems impossible. Freedom? In the wilderness? Led by a murderer? Who already ran away once? How can this be? These are the questions that God answers again and again, making a way where none seem possible, making a pillar of fire by night and a pillar of cloud by day, parting the waters, putting prophetic words into the mouths of mortals, and in these ways repeatedly bringing down the mighty and lifting up the lowly. All people need to hear this story, for all of us are in captivity to something not liberating. All people need hope.

ISAIAH 4:2-6 (BCP)

Jerusalem's Restoration. The BCP Old Testament readings move from the story of the exodus to this vision of what will follow the Lord's judgment of Israel. It is a portrait of joy and calm: "whoever is left . . . will be called holy" and the familiar images of a pillar of cloud and a pillar of fire will return. The people will be shaded and given shelter. They shall be deemed beautiful. This is a promise of home-coming and it extends imagistically the rescue across the sea and into the wilderness.

ISAIAH 54:5-14 (LFM)

Song of Assurance. Following the exodus story, this song celebrates God's steadfast promises to a people who had felt abandoned. The familiar depiction of the Lord as husband calling the previously cast-off wife back into relationship offers assurances of the Lord's compassion. Despite the obvious problems of this patriarchal image, it exudes a clarity about the difficulty of relationships, the work involved in remaining faithful, and in the end paints a picture of stunning beauty replete with precious gems: "I am about to . . . lay your foundations with sapphires" (Isa. 54:11). Such a commitment from the Lord cannot be lightly taken. It comes as a bridge here between the exodus and the Isaiah 55 text laden with food.

ISAIAH 55:1-11 (RCL, BCP, LFM)

Salvation Freely Offered to All. When the people arrive at the impossible restoration, they must sing! And this is the hymn! Everyone is welcome in this place of rich food, water, wine, and milk. This is the consummation of God's promises to deliver the people into bounty. God's word "shall not return . . . empty" but will accomplish what God's purpose sets forth.

PROVERBS 8:1-8, 19-21; 9:4b-6 (RCL)

The Wisdom of God. Here is the personification of divine wisdom: Lady Wisdom, the feminine noun *hokmah.* She is calling from every possible place where her invitation might be heard; calling all the people to listen to her truth and receive her gifts of rich fruit. She promises to shower those who walk with her the treasures only wisdom can bestow. The hearers are invited to feast and to live.

Most intriguingly, the speech from Lady Wisdom, by juxtaposing food, riches, and insight, offers up thorough bounty—body, mind, and spirit—to those who walk with her. The freedoms and pleasures, the relief (!) experienced by the Israelites who crossed the Red Sea are, here in this invitation, offered to everyone.

BARUCH 3:9-15, 32—4:4 (RCL alt., LFM)

The Wisdom of God. More specifically, this poem identifies wisdom as Torah. Wisdom has, in fact, "appeared on earth and lived with humankind. She is the book of the commandments of God . . ." (3:37—4:1). The onus is on the people to "learn where there is wisdom, where there is strength . . ." (3:14), so that they may have life. This is an instructing word, guiding the people to the place—the Torah—where wisdom is to be found.

EZEKIEL 36:24-28 (RCL, BCP)
EZEKIEL 36:16-17a, 18-28 (LFM)

A New Heart and a New Spirit. What will happen to the scattered and broken people for whom God has special concern? They will be gathered, washed, given a new heart and spirit, and they will be God's people who live in their own land and follow God's commands. This is a picture of restoration and new beginnings.

EZEKIEL 37:1-14 (RCL, BCP)

Valley of the Dry Bones. What God promises as restoration is amazing enough, but in this vision the wild transformation is deepened: even into a valley full of dry bones, the breath of life will blow and the people will have new life. Ezekiel speaks to the bones the word of God and the word itself brings about the re-membering of the bones. The people are made whole, reconnected by the breath of the prophet. Hope is never lost because the word of the Lord in the mouth of the prophet creates a new reality.

ZEPHANIAH 3:14-20 (RCL)
ZEPHANIAH 3:12-20 (BCP)

The Gathering of God's People. The prophet has been speaking to the nations and turns now to speak of Israel's special place in the midst of the nation. The Israelites will become resident among the nations that had previously persecuted them. In that place, the Lord's power will bring rejoicing. Is this not the state of all faithful people living in a world at odds with the promises of the Lord? Believing that the Lord will, indeed, "remove disaster" (v. 18), "deal with . . . oppressors," and "save the lame and gather the outcast" (v. 19), people of faith are renewed. Dry bones are knit together.

JONAH 1:1—2:1 (ELW)

The Deliverance of Jonah. An evocative narrative—one that is true and preposterous at the same time—can be a great gift for someone sitting in the dark of flickering candles. Jonah's story is such an offering, beginning with Jonah's very human fleeing from God's intentions for him and ending with Jonah's prayer in the belly of a dilemma.

Who among us has not known this experience? The story is an image of every human life tossed by storms and doubts, questioned about past guilt, looked to for answers, and finally served up as a sacrifice in some way. For Jonah, as for us, God has another new beginning. In the pattern of the truly heroic tale, Jonah first endures a kind of death that mirrors the three days' tomb for Lazarus and for Jesus. Such are archetypes: rich with echoes of others' tales. And so, in the dark, the listeners hear their own story, too, of God's rescue and correction. This story is for some the dramatic climax of the night of listening, for the emotional rollercoaster hits bottom in the whale's belly and from there gradually rises into the final light.

ISAIAH 61:1-4, 9-11 (ELW)

Clothed in the Garments of Salvation. And then, the words in the dark of the sanctuary on this night become poetry, become words the congregation recognizes from the mouth of God's own Son: "the LORD has anointed me . . . sent me to bring good news . . . to bind up the brokenhearted . . . to proclaim liberty . . ." In Isaiah's words, the people also can hear Jonah's voice, finally calling to the people of Nineveh. We remember that Jonah cried, "Repent," but behind that summons was the promise, as it always is, of God's mercy: the "garland instead of ashes, the oil of gladness instead of mourning . . ." We know that behind the law stands the gospel (in the same way that we could also say behind the gospel stands the law). Here it is for Israel and for the individual, too, who sings, "I will greatly rejoice in the LORD." It is as if the previous ten readings have prepared a context for this bursting out in rejoicing. The turmoil that has gone before from creation to flood, the near sacrifice of a child, slaves brought to freedom, promises of feasting and of healing even dry bones, became Jonah's running away and now the denouement of soothing images of rest.

DANIEL 3:1-29 (ELW)

Deliverance from the Fiery Furnace. But the ear needs a more penetrating reprieve, and the story of the three young men in the fiery furnace with its comic repetitions, its repetitive language, and its mockery of the ridiculous (but dangerous) king deflates all the heights of the narratives. Where would we be without humor? And why should the night of the vigil—which will end in an elaborate and unbelievable joy—not remind us of mirth?

Tonight we are going to tell our name—to ourselves, by way of reminder, to those who will become part of us this night through baptism and confirmation, and to those of the world who will listen, who will take the time to hear what our name is. And our name is a very long one, one that has been growing since the creation of the world.
—Brian Helge[1]

By this story we are ushered back into the land of our own lives where irony surrounds the tragic and comedy brings down foolish emperors. This is a story of what it is like to be alive as a human being in every age. Here is Act Two of the denouement, but only to bring the first revelation—the experience of God reflected in the Old Testament—to a close so that what is written in the next testament, the New Testament, can be heard.

RESPONSIVE READING
PSALM 114 (RCL, BCP)

In the middle of this song, the waters of the Jordan part and the mountains and hills frolic. These images are repeated; so important are they for the psalmist. Verses 3 and 4 assert the strange behavior (fleeing, skipping) of the elements, and verses 5 and 6 ask the sea and the mountains why it is they behave in this way. Nature itself is queried for its powerful witness to the liberation of the Hebrew people. Whether this is an enthronement hymn or part of the Passover liturgy, it is a strong echo of the founding motif of the Israelites: release from captivity. As a response to the Old Testament readings, it is a fitting song of joy.

PSALM 118:1-2, 16-17, 22-23 (LFM)

Believed to be a song for a liturgy of thanksgiving, this psalm turns the congregation to the one appropriate response to the Old Testament readings: "Give thanks to the LORD . . ." This thanksgiving turns the song into proclamation of the Lord's rescue, leading to the proclamation that the singer will live and tell of the Lord's deeds. The final two verses anticipate the language used by followers of Jesus to describe him as a cornerstone rejected and yet exalted.

SECOND READING
ROMANS 6:3-11 (RCL, BCP, LFM)

It is fitting that the first New Testament reading for this Vigil night is language we hear most often at funerals, speaking of Jesus Christ: "If we have been united with him in a death like his, we will certainly be united with him in a resurrection like his" (v. 5). This text also begins with baptism, thus linking baptism and death and resurrection together into one whole. We have been buried by baptism into death so that, with Christ, we might have resurrected life.

This is complex and simple at the same time. Baptism is the entrée into "walking in newness" (v. 4b). Baptism is how we are united with Christ. That word, *sumphutoi*, is literally "grafted," and so the use of the word *united*, while appropriate, is not exactly strong enough. The vine and branches—and tree of life!—come to mind. We are united to that without which we could not and

Baptism is a sacrament of truth and holiness; and it is a sacrament, because it is the sign which directs us to God's revelation of eternal life and declares, not merely the Christian "myth", but—the Word of God. It does not merely signify eternal reality, but is eternal reality, because it points significantly beyond its own concreteness. Baptism mediates the new creation: it is not itself grace, but from first to last a means of grace.
—Karl Barth[2]

would not thrive as we do when part of the larger, mothering, fathering, nourishing, Risen One we know as Christ Jesus.

Many churches today, struggling to make Sunday morning welcoming to strangers, have moved toward opening communion to all who are present, regardless of whether they have been baptized. While the desire to be welcoming is commendable, this change loosens the confessional role of baptism in the church's life, leaving baptism to be something other than the sacrament of initiation into the body of Christ. Because of the Vigil's close identification with baptism, this night may be an auspicious time for the sermon to assert the gift of *sacramental* welcome to communion with the whole body of Christ—welcome to all people through the sign of God's faithfulness that is not dependent on human cognitive embrace.

The avoidance of—or embarrassment over?—baptism's significance, seen in our time, was also a problem in the sixteenth century. Martin Luther's *Large Catechism* rails against a diminished notion of the sacrament: "[W]e are not to regard [baptism] as an indifferent matter, like putting on a new red coat. It is of the greatest importance that we regard baptism as excellent, glorious, and exalted. It is the chief cause of our contentions and battles because the world is now full of sects who scream that baptism is an external thing and that external things are of no use."[3] Here it sounds as if our age and Luther's time share an inability (among some Christians) to take seriously the divine origin of baptism, willingly setting it aside as if it was a human ritual indifferently concocted and easily let go.

The water is not merely water, but water infused with God's Word. It is the Word, Luther tells us, that effects the baptism "and this shows also . . . that God's name is *in* it. And where God's name is, there must also be life and salvation. Thus it is well described as a divine, blessed, fruitful, and gracious water, for it is through the Word that it receives the power to become the 'washing of regeneration,' as St. Paul calls it in Titus 3[:5]"[4] (emphasis mine). It is entirely appropriate at the Easter Vigil for the sermon to lean into the meaning of baptism for knowing Christ and his resurrection as realities for our own lives, as realities *in* which the baptized live and move and have our being.

How does baptism achieve all this? Baptism is the negation of what is negative so that the old self—living under the illusions of temporal reality that cannot see beyond its own space/time arena—dies into a new continuum that has no end. What is negated creates the ultimate positive: "the mysterious possibility emerges of my regarding myself as an object not identical with myself."[5] Baptism is the sign from God that we who are baptized are ushered into new identity (passive voice in the verbs here is intentional), a self beyond the self. What is let go leaves room for a new creation to come into being by the mercy of God. "Expecting resurrection, and discerning my identity . . . beyond the death of Christ, I must, I can, I ought, and I will, not be a sinner."[6]

The great gift of this Christian faith, signified on a cross and in an empty tomb, is that our faith comes out of what seem to be extreme polarities: death/life, blindness/seeing, bondage/liberation, sin/unity, and so forth. Faith in Christ Jesus "consists in the perception that the line of death which runs through the life of Jesus is in fact the law and necessity of all human life. We perceive that we are dead with Christ, that in relation to God we are ignorant, and that before Him we can only cease to move and speak, we can only worship."[7]

We can only worship. There is, then, nothing better for us on the day when we await the joy of resurrection than to come together in, with, and under the Word that enters our ears and mouths. That is worship. The people—made into one body by the sacraments of grace—hear, give thanks, sing, pray, and eat together. It's quite simple, and very profound. Paul's word on how we come to be together in these things is the utterly appropriate way to draw us further into the mystery of the Old Testament readings and refocus on the mystery of the resurrection.

The Gospel
MATTHEW 28:1-10 (RCL, BCP, LFM)

Worship is also at the heart of the Gospel story for this pivotal day: when Jesus appeared to the women, "they came to him, took hold of his feet, and worshiped him" (v. 9). Worship is the absence of fear because it is a uniting event. Worship is the negation of loneliness and alienated estrangement. The impetus to worship may grow out of an awe formed at least in part by fear, but worship does not actually either invite or condone that sort of self-protection.

On this Matthean Sabbath morning, the story is an apocalyptic one: an earthquake reminiscent of the earthquake at the moment of Jesus' death (27:51) and of the birth pangs of a new beginning (24:7-8) and of several moments in Revelation (6:12; 8:5; 11:13, 19; and 16:18). An utterly unique event is in process, announcing itself with the very shaking of the foundations. Such is what defines a world-shattering change.

Mary Magdalene and "the other Mary" have been through the entire crucifixion experience with Jesus, watching him die, watching him buried, and now suddenly seeing the stone rolled away. They are said here to see an angel who then, in characteristic and exquisite detail, sits on the stone and speaks to them. The Roman guards have been shocked to death. Although perhaps not actually dead, they are *like* the dead. Angels do not speak to such persons. Perhaps angels cannot be heard by persons who have no ability to respond. This definition of being-as-if-dead is quite familiar as a description of some people and of all of us at some points in our lives when we have lost hope or suddenly realize we have never known true hope.

The angel's words are a direct address to the most prominent experience the women have upon seeing all this. Indeed, the words are exactly what we who are hearing about this event even in the comfort of our cushioned pews at the Easter Vigil in the year 2008 might well be feeling: "This is outside my knowledge/I cannot believe this/What am I doing here? I am afraid of myself and of God." The angel says what is, in fact, almost always true: along with the women at the tomb, we also are looking for Jesus, and we are looking in the wrong place. This is enough to give us fear. If we are wrong about where to look, how can we be set right? And the angel answers that as well: "See where Jesus *was* and then go on to where you will find him, where he said he would go." For Jesus did tell the disciples he would go on ahead of them to Galilee (Matt. 26:32; 28:16).

Where did Jesus tell us he could be found?

Christ Jesus is in the meal. His words about his own body are proclaimed in worship whenever we "do this in remembrance" of him: "This is my body; this is my blood . . ." (Matt. 26:26-28).

Christ Jesus is in the body gathered as the church. "Wherever two or three are gathered in my name, there am I in the midst . . ." (Matt. 18:20).

Christ Jesus is present in those who have needs. "Whatever you do for the least of these, you do for me . . ." (Matt. 25:45). He is where we meet the needs of our communities, which includes the meeting of the needs of all members. The church is made up not just of people who have something to give for the sake of others but people who also receive the gifts of others for their needs. We gather together in order to be receivers and givers.

We do not worship in order to be filled with the capacity to go out and *do* to others (although this is an outcome of our worship, to be sure); we worship because, as Karl Barth wrote, that is all we can do in the presence of the One who went to the grave for us. We worship because we must. It is the same response the women had to the risen Jesus.

Notice that when Jesus met them on that morning, his first word was, "Greetings!" The women displayed their honor and fear to which Jesus then spoke words of comfort. But he first said, "Good morning" or "Hello" (*chairete* —a word used in normal conversation when one encounters friends). Jesus' resurrection appearances are occasions when a friend sees his friends or when the friends who have seen the death are confronted with a reality that is both familiar and strange. They know him and yet . . . they come to the knowing out of a fear so intense he has to tell them himself not to be afraid. Something about seeing him is frightening.

> *Yesterday I was crucified with Christ;*
> *today I am glorified with him.*
> *Yesterday I was dead with Christ;*
> *today I am sharing in his resurrection.*
> *Yesterday I was buried with him;*
> *today I am waking with him from the sleep*
> *of death.*
> —Gregory of Nazianzus[8]

Here is the paradox of faith: fear and joy at the same time. Out of this paradox comes the sermon for this Resurrection of Our Lord at the summit of the Easter Vigil.

JOHN 20:1-18 (ELW)

Lectionaries diverge on the Gospel readings for the Vigil and for Easter Sunday. The RCL appoints Matthew 28 for the Vigil and John 20 for Easter Day with Matthew 28:1-10 as a possible alternative. The *ELW* lectionary, however, appoints John 20:1-18 for the Vigil[9] and Matthew 28 for Easter Day with John 20 as an alternative. The point is that the Gospel readings for the Vigil and Easter Sunday ought to include these two readings.

Both texts recall the first experiences of the resurrection in the vicinity of the empty tomb. In the Matthew text (see above), the women hear from an angel about Jesus' rising. The John 20 text contains two scenes: (1) the disciples, Peter and John, differ in their responses to the empty tomb, and (2) Mary Magdalene is met by the Risen One himself.

Mary Magdalene summons Peter and John to the tomb. They run to see what she has seen. Peter sees the cloths, registering perhaps that this empty tomb is not like Lazarus's. (When he came out of his tomb, he needed to be unbound.) The body that was laid in Jesus' tomb has left its cloths. Peter is not said to believe; the reader is not told Peter's response. The Beloved Disciple, however, sees the cloths and believes. What it is exactly to which that belief is directed, the reader is not told. We are given, at any rate, the two possible responses to an unbelievable marvel: incomprehension (on Peter's part) and belief (the other disciple). The two return home.

Mary stays weeping. Her response constitutes a third way of responding to a mystery: full-bodied immersion, remaining present in the place where the incongruity has become manifest. She is neither said to believe nor to disbelieve. She remains in the vortex of existential openness. She does not run home. Neither does she proclaim. Instead, she waits.

> Resurrection doesn't happen *to* persons; it happens *between and among* them.
> —Marianne Sawicki[10]

What this scene may call up in the hearer is a recognition of our own relationship with tragedy and mystery, with helplessness and despair. With Mary in the garden, we too behold and do not see, weep and cannot know. It is only when Jesus the gardener/rabbi speaks her name that Mary is enabled to see through her tears. The command to her from Jesus, then, is to go to the other disciples and say that he is ascending to the Father. By the time she reaches the other disciples, the impossible has taken on the shape of a personal assertion: "I have seen the Lord." These words become the witness of the whole catholic, apostolic church throughout the ages, with all of the attendant language striving to explain and define their meaning.

The mystery remains, while the assertion lives. This is the beauty of the gospel.

PREACHING THE HEART OF THE GOSPEL

Preaching at the Easter Vigil comes at the end of the long story told through Scripture readings from the Old Testament. Depending on your congregation or the lectionary to which you are adhering, the congregation may be given seven to twelve readings. Those who have become accustomed to a full Vigil with all twelve readings will attest to the loss they feel when any of the readings is omitted, but every context will have to determine what would best introduce or help an assembly keep the Vigil year after year.

The twelve readings take the assembly from the beginning of all things—the creation of the world—to the moment when the ruler of this world at the time of Daniel, who meant to bring all things under his control, found that the three faithful servants of God—Shadrach, Meshach, and Abednego—were not consumed by the hottest fire the ruler could muster. They were, instead, protected. Their survival itself preached to the ruler, King Nebuchadnezzar, that the God they served was worthy also of his praise.

In other words, the story of God's power and steadfast commitment to the creatures who live on and in this world begins in the very stuff of life and explodes to include even the most mysterious and "otherworldly" occurrences that no science, no reasoning, no mortal argument can comprehend. To sit in the candlelight for the time it takes to hear the twelve readings is to be infused with the overwhelming abundance of God's help throughout the ages. Different people from ourselves in different times and places have, in fact, experienced a power beyond our knowing. These stories and poems, songs, and even funny language (for Daniel is at least that!) brought to ours ears on one night, in the company of other people who care to hold vigil at the tomb, drive into us the great significance of that for which we are waiting. All of the readings speak of something too big to grasp, and yet there is something even more to be described: the resurrection.

By the time we have heard the stories, and welcomed the newly baptized or spoken our Affirmation of Baptism, we settle in for the culminating words: a reading from Romans that says we are dead to sin and alive again and the story of Jesus' appearing to the women who proclaim his resurrection to the other disciples, replete with admonitions from angels and Jesus himself—"Do not be afraid."

It is as if, on this night, the primary reason for our gathering together is to hear—in a stretched-out, detailed, interesting, and mysterious way—that God's fundamental message to us in all these forms is peace without fear. Although calamities and injustices have taken place and will and do take place every day in this world, we have been made alive to a different way of understanding ourselves and this world and the next. We have been given a vision of something utterly new, always new, absolutely unbelievable (literally not to be believed), and so every year we have to gather together and on one night hear the entire scope lest we take it in only piecemeal and perhaps never see the forest for the trees. We need to hear the stories, not so much to use them for just the right moment or because we can glean from them rules for living but because every moment—no matter how much or how little we have studied—we need to hear the context in which God has located us.

Karl Barth's meditation on Romans tells us that the crucifixion and resurrection create for us an "invisible point of observation" which lets us stand in a place beyond ourselves. From there we can more clearly see the "closed circle" in which we live.[11] It is a circumscribed world full of beauty, to be sure, but also of struggles, our own failings, our disappointments over others, and awe at those who by conviction and love become icons of courage, stories in their own right, including the stories of our own lives, also a piece of that context.

Every Sunday—and especially on this night—when we hear the prayer of thanksgiving said over the bread and the wine, the one who prays invites the assembly to respond with words that express the core mystery of our faith: "Christ has died. Christ is risen. Christ will come again." That proclamation is so ripe with meaning that it needs thousands of images to pull at it, to give it edges, to round it out, and to fill us with hope that Christ *is* risen and will come again. The assembly's proclamation needs a huge context in order to be even barely understood. The building up of that context takes weeks and weeks and years and years of hearing and speaking images and incidents, characters and stories in order to make sense at all. In the three short phrases spoken by the assembly every Sunday, the *herzpunkt* of Christian faith is proclaimed.

On this night, the message toward which all of the images pull the assembly is this: Do not be afraid. That is what the sermon might best say at the Vigil of Easter.

You could "see him" only by coming into contact with hunger: by being hungry and by feeding the hungry. You could "enter the kingdom" only if you rooted and snuffled around for it like a hungry infant wanting to nurse. God's kingdom was imaged as the table where there are places for everyone, and everyone has the place of honor, and everyone gets enough. The only table like that is the breast, the table where someone smiles and says, Eat my body, and where the little child has the place of honor forever.
—Marianne Sawicki[12]

Notes

1. Brian Helge, quoted in Gabe Huck and Mary Ann Simcoe, eds., *The Triduum Sourcebook* (Chicago: Liturgy Training Publications, 1983), 78.

2. Karl Barth, *The Epistle to the Romans* (Oxford: Oxford University Press, 1933), 192.

3. Martin Luther, *The Large Catechism*, in *The Book of Concord*, ed. Robert Kolb and Timothy J. Wengert (Minneapolis: Fortress Press, 2000), 457.7.

4. Ibid., 459–60.26–27.

5. Barth, *The Epistle to the Romans*, 199.

6. Ibid., 200.

7. Ibid., 202.

8. Gregory of Nazianzus, in *Celebrating the Seasons: Daily Spiritual Readings for the Christian Year*, ed. Robert Atwell (Harrisburg, Pa.: Morehouse, 2001), 223.

9. See *Evangelical Lutheran Worship* (Minneapolis: Augsburg Fortress, 2006), 31.

10. Marianne Sawicki, *Seeing the Lord: Resurrection and Early Christian Practices* (Minneapolis: Fortress Press, 1994), 79.

11. Barth, *The Epistle to the Romans,* 198.

12. Sawicki, *Seeing the Lord*, 291.

DECEMBER 2007

Sunday	Monday	Tuesday	Wednesday	Thursday	Friday	Saturday
						1
2 1 Advent	3	4	5	6	7	8
9 2 Advent	10	11	12	13	14	15
16 3 Advent	17	18	19	20	21	22
23 4 Advent	24 Christmas Eve	25 Christmas Day	26	27	28	29
30 1 Christmas	31 New Year's Eve					

JANUARY 2008

Sunday	Monday	Tuesday	Wednesday	Thursday	Friday	Saturday
		1 Holy Name of Jesus	2	3	4	5
6 Epiphany	7	8	9	10	11	12
13 1 Epiphany	14	15	16	17	18	19
20 2 Epiphany	21	22	23	24	25	26
27 3 Epiphany	28	29	30	31		

FEBRUARY 2008

Sunday	Monday	Tuesday	Wednesday	Thursday	Friday	Saturday
					1	2
3 4 Epiphany / Transfiguration of Our Lord	4	5	6 Ash Wednesday	7	8	9
10 1 Lent	11	12	13	14	15	16
17 2 Lent	18	19	20	21	22	23
24 3 Lent	25	26	27	28	29	30

MARCH 2008

Sunday	Monday	Tuesday	Wednesday	Thursday	Friday	Saturday
						1
2 4 Lent	3	4	5	6	7	8
9 5 Lent	10	11	12	13	14	15
16 Palm Sunday / Passion Sunday	17 Monday of Holy Week	18 Tuesday of Holy Week	19 Wednesday of Holy Week	20 Maundy Thursday	21 Good Friday	22 Holy Saturday / Easter Vigil
23 Easter Sunday 30	24 31	25	26	27	28	29